CHALLENGE

How to Succeed Beyond Your Dreams

The autobiography of sports icon

Hobie Billingsley

"The greatest diving coach in the history of the sport"

To Cathy — nice to know you, and happy you Enjoy the book!!
Sincerely
Hobie Billingsley

TRIUS PUBLISHING
San Diego

CHALLENGE - HOW TO SUCCEED BEYOND YOUR DREAMS

The autobiography of Hobie Billingsley

The World's Greatest Diving Coach and Sports Icon

Published in the United States of America by:

Trius Publishing, P.O. Box 600801, San Diego, CA 92160

This is the autobiography of the life and times of Hobert Sherwood Billingsley who at the age of 85 began to recall events from his life. He apologizes if his stories are not depicted exactly as you may recall. To learn more and find personal stories and pictures provided by his athletes about this sports icon go to his website. http://www.HobieBillingsley.com.

ISBN: 978-0-9986357-0-5 52995 paperback

Table of Contents

CHALLENGE

How to Succeed Beyond Your Dreams

ACKNOWLEDGMENTS

I want to give credit to my family, my significant others and friends, and all my divers and students who made my accomplishments possible. There are far too many to include in my autobiography, but know that I remember each of you in a special way.

I did not start to write my autobiography until I was 85. It has taken me five more years to put my life in order. I wish I had the memory of a teenager, but I have done the best I can to recall people, places, and events as I saw them at the time.

I apologize if I have misrepresented the facts or saw them differently from your account. It was not my intent to embarrass or harm anyone, but to praise effort responding to my challenge.

Most of the photographs are from my personal collection. I also want to thank Indiana University Archives for use of a few others that are credited in the book.

I want to thank Bob Schneider, who was one of my first divers I coached at Ohio University, for his first edit of the manuscript, to put everything in a positive light. I want to thank Dr. Pete Andersen, who was a 5-time All-American swimmer, and has known me and our divers since 1961 for his editing and fact checking of the final manuscript.

As I could recall people, places, and events, I simply started to type them on my laptop computer without regard for grammar and punctuation. Dr. Pete has put my thoughts into a readable format. No other editor I know could have been as familiar with the people or places. He has tried to research the facts to spell names correctly, and locate results of competitions. He is aware of the physics principles I learned to apply to coach my divers, and knows the history of the swimming and diving programs at Indiana University.

For more stories and photos, you can submit to share and enjoy, go to:

www.HobieBillingsley.com

You can submit your content to Dr. Pete (**drpete@drpeteandersen.com**) to post on the website, where your friends can use PayPal to purchase this book, my other authored works, and the acclaimed film, **Hobie's Heroes**, is also available.

FORWARD

This is the autobiography of Hobie Billingsley, "The greatest diving coach in the history of the sport," and legend in his own time. His motivation to seek diving perfection was guided by this quote:
"No move should be made unless it contributes to the execution of the dive."

How It All Started

Curt Simic, the former president of the Indiana University Foundation and dear friend, asked me to write the story of my life. I accomplished a lot as the diving coach at Indiana University, but Curt wanted to know how and where I developed the initiative and character to do what seemed impossible at the time.

When I started to write my autobiography, I realized that I wasn't only writing about myself, but also the effect of the times in which I lived. Readers will get a better concept of what I accomplished in my life by learning what the world was like during that era. The world has unbelievably changed a lot in a short time.

The more I wrote, I realized how fortunate I was to be born in the United States of America. The greatest country on earth let me be free and blessed with opportunity others didn't and still don't have to accomplish their dreams.

My life is a testament to how a person born in total poverty from a broken family with little or no chance of ever accomplishing much in life could rise-up and fulfill dreams that had been pure fantasy.

I quickly learned that through determination, persistence, hard work, faith, hero worship, belief in God, and accepting guidance from others who cared for me that I could gain the confidence to succeed. I looked forward to new challenges, counted my blessings, and never looked backward to what I didn't have.

That early realization made it possible for me to reach a level that not only appeared impossible to me as a child, but also to my mother and friends. I've lived an amazing life that included a Depression, World Wars, divorce, and a time when people had the desire and sense to want to improve themselves through hard work all of which occurred and has changed in less than a hundred years.

Something to Think About

I lived in a time when you had to use your imagination to create your own entertainment. There was discipline in the schools, and parents backed up the teachers. We were taught how to think, act, and do for ourselves and help others.

Communication and travel were far different than today. We didn't have cell phones or jet planes. You got the news and entertaining programs from your radio because there was no TV. You paid cash for your purchases because there were no credit cards.

Men went to work and women stayed at home to raise the kids and manage the household. And it was proven that early discipline in the home effected by the mother created more successful children and adults. Divorce and pre-marital sex were frowned upon.

You had respect for most of those in office, the police, and those in the service. You had to be a citizen to live in America. Most of the people were Americans who were Christians, attended churches, and believed in God.

You had to work for nearly everything you had, and if you didn't have the money to buy it you went without including food and housing. I was born three years before the Great Depression when many people who had a high quality of life lost everything. You couldn't go to your relatives or neighbors for help because they were in the same predicament.

There were no automatic washing machines and dryers. You hung your clothes out on a line to dry in your back yard. Gasoline was eleven cents a gallon. Streetcars and buses were used because people couldn't afford cars, and Interstate highways didn't exist. Trains were a main source of transportation.

Movies were a treat. The good guys always won over evil, and there was no foul language. Cartoon and cowboy movies were popular Saturday matinees for only a quarter. You believed in the Ten Commandments, the Constitution, and obeyed laws. You had to use good common sense or suffer the consequences of bad decisions. You were honored for service to your country.

Nearly every family had a mother and father that taught the difference between right and wrong. Parents where praised for disciplining their children and honoring their teachers. There was no DCFS agency taking away your children for disciplining them. Families held their children accountable for their actions, and teenagers rarely stayed out later than 10 o'clock.

Prayers were given in schools along with the Pledge of Allegiance to the flag every morning, and the National Anthem and God Bless America were often sung. Grade schools with playgrounds had recess twice a day.

Students respected their teachers who taught subjects that didn't include politics. Shootings by students in schools were unheard of. Most students walked or rode a bicycle to school, and carried their books or put them in a basket attached to the handle bars on their bike. Back packs didn't exist.

Children and women could walk down the street at any time of day and night with no fear of being molested. Few locked up their houses because there was little to steal. There were no street gangs, but mobsters and Mafia created crime syndicates. The use of drugs was very rare. It's remarkable how much has changed in one-hundred years.

CHAPTER 1

My Home Town

Erie, Pennsylvania had a population around 119,000 when I was born in 1926, but with hard economic times I think it is less than 100,000 now. Erie is in an area of the state that is shaped like a house with a smoke stack in the upper northwest corner on the shores of Lake Erie. It's the only lake port in Pennsylvania, approximately 100 miles East of Cleveland, Ohio, and 90 miles West of Buffalo, New York.

All the cities on the shores of Lake Erie usually have very cold and long winters with yards of lake effect snow. Erie is interesting in that it consists of many different nationalities that congregate in their own communities throughout the city.

State Street is the main street with stores and business buildings that run north and south through the center of the city. In my day, most of the poor people, who were Russian, Polish, and African-American, lived on the East side of town, and the wealthier people, who were Italian, German, English, Jewish, and Portuguese, lived on the West side.

The city dock overlooks Presque Isle Bay that is separated from the lake by a beautiful eight-mile-long peninsula that provides breath-taking sandy beaches on its north side, and some boat marinas on the south west side.

The bay empties out into Lake Erie through a navigational channel where a Coast Guard station directs boat traffic and rescues boats and ships in distress. The bay and lake freeze over during the winter months so boats cannot pass through the slip until spring.

Large lake freighters often pass through the slip carrying coal, sand, and other products when the weather permits. The bay once had about five or six old rusted lake ships moored together near the dock where they sat through the Depression and World War II, and they did little to improve the beauty of the bay and the city.

The area also offers some historical interest. On this bay, Commodore Oliver Perry built his fleet in 1812 to engage the British fleet in the "Battle of Lake Erie." He returned to the peninsula after he defeated the British and sunk the remainder of his fleet, except for the U.S.S. Wolverine that is in a small cove known as "Misery Bay" where there's a monument to Perry and his men.

The U.S.S. Wolverine built in Erie was the first iron clad battle ship of the U.S. Navy and is now a memorial. Fishing in Erie was also a feature in the early 1900's, and most of the fishermen were Russians who sold their catch on the dock nearly every morning.

Most the people in Erie were Catholic, and the city government was run by Italians. Erie has Gannon College attended mostly by local students. It was founded in the 1950's, and started in a mansion owned by the Strong family who were the wealthiest in Erie in the early 1900's.

The home was given to the city after they passed away, and though a small college at first, it has now grown to include several buildings that offer a variety of subjects. Most of the mansions owned by wealthy people that surround the college have long been converted into offices and apartments because few people could afford to reside in them. The town had five high schools up until World War II when they added two new ones and lost one.

Erie has four distinct seasons with winter lasting the longest. The spring and fall seasons display extraordinary beauty when Mother Nature's leaves turn and fall from the trees. Though summer is normally short, it often gets very hot.

The only entrance to the peninsula is a road on the west side of town that passes Waldamere Park, a large summer entertainment center, that offers rides, games, picnic grounds, etc. The park is also located on a high level where the road winds down a steep hill to the entrance of the peninsula. The road then widens slightly to provide space for cars, bicycles, and walking space along the water's edge as it circles completely around the peninsula.

Native Americans were the first humans to occupy the peninsula, but they were eventually driven off by the white man years-ago. The Peninsula is an aquatic paradise that draws thousands of tourists each summer from many neighboring states for swimming, surfing, boating, camping, picnicking, fishing, and hiking.

Lake Erie is a shallow lake where storms often occur without warning, and can produce waves up to 20 feet high. Stone jetties were built along the north shore of the beaches on the peninsula to keep the sand from being washed away by storms and winter ice when the lake freezes over. Erie is a fine place to visit for winter activities skiing, ice skating, snowboarding, and great tourist accommodations.

Erie is known for many things one being its fruit production that includes grapes, apples, cherries, peaches, plums, wine, and a few more. The weather and soil are ideal and as good as anywhere in the country. Welch's Grape Juice, for one, obtains their grapes from Erie.

Erie used to be a large industrial town because of the lake, but most of the big companies have moved away leaving industrial buildings as vacant eyesores. However, the General Electric Company has remained and employs many residents.

My Birth and That of My Family

I was born on December 2, 1926, three years before the stock market crash, in Hamot Hospital located atop a high hill on the north side of State Street overlooking the city dock, Presque Isle Bay, and the peninsula. The hill next to the hospital on State Street is used for the Soap Box Derby races every summer.

My mother was born in Jamestown, New York on September 9, 1900 and had two sons by my father. My older brother, James Harrison Billingsley, was also born in the Hamot Hospital on November 6, 1923 three years before me.

I don't remember where or when my father was born, but I believe he was about a year older than my mother.

My Mother and Her Family

My mother came from an upper middle class family that owned a music store where my grandfather also tuned pianos. I don't remember ever meeting him because he may have died before I was born.

However, I do remember my grandmother who was a very elegant person, and wore beautiful clothes with great dignity. She also demanded respect from her children and friends. My only recollection of her was when she was standing in her bedroom when I was very young.

She had a great taste for the good things in life, and thought nothing of going out and buying an $18.00 hat that, in those days, was equal to a man's weekly wages. She died when I was four years old.

My mother was 5'9" tall with beautiful long legs and a very nice figure. She was so flexible that she could put her leg over her head until she was well over seventy years old. She was also an attractive young woman, but lost most of her beauty when she decided to work in machine shops that made armatures to help the troops during the First World War.

Except for the period that she lived with my father and us kids until I was five years old and my father walked out on us, she continued to work outside of the home. She had a stroke at the age of eighty and passed away a year later. She is pictured here with my older brother Jimmy.

She was a very giving person who had a personality that attracted people to her. She was also extremely intelligent with a great love for flowers, music, and books. She would go around to garage sales and second-hand stores in her later life, and buy all sorts of books most of which were fictional but also included poetry and literature.

I remember coming home for a visit from college and found her closet filled with books. When asked about the books, she said that was where she put them after reading them. Her taste changed a little later when she started to collect recordings of the big band era, semi-classical records, musical shows, and other sorts of good music.

She collected well over a thousand records before her death, and I managed to gather up many of them when we closed her apartment. She also possessed a hidden talent.

She met a man who took a liking to her when she was around sixty years old, and he hung around her house for about a year.

Being a good-looking man, my mother decided, for some unknown reason, to do a bust of his head so she purchased the clay and other necessities needed to make the bust, and finished it in a little more than a month. My brother Jimmy came home from Oberlin, Ohio where he was directing a band at Oberlin College, and was flabbergasted when he saw what she had done.

The bust looked more like the man than he did. Jimmy was so impressed with the bust that he took it back to Oberlin and showed it to the head of the Art Department. The Dean of the fine arts department was nationally known and astonished after examining the bust. He asked Jim who his mother had studied under. When Jim said no one, the Dean said that it was not possible to make such a magnificent piece of work without the aid of someone who was far advanced in the profession. Unfortunately, that was the first and last bust she ever made.

My mother had five sisters and my father had four brothers and a sister.

Bob Davis, my cousin, joined the army to fight for his country soon after the bombing of Pearl Harbor. He was a very handsome youngster who was a crack shot with a rifle. He also had great pride in himself and was the type that would never give up in a fight.

He was a paratrooper with the 101st Airborne in Germany, and was captured fighting in the Battle of the Bulge in late 1943. The Germans put him in a concentration camp where they tortured and starved him along with many others for months until they thought they were dead. Then they threw the dead bodies onto trucks and drove to an area where they dumped them into large open graves.

Bob was thrown on top of the dead bodies on one of the trucks when a German officer heard him groaning and climbed up and found him still alive. Looking at Bob's dog tags and seeing his name was "Bob Davis," the officer asked him if he was related to Betty Davis, the movie star? When Bob replied that she was his sister, the officer pulled him down from the pile, and put him back in prison until he was liberated near the end of the war.

Not one to talk about that part of his life, Bob was one of the prisoners whose picture was on the cover of Life Magazine in early 1945 when the prisoners were being liberated from the German torture and death camps. He was a very talented artist. After returning from the war he attended the University of Florida and graduated in Architecture.

The school was so impressed with his work that they hired him on their staff as an instructor, and after a time he got married and had two children. A broken man from being tortured, he would dive under a table and tremble with fear whenever a thunder storm occurred. He later died in the 1960's after I saw him for a short time when my diving team and I were headed for Ft. Lauderdale to train over Christmas vacation.

Fay was the oldest of my mother's sisters. She was a talented artist, and painted a life size picture of Santa Claus for the Coca Cola Company in 1933 that I believe is still being used by them during the Christmas holidays.

My Father and His Family

The Billingsley clan apparently started in Pittsburgh, Pennsylvania. A Billingsley from Texas informed me years later that he was doing a study of the Billingsley family tree. He found that I had a cousin six times removed who came up with the slogan "remember the Alamo."

I never liked my grandparents on my father's side because they were cruel, wicked, self-centered, and selfish people who had no regard for anyone but themselves.

My father had four brothers and a sister. I was named Hobert after the second oldest son, who had stuck his head in an oven, turned on the gas, and killed himself before I was born. Gee, what an honor to be named after someone who was such a great guy.

My father was the third oldest brother, and was the best sign painter in the family. He did gold lettering on the windows of banks and businesses. I never got to know my father because I never spent any time with him.

In those times, no one thought a family was dysfunctional. But all that had a lasting effect on my personality. I wanted to be kind and help people.

CHAPTER 2

Starting My Life as Far Back as I Can Remember

My dear friend Curt Simic, the former president of the Indiana University Foundation, suggested that I write my autobiography. He said it was important because no one had ever written anything about Doc Councilman, the great swimming coach at Indiana University, except for his accomplishments. Very little was known about Doc, and he didn't want that to happen to me.

When I asked Curt when in my life should I start, he said from the time I remembered anything after I was born. So, the first recollection I had was when I was three years old, and our family of four was living behind a store on Eighth and Chestnut Street on the west side of town. I am pictured here with my older brother, Jimmy.

The Innocent Child

It was a usual winter in Erie, PA, with about two feet of snow on the ground. While playing with my brother, who was three years older than me, I had to pee. My brother got upset when he saw what I was doing, and took me into the house and told my mother.

I remember her standing in the kitchen and looking down at me with her arms folded with a stern look on her face when she said, "Hobie, how could you have done such a thing; aren't you ashamed of yourself? What would you say to God if you went up to heaven - what would you say to him?" Thinking for a moment, I replied, "Howdy Folks" and my mother and brother broke out in laughter.

My father did not drink alcohol but like most people in those days, he did smoke "Lucky Strikes" and "Camel" cigarettes. He was not a violent person, and never hit us kids except once when I was four years old. We moved from Eighth and Chestnut Street up to 22nd and Holland Street into a ground floor two-bedroom flat on the Southeast side of town.

My brother and I were visiting the people in the flat above us. I saw a jack knife sitting on the table, and picked it up and put it in my pocket. A little later the people upstairs told my mother about the missing knife. That night, while eating supper, my mother told my dad about the missing knife that she had returned to the owners.

14

Thinking that my older brother Jimmy was the thief, my father suddenly jumped up from the table, and smacked Jimmy across the face so hard he knocked him out of his chair before he found out I was the culprit. I don't remember my father ever hitting me, or for that matter, even touching me for any reason.

My Home Life

We really liked living in that house because it had a big cherry tree in the yard next to our house. My brother and I would sit on its branches, and eat big juicy cherries when in season. We also enjoyed the fresh sweet sugar coated doughnuts that we bought from the store across the street that cost fifteen cents a dozen.

One day, a big beautiful stray but very tame dog showed up at our house. We named it "Whitey" and loved it to death. But we had to move again and couldn't take Whitey with us. My father was going to prison soon for painting over the numbers of a license plate of a car that some of his friends had stolen and got caught. When we moved to a five-room house on Eighth and Holland Street we saw Whitey running after our moving van for miles. He became so exhausted he stopped, and we never saw the dog again.

The single floor house had a piano that my brother and I never played except chop sticks. I remember my father bringing home a toy dirigible (blimp) that he attached to the hanging light cord in the kitchen. We'd watch it circle around and around after winding it up.

We also had a Victrola (phonograph) you had to wind up with a crank that played wax records. My mom loved to play her favorite song, "My Blue Heaven" all the time, and I never got tired listening to it. We lived there for only a short time because my father went to prison for a year.

We didn't have the money to pay the rent for our house. Having no money and with my father in jail, my mother could not take care of two children so she sent my brother up to live with my grandparents, Mum and Pappy.

My evil grandmother liked having my brother Jimmy stay with them because he was a beautiful child with curly brown hair and a baby face while I was just the opposite. I was a rough looking kid, and when I walked across a room I knocked into chairs or a table.

With no money, no job, and no place to live, my mother decided to take me to an orphanage. When we arrived at the front door, she couldn't make herself take me inside. She sat down on the orphanage steps and cried. We walked down the street where she found a rooming house one block away from where I was born.

The rent was five dollars a week, and we moved into a one room apartment on the second floor with a big bay window. We had a great view of the bay, the dock, and the peninsula. My mother walked five blocks over to West Sixth Street, where all the rich people lived going door to door asking people if she could clean their house, do their washing and ironing, cook their meals or any other chores.

Mom finally found a family who agreed to pay her seven dollars a week to do their washing and ironing. At five years-old and staying home alone, one morning I decided to cook eggs for my breakfast and caught the trash in the closet on fire. Thankfully, I had the sense to throw a pan of water on the fire before it caught the whole house on fire and endangered five or six other tenants.

Mum and Pappy understood we didn't have any money. Occasionally they would put their food scraps in a brown paper bag, and drive about ten miles in one of their four big cars over to our house to give us their scraps.   I remember one time they gave us a pork chop with only one bite out of it.   We gladly accepted it because it was better than starving. I guess they felt guilty and pitied us, and it was better for them not to waste their garbage and think they were being kind to us.

I liked where we were living because I could open the window a notch at night and enjoy the fresh air and sound of the fog horn on the Peninsula. I can still hear it sounding more often when it was foggy to give direction to ships out in the lake.

Since Erie is a lake port, trains ran by only a few yards away from our house. They carried coal and other goods that were taken to other locations. The trains were usually overloaded so it took two engines to move the load. The wheels on the engines would often slip while trying to start, and it sounded like a human painfully struggling to crawl.

There was a four-foot-high circular water trough across the street from our house that provided fresh cold water from a spring for thirsty horses. Never seeing a horse use the trough, I used to go over a couple of times a day and get a good cold drink.

A big park on a steep hill north of our house led down to a flat area near the train tracks where teenage boys often played baseball on the field. My mother came home from work one day, and couldn't find me. She went down to the field, and found me behind the batter's box with a big right-hand catcher's mitt on my hand yelling at the pitcher, "put it in here you son-of-a bitch."

We lived in the apartment for a year until my father got out of jail. He immediately went to his mother's house for a week before coming to our place to see my mother. He and my mother went to the park and sat on a bench while I sat on the grass near them. I heard my father tell my mom that he was going to leave her and live with Ester, who was a prostitute.

Her profession was obvious because in those days, prostitutes wore satin dresses with low cut neck lines. Though I was only five years old, I remembered every word he said to her.

I started crying, and my mother asked him since we had next to nothing to live on, "how were we going to live?" He told her that she would have to figure that out for herself, and got up and left.   He never tried to locate us for years though we did try to locate him for alimony which we rarely received. My mother learned that he left Ester a few months later when she stabbed him with an ice pick.

Paying $5.00 a week rent, and trying to save enough for food living on two dollars a week, my mom and I were forced to move out. She found another small one room apartment on Eleventh and Cherry Street. She took me to Lafayette Grade School within walking distance only a couple of blocks away.

My mother pleaded with the school officials to put me in kindergarten because I was only five years old and under age so she could look for work. They finally gave in.

Christmas season was fast approaching and I still believed in Santa Claus. My mother would look out the window nearly every night, and tell me that she thought she saw Santa Claus go by in his sleigh. She told me if I was a good boy, Santa would bring me some presents.

She went out in a cold snowy night on Christmas Eve with less than a dollar in her purse, and bought a small Christmas tree for twenty-five cents. She trimmed it with ornaments that she borrowed from her sister, Boo. Then she realized that she didn't have any money to buy me any presents. Mom learned how to be resourceful, and was a great knitter. She stayed up all night knitting me a sweater and carefully wrapped it up in a box, and put it under the tree.

When I woke up Christmas morning, I ran over to the tree and ripped open the box and found the sweater. Not knowing any better, I started to cry and asked her why I didn't get any toys since I had been such a good boy and added, through tears, "doesn't Santa Claus like me?" That made my mother break down and she cried and cried. I believe that it was probably one of the saddest moments in her whole life.

We had to move again after a few months due to not having the money to pay the rent. We had only one room again in this house on Eighth Street between Holland and French Streets, and one block from State Street, the main street in town.

School Days

My mom put me in first grade along with thirty other kids in Jones School only a block away. I liked school because each morning, all six grades would go to a big hall where we stood in a designated place, and pledged allegiance to the flag before reporting to our home rooms.

A bell rang ten minutes later to tell us to go to our first class for fifty-five minutes. When the bell rang again we had five minutes to get to our next class. We had six classes each day with a half hour recess in the middle of the morning and afternoon. We would play field tag and other games that required a lot of running.

The best-looking girls in school were Edna Carlson and Billy Jean Kingsley, and all the boys were crazy about them so we would do all kinds of crazy things to get their attention. I think we were too young for either of the two girls to develop a real crush on any single boy because they were getting all the attention they wanted and enjoyed every single minute of it.

Making Ends Meet

My mom got a job near the end of the year with the Community Chest charity making $7.50 a week working eight hours a day. We were living under $500 a year. I remember that my brother was coming home from our grandparents. That gave my mother a lot of grief because they wanted to keep him, but she finally won out.

We quickly found they had terribly spoiled him when we sat down for dinner on his first night at home. My mother served macaroni and cheese and some vegetables. When she put the food on his plate he looked at her and said he wasn't going to eat that garbage.

So, my mother reached over and grabbed his plate and scooped half of his plate on to mine and the other half on to hers. When we started to eat, Jimmy started to yell what was he supposed to eat and my mother said if the food wasn't good enough to eat, then he could go without because that was all we had.

Jimmy went to bed hungry that night and never once complained about his food again. I remember that evening well because my mom made some vanilla pudding as a special treat for Jimmy's home coming, and put it on the window sill to cool and when she went to fetch it, someone had stolen all three dishes.

My mother also took a summer job for several years working at the Waldermere amusement park on the peninsula. She worked there during the day on weekends and the evenings during the week. She took tickets for the various rides, and one was the "Ravine Flyer" that was a roller coaster.

She used to put me in the back seat of the last car where I remained until she was relieved. So, while people were screaming their heads off during the ride, I could be found in the rear car, asleep.

The roller coaster ran on a wooden structure that passed over the highway that went down to the peninsula. The structure rotted a few years later and the cars on the ride crashed on the highway killing several people. The ride was retired for several years before they remade the structure with steel supports.

My brother was taking care of me at home when she had to work late one night, and missed the last bus to town. One of the workers came along and seeing the problem, offered to take her home in his car. Having a nice figure and an enormous bust, she quickly found herself in trouble because he suddenly turned off the highway onto a dirt road and started to make advances on her.

A quick thinker, she started to cough violently and pulled out her handkerchief and rubbed her lipstick all over it. She excused herself telling the man that she had an acute case of tuberculosis, and showed him the bloody handkerchief. The guy started up the car and took her home without uttering a word, and he never bothered her again.

I helped my mom going door to door selling Liberty and the Saturday Evening Post magazines for a nickel when I was eight years old. I earned a penny for every magazine I sold. I also sold weekly advertisements and a local newspaper called the Starret Weekly. I stood in line in an alley at six o'clock every Saturday morning where about 75 grownups and some children were given fifty papers each for free. We would go around town and sell them on the street, hollering "Starret Weekly, Starret Weekly, one cent." I remember how cold those Saturday mornings were in the fall and winter, but it was worth the money. I usually sold most of my papers and sometimes got a tip from some people who would give me an extra penny and even a nickel on occasion which was a real bonus. I made around 35 to 50 cents which was a small fortune to me in those days.

I joined the Boys Club bugle corps a block away from our house. I bought myself a new bugle for five dollars with the money I saved, and blew it all the way home on the street after practice. I'm sure the neighbors really loved to hear me coming.

We lived in that apartment for nearly a year when I came down with a cold one night that turned into double pneumonia. Doctors made home visits in those days, and by sheer luck someone called a doctor who came and saved my life. He told my mother that if he hadn't shown up when he did, I would have died in the next hour or two. I was in bed for two weeks.

The Bully

We were all poor kids who could run all over town with little danger of being molested. Few people locked their doors because they didn't have anything worth stealing. Most of the kids looked forward to going to school so they could be with their friends and like most schools, Jones School had a bully who would pick on the younger and weaker kids. Chuck Norris would tell me nearly every day, when I was in the fourth grade, that when he got the chance after school, he was going to beat me up. So, being bigger and stronger than me, I would run home as fast as I could after school so he wouldn't catch me. This went on for a couple of months until one day, I decided that, win or lose, I was going to have to face him no matter what because I wasn't getting any sleep at night. I had a real tough time at school that day as I watched the school clock slowly tick away during each class. Realizing that I was probably going to get the crap kicked out of me after school, I met Chuck on the playground. Half of my class showed up to watch.

I picked up a stick and put it on my shoulder and dared him to knock it off. In disbelief, he backed off and walked away, and everyone started to cheer. He asked me the next day where I learned to be so tough. He turned out be a good friend until I left Jones School after the fifth grade to attend a different school, and years later he became a state champion weight lifter.

Miss White was my fifth-grade teacher, and a witch. I was left handed, and she insisted that I learn to write using my right hand. Since I couldn't do that, she would demand that I put my left hand on the desk, and with a wooden pointer, smack my hand across the knuckles a couple of times nearly every day until they would bleed. She never succeeded in changing me to write with my right hand. She didn't like any of us, and we couldn't figure out why she was a teacher. I think it was because of the Depression when only a few people had jobs and teaching was probably the only one she could get.

I went down to the Jones School gravel playground after selling papers on Saturday morning, and played football with a bunch of kids that were all older and taller than me. They played rough, but I was a wizard at catching the ball. They would all jump up to catch a pass, and knock the ball in my direction where I caught it and ran like hell. That technique helped me be one of the first picked when choosing up sides for games.

Tough Life

My mother and I picked cherries, apples, and peaches, when in season, at the fruit farms located in North East, a suburb of Erie. I wasn't very good at the job because I usually ate more than I put in the basket. The Tyler family, who lived behind us, had a car, and would take us out to pick the fruit for a small fee.

When my brother and I went back to school after the season was over, the Tylers took my mom out to pick grapes. That was a tough job because she had to cut the stems with the use of shears. I remember her coming home time after time with bruised and bleeding hands from shearing the grapes.

The Tylers also took us out to pick violets after the fruit season was over, and that was also a tough job, too. You had to bend over and pick one little flower at a time which was hard on your back. The Tylers made small flower bouquets, and wrapped them in cellophane paper tied with a rubber band. I would take the violet bouquets and stand in front of the Warner movie theater at night where I sold them to people that came out of the show. I remember how embarrassed I was selling them because none of my friends were doing anything like I was. If I saw a friend approaching me, I would hide behind the "coming attractions" sign in front of the entrance until my friend passed by. I sold the flowers for ten cents a bunch. The Tylers made six cents a bunch because they furnished the transportation to pick the violets and wrapped them into a bouquet.

We moved again to 306 East Eighth Street when I was eight years old. We lived there for two years in a one room apartment on the second floor. I made friends with a boy named Pete Deturk who lived across the street. His father was a doctor, and had an office attached to their home. Pete was about nine years older than me. One day, when not getting enough to eat, he invited me over to his house where his mother served us lunch. For months after that I went over to his back door, and would whistle and sing hoping they would hear me and give me something to eat.

My mom wasn't earning enough money to feed us so we made a deal with the grocer next door who put us on a charge account. His name was Mr. Mutlinger, and I would guess that he had a similar understanding with half the people in the neighborhood, most of whom probably never paid him back.

When my brother turned sixteen, he got a job with the Bliley Electric Company, and he saved every cent he earned. Our bill with the grocer had amounted to around a hundred dollars over the years which might just as well been the national debt. Jimmy went over to the grocer one day, and handed Mr. Mutlinger the money that paid our debt in full. He stood there staring at my brother, then broke down and cried. What a wonderful and kind man.

While walking home from Jones School one day, I passed the Hill Mill Ice Cream Store one block away, and for some reason I turned into the alley and entered the store through a side door. I stood there for a while watching some of the employees chop up 300-pound ice kegs into 25 and 50 pound chunks. These were sold to people for their ice boxes when electric refrigerators weren't on the market yet.

Other workers bottled half pints of white and chocolate milk, and put them in cases to be delivered to the schools and stores in the area. I walked over to one of the men, and started to help him load the cases on a motorcycle side car to deliver to the local grade and high schools the next morning before school started. The man was really surprised, and yelled out to some of the other workers something like, "Hey you guys, look at my new helper."

Feeling good about that, I started to stop by the Hill Mill every day after school, and worked my tail off. One of the workers later took me to the front end of the store where they made the ice cream. As a reward, he put some soft ice cream on a small paper plate for me to eat, and boy was that ever good.

I tried for months to figure out why they didn't sell soft ice cream when it tasted so much better than hard ice cream, and companies finally figured that out a few years later. One of the workmen took a liking to me, and asked if I would come early in the morning and ride on the side car to deliver milk to the schools.

One morning I got on the side car, and sat on top of the cases of milk. We took off in a blizzard with snow a couple of feet deep. The motorcycle suddenly hit a big bump, and I went flying off the side car into a snow bank on the street. The driver didn't realize I had been thrown off until he drove a block or two. He turned around and found me unhurt lying in a snow drift.

I continued to hang around the Hill Mill for around a year because they gave me a gallon of ice cream to take home to my family every week, and besides, I also liked the people and the job.

Mr. Brown was the next-door neighbor who owned a floral store in his house, and used to have me get him a 25-pound block of ice every week for his ice box. I would go down to the Hill Mill store with my wagon a block away to get the ice, and he always gave me a nickel tip. One day, I did something wrong at home and my mother got so mad at me that she gave me a swat across one of my legs with a wooden curtain rod that contained springs.

The curtain rod springs sounded like it was killing me so I started to cry. Just then, Mr. Brown came out of his house, and yelled up for me to get him some ice. I walked over to the open window in our apartment hobbling on my left leg, and told him I would. Still sobbing, I turned around to get my wagon limping on my right leg. My mother quickly caught on, and stood there laughing which made me sob even more.

Kid Games

Every kid in those days played with marbles that were often called "bunkers" or "glassies." They were very popular and made of glass that came in single and different colors that could be purchased at any five and ten cent store in bags of 25 for a nickel.

21

You could also buy bigger ones that were about the size of a quarter, and get ten in a bag for the same price.

Another type of marble was made of steel called "steelies." These steel balls were not available in stores, but rather obtained from the bearings found in the hubs of all kinds of wheels used for transportation. The steel balls were obtained by breaking the bearings open with a hammer, and since they were so hard to obtain, they were traded one for two or more glassies. There was a big Ford dealership right next to the Hill Mill. I started to hang around that group who saved all the worn-out bearings for me, so I had more than any of my friends, and traded them for glassies.

The neighborhood kids used to get together at night to play many games in the dark such as kick-the-can, capture-the-flag, hide-and-seek, and others that had us running all over the neighborhood. One neighbor didn't like any of us, and was constantly running out of his house and yelling for us to stay away from his house. One time during Halloween, we knocked on the old grouch's' door and said, "Trick or Treat." He told us to get the hell off his porch, and if we bothered him again, he would call the police.

He was so mean that we all decided to urinate in a milk bottle. After filling it, we snuck up on his porch and placed the bottle tilted against his door, and rang his door bell. Then we ran away and hid, and when he opened the door, all that urine would spill all over his feet. Only a few times in my life have I ever seen a person get so mad. We were basically good kids and none of us ever got in trouble with the law during those years.

Frank Wendell "Wendy" Sheldon

"Wendy" was my best friend who lived on German Street around the corner from me. We were inseparable and played together every day except when I spent time at the Hill Mill. We played a lot of games like "mumbly peg," and did a variety of stunts. We flew kites from atop a slanted roof of a business building two stories high, walked across the top of billboards on a dare, went sledding in the winter time, and jumped off Wendy's garage roof landing on our stomachs in a pile of leaves in the fall. We thought that the leaves would soften our landing, but most of the time they didn't.

We also played monopoly, and saved baseball cards that included a thin sheet of bubble gum for a penny. We never dreamed that some of those penny baseball cards would be worth thousands of dollars later. We also attended the Y.M.C.A. and played a lot of ping pong in the boy's department. Wendy didn't have an interest in swimming or tumbling so we never got together when I was busy in the pool or in the gym.

Wendy and his family moved over to 714 West 7th Street after finishing sixth grade at Jones School so I only saw him at the Y.M.C.A., and on occasion at his house. After the tenth grade, I changed high schools from East High to Strong Vincent where Wendy also attended, and we continued our friendship.

Wendy's grandfather, Mr. Hotchkiss, owned a 110-acre farm. My mother paid him five dollars every two weeks to let me work on their farm for the summer along with Wendy.

He was a very competitive guy and we would see who could hoe corn, pitch hay, and some other farm chores the quickest.

We both worked our butts off all summer and we would go down to the creek and play tag in the muddy water at the end of the day. We also went fishing for catfish in the creek around sun down. We put five hooks on a line with night crawlers, and then after running around in the woods for an hour or two, we'd go back to check our fishing lines, and usually found four or five catfish on each line. At first, we put them in a bucket for Mrs. Hotchkiss to cook, but she never wanted to clean the fish so we didn't take them to her anymore.

One night the Hotchkiss family got together, and took me out in the woods to go "snipe" hunting. Being a city boy, I didn't know anything about snipes. They told me that it was a rare bird that flew backwards, and all I had to do was take a large burlap bag, hold a flashlight over it, and the bird would fly into the bag when they saw the light.

They set me up with the trap in the woods, and told me they would be back in a couple of hours. They returned about three hours later, and asked me if I had caught any snipes. I was embarrassed and said I nearly caught one, but it got away. I still didn't get the joke until a couple of days later when they wanted to take me out again, and I finally caught on when they broke out laughing.

The farmers milked cows by hand in those days, and it took me a while to learn how to milk them. One day, while Wendy and I were milking the cows, the one I was milking suddenly relieved herself and stepped backwards into one of the "cow pies," and then put that leg in my milk bucket. Wendy and I didn't know what to do because if we told Mr. Hotchkiss, he would be very upset.

We decided to say nothing about it to anyone, and hoped that the milk strainer would clean the ingredients out of the milk. Holding our breath over that episode for a couple of days, we never heard a word from Mrs. Hotchkiss and that gave us a lot of relief.

Another time, Mr. Hotchkiss had filled a wheel barrow full of cow manure, and asked me to empty it out in a pile near the pig pen. On the way, I suddenly slipped and went head first into the wheel barrow. It took a couple of days to rid myself of the terrible stench while everyone had a good laugh, and didn't get near me.

Wendy was drafted into the army after finishing high school, and fought the Germans in Europe for three years. He was a crack shot, and wrote me a letter to tell me that he had stepped over fifteen German bodies he had killed one day.

He ended up in three companies because most of the men in each company were killed. He attended the University of Pittsburgh when he got out of the service, but he was never the same after returning home from the war. He started to drink and smoke a lot, and at times was not one to fool around with.

I went out with him one night after he had returned from the war, and we went to a bar where he got drunk. Erie had a terrible snow storm that night, and it was about midnight when we left the bar with hardly anyone out on the roads. He insisted on driving and drove his car down to the city dock, and after sitting there for a while, he suddenly took off driving with the accelerator wide open.

He drove on the wrong side of the road up State Street, and went through every stop light for nearly four miles until he reached the football stadium on 26th street when he stopped and passed out. I screamed at him the whole way to stop the car, but he refused to respond. It was a miracle we weren't killed, and I knew at that time he could have cared less.

He got married soon after finishing college, and went into a carpet business with his father. They had four sons who eventually took over the business years later. His oldest son, a sky diver with over 1500 jumps, was later killed when his parachute opened just as he hit the ground. No one in and out of the family ever got over that tragedy. Of course, I always visited Wendy and John Wolford when I went home to Erie. The last time I saw him he was on oxygen, and we knew his time was up soon.

We decided to visit his grandfather's farm once again, and talk about old times before he passed away in 2005. One note worth mentioning, Wendy was not a very handsome guy, and was sort of shy around girls. We went to our high school reunion just before he died, and learned that the best-looking girl at Strong Vincent High that every boy in school wanted to date but never did, was stuck on him.

CHAPTER 3

The Y.M.C.A.

I was running the streets when I was seven years old, and my mother became concerned with my welfare. She was afraid that I was going to get into trouble, so she went to the Y.M.C.A. to see if they could give me a membership.

You had to be at least eight years old to join the "Y", and the fee for one year was six dollars. Not having any money, my mother convinced them to make an exception for the sake of my life, and they finally gave me a one year hardship membership. I took to the "Y" like fish to water for I now had a place where I could play all sorts of games with other kids.

Role Models

The director of the Boy's department was Max Darone and his assistant was Tel Epley. These two men were largely responsible for the person I turned out to be today. They were role models and leaders with a purpose who loved children, and gave so much to hundreds of young boys from all walks of life.

I was told that I could no longer be admitted to the boy's department when my membership ran out a year later. However, I began to sneak in and when they saw me back in the boy's department, playing pool, they tossed me out only to find me playing ping pong a little later and threw me out again.

This went on every day for months until a time came when they sort of gave up, and ignored me because they couldn't keep me out. I snuck into the "Y" for nine years after my membership ran out. I was thankful to the "Y" and those men for taking a kid like me in who was caught up in the grips of the Depression, or I probably would have ended up in prison.

For some reason, my mother told me that she didn't believe in God. Knowing that I was not a member of the "Y", Tel Epley asked me if I would like to go to church with him. I asked my mother if I could go with him, and she agreed. Nobody in my family had ever seen the inside of a church, and I was the first in my family.

He took me to the Evangelical Christian Church every Sunday for the next three or four years. We never missed a week because my mother gave me eleven cents, the price of admission, to attend the Regent Movie Theater on Sunday.

Tel had had polio as a young boy and walked with a limp. He was a very special person who loved and cared for kids, and believed in the Y.M.C.A.'s motto "Spirit, Mind, and Body." I think he was out to save some child's soul...mine.

The neighborhood cinema showed a main feature, a cowboy movie, a chapter, a cartoon, and a news reel. Most of the kids would stay to see the movies twice. When you walked by the theater, you could tell exactly what movie was on, and what exciting event was occurring by the yelling and stamping of the kid's feet on the wooden floor inside.

The chapter movie was a fifteen-week series that starred Buster Crabbe as Flash Gordon. I never dreamed that later in my life I would get to know him and Johnny Weissmuller who played "Tarzan."

All of us kids rarely missed going back to the theater because we had to find out how our hero escaped certain death in each dangerous episode. When we came back the next week, we found that the death scene was altered to allow our hero to escape death and didn't seem to bother any of us.

Max Darone was loved by all of the boys at the "Y." He was bald headed, and everyone made fun of it, but he took it with a sense of humor. He was fantastic working with kids and directed thousands of them to live good lives. He knew how to motivate and encourage us into being better citizens.

Summer Camp

Max was also the director of the "Y" summer camp that was located sixteen miles west of Erie right on the Lake Erie shore. My brother and I attended the camp for two years, and worked in the kitchen for our room and board because we didn't have the money to pay the camper's fee.

Jimmy was one of the chefs, and got paid extra for his efforts. I was the head dishwasher. I remember the dish washers got mad at me for something one day, and they all walked out and left me to wash all the dishes for the whole camp that took me all afternoon.

Ten campers occupied ten tents each. They had wooden floors with foot lockers and single cots. The grounds were great with one very large field used for all sorts of games, sports, and activities such as football, soccer, tennis, and track. Everyone went down to the beach on the lake in the morning and late afternoon to swim, and take part in some boating activities.

Every tent had a camp leader who took care of his group morning and night. One of the leader's names was George Steck, who was thought to be the best-looking guy that anyone had ever seen. Everyone in camp idolized him because he was not only an extraordinarily handsome person, but a master tennis player with a magnificent build, great personality and a born leader.

Twenty-five years later I was doing a clown water show in Toledo, Ohio. When the show was over, I got a tap on my shoulder, and when I turned around, I was looking at a person who asked, "Who am I?" Without hesitation, I said "George Steck." He said he couldn't believe that I would remember him so easily after not seeing him for such a long of time.

The camp was the best one that anyone could ask for mainly because of the people who ran it. They were completely organized in handling the programs and activities that suited everyone. They had a nice mess hall that served good food, and had a camp fire every night where everyone gathered around listening to all kinds of stories followed by some great camp songs like "The Old Rugged Cross."

I never met anyone who wanted to go home early. The camp was set up on a weekly basis that lasted for six weeks with many staying for the whole summer. The camp was always full, and some came back to camp year after year where many lifelong friendships were made.

I learned during the second year at the "Y" that they had a tumbling team that met at seven o'clock in the evening on Monday, Wednesday, and Friday nights. I joined the team when I was eight years old. The team had eight members who were much older than me with the next youngest being about fifteen years old.

Since I was so young and very small, they called me "Peanuts". I learned to perform all the basic tumbling stunts that included a head and hand spring, a cartwheel, and several simple routines. I learned to perform more difficult stunts as time went by that included a forward somersault in the air, a back handspring, and a back somersault.

The team gave exhibitions for various social groups in some of the smaller towns in the area, and I was taken along probably more as a mascot and a novelty than for my tumbling routines. Skeets Means was probably one of the finest tumblers in the country. He was our best tumbler by far, and had performed in a circus for a few years.

I remember he came out to the beach one day a few years later when he was asked by Doc Ainsworth to do a tumbling routine. He did a round off, three back handsprings, and into a back somersault with two twists in the sand with all his clothes on wearing shoes! He was one of my heroes, and I wanted to be like him.

Doc Ainsworth was a former director of the Y.M.C.A., and everyone had great respect and love for him. He had to walk with a cane due to his age, but still came to the "Y" when some special activity took place. He and I became very close friends over the years. He had a beautiful gold ring with a diamond in it that he wanted me to have when he passed away, but I never got it.

I was ten years old and finishing fifth grade when my mother decided to move to 258 East Eleventh Street. We lived on the first floor behind a barber shop where we got a haircut for twenty-five cents. We had to walk down a long hall to get to our apartment that was separated from a bar next door by a thin wall. Unfortunately, we could hear almost everything that was going on in the bar that remained open every night until two A.M. except Sunday.

One night someone got drunk and started a fight that ended up outside the back of the bar with one guy getting shot to death. Our apartment included two bedrooms, a living

27

room, and a kitchen. We heated the apartment with the kitchen wood stove to keep us warm. My brother and I scrounged around the neighborhood for wood to heat it.

I used to lay on the couch with my feet propped up on the wall listening to the radio that was the big thing in those days because it was the main source for news and entertainment. There were all kinds of fifteen minute, and half hour programs on every afternoon during the week such as Terry and the Pirates, Sky King, The Shadow, Red Skelton, and many others that were fun to listen to by kids around our age.

One hour programs were heard in the evenings. Sunday nights were very special when the whole country listened to Bob Hope, Jack Benny, Fibber Magee and Molly, Grand Central Station, and many more. You could walk down the street on Sunday evenings, and not find any people out on the streets because they were all home listening to the radio.

One radio program came on at eleven o'clock Sunday night called "The Mummers" that was a horror program, and it used to scare the daylights out of my brother and me. What was so great about all these programs was that the listeners had to use their imagination to see what was occurring.

Marshall Grade School

I had to change schools when we moved to 258 East 11th Street. I went to Marshall Grade School on Twelfth Street for my sixth grade that was just a block from my house. It was hard to leave my friends at Jones School, and equally hard to make new friends in my neighborhood and at Marshall. I eventually made friends with two kids across the street, and we played Monopoly with the game sometimes lasting a week.

John Duda and John Dodick were two boys in my class who were thieves. They broke into houses at night, and would come to school and tell us kids what they were doing. They were also bullies, and would beat up on weak and smaller kids demanding their lunch money. Another boy in my class was a Greek named Nick Grico who was a lot tougher than either of the two thieves, and they knew it so they wouldn't bother him. I immediately made friends with Nick so the two crooks never bothered me.

One day, our female teacher tried to control the two bad guys who were acting up in class. They suddenly physically beat the day-lights out of her as the rest of us in class watched and were afraid to interfere. They were expelled from school, and I never saw them again.

I was coming home from school one day in a very bad snow storm that was so bad I couldn't see two feet in front of me. I was hit by a car as I started to cross the street right in front of my house. I had a large geography book protecting my face from the storm. The driver never slowed down before hitting me because he didn't see me.

The front car door had a pointed knob facing forward, and it punched a hole through the geography book that I was holding up, and then hit the back of my head. The blow knocked me down, but I got up and pulled my book off the door knob when the man stopped the car and asked if I was all right. I told him I was all right, and he drove off and never made a move to help me.

28

The accident called for a few stitches leaving me with a head ache for a few days, but I'll never forget how fortunate I was to have that geography book protecting my face from the blizzard because the blow to my head without that book would have probably killed me. That made me think God had a purpose for me.

My father was living with another woman who lived only a block down the street from our house. Sometimes my brother and I would walk to school with her two children. One day my mom asked me if I would go down to see my dad, and get the eleven-dollars alimony he was supposed to give us by court order.

I went to her house and knocked on the front door and when one of her kids opened it, the first thing I saw was my dad lying in bed with this woman. I went over to the bed and asked him for the alimony, and he told me to hand him his pants hanging from the bed post. He reached in his pants pocket, and handed me thirty-seven cents. When I asked him how we were supposed to live on that, he told me to come back next week and maybe he could give me more. He then rolled over with his back to me, and cuddled up to the woman as I walked out.

We Were On Relief

We were on relief during that time which meant the government gave food to people who had little or no income. I used to go down to the relief station with my wagon or sled and pick up a couple of bags of food that included a sack of potatoes, canned milk, oleo margarine, bread, a box of raisons, a bag of applies, and some canned vegetables.

I was so embarrassed picking up the food that I would go down an alley to the relief station. But I soon found that it was dumb for me to get embarrassed because everyone in the neighborhood was doing the same thing. My brother and I were so ashamed of where we lived that we would tell friends who drove us home on occasion to leave us off at the corner or at the grocery store nearby so they wouldn't see where we lived.

My mother wanted me to learn how to play the piano. She found a used one for five dollars, and they had to take out a back window to get it into the house. My mother got me a piano teacher for a dollar a lesson who would often ask me, after a few lessons, if I had practiced my lesson. I would tell her that I did, but I practiced swimming, diving, gymnastics, and ping pong instead. My lessons didn't last long, and the only song I ever learned to play was "Long Long Ago" that I could play for around 30 years.

My mother didn't have a washing machine, and I remember how many times her hands were bleeding after doing laundry with a wash board down in the cellar. She also used to make root beer. But it never got totally fermented because the kids in the neighborhood would hear about it, and bring up the bottles from the cellar to our kitchen. They would shake them up and shoot root beer all over the ceiling and walls, but my mom never scolded them.

Learning to Swim and Joining the YMCA Swim Team

I learned to swim when I was nine years old after I learned to put my head under water playing in the water fountain on Sixth and State Street. I went to the "Y" and started to take my feet off the pool bottom while making some primitive moves with my arms.

I managed to kick my legs and move my arms well enough to swim across the shallow end of the pool. With more practice but no instruction, I started to breathe with each stroke so I could swim several lengths of the pool in no time. I also learned to swim all four strokes well.

I joined the "Y" swimming team when I don't think Bob Fields knew I wasn't a member. I started to swim in the workouts, and got good enough to compete in some of their meets. I continued to improve enough to win a couple of the forty-yard events for boys twelve years and under in the city championships.

(I am in the middle of the back row)

While at the meet, a teammate, Fred Abbot, asked me if I would swim the forty-yard breast stroke slow enough for him to win because he knew I could beat him and he hadn't won anything. Like a true friend, I deliberately let him beat me and took second place.

Few people had any interest in our meets because of our age so we received little notice in the newspapers when the results were very small print. However, this time, the Erie Daily Times came up with a big spread on how Fred Abbot had won the breast stroke event, and put his picture in the paper. I learned a lesson from that occurrence and, from then on, I always gave it my best shot in any competition I encountered.

I Try Out Diving

The "Y" swimming team was preparing for a dual meet when I was around eleven years old. They lost their diver, Alan Cokefair, who got sick, and couldn't compete. We didn't have another diver, and one of the swimmers suggested that since I was a tumbler I might be able to dive.

Bob Fields was the "Y" swimming coach when I told him I didn't have any diving experience, but I could do some basic somersault dives and he said that would be fine. I practiced six dives while the swimmers were in the pool and swam under the board. Soon I could win all the diving events at meets including beating Alan Cokefair because he couldn't dive worth a lick.

No women were allowed in the pool since the "Y" was only for men and boys so we all swam in the nude. But I usually wore a tank suit while practicing and competing in diving for obvious reasons. I remember competing at the local Boy's Club when after a couple of swimming races, I came out on the board nude and started to put my suit on for the diving event. Everyone in the pool area started to laugh because there were some ladies in the crowd, and I shot out of there like a bullet to put my suit on in the locker room.

Bob Fields was the swimming coach and didn't know a thing about diving. I don't think he knew much about coaching swimming either, but he thought he was a great coach. Unfortunately, our results didn't prove that.

He informed the team on one Monday that we were all going to Buffalo on Saturday for a swimming meet followed by a tour of Buffalo and Niagara Falls. He said he would put the names of those making the trip on the bulletin board on Friday, and I got really excited about going because I was by far the best diver on the team. I had never been out of Erie much further than twenty miles, and Buffalo was nearly a hundred miles away so I had trouble getting to sleep for the rest of the week while dreaming about all the fun we were going to have.

However, when I went to the bulletin board on Friday my name was missing. I went to Coach Fields and told him that he must have made a mistake because I had won every diving contest the whole season, and he was taking Cokefair who had never won anything. Coach Fields looked at me, and said he decided to take Cokefair because he didn't think I was cut out to be a diver.

That kind of rejection was very painful for a twelve-year-old boy, and it really hurt when I went to the "Y" the next morning and watched all my friends board the bus while carrying their lunches and swim gear and whooping it up. Broken hearted, I stood on the sidewalk crying my eyes out, and waved at them as the bus drove off. That was another painful lesson I would never forget, and I wanted to make sure I'd never do anything like that to anyone.

As I slowly walked home, I said to myself, "So he doesn't think I'll make a diver, well we'll see about that." The next week I started to dive three or four hours a day by myself in the "Y" pool when the swimmers were not around. I was out to prove that Bob Fields was wrong about me. In fact, I skipped Thursdays attending junior high school to practice diving because they didn't have any gym classes at East High on that day.

I didn't realize it at the time that I was trying to learn under several handicaps. The first was that I didn't have a coach. I would ask anyone that came into the pool to tell me if I was making certain moves properly which wasn't much help because they knew nothing about diving. The only other assistance I had was some drawings of dives that were taken from the diving rule book on the bulletin board. The problem with that was the drawings were made in 1908, and the only ones that could perform the dives in the drawing were God and superman.

I walked into the "Y" gym when I was twelve, and saw a new gymnastic apparatus known as a trampoline that was usually only seen in circuses. George Nissen, from Cedar Rapids, Iowa was the maker of gymnastic equipment since the 1930's, and decided to make and sell trampolines to the public as a form of recreation. The Y.M.C.A. bought one and I was one of the first persons in Erie to try it out.

The landing bed was made with two canvas covers and after some use, the lower canvas sheet would split and had to be replaced with a new bed. The bed was attached to the metal frame with metal springs that didn't offer much spring to the user. But it was springier than the diving board in the pool so I could learn more dives with higher degrees of difficulty.

The Army used trampolines for conditioning troops during the Second World War, and soon after, gymnastic teams all over the world started to use it as one of the events in gymnastic meets. The metal springs and bed were improved, and replaced with a nylon web that over the years allowed the athlete to jump as high as twenty feet while performing difficult stunts in sequences.

Unfortunately, it was found to be dangerous when sold to the public so most of the high schools and clubs in the country banned them. But they are still used as an event in colleges, clubs, and in the Olympic Games while a different version of the trampoline can still be purchased by the public.

Learning to dive on a regulation diving board was also a handicap. The board was 16 feet long and 15 inches wide, and tapered from three inches at the back end to 1½ inches thick in the front end to give it some flexibility and spring. The boards in those days were made of laminated wood pieces glued together, and covered with cocoa matting to prevent a diver from slipping.

They were normally mounted on a metal stand that extended the board six feet over the edge of the pool, and one meter above the water surface. The "Y" swimming pool was twenty yards long, and had a crummy diving board that was 12 feet long and 13 inches wide. The back end of the wooden board was about 4 inches thick and tapered down to about 2½ inches at the front end.

The board was also attached to the deck with bolts in the back end and a four-inch-wide steel band wrapped over the board near the edge of the pool that was used as a fulcrum. The tip of the board was about two feet above the water where the pool depth was only eight feet and the ceiling was 9 feet above the board.

The spring from the board was minimal and only slightly better than jumping off the ground. The board didn't offer much spring and because of the low ceiling, I eventually could touch it with my stomach when performing a reverse dive layout. To say that the diving equipment was primitive was a great understatement. However, I made the best of it, and took the challenge while not having a real concept on how the dives should be performed.

My High School Team

The city swimming and diving championships were again held at Strong Vincent High School because it had the best swimming and diving facility in Erie. A very special treat was given to us at the meet when Mike Peppe, from Ohio State University, and recognized as the swimming coach and greatest diving coach in the world brought along his top diver, Al Patnik, to give a diving exhibition. Patnik was the winner of twenty consecutive national diving championships, and the best springboard diver in the world.

Patnik did a superb job diving from a poor diving facility into a pool that was only eight feet deep when pools were normally at least ten feet deep. I won the city diving championship at the meet, and Patnik gave me his autograph on the box that contained my medal that I still have today. I was awed by him and his performance, and began to feel I wanted to be just like him and never dreamed that we would later become very good friends.

The best high school swimmers from Erie at that time were Achilles Poulakis from East High School and Jimmy Duke from Academy High School, and the best diver was Benny Strand from Tech High School who finished his diving career as I was seriously starting mine. Poulakis and Duke were sprinters and middle distance swimmers that had won city and state championships three years in a row. They competed against each other in several events at the city championships, and the stands were always packed when the two swam against each other.

Poulakis came from a wealthy family that owned a candy store at 926 State Street. Gus Poulakis was his father and owner who was nationally known because he made chocolate figures, like the ones we now see made from ice on television. They were displayed for years in the front windows of his store over the Easter and Christmas holidays that attracted people from all over the country.

Gus took a great interest in the Erie "Y" and their swimmers over the years that, of course, included his son, Achilles, who later swam for the University of Michigan before going into the Navy for a couple of years during the war. He eventually took over his father's store when he graduated from Michigan, and like his father, made candy and national displays and was recognized as the best candy maker in the country.

Gus was made "Erie's Man of the Year" in 1974 when a banquet was given in his honor. Not able to attend the occasion, I sent him a telegram that read "Very few people have unselfishly contributed more of themselves to the young boys of Erie than you Gus Poulakis. Though busy with your store, you always found the time, energy and patience to offer guidance and direction to many under privileged children like myself. I and many others will be forever indebted to you for making us realize that life has many fine things to offer if we are willing to work for it. Erie is a fine city to live in because of people like you, Doc Ainsworth, and Art Weibel who have made it so. Though I can't be with you tonight, I wish to extend my best wishes, and thanks to a father of many." Thinking that this message revealed the whole story of the man being honored, Max Darone, the boys Director of the Erie Y.M.C.A. suggested that Gus write a book about some of his best moments in his life because of a telegram sent to him from a boy that was forgotten and became a real man.

Jimmy Duke was a quiet good looking youngster whose parents never took an interest in his swimming. He ended up going to Michigan State University where he was an All-American swimmer. He joined the F.B.I. after graduating, and was never seen again in Erie.

Benny Strand was a much better diver than I was, but he never went to college and ended his diving career as I was beginning mine. He was a great friend of mine, and followed my career for nearly fifty years by attending the national championships and several Olympic Games to watch me coach.

CHAPTER 4

My High School Career

East High School and Strong Vincent High School

I started junior high school at East High School after leaving sixth grade and Marshal School. East High was about three miles directly east of our house at 258 East 11th Street. My older brother, Jimmy, also attended East High and was going into ninth grade so we always rode our bicycles to school together.

We usually took our lunches to school because we couldn't afford to buy them in the school cafeteria. Mother was great at making peanut butter and banana sandwiches. Never ones to complain, we also got an apple or fruit with our lunches. I liked East High right away, and found most of the students were Polish and Russians from hard working families that made for a very loyal close-knit group in school.

The sports programs included the junior varsity for the seventh and eighth grades, and the varsity was for athletes that were in ninth through twelfth grade. I was too small to play junior varsity football and too short for basketball, and I had no interest in participating in either one. I thought there might be some event in track that I could compete in, but my legs were too short to run fast.

The only event I thought I could pursue in track was pole vaulting, but I never got any encouragement to try out. Besides, I wanted to continue to dive so the only activity I thought I could participate in besides diving was cheerleading.

I Make the Cheerleading Squad

I made the cheerleading squad in eighth grade. It was made up of four boys and four girls, and we led cheers in assemblies for the junior high football teams. One day, our head cheerleader got sick and couldn't lead the cheers, so they asked me to take his place.

I was scared to death because I had never addressed a large group of people before. I got so excited that I made all kinds of mistakes and the students started to laugh and went wild. I got them to yell so loud that we thought it might break the windows in the auditorium.

The noise also interrupted a few of the older student class rooms. The students enjoyed themselves so much that the teachers asked me to also lead cheers for the upper-class students that followed the junior assembly, and they reacted in the same way as the younger class.

This resulted in me leading cheers for both the junior varsity and senior varsity assemblies and the varsity football games. It got so good that if the students didn't have a hoarse throat after the assemblies, they hadn't yelled loud enough. Suddenly I became the most popular student at East High even though I felt so shy.

Shirley Friar was my cheerleading partner and two years ahead of me when I was in the ninth grade. She started to date my brother while both were in the eleventh grade. East High played Massillon High School from Massillon, Ohio and was known to have one of the best high school football teams in the country.

They beat our team in Erie 66-0 then came back the next year and beat us 73-0. When they came back the third year, they beat us 13-6 and never came back again. Twenty thousand fans packed the stadium for all three games not to watch the football games, but to be entertained by their marching band.

Their band was the best band any of us had ever seen and ranked with the best in the country. When we played them for the third time, our cheerleading director wanted me to dress up in an Indian Chief outfit that was our logo, to fight the Massillon tiger mascot during half time.

Unfortunately, the temperature at the game that night was about eight degrees above zero so she suggested we cancel the skit. I pleaded with her to let me try and if I found it to be too cold, I would go inside. So I took the challenge and it turned out to be a very entertaining half time.

Tough Teacher

Miss Laughey was my tenth-grade teacher who often came to school drunk. She usually had a hangover when she came to class and one day when she had a bad one, she decided to take it out on our class. If she had a tough night that left her with a splitting headache then she told our class that if we made any noise she would punish us.

I happened to drop my pencil on the floor as she was walking toward me, and as I started to pick it up she slapped me across the face hard enough to knock me to the floor. She told the class that if anyone else caused a disturbance, they would get some of the same. I ran into my brother in the hall after class and he asked me where I got the bruised face, and I told him what had happened.

The next day while attending her class, my brother came walking into the room, walked up to her desk, and bent over with his face about six inches from hers. He told her that if she ever landed a hand on me again, he would come back and beat the living crap out of her. She came to school sober every day for the rest of the semester, and never threatened any members of the class again.

I Joined the Swimming Team

I made the swimming team in ninth grade and joined the swimmers with names like Jakabowski, Melninski, Robaski, Popodinski, Ropoluski, Sokolov, Etter, Brugger, and Poulakis. With all those Polish kids, one German, one Greek, and one English teammate, we went on to win the Pennsylvania State High School Championships when I was in tenth grade. I added my effort to winning the title by taking fifth in diving.

The diving equipment at East High was the worst I had ever seen. There was a balcony above the back end of the board that was so low that I had to stand, bent over, until taking two forward steps on the board. Then I could stand up to finish the approach and perform a dive. Art Arrowsmith was the swimming coach and a nice guy but knew less about swimming and diving than Bob Fields, the coach at the "Y." The team won the state meet because we were talented.

Conflicts with My Dad

A couple of years later, I was walking down State Street when I saw my father coming toward me from the other direction. When passing me, he looked straight into my eyes with no sign that he recognized me. I was fifteen years old when my brother got the idea that maybe our father wasn't as bad as we thought, and encouraged my mother to take him back to live with us.

This went on for a couple of weeks when she finally gave in and he moved in the next week. I had just come home from the "Y" where I was taking a martial arts class, when my father and I had a little discussion. He was telling me who was the boss of the family when he grabbed my arm and twisted it to the point of pain.

I suddenly grabbed him by the wrist and bent it backwards which forced him to the floor face down. I put my foot on his elbow, as he yelled with pain, and told him that if he so much as breathed deep, I would break his arm. I told my mother, without raising my voice, that I was leaving the house and wouldn't return until he was gone.

I went down to Wendy's house for a couple of days and got in touch with my mom later when she told me that he had left. I later found that I had twisted his wrist so bad that he couldn't work for a week. Sorry to say, I never regretted what I did and I never spoke to him again.

Years later my brother made amends with him and told him that he should try to get to know me when he replied, "Let Hobie live his life and I'll live mine." No wonder, when my mother called me to inform me of his death in 1973, I said, "So what else is new, mom?" Even though many other youngsters had even worse times with their parents, I can honestly say that similar incidents leave a scar on the victim forever.

Soon after my father left our house, my mother met a nice man out at Waldamere Park who took her out for lunch and she invited him to our house to meet my brother and me after going out with him a few times. His name was Howard Holder, and we liked him a lot when he started to come to dinner every night. He would study the horse racing newspapers that he often bet on, and then go home.

About fifty years old with real thick eyebrows and a pleasant personality, he had a good job working as a supervisor near the city dock where the ships brought in coal. When he won on a horse race, he would bring us food and other things needed around the house. Howard hung around our house for around seven years and showed a genuine interest in my mother and us kids, but we never saw him ever make any romantic moves toward her.

Thinking that he would someday ask our mother to marry him, he never did and that led us to believe that being a Catholic, he didn't believe in divorce. We also thought that he might have been married before and his wife might have died.

Then one day, he developed a bad case of hiccoughs that continued to get worse over a year. He finally went to a specialist in Cleveland who sent him to the Mayo Clinic in Minnesota for tests and treatments, but they couldn't help him and he passed away about six months later. He was a wonderful man who was as close to being a father to us than anyone we ever knew. I remember that he gave me forty-seven dollars for my first quarter tuition at Ohio State just before he passed away.

Pearl Harbor is Bombed

One night as I came out of the movie theater that was across the street from the "Y," I saw newspaper boys running up and down the street hollering "Extra, Extra. Pearl Harbor bombed." I had no idea where Pearl Harbor was. I'll never forget the fear I suddenly felt. I knew that if my brother would have to go off to war, I would be following him when I turned 18 if the war lasted long enough.

My Older Brother Jimmy

I was fifteen when, as expected, my brother was called up to serve in the army. He was in the infantry and later switched over to the paratroopers and served in the 11th Airborne and ended up fighting the Japanese in the Philippine Islands. Shirley Fryer, my brother's girlfriend, wrote him a letter every single day for 3½ years during which time he was awarded the Silver Star for bravery, one grade below The Congressional Medal of Honor.

I was at a movie one night when a news review showed American paratroopers dropping down and shooting the Japanese on the ground in the Rizal Stadium in Manila, the capital of the Philippines. A few years later I was in that same Rizal Stadium where my brother was in the group I had seen in that news reel.

Shirley and Jimmy got married when he returned from the war. He then went to DePauw University in Indiana where he majored in music, and later attended Indiana State where he got his master's degree. He took a teaching job in 1953 at Saegertown, Pennsylvania which is a little town located in the rolling countryside of Crawford County about forty miles south of Erie with a population of around nine hundred people.

He started out as a music teacher and was later asked to be the band director for twenty-six students who were in such a bad way that they had to buy their own instruments and wore capes as uniforms when performing at half time during their football games.

Having no experience in directing marching bands because he was an orchestral music teacher, he made up his own formations when the band danced and marched in triple time rather than double time that made it exciting and very entertaining to watch. It wasn't long before his band grew to seventy students and it was so good that some of the football players quit the team to join the band.

The band first practiced on a stage in the gym that was separated by a curtain that made it very difficult to teach so they moved into a garage nearby. The band became so good that the school built a separate building attached to the school. They performed for different social groups all over northern Pennsylvania, and won several competitive band awards. Jim and his band soon received national attention and played at half time in two NFL professional football bowl games, one of which President Nixon came out of the stands and invited him and his band to play in the Spring Festival in Washington, D.C.

Most people leave their seats to get refreshments, but this time when hearing the band playing at the half for the first pro-game, the people turned around to see what was going on and returned to their seats. With the game being televised nationally, all the commercials were cut to watch his show that went on for nearly twenty minutes. It wasn't long before he was recognized as having the best high school marching band east of the Mississippi River.

It was not unusual to see hundreds of cars following the school buses loaded with the band going somewhere to present a concert. I often thought what he might have done if he was the band director at Indiana University because if he had, the football stadium would have been packed for every game for years. However, having the reputation for great bands, Massillon High School, that was known to have one of the best high school bands in the country, hired him where he remained for over twenty years.

Strong Vincent High School

I made three great friends in John Wolford, John Boyd, and Jim Pflueger while competing for the "Y" swimming team when I was very young. They attended Strong Vincent High School and suggested for years that I change from East High School to their school because they had the best swimming coach in Erie.

Changing schools meant that my mother and I would have to move to the west side, and I would lose a year of competition for changing schools. When I finished the tenth grade in 1942 and my brother was graduating and leaving for Fort Benning, Georgia, to take part in the war, I pleaded with my mother to move to the west side where I could get some real coaching and go someplace with my diving.

My mother kept asking me why I needed to dive when it would never do me any good. Finally, realizing that it was important to me, she consented to move, but only if she could find a place that we could afford and thankfully, she eventually did. The students at East High School started to call me a traitor when it was found that I was going to attend Strong Vincent High School. But they didn't understand the reason for my changing schools.

Later when both schools started to have alumni reunions, East High always invited me to theirs even when I had only attended up to the eleventh grade. In fact, I was invited as a guest speaker at their reunion on two occasions and recently went to our 65th and last high school reunion.

Wolford, Pflueger, Boyd and I became lifeguards on the Peninsula following my sophomore year at East. We were only sixteen years old when most of the older boys were in the service, so they offered us the job. In the meantime, the Y.M.C.A. got me a job guarding young children at the Erie Bible Camp for two weeks near the beginning of summer, so I didn't start guarding on the peninsula until a little later in the summer.

The camp was located on the shore of Lake Erie, about four miles west of Erie and my job was to guard about a hundred small children aging from six to twelve years in a swimming area marked off in the lake with ropes and buoys. Since I had to guard them once in the morning and once in the late afternoon, it made no sense for me to leave the area, and go back to town on a bus between sessions. So, out of boredom, I started to attend some of the Bible classes but they didn't impress me.

While walking on the dirt road from the camp to catch the bus on the main road for home, out of nowhere, a change came over me like a bolt of lightning. Knowing little about religion, I suddenly became a true believer in Jesus Christ and God. It felt like my feet were off the ground for a very long time.

I had never been a Christian before because my family never attended church. I was so infatuated with this strange change in my life that from that time on, I never cussed, smoked, drank alcohol, or had any sexual experiences until I was discharged from the service years later.

I will say that I swore only once in all that time over an incident that happened to me while in the service. My reaction was so strong that I began to wear a celluloid collar, black shoes, and black socks and when changing schools from East High to Strong Vincent the students at first thought I was a little weird.

But they heard of my cheerleading reputation, and I was made their head cheerleader. I knew that most of the kids at Strong Vincent thought that they were being led in cheers by a real nut case, and they were probably right. I eventually returned to wearing normal clothing and life, but I never lost my religious faith nor did I try to push my beliefs onto anyone else during my teaching and coaching career.

After lifeguarding on the peninsula for about a month, I was checking out at beach headquarters to go home when a call came in that a young girl had drowned on the Waldermere Beach that had no lifeguards. I went out on the road on a Sunday that was really crowded and hailed a car with my whistle, and we forced our way through the traffic for about a mile to the Waldermere beach.

The girl was about fifteen years old, and didn't know how to swim. Unfortunately, she jumped off the side of the pier on the deeper side thinking that the water was shallow.

Due to the wind and currents in Lake Erie, the pier had deep water on one side and shallow water on the other side. The current and waves pulled her away from the pier.

A man dived in and swam to her when she hollered for help, but he swam so fast that he was exhausted by the time he approached her and couldn't make the rescue. Another man then went out and pulled her to shore where she was lying face down on the sand when I arrived. I immediately pulled out her tongue and applied artificial respiration using the Holger-Nielsen method. That was the only method offered by the Red Cross in those days. I worked on her for about twenty minutes as her parents watched my efforts, and I'll never forget their contorted faces when they realized that I had arrived too late and she was dead.

I had a dream about a beautiful blond girl one night, and it was so real that it stayed with me for a few days. Unbelievably, another guard and I were stationed on Third Beach the following Sunday when it started to rain so hard that we decided to close the beach and hitchhike back to the beach headquarters and go home after checking out. With little traffic, a car came along and stopped to give us a ride. When we got in the back seat, the girl in the front seat turned around, I looked up and saw the same girl that I had seen in my dream. It is difficult to describe my feeling at that moment. But on the ride back to headquarters, I found out that her name was Ruthie and her father was a minister in a Swedish church one block from where I used to live on the East side of town.

I was working on First Beach, the first beach coming onto the peninsula, the next day. Being Monday morning, no one had arrived on the beach, so I was sitting on some rocks watching the waves wash in. I turned around and saw Ruthie getting off her bicycle, and walking toward me. I could hardly believe my eyes and when I asked her what she was doing here she said she came out to see me...WOW!

This was truly amazing because she had no idea at which beach I would be guarding that covered a ten-mile stretch. We spent the morning and early afternoon talking and getting acquainted, and it was nice to find that she also attended Strong Vincent and was a grade behind me.

That day was the beginning of a romance with the first girlfriend I ever had. Ruthie was by far the prettiest girl at Strong Vincent, and when cheerleading at a night football game, it was very easy to spot her in the stands because of her beautiful platinum blond hair. (pictured standing on the right)

Ruthie lived on Lincoln Avenue only a few houses away from John Boyd's house, and about a half mile from the High School. I went over to her house a few times, and got to know her mother and two younger sisters all of whom were wonderful people. About six months later, her father, a Navy chaplain, was suddenly assigned to a station in

Daytona Beach, Florida and the whole family went with him. That made me one sad boy.

A year went by before she and her family returned to Erie, but things had changed. Though we remained friends, we both started to date other people and went our separate ways. Ruthie graduated from Strong Vincent and a couple of years later I went to visit her in Detroit where she was in school to become an airline hostess. Ruthie was made Homecoming Queen, and later was Queen of Queens in a contest with 10 other queens.

We were having a candle light dinner, and I was shocked when she asked me if the reason I had come to see her was to find out if I was still in love with her. After some thought, I told her I was but not in the same way that I had been when she was a sixteen-year-old girl back in Erie.

We went on with our lives but never lost touch with each other. She got married years later to a prominent insurance man, and they had four blond-haired boys. I met the boys a couple of times when they were in their late teens and early twenties. Her husband had a heart attack later, and passed away. I didn't see her again until many years later.

When we met, we had a long talk and she asked me if I wanted to marry her. I declined again, but we continued to be everlasting friends. She later married Leo, her next-door neighbor, and I got to meet him. He was well over six feet tall, and a wonderful guy. He later wrote me a letter telling me he was a diver growing up in school, and I was his hero. I talked to him on the phone a couple times, and he said he understood my friendship with Ruthie. She later developed cancer and passed away in 2006. Though I never kissed her we had been dear friends for sixty-five years.

Wolford, Pflueger, Boyd, and I decided to buy a car, after meeting Ruthie, so we wouldn't have to ride our bikes out to the beach to guard every day. We finally found one owned by the McClenathen brothers who were former Vincent swimmers.

They owned a 1930 four door Dodge sedan and after some bargaining, they sold it to us for 75 dollars. My friends gave me their share of the money and while working at the beach, they told me to go downtown to a garage located a half block off State Street and pick up the car. After paying for the car, I asked one of the McClenathen brothers how I was going to get the car out to the peninsula, and he said that I should drive it out.

I told him I didn't know how to drive so he showed me where the accelerator, brake, clutch and stick gear shift were, and explained the procedure used when switching the gears. He then handed me the keys and sales slip, started the car, and wished me good luck and left. Having never been behind the wheel of a car, with the grace of God, I drove the car out of the garage. In a bucking bronco style, while trying to shift gears, I managed to get through the city stopping for the traffic lights during the busy hours of the day, and got to the beach alive.

We decided to give the car a name and agreed to name her "Esmerelda" and painted the name in big white letters on the back end just below the rear window. Gasoline and tires were rationed in those days, and we bought our gasoline for five gallons a dollar using black-market gas coupons. Tires and inner tubes were out of the question. When the tires wore down to the point that the inner tube showed, we put cardboard in the holes to prevent a blow out or a flat tire.

Fixing a flat tire in those days took about a half days' work because you had to remove the tire, take it off the rim and pull out the inner tube to fix the hole. Then you had to put the tube back in the tire, fill it up with air, put it back on the rim, and replace it on the car. Getting the tire off and on the rim was a real chore and unbelievably, we never had a flat for nearly a year.

The car became very popular with the lifeguards, the people on the beach, and especially with the students at Vincent when school started in the fall. We used to charge students who lived near the school a dollar a week to pick them up in the morning and take them to school and that helped pay for the gas. Everyone wanted to take a ride in Esmerelda and most of them did for a couple of years.

One time, we had a football game with a high school in Girard, New York, that was about forty miles away from Erie. We loaded the car up with students and drove over for the game. We had cardboard in the front tires and luckily didn't have a flat because if we had, we would have been stranded because we didn't have a spare tire.

The roof on the car was made of black canvas material that developed a small hole that gradually increased to the point where the roof blew off from a strong wind in a rain storm. It left nothing but chicken wire on the top. From then on, we would park under a tree, and put a blanket over the chicken wire when it started to rain.

Wolford and Pflueger went into the service a few months later, so I kept the car in a garage behind our house. One day, I left the back door on the right side of the car slightly open, and when backing out of the alley to the street, the back door caught on to the rain pipe on the house and sprung the door. John Boyd and I managed to get the door closed, but if anyone wanted to get in the back seat on the right side of the car, they had to crawl through the window.

I gave the car to Boyd when I graduated, and when he graduated he sold the car to three lower class boys for five dollars so that he could go into the service. I tried to buy the car back from them when I returned from the service a couple of years later, but they wouldn't sell it to me.

Frank Petinato was the head lifeguard out on the peninsula and rode around in a little red car to check out all the beaches every day. He was also a teacher at Academy High School and everyone liked him. He had a cottage and when we finished our first season as lifeguards on the beach, he asked us to get permission from our parents to attend a party at his cottage that would probably last all night. All our parents agreed and when we all showed up, we found that he was serving us beer. I believe a few of us had never tasted it before.

43

We all got drunk and had to sleep it off before going home and promised him that we

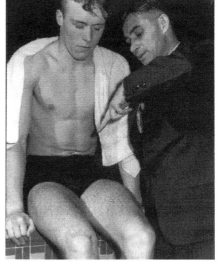

would not tell our parents about the drinking. He got away with it with the war on, but he would have gone to jail if such an incident occurred today because nearly all of us were only sixteen years old. He kept his job on the beach for around forty years until he passed away around the turn of the century and had a beach named after him.

When starting school at Strong Vincent High School in my junior year, I received instructions from Art Weibel, the swimming coach, a man who changed my life. He was a graduate from Springfield College in Springfield, Massachusetts, which is a great school for those who wish to major in physical education. He was also an honorable man and one tough teacher and coach. He took no nonsense from anyone while being firm but fair with his athletes and students. This was our Strong Vincent High School swimming team in 1943.

I am second from left in middle row next to Swede Carlson on my left.

He took a liking to me, but soon found it was not possible for him to coach one diver while also trying to coach a bunch of swimmers who were swimming back and forth

44

under the diving board during practice. So, he decided to coach me for an hour after swimming practice that meant he gave up an hour or more of his time every day to help me with my diving and that resulted in him eating dinner at home an hour later than usual.

With the war on and having fought in the First World War, he took our team out to the beach about once or twice a month and taught us how to fight hand to hand. He also put us through rigorous exercises, and ran us through obstacle courses. His purpose was to get us in the best mental and physical shape possible in preparation for when we would be called for military duty.

To show how serious he was about coaching, one day while I was sitting at the counter drinking a milkshake with another swimmer in the drug store next to our school, he walked in and without saying a word, swiped the milkshakes off the counter onto the floor and walked out. In his silent way, he was telling us not to try and get into shape by drinking milk shakes.

I soon learned another great lesson from him when he was teaching us how to march in the gym, and a man came in to talk to him. He told me to take over the marching while he talked to his visitor, and when I hesitated for a moment by saying, "I guess so," he immediately told John Wolford to take over. I remember how embarrassed I was that he handled it that way in front of my friends. However, I learned that he did not want a flimsy vague answer, but a straight "yes" or "no" which was a philosophy I followed when I became a teacher and coach.

Vincent had just bought a new one-meter wooden diving board and stand with a non-moveable fulcrum when I arrived. The new diving board was stiff and covered with cocoa matting, and it tilted upward about four inches more than the standard requirement. Weibel went to the athletic director with a request to loosen the bolts holding the fulcrum, and move it back a few inches to give the board more spring. The athletic director denied his request, but we changed it anyway and replaced the fulcrum back to its original position after each practice and no one ever caught us.

Coach Weibel invited me to his house for a talk when nearing the end of the swimming season in my junior year, and I was really scared because I thought I had done something wrong. But when I sat down with him in his living room, he informed me that he had taught me all he knew about diving, and I would have to go elsewhere to learn more about the sport.

When asked if he had any idea where I could go, he suggested that I compete in the 1943 Senior National A.A.U. Championships that were being staged at the New York Athletic Club in New York City during the first week in April. At first, I thought he was kidding or he was crazy, but it became apparent that he was serious.

I told him I couldn't possibly go because I didn't have any money. He suggested that I go home and talk to my mother, and see if she could raise fifty dollars which he figured would be the cost of the trip. She answered me exactly the way I thought she would when I told her what I needed. She said she couldn't possibly find that kind of money which was like five-hundred dollars today.

I was disappointed but I told her I understood. Never in my short life was I ever so shocked when a couple of days later she said she had scraped up the money. I never did learn where she got the money, but I am sure that she made some sort of sacrifice to get it.

I informed Coach Weibel that my mother got the money. He advised me to seek out the good divers at the meet when I arrived and ask them if they could make some suggestions on how I could improve my diving. I was to write down everything they told me. He then instructed me to bring back all the information I could get so he could use it to coach me for the state championships in the coming year.

I was sixteen years old and had never been further than a few miles from Erie in my life when I bought a round-trip ticket on the Greyhound bus to New York City for eleven dollars. I went to the 63rd Street Branch Y.M.C.A., and rented a room for $2.50 a night. When I arrived at the "Big City," I only needed to walk a block or two from the bus terminal to the New York City Athletic Club across the street from Central Park.

I thought New York City was a beautiful city back in 1943 because I never saw any pimps, drug addicts, pick pockets, pan handlers begging for money, drunks laying in the alleys, prostitutes, dirty movie theaters, the homeless begging for food, graffiti, or any noticeable crime. The taxis cost the passengers five cents per quarter mile, so I rode the bus and the subways for a nickel.

I cut through Central Park after practice each day with no fear of being mugged or molested while enjoying the fresh air, birds, fountains, trees, and friendly people. I stopped a man walking down the street one day, and asked him if he could tell me where I could find the Empire State Building. The man gave me a funny look then looked straight up, as did I, to find that I was standing directly in front of it.

I entered the extravagant athletic club once I got settled in, and was a little scared walking into the pool. I had only seen one great diver in my life who was Al Patnik when he gave a diving exhibition at Vincent, and now I was going to try and compete against the best in the land. With the war on, there were only sixteen divers competing in the meet, and I soon found that two of them, Charlie Batterman and Frank Dempsey, were national champions from Ohio State. They are seated in front row.

I immediately introduced myself and asked if they would kindly help me with my diving. Being the youngest diver there, and never dreaming that they would later be very good friends of mine, they agreed to give me a few pointers during practice sessions. I worked out twice a day with my two heroes and wrote down everything they told me about my dives.

I went to a movie or just walked around the Times Square area taking in the sights when I was not in the pool. I treated myself to a show at Radio City Hall where they showed a movie followed by a live show featuring the famous Rockettes dancers. What a thrill and all for just eighty-eight cents!

1943
WESTERN CONFERENCE
NATIONAL INTERCOLLEGIATE
NATIONAL A.A.U. (INDOOR)
NATIONAL A.A.U. (OUTDOOR)
CHAMPIONS

OM ROW: CHARLES BATTERMAN,   FRANK L. DEMPSEY,   MILLER A. ANDERSON   JOHN L. NOVAK
E ROW: MICHAEL PEPPE (COACH), VERNON H. REISS, JOHN F. RYAN, DONALD E. COOLAHAN, CAPT. MARK A. FOLLANSBEE, JACK A. MARTIN
WILLIAM F. RYAN, EMIL MAMALIGA, HAROLD BIGGS (TRAINER)
ROW: CARL J. WIRTHWEIN (ASSISTANT COACH), KEO NAKAMA, BIRKBY A. LEIP, JAMES E. COUNSILMAN, HARRY F. SULLIVAN, THEODORE
K. HOBERT, THOMAS R. HEDGES, MYRON VOLK, ROBERT S. AGATSTON (MANAGER)
RT: DONALD B. SCHNABEL, WILLIAM M. SMITH, JAMES STRONG   STANLEY PRAVER, JACK HILL

Who showed up a couple of days later but John Boyd and a couple of our swimmers from Vincent to watch me compete. I couldn't spend much time with them because of practice, so they spent their time taking in the sights in New York City. I was in fifth place after performing the five basic dives from the one-meter board, but I missed a front double somersault badly when performing the optional dives and didn't qualify for the finals. I ended up in thirteenth place.

I saw John Boyd and the swimmers after the meet and told them how sorry I was that they had come all that way only to see me foul up. They started to laugh and said it was okay because they didn't show up in time to see me perform because they had gotten involved with some sightseeing. I was upset with them at first but got over it in a couple of days.

I gave coach Weibel all the information that I had gathered from Batterman and Dempsey when I arrived home. He coached me through my senior year which made it possible for me to win every meet including the Pennsylvania State High School Championship. After returning from the state meet Weible suggested that I compete in the National A.A.U. Championships again. They were being held at the University of Michigan in Ann Arbor a couple of weeks later.

47

This time I didn't tell him that I didn't have the funds for the trip, but I did have enough to buy a bus ticket to Ann Arbor and a dollar for food. I arrived on Wednesday and went to the pool on Thursday morning to practice and was surprised to find Charlie Batterman who had helped me in New York.

We worked out together and after practice, he suggested we go out for lunch. Though thrilled with the chance to be with Charlie, I started to make excuses before he interrupted me and asked me how much money I had in my pocket. Not wanting to tell him, he asked me again and I finally told him I only had a nickel. He then asked me where I had stayed the night before, and I told him I stayed at the "Y."

Still curious, he asked me in what room I had stayed and I gave him some dumb excuse but finally confessed that I snuck into the "Y" and found a closet full of dirty bed sheets where I slept for the night. Batterman then told me that he was attending grad school at Columbia University. The school was paying his expenses for the meet, so he invited me to stay and eat with him at the Michigan Union for the duration of my stay.

The one meter event was on Friday. The contest occurred in April of 1944 when our country was at war with Germany and Japan, and most of the good divers in America were in the service. Strother Martin, better known as "T-bone" was an officer in the Navy when competing and went on to be a very famous movie actor after the war when he was nominated for an Oscar award as a supporting actor in the movie "Butch Cassidy and the Sun Dance Kid." He was in several great movies and usually appeared as a person much older than he was.

I have never forgotten Charlie Batterman for his kindness and concern and though he recently passed away, he remains to be my hero and true friend for over sixty years. I know that if he hadn't taken me in, I would have gone without food for two days, and that would have greatly affected my performance and I probably would have never taken third place and gone to college.

I remember walking home about three miles in a rain storm after getting off the bus from Ann Arbor on late Sunday night. I thought, how I should act when attending school on Monday morning? I didn't know if the newspaper knew of my accomplishment. But as soon as I walked in the door my mother welcomed me with a copy of the local Sunday paper.

On the front page in the sports section they printed a picture of me performing a swan dive along with a nice write up. Looking at that made me even more afraid of what to expect from my school friends, but I was relieved when they didn't say much.

Coach Weibel invited me to his home again about a week later to inform me that he felt I should go to college where I could get an education while using my diving talents. I told him that I didn't have any money, and since colleges didn't give scholarships until after the Second World War, college was out of the question.

Besides, I hadn't taken enough college prep courses in high school to qualify. I wasn't aware the swimming coaches from the University of Michigan and Ohio State University were interested in me. And even if I had known, it wouldn't have mattered because we didn't have any funds for college.

Unaffected by my excuses, oach Weibel continued to encourage me to take courses that would get me into college that included two years of a language. That didn't seem possible because I was already half way through my senior year. But coach Weibel knew the German teacher at Vincent, and convinced her to let me take German one, two, three, and four in my last semester.

I soon found myself taking German "one" and learning the meaning of die, das, and der, and then trying to read German when taking German 'four' in another class. The German teacher thought it would help if I joined the German club so she made me the president of the Club, and classmate Ann B. Davis (later known as Alice of the Brady Bunch TV series), the vice-president. I finally graduated with a little above grade "C" average, but that was good enough to qualify me for college. My high school graduation photo is below.

Matt Mann, the swimming coach at Michigan, saw me compete at the nationals and told Achilles Poulakis, who was on my team at East High and their swimming team, to recruit me. Achilles told his dad Gus, and he offered to pay my way through college if I would attend the University of Michigan. I was invited to visit Michigan and check out their swim team, the courses given, and the campus. But when talking to Matt Mann, I realized he knew nothing about diving and my diving would never improve, so I wasn't too anxious to attend there.

After returning home from the nationals at Michigan and my campus visit, I received a letter from coach Mike Peppe who invited me to visit Ohio State. I hitch-hiked down to Columbus, Ohio from Erie to look over their facilities, campus, and diving program. This program had produced the best divers in the United States and the world.

The pool at Ohio State had the largest seating capacity I had ever seen. I was also impressed with the pictures of the great divers on the walls around the pool, especially the ones of Al Patnik, Charlie Batterman, and Frank Dempsey who I knew. It was apparent that all the good divers in the country went to Ohio State.

I told Coach Peppe before I left for home that I had decided to attend Ohio State, but I didn't have any money. He said he couldn't offer me any financial aid, but he could get me a job as a lifeguard at the Scioto Country Club in the summer and I could save around $150.

He also said I could work at the Ohio State varsity pool for twenty-five cents an hour, and wash dishes in a fraternity or sorority for my meals. That did it. I was used to working hard to get what I wanted because very little was ever given to me, and I decided that Ohio State was the place for me.

Mike Peppe was known as one of the best diving coaches in the world because he had the world's best divers. Not realizing it at the time, Ohio State was creating a diving dynasty that eventually became well known because of all the great divers that performed for Ohio State since 1937. So, I enrolled at Ohio State in the summer of 1944.

It was amazing that I ever made it to Ohio State. In fact, it was a miracle that I could go to any college since I had grown up in poverty during the Depression and didn't have enough money to live on or the credentials for college. Fortunately, I also didn't have to take a college entrance exam because of the war.

CHAPTER 5

Mike Peppe and The Divers Before I Enrolled at Ohio State

The Coach and His Divers

Mike Peppe was from Columbus, Ohio and known to be a diver before he was made the swimming coach at Ohio State in 1931. He had, at best, average swim teams until 1937. He seemed to know something about diving and recruiting. His first great diver was Jim Patterson pictured here who won the N.C.A.A. Championship one-meter title.

Patterson couldn't point his toes which was an important feature when judging form in those days, but still became an outstanding diver. He was the first diver to ever perform a forward 3½ somersault from the ten-meter platform in 1931, and a 4½ somersault in 1941. He also did a forward 3½ somersault in the tuck position, then added a full twist to the dive before entering the water which no other diver has ever performed to this day.

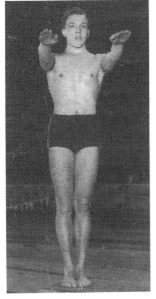

Patterson was still competing for Ohio State when he met Al Patnik, pictured on the left, who was a senior, and an outstanding diver for a Cleveland High School. Patterson convinced him to attend Ohio State. Patnik was a superb diver and the "Greg Louganis" of his time. With long legs and an excellent toe point, he went on to win twenty consecutive springboard national titles between 1938 and 1942.

That drew the attention of all the best high school divers in the country. He was, by far, the best diver in the world in his day. But unfortunately, never had the chance to show his talents internationally because of the absence of the 1940 and 1944 Olympic Games during the Second World War. Tower diving didn't become a college event until the early 1990's, so Patnik never dived tower. But I'm sure that if he had, he would have won a lot more gold medals.

Coach Peppe became aware of how valuable a good diving program was to the swimming team when the rest of the collegiate swimming coaches in the country made little attempt to recruit divers. Few of them knew anything about coaching divers, and didn't want to take the time to try and coach two or three divers while coaching thirty, forty or more swimmers.

Some college swimming coaches in the country tried to have diving eliminated from their swimming programs for years, but never succeeded because diving is an Olympic event. With Al Patnik's reputation and Mike's personality, he began to recruit other good divers who helped him draw swimmers and divers to Ohio State. It wasn't long before Mike was known as the first college coach to recognize the value of diving in swimming meets.

When Al Patnik was a junior at Ohio State he met Earl Clark, pictured here with me and Coach Ron O'Brien, while training in Ft. Lauderdale over the Christmas holidays, and they became good friends. Al talked Earl into attending Ohio State in 1939 after graduating from high school, and he turned out to be an outstanding diver on the one and three meter springboards, and particularly the ten-meter platform.

All the good divers performed the forward 1½ somersault with a full twist as their twisting optional dive up until Clark's era because it was the most difficult twisting somersault dive listed in all the diving rules books until 1947. Divers performed the dive with a slow twisting action because the twist was performed while the diver remained in the pike position throughout the whole dive, but that soon became obsolete.

Clark was bouncing up and down on the one-meter board one day when he flew off the board with the intent to perform a front dive with one twist in the layout position. He suddenly realized he was going to over rotate after performing the twist so he ducked over into a pike position, and entered the water feet first to prevent landing on his back.

Startled by the quickness of the twist, he decided to perform the dive with the same action again, but intentionally rotated the somersault more so he could enter the water head first. That would perform the forward 1½ somersault with one twist dive - a new and improved way.

Clark went on to perfect the dive using the new twisting technique, and performed it from the three-meter board against his teammate, Al Patnik, in the 1940 National A.A.U. Championships. He received perfect scores from all the judges for the dive, and beat Al Patnik who had never been beaten before.

The new technique of performing the dive was so amazing that it was featured in the April 1940 issue of Life Magazine showing Clark performing the dive in sequence. Clark's new style is still used to this very day in all twisting somersault dives performed by all divers worldwide. Clark went on to be the first diver to ever make a grand slam in diving when he won every available national title from the one and three meter springboards, and the ten-meter tower indoor and outdoor events.

The Scioto Country Club

When I arrived in Columbus, Mike Peppe took me out to the Scioto Country Club where he got me a summer job as a lifeguard. It was one of the finest places I had ever seen. It had an eighteen-hole golf course with beautiful lawns, a lavish dining room with menus that offered very good food, a bar that was always busy, and a twenty-five-yard swimming pool with one-meter and three-meter boards.

I was given a cot to sleep on in a small area under the deck of the pool where I used card board boxes to store my clothes. The area was also used to store all the food and drinks sold at the pool concession stand.

I ate in the kitchen for free every day to save money, but for some reason, the cook didn't like me. He fed me the burnt sides of the meat with fat that often made me gag. Obviously, my diet never improved over the summer.

I really liked my job at the club because I love children, and taught many of them how to swim and dive. I used to swing them around by the arm, and then throw them into the pool where they often landed on their stomachs and backs. This caused some concern with the parents, but since their kids were having so much fun, none of them ever complained.

The Scioto Country Club was only for the elite people like doctors, lawyers and business administrators who lived in Upper Arlington, a suburb of Columbus. In those days, Jews and black people were not permitted to live in that community.

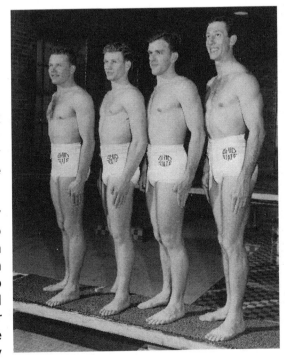

Black people did most of the domestic work in the large homes and mansions, but were not allowed to be seen on the street after six o'clock waiting for a bus. After spending some time at the country club, I found that most of the members were very kind and considerate. It appeared that no one had a hang up about anything for it was just the way things were at that time, and everyone accepted it.

I was working as a lifeguard one Sunday morning when Mike Peppe walked into the pool with some camera men, and a very handsome lieutenant in the uniform of the Army Air Corps. I asked Mike who the good-looking guy was, and he told me he was Miller Anderson. Pictured far left in photo. I had memorized all the names of the good divers in the country listed in the diving rules guides for the last ten years, and immediately recognized Miller's name as the present national diving champion. Awed by his presence because he looked like Alan Ladd, the famous movie star, I asked Mike why was he here, and he said that I would soon find out.

Miller went downstairs and changed into a swim suit. When he returned, he went up on the three-meter board where he performed a couple of simple dives, then yelled down to Mike that he was ready. Mike gave the okay to the camera men, and Miller took off from the board and performed a near-perfect forward 1½ somersault with two twists.

Watching that dive, I nearly fell over because up to that time, all the divers in the world were only performing a forward 1½ somersault with one twist. Miller used Clark's new technique to greatly increase the speed of the twist in the layout position so he could add another twist. That action made the dive appear amazing and unbelievable.

Miller Anderson was from Chicago when he enrolled at Ohio State in the Spring of 1943. He had natural talent for a diver, and won the National A.A.U. Championship title from the three-meter board as a freshman. He then joined the Army Air Corps to fight in World War Two, and became a fighter pilot.

After his pilot training, he was sent to Italy where he flew a P-47 fighter plane for over one hundred missions before he was shot down. His leg and head hit the plane's tail, and it knocked him out as he pulled the rip cord to open his parachute before it crashed. When he woke up on the ground, he looked up to find a German officer standing over him with a Lugar pistol pointed at his head.

Germans were taking few prisoners at that time, and after Miller pleaded for his life, the German took him to a German hospital where he was treated for his wounds. Miller was later liberated, and placed in an American hospital where the doctors found he had gangrene in his leg.

They decided to amputate his leg, but he convinced them not to cut it off even if he couldn't use it. They put a silver plate in his thigh with no guarantee that it would give him any support to walk again. He went through a painful rehabilitation program after the operation, and with great determination, learned to walk again.

After being discharged from the service, he returned to Ohio State. He decided to try and dive, but found he had little strength in his hurdle leg so he changed his approach by hurdling with his good leg.

Frank Dempsey and Charlie Batterman competed and both won national diving titles in 1943 and 1944 before Miller returned to Ohio State from the service. Miller went on to win six national diving championships and place second on the springboard in two Olympic Games. Few could ever say that Miller Anderson wasn't a war hero.

Frank Dempsey joined the Navy in 1943 after I went to New York while in high school to compete in the National A.A.U. Championships, and to get technical diving information. Frank was made an officer, but never went overseas.

Charlie Batterman never went into the service, but went on to get his master's degree at Columbia University when I placed third in the nationals at Michigan my high school senior year. He ended up as the diving coach at the University of Massachusetts Institute of Technology many years later.

I had never dived from a three-meter board so I taught myself during the summer at the Scioto Club because it was a required collegiate event. At the Scioto club, I had a lot of access to a three-meter board. I learned to perform the same basic dives I used on the one-meter board in competition with no problem.

Mike came out to the pool a few times during the summer, and coached me a little. But after overcoming some of my fears of height, I learned to perform a full list of optional dives that I could use in competition. While learning a full list of dives, the optional dive that scared me most was the forward 2½ somersault. I remember losing several nights' sleep before I finally mustered up enough courage to attempt the dive. And when I finally went for it, I found it to be quite easy.

I had only read school textbooks in my life except for the diving rule book with its sequence pictures when I started to lifeguard at Scioto. A lady at the pool found I was religious, and gave me a book that she thought I would enjoy reading entitled, "The Robe" by Lloyd C. Douglas.

I took her up on it and after I had read a few pages, I got so wrapped in it that I kept reading it every chance I got when not working. It took me about a week to finish the book because I was a slow reader, and when I saw the lady again, I thanked her for helping me.

I saw her again a couple of days later when she gave me another book, "Keys of the Kingdom" by Sir Arthur Cannon Doyle, and that one took me to the end of the summer to read. I later got a chance to thank her for opening a whole new world for me and started to read almost anything I could find that offered a religious message.

During the summer, I watched a young tow-headed boy, about five years old, come off the golf course nearly every day with a large white bag of golf clubs. But he never came near the pool. One day, as the boy passed us on the way to the dressing room, I asked someone who that kid was, and he said his name was Jack Nicklaus.

CHAPTER 6

Attending Ohio State University Before Entering the Service

Finding a Place to Live

I went back home to Erie for a few days after finishing the summer at the Scioto Country Club. My mother had bought me a present: a trunk for forty dollars. I packed it up with all my clothes and articles that I thought I needed for college, and sent it down to the Delta Upsilon fraternity where Keo Nakama was a member.

Captain Keo Nakama

Keo was a great swimmer from Hawaii who had won several national and world championships in long distance races and only weighed about 130 pounds. Keo and I became good friends during the summer when he came out to the Scioto Country Club to practice.

It was early in June when I called Mike Peppe that I was coming to Ohio State. My mother gave me five dollars to help me with my expenses, and I took a small bag of clothes so I could save money and I hitch-hiked to Columbus to start school.

I immediately went to the Delta Upsilon house to meet Keo. When he found out that I didn't have any place to stay, he suggested that I sneak into his fraternity near midnight and sleep on the couch. I could get up early and go down to the pool where I could take a shower and change my clothes, and nobody would know the difference.

I did this for about six weeks before getting caught by some of the Delta Upsilon members who threw me out. Not knowing it at the time, all the good divers who attended Ohio State belonged to the Sigma Chi fraternity. I didn't know where to go, and one of the swimmers on the team suggested I go up to the Sigma Chi house and see if they could help me out.

So, I went to the president of Sigma Chi and told him I was a diver and would like a job washing dishes, serving the food, and helping with some of the house chores for my room and board. I told him I didn't have any money but would gladly work, and he took me in. I got along with the members well, and they asked me if I would pledge and continue to work there even though I didn't have any money except for what I had saved over the summer for my tuition.

Using my Cheerleading Experience

I was a cheerleader at East and Strong Vincent High Schools for six years. I thought it would be fun to try out for the Cheerleading squad at Ohio State.

I gave them a couple of cheers that I used in high school, and made the team. They liked my cheers and enthusiasm and decided to use them, and made me the head cheerleader. One cheer was called the "locomotive" that Ohio State used for over 72 years.

All the cheerleaders were boys, and that tradition remained until I returned from the service two years later. The cheerleaders decided to have a mock king and queen for the homecoming game with Michigan in 1944.

Bill Meeks, who was a little over five feet tall and too short to get into the service was chosen to be the king, and I was chosen to be the queen. Bill got dressed up in a zoot suit with a long watch chain down to his knees, an oversized neck tie, a huge round hat, and a pair of baggy pants that were real tight around the ankles.

I dressed up as a girl with a long dress, grape fruits for a bust, make up with red lipstick, a bonnet, and a pair of size 22 army combat shoes. Someone found an old Model "T" Ford convertible car to drive us into the stadium, and around the track. We sat on top of the back seat waving at 83,000 fans during half time. The fans applauded their approval of our performance of too young or too ugly, and mentally unqualified for service.

The number of students attending Ohio State in 1944 was five-thousand. There were four-thousand girls and only one-thousand boys. Nearly every healthy male was in the service unless he was 4-F (physically unable to be in the service).

Ohio State was on a quarter system instead of the semester system that meant excluding summer school, students normally attended three quarters a year instead of two semesters. The difference was that students selected subjects three times a year instead of two times.

At that time because of the war, Ohio State didn't require taking any tests to qualify for college. I was a little confused as to what courses I should take in my first quarter. I was interested in becoming a minister, but Ohio State didn't have a divinity school. I had two years of schooling ahead of me to decide what I would do with my life, and I chose the Art and Science school taking general education courses in algebra, physics, hygiene, physical education, and R.O.T.C. for the first quarter.

I thought I could do well in those courses, but soon found that I was wrong. I didn't have the high school preparation courses I needed, and quickly found that I was a poor student because I didn't know how to study. I began to feel like I didn't qualify to be in college because I lacked basic skills.

The reason I selected algebra in my first quarter was because I had done well in high school, but I didn't do well in college and received a "D" grade. I also took physics and only scored 23 out of a 100 on my final exam. The instructor must have thought the school needed my money because he gave me a passing "D" grade. Thanks to the physical education, hygiene, and R.O.T.C. courses, I managed to get a 1.7 on a four-point system which was a poor grade and put me on probation. This meant that if I didn't get at least a two point in my second quarter, I would flunk out.

With such poor grades in my first quarter, I dropped out of the Sigma Chi Fraternity, and moved into a single room on the third floor of a rooming house on Chittenden Avenue that was across the street from the entrance to the campus. I got a job as a bus boy and washed dishes in a sorority house that fed and paid me a small fee. Some girls in the sorority found out that I was the head cheerleader and wanted to date me, but I was too busy with my classes, diving, and cheerleading to date.

Changing Majors for Good Reason

I changed my major in the second quarter. I had no idea what I wanted to do with my life, but decided to see if I had a business head and took a basic course in economics. I worked hard at the course and read the complete text, but was not prepared to take the final exam in a blue book. This meant I had to write out my answers to each of the questions.

My mind went blank. I couldn't answer any of the questions. So, the only thing I could do was write down what I had learned from reading the text. I think my instructor felt sorry for me because he gave me a "C "grade. I also received the same grade in English and an "A" in three activity classes, and ended up with a 2.2. That moved my grade point average up from a 1.7 to a two point that qualified me for further study. Unfortunately, my college life was interrupted half way through the third quarter when I was called to enter the Army Air Corps.

Our Ohio State Diving Team

Our diving team included Ted Christakos, Bob Stone and me. Being a Greek, Ted had hair all over his body, and when he competed in a meet, some people would comment on how much he looked like a hairy ape. Bob Stone was from Chicago and was 4-F because he had a bad case of asthma and very poor eye sight. He was sort of short and skinny, but not afraid to try any kind of dive. Our practice periods were not fun because the pool was not heated due to the war. Since there were no women allowed in our practices, we dived at first without a suit. But this wasn't ideal especially when performing dives that required feet first entry or dives that involved twists.

Billingsley, Stone, Christakos, divers

We sat in the bleachers under blankets to keep warm until it was our turn to dive. We'd jump over the railing, run to the board, perform our dive, and then run back to the bleachers to dry off before getting under the blankets again. The pool had green moss all over the bottom because the circulation pumps were turned off to save electricity. The janitors poured chlorine from canisters around the pool almost daily to keep the water sanitary. The only warm water in the building was in the showers at the other end of the pool, and we'd run several times during a workout to warm up so we wouldn't shiver trying to dive.

The competitive season started with several dual meets in late fall, and the important swimming meets were held in the winter season ending with the Big Ten Conference Championships in late February. The N.C.A.A. Championships were in the middle of March, and the National A.A.U. meet was in early April.

I won the one-meter Big 10 Conference at Northwestern University in Chicago by beating my two teammates on the last dive. Northwestern didn't have a three-meter facility so no contest was offered at that height. The N.C.A.A. Championships were held at the University of Michigan the next week. We had a good chance to win the N.C.A.A meet, and Mike Peppe asked me if I knew of any swimmer who could swim a fifty-yard freestyle sprint in a time of around 25 seconds. I told him that I dived with a guy on our team at Vincent named Ray Grode who might be able to swim that fast, but he was still a senior in high school.

Mike told me to call the kid up, and tell him to take a bus down to Columbus. When I asked Mike why he wanted him, he said to never mind. The next day Ray showed up at the pool. Mike had Ray swim a fifty-yard dash, and he did it near the 25 second mark. With that, Mike took Ray with our team to the N.C.A.A. Championships at the University of Michigan where he placed fourth in the fifty-yard dash, and fourth in the two-hundred-yard free relay.

Those were enough points for us to win the N.C.A.A. Swimming and Diving Championships. Grode then returned to Ohio State with our team before taking a bus back to Erie to finish his senior year at Strong Vincent High School, and later attended the University of Iowa. That incident was never known by anyone except the members on our team, but I am sure that a lot of other coaches pulled similar shenanigans during the war years.

CHAPTER 7

The Misfit

At the Nationals

The last big meet of the swimming season was the indoor National A.A.U. Championships the first weekend in April that was, again by coincidence, held at the New York Athletic Club in the same pool that I had dived in while a junior at Strong-Vincent. I took second place in the one-meter competition that was won by my teammate, Ted Christakos. I also took second in the three-meter competition behind Frank McWiggen, a naval officer from California.

Bob Kiphuth, the swimming coach at Yale University, came up to me while we were standing on the deck after the three-meter competition. He had heard I was interested in divinity school, and since Ohio State didn't have this school, would I be interested in changing schools and attending Yale?

Kiphuth was recognized as the best swimming coach in the country, and his track record with swimming teams was winning a couple hundred dual meets in a row. He only competed against teams that were inferior to his. He obviously wanted me to change universities because it would strengthen his team while greatly reducing the strength of Ohio State's diving dynasty. That diving dynasty was responsible for scoring points and for Ohio State winning several national championships. I told him I was willing to make the change. He asked when, and I said, "Right now."

A Not So Funny True Story

I wasn't aware that Mike Peppe was standing behind us during the conversation. He stepped up, and handed me a telegram from my mother that read, "You are to report to your induction center for the Army Air Corps at Indian Town Gap, Pennsylvania on April 7, 1945."

Earlier in high school my teammate, John Boyd, and I had gone down to the armory in May of 1944 and we had taken a test to join the Army Air Corps. I was a senior and John was a junior. We both barely passed the test, but it was good enough for us to be inducted into the Army. They said they would induct us a year later.

After reading the telegram, I told Mike that the telegram was already a week old and today was April 7th so why didn't he give me the telegram last week? He asked me if I would I have dived in the contest had he given me the telegram. I said, "No! because I was A.W.O.L. and in a lot of trouble."

Mike said that they would understand for my being late, but he was wrong. The Army didn't accept any excuses. Looking back now, if I could have gone to Yale the following Monday, and attended one class at Yale before going into the service, I would have most likely become a minister.

I was shocked to receive the telegram because the Army had promised John Boyd and me that it would be a year before they would call us for duty. But they lied because we took the test in May, and they had called me up the following April which was not a full year. I would have finished three quarters at Ohio State if they had let me finish that last month. I didn't find out until much later that John Boyd was also called to duty, but not until he graduated from Strong Vincent High School in June.

I immediately returned to Ohio State on Sunday morning April 8th and packed up my belongings and had a friend ship my trunk home. I had to wait until Monday, April 9th, to go to the office of the Education Department, and inform them that I was leaving for the Army. I then took a bus back to Erie and spent the rest of Monday with my mom.

I Report for Duty

I left Erie on a train Tuesday morning, April 10th, bound for Indian Town Gap. Indian Town Gap seemed to be in the middle of nowhere when I got off the train. I followed a fence to an entrance where I was met by a very large sergeant.

He looked at the date on the telegram, and stared at me asking where in the hell had I been? He cut me off when I tried to explain, and told me to get my ass up to the orderly room where I was met by two non-commissioned officers. They read the telegram before asking me where in the hell I had been.

When I explained to them what had caused my delay, they were nice to me and explained what was going on in the reception center. They told me that the center was for those that had enlisted to serve in the Army, Navy, Marines, Coast Guard, and Air Force in the state of Pennsylvania and were all brought to Indian Town Gap to go through a processing program that included getting a medical exam, some uniform and other pieces of clothing, a haircut, dog tags, etc. that took five days. They also said that after being processed, I would be shipped out to an Army Air Corps base where I would take basic training for around six weeks.

The group I was originally assigned to was nearly finished with processing and ready to be shipped out, so the sergeants tried to find another army air corps group I could join. They finally decided that I could join Flight 178 which had already started their processing a couple of days earlier, but I could catch up.

I was told where to find Flight 178 and to go with them during the rest of their processing. The reception center had only one loud speaker that was heard by around five-thousand soldiers being processed all day long. With that, the loud speaker ordered Flight 178 and "Billingsley" to report to some processing destination. The loud speaker then instructed "Billingsley" to report to the orderly room.

After getting to the orderly room as fast an I could, they asked me where in the hell I had been. When I told them my story, they said to get my ass back to my unit, which I did until Flight 178 and "Billingsley" was again ordered to report to somewhere else when we would go through the whole ordeal again.

This went on all day long, and after a day or two, people in camp began to ask who was this guy Billingsley that is getting such special attention. I never said a word to anyone the whole time I was there, but the troops I was being processed with got a big kick out of it.

I later thought that maybe the sergeants were doing it on purpose to get even with me for being late in reporting for service. The processing finished each day at five o'clock and then we had time to relax. There was no town close to the camp so none of us could leave the camp and go anywhere else.

They had a P.X. and canteen where many could drink beer, listen to the radio, and play cards as our only source of information and entertainment because television wasn't available until 1950. While listening to the radio in the canteen one night on April 12, 1944, the radio announced that President Roosevelt died, and the whole camp became very quiet for the rest of the evening.

Basic Training Wichita Falls, Texas

After I finished being processed, the sergeants put me on a train that was headed for Sheppard Field in Wichita Falls, Texas. Shepherd Field was a helicopter base and a training center for those who had enlisted in the Army Air Corps. The train included six-hundred black troops and six-hundred white troops, and since I didn't belong to any group, a captain grabbed me and started to put me on the train.

As I stepped up to get on board, a major, who was the troop commander for the train, yelled at the captain why he was putting me in with the black troops that might kill me. The major then led me down to another car where I boarded the train with the white troops that might have been a move that saved my life.

A sergeant came through the cars after we boarded and asked for volunteers to help serve food to the troops. I had always been told to never volunteer for K.P. if you join the service. But, the idiot I was, I volunteered. The mess sergeant said it would take us about five days to cover approximately 1200 miles to Sheppard Field so we should relax and enjoy the trip. He was right about the five days because the train stopped for a couple of hours every hundred miles.

Everything went well over the five days, and I really enjoyed doing K.P. even though we slept on the kitchen tables every night. Once the troops were fed, the mess sergeant would say, "All right you guys, let's bring out the real food." Never in my life did I ever taste better steaks than when making that trip to Texas.

When I arrived at Sheppard Field, I was put in a barracks with Flight 256 along with eighty-nine other teenagers. There were thirty-thousand enlisted teenagers on our base who were to take a six-week basic training that included taking several tests to qualify for air cadets. Those who qualified were sent to a school at another base in the country where they would be trained to be a fighter or bomber pilot, a navigator, or a flight engineer.

They were made officers after finishing school, and given the rank of lieutenant before being assigned to an air base where they would remain until being sent overseas to engage the enemy. They would be assigned to a group that was active in fighting the enemy or given some other duty.

Those who didn't qualify to be an air cadet were shipped out after basic training and sent to an air force base where they would be schooled to be a radio operator, a gunner, or a bombardier. Once through school, they were also assigned to an air force base where they remained until assigned to a permanent location that could be overseas connected to a combat group, or remain in the states at a base where they would be assigned duties related to their qualifications.

The grade scale for the tests were known as a stanine, and nine was the highest score. A stanine of seven was needed to qualify for air cadets. One of the tests was on the Morse code that started out slowly with dots and dashes for letters, then increased in speed that made it very difficult to recognize.

Another test, known as a psycho-motive test, was one with two thin ropes attached to two wooden blocks on a slide about 25 feet away. You had to line up the blocks side by side to test our vision. We were also given a test that showed pictures of different terrains on the ground taken from an airplane from around ten to fifteen thousand feet, and had to identify various slopes, hills, valleys, and other terrain.

One difficult test to pass required turning a wheel in the opposite direction using a lathe. After taking tests, we were taken to a dry firing range and taught how to fire a 45-caliber revolver, a 1903 Springfield rifle, and a gun that was much like a machine gun. This weapon had no kickback when fired. You could place an egg between your nose and the back end of the weapon and not break the egg when firing several rounds.

We often went to the med center to receive different shots in the arm for preventive measure. When I arrived at the center the first time, we gathered around the doctor standing on a table explaining the process. He held up a syringe, and shot a couple of drops out of the needle while explaining how simple the process.

Just then a big muscular guy standing behind me suddenly fainted, and fell on the floor right on his face. We also visited the med center on a regular basis to get checked for any venereal diseases that was called a "short arm" inspection. This required pulling the foreskin of the uncircumcised penis back and forth a couple of times to see if any pus appeared. If none did, you didn't have gonorrhea.

It seemed like we went through that procedure three or four times a week, and one day when we were taken to the med center we had to stand in line for a long time. I was talking to the guy behind me in line and asked him why we here, and he said he thought it was for another short arm inspection.

So, when I walked through the door into the medical room, I took out my penis and the nurse looked at me in shock, and asked me what in the hell I was doing because we were there to receive a shot in the arm. I was as shocked as she was while a couple of other nurses got a big laugh out of my mistake.

The drill instructor for our flight was a little guy about five feet five inches tall who wore a blue plastic helmet liner like all the other drill instructors. All the troops wore olive drab helmet liners, but no steel helmets. We called him "Little Caesar" because that was exactly what he turned out to be. He was tough with no sense of humor and wore his helmet tipped forward down over his eyes so they could hardly be seen.

He would stand out in front of the barracks every morning and yell "Flight 256 fall out" and we would all come running out and get in formation. One morning when he called us out, one of the men in our flight leaned out the window and gave Caesar the razz berries blowing on his trombone that really irritated him.

He got the razz berries again the next morning, and got more irritated when we came running out of the barracks laughing as we lined up out on the street. That little stunt resulted in us taking a long hike the next morning. Caesar would have us count off to make sure everyone was present then march us to a field where we did physical training (PT) before taking us to the mess hall for breakfast. After breakfast, we would meet back at the barracks where Caesar would march us to certain locations on the base to take tests to qualify for the air cadets.

We had physical training in the form of calisthenics every morning that lasted one and a half hours every day except on Sunday. We also ran the obstacle course twice a week, and a ten-mile hike about once a week. Most of the hikes were in the heat of the day when the temperature was around 110 degrees in the shade. We took a five-minute break after walking every hour and because of the heat, we laid on the road and used our helmet liners as a pillow while trying to sleep four of the five minutes. We also filled our canteens with water before marching that helped protect us from having a sun or heat stroke.

I rarely took leave to town on the weekends like most of the soldiers who usually ended up going to a bar or looking for other forms of entertainment. Most of the troops at Shepherd Field called the base and the town "the cesspool of the universe" but, personally, I liked the place. The land was flat and dry and the town had little to offer the troops, but most of the town people accepted the military that spent a lot of money in their shops, restaurants, gas stations, and many other places.

The USO in town was visited by nearly every soldier on the base. The female receptionists in the canteen were very friendly, and helped those who were homesick. All the town people seemed to sense the feelings of the soldiers, and treated us with respect and kindness. They tried to inform us that they understood why we were in the service, and were trying to keep our country free. They made me feel like it was a great time to be alive, and live in this country that was well worth dying for. As I said then and I still say, "We were living at the greatest time, and in the greatest country in all history."

I was known as a loner during the six weeks in basic training because I didn't mix very well with my fellow trainees. I took the advice of my mother who told me not to look for my friends because they would come to me. I did as she suggested so when I was in the barracks at night, I would sit on my cot and read the New Testament or some other book.

One night one of the men a few bunks away from mine started to harass me by voicing to all the soldiers on the second floor what a weirdo I was because I always kept to myself and was always reading. Feeling that I had had enough of his crap one night, I told him to shut his mouth but that only encouraged him to harass me more. After a few more minutes of his insults, I told him that he had better shut his mouth or I would shut it for him.

He laughed and kept right on teasing me until I got up and went over to his cot where he was lying down. Just as he started to get up from the cot, I hit him on the forehead with my first so hard that it split it open with blood spattering everywhere. I grabbed him by his shirt, pulled him to his feet, and took him over to the top of the stairs. With a very quiet voice, I told him that if he so much as breathed loud around me again, I would throw him down the stairs. I thought I would probably be court martialed, but nothing was ever made of it and no one bothered me again.

I set up a schedule for myself about halfway through basic training that followed our five o'clock evening meal. I would go over to the canteen and listen to classical and semi-classical music for an hour while digesting my food. Then go to the gym for a workout with weights and vigorous calisthenics for over an hour before going back to the barracks to read.

Occasionally I took a long walk around the base that included the marching field where I enjoyed the cool air every night. Following my schedule for a couple of weeks, I ran into Dick Desinger, also from Erie. He became curious what I was doing with my time at night. When I told him, he decided to join me and we became good friends.

Soon three other guys in our barracks learned what we were doing and joined us. Candidly, we discover that all five of us were thinking of becoming ministers when we returned home. We took great comfort talking about our lives in the barracks, canteen, or after leaving the gym nearly every week night.

We agreed that we wanted to be in the best physical shape possible if we were ever to engage the enemy. So, when taking P.T., we stood up front doing the exercises in double time while some of those in our outfit were hiding in the back flapping their arms up and down pretending to be doing jumping jacks or some other exercise.

The five of us would also wait until everyone had started to run the obstacle course, and then we would try to catch up with them before they reached the finish line. Our lazy members would start the run and when out of sight of our superiors, they would cut through the bushes and run to the end of the course acting like they were exhausted.

We tried to stay away from the slackers and knew that if we were ever in a tough spot, we wouldn't get near them. Obviously, the slackers had a different philosophy and purpose for taking basic training and being in the armed forces than we did. We five ran around together until we were shipped out to different bases.

V-E Day May 8, 1945

The war with Germany ended while we were in basic training, but the war with Japan continued. We were all called to appear in a huge hanger for helicopters soon after Germany surrendered where we were told that those who qualified as cadets could return home. And those who did not qualify for air cadets had to remain in the service and be shipped out to other air bases where they would be assigned to other duties.

All but eight of 30,000 of the original group of enlisted men were shipped out after finishing basic training, and replaced with draftees many of whom were in their twenties and some older. Unfortunately, Dick Desinger and I were two of the eight that remained. Thinking we would be shipped out to another base soon, we were informed that we would have to take basic training again and we never did find out why.

Thankfully, it was ordered that we were not going to take basic training again, and were assigned to different duties on the base for six weeks. I was given the job of directing the troops on the dry firing range where I stood on a stand and yelled out directions to the troops as they approached the range. That position lasted for a couple of weeks when they placed me in an office working with A-20 forms which were the records of the enlistees that were leaving the base to be discharged or be shipped out to some other base.

I recommended Dick Desinger to be assigned to the post office while working in the office, and he got the job a couple of days later. I can't remember what happened, but I ended up on permanent K.P. for a couple of weeks before the training period ended. I didn't get along very well with the cooks because I would disappear when cleaning the tables. After looking all over the mess hall, they would find me under one of the tables reading my New Testament.

The 1945 National A.A.U. Diving Championships

During that time, I found out that the National A.A.U. Diving Championships were to be held in Cuyahoga Falls, Ohio, a suburb of Akron. Not doing much of anything but working in the mess hall, I went to headquarters and asked the commanding officer of the base if I could get a five-day pass to compete in the meet.

Unbelievably, he granted me the pass, and I went out to the airfield on the base and asked if they had any planes going my way. I found a pilot who was flying a B-24 bomber to St. Louis and he said I could go with him and the crew. The plane flew about three or four thousand feet above the ground all the way to St. Lewis. I could stand in the open area where the gunners stood, and get a great view of the terrain below.

It was a thrilling experience for me because it was the first time I had ever flown in an airplane, and the crew were great guys. After landing in St Louis I immediately proceeded to hitchhike to Akro, because the diving contest started the next day in Cuyahoga Falls. I got lucky hitching a ride in a big truck late at night that took me all the way to Akron. I found my way to the pool about an hour before my event was to begin and after explaining my position with the diving referee, he permitted me to make out my diving form.

I could practice only a couple of dives twenty minutes before the event. That didn't give me enough time to practice any of the five optional dives with higher degrees of difficulty. So, I had to perform dives that I hadn't done since diving at the nationals in New York City three months earlier.

I did well, considering that I had so little preparation, and had been up all night hitchhiking without any sleep. I felt good placing fifth getting beat by Bruce Harlan and Miller Anderson who later placed first and second at the 1948 Olympics. Incidentally, it was the first meet for Miller Anderson after coming back from the war, and the first for Bruce Harlan after learning to dive in the Navy. I immediately hitchhiked home to Erie to visit my mother for a couple of days before taking a bus back to Shepherd Field.

When I returned, the base was in a horrible heat wave with temperatures well over a hundred degrees in the shade. The heat wave continued for a couple more days when clouds started to form. Hail stones the size of golf balls began to drop down and hit us on the head so quickly that we had to wear our helmet liners to keep from getting injured running for shelter. A strong wind well over a hundred miles an hour came upon us followed by a terrific rain storm that lasted long enough for two soldiers to drown in the drainage ditches next to the road.

Assigned to Truex Field, Madison, Wisconsin

I was finally shipped out to Truex Field in Madison, Wisconsin after the basic training session was finished, and was assigned to a radio operator school that was to prepare me to fly on a B-25 bomber - the same plane Jimmy Doolittle flew bombing Tokyo. My enthusiasm was immediately squashed when I was informed that they closed the radio school because they no longer needed any more radio operators.

So, not knowing what to do with me, they put me on permanent K.P. The barracks and buildings at Truex Field were in terrible shape, unheated, and very cold in late September. Even worse, the cook assigned me to clean six stoves fueled with wood and coal that he claimed were always dirty. He would come around after I cleaned the stoves, run his finger across one of them, and tell me I did a lousy job and clean them again just to keep me busy.

Then one day a notice came out that the farmers needed help to pick corn because nearly every able-bodied male person was in the service, and there was a great need to get the crops in before winter. The farmers were willing to pay eight dollars a day for anyone who could help, so I jumped to help.

Picking corn was a heck of a lot better than cleaning stoves over and over and besides, I was also being paid for my efforts. The weather got cold during that time, and I nearly froze to death sleeping in unheated barracks.

Transferred to Travis Air Force Base

I spent most of my spare time at the University of Wisconsin library reading books, and enjoying a good college atmosphere. I was finally shipped out on a train to Travis Air Force Base located north of San Francisco. I immediately went through processing with 2400 soldiers. They didn't tell us where we were going when two days later we boarded the U.S.S. Altman that was made into a troop ship when the war first started.

I remember leaving San Francisco and passing under the Golden Gate Bridge. I looked back to see "Welcome Home, Job Well Done" displayed in huge letters on the hill across the bay. I had to laugh because we were just leaving as the combat troops were returning home. About half of the troops on the ship began to get sea sick when we reached the seven mile swells outside of San Francisco Bay. They crowded the railings and vomited over the sides and on each other. Having lived on Lake Erie all my life, I didn't see that such little movement of the ocean was anything to get sick about. Unfortunately, the smell of vomit remained with us for a few days as we continued to move out to sea.

I was one of the first to go below decks when boarding the ship. I entered a very large area, and found it filled with sleeping bunks that were stacked four high. I chose one of the top bunks, but soon found I chose the wrong one because it had an air vent above it that started to blow cold air and nearly knocked me off the bed that evening.

Finding no other vacant bunk, I asked those who stayed up most of the night playing cards if I could sleep in their bed until they decided to retire. I soon found another soldier that had the same problem, so we decided to take our blankets and pillows and sleep up on the top deck.

I don't believe anyone knew where we were sleeping because no one ever said a word to us. Sleeping this way was great because we enjoyed a nice breeze, and listened to soft music that was played over the P.A. system every night. We also enjoyed watching the flying fish jumping alongside the ship, and shooting stars during the night.

No lights were on during the night except a small pilot light up on the bridge. Though the war with Japan ended a short time before we shipped out, a small aircraft carrier escorted us all the way to our destination because many Japanese refused to believe the war was over, so no regular lights were on that could attract a Japanese submarine.

After we were out at sea for five or six days, we learned that we were going to Okinawa. I don't believe anyone aboard ship ever heard of the place, but we soon found that it was on the other side of the Pacific Ocean in the East China Sea. It took us twenty-two days to reach our destination because the ship did a lot of zigzagging all the way across the ocean to avoid any enemy submarines. Most of the troops spent their time reading, sleeping, and gambling while I spent most of my time reading and trying to memorize words from a book I had read and didn't know their meaning.

My Service in Okinawa

The ship anchored in Okinawa, and we were ordered to climb down a cargo net that hung over the sides to board some boats that had come alongside.   Some of the soldiers were too lazy to carry their duffle bags down the cargo net, and threw them thirty feet below into the boats. Many of the duffle bags unfortunately split open hitting the deck, and clothes were thrown all over the place. That created a big mess when the soldiers tried to figure out who owned what.

I climbed down the net with my bag half filled with books, and a slide rule clenched in my mouth. I was told that the capital of Okinawa was Naha and as the boat headed for shore, I asked one of the navy crew where was Naha. He started to laugh as he told me that I would find out in a minute. When the boat hit the beach and the landing door dropped down, the sailor said, "that's Naha." I was looking at a mass of rubble with nothing standing but a set of stairs that went up one floor and a damaged smoke stack. It was all that was left of a town of sixty- six thousand residents that had been bombed flat.

A sergeant started to call out the names of different groups that were to assemble to be taken to their destinations once on shore. I went to my area and found about a dozen other soldiers, and boarded a huge truck that took off for the hills for around two hours. We finally pulled into an area near the beach that had some small buildings and a few quonset huts.

We reported to the office and learned we had just been assigned to the 317th Fighter Squadron, and the name of our base was Lolly Beach. The squadron was made up of 108 men that included around a dozen fighter pilots who flew P-40's and P-47 fighter planes. Lolly Beach was on the shore overlooking the East China Sea, and next to a leper colony guarded by the marines and off limits to all outsiders.

We could see a small island from our base called Iwo Jima that had a monument honoring the great G.I. news columnist, Ernie Pyle, who was killed by a Japanese sniper. At his request, he's buried on the exact spot where it happened. He had gone through the entire European campaign with our American soldiers, and wrote stories published in newspapers all over the United States about what they were going through fighting the enemy all over Europe.

He joined the Japanese campaign after the war in Europe was over, and only a short time before his death. He graduated from Indiana University before the war started in 1941 and the university named the journalism building after him when the Japanese surrendered.

Our commanding officer was Captain Bill Michaels from Cincinnati, Ohio, and an insurance agent before entering the service. He made it real clear in our first meeting with him that we were to all stay away from the leper colony. If we crossed the line, the Marines were ordered to shoot on sight. We were assigned to a quonset hut, and I slept on a cot covered with mosquito netting that protected us from getting malaria.

No one had to wear a designated uniform that showed their rank since the war was over, and we were forty miles away from headquarters near Naha. We usually wore

T- shirts and khaki pants, addressed each other by our first name, and didn't salute the officers. I later put five mattresses on my cot that made it a little more comfortable.

We didn't have any latrines or showers when I first arrived, but we did have an outhouse. We also had some five-inch shell casings installed in the ground around the base that were used for us to urinate in. I remember the first time I used a shell casing. I looked down to see a female native digging up potatoes not five feet away from me. She simply looked up at me and smiled when she saw how embarrassed I was.

There was no entertainment at Lolly Beach except for the radio. There were no American females on the island except the nurses who were stationed at the hospital down at headquarters. Of course, there were females in the various villages around our base some of whom came to our base to do some domestic work.

Some in our group were willing to take a chance and have sex with the Okinawa women knowing sixty percent of them had syphilis. You could recognize a male from the female natives when walking behind them on the road. The women had broad shoulders because they did all the farming, and those with narrow shoulders were the men who did the fishing.

Latrines were built soon after I arrived at Lolly Beach. They were needed because Lolly Beach was going to be used as a rest camp for the combat soldiers who were waiting for their ships to take them home to be discharged. Many of the soldiers had fought through the European campaign, and were transferred to fight in the Japanese campaign.

Some of these soldiers had been killing people since they enlisted soon after Pearl Harbor, and a point system was used to determine who qualified to return home. A soldier received one point for every month in service, two points for every month overseas, and five points for every month in combat. The ones with the highest number of points were the first to board a ship home.

Some of the soldiers were already coming to Lolly Beach when I arrived. One day while having lunch, one of the soldiers came in the mess hall and sat across from me to eat. He had been in combat for around four years, and he was 23 years old. He had gray hair and expressionless eyes that made him look like he was fifty years old.

Attempting to be friendly with him, I asked him how many points he had and with a little thought, he replied that he had 223 points. He then asked me how many points I had, and when I told him I had six points, he nearly fell off the bench with laughter. He suddenly jumped up and yelled to some of his buddies in the mess hall to look at this poor son-of-a-bitch sitting across from him that had six points, and probably wouldn't be qualified to go home until the end of the century.

After that, when I would see one of the soldiers on the base, they would point their finger at me and laugh. I didn't mind their laughter because it was probably the first time they had laughed in a long time, and I felt that it was great therapy for them after all they had gone through. The combat soldiers continued to come to Lolly Beach for about two months before they were all processed from our station, and were sent home on ships.

One of the first assignments given to us non-commissioned soldiers was to help tear down some of the hangers that were no longer in use. For some unknown reason, Captain Michaels didn't assign me to this task. Instead, he had me drive a six by truck down to headquarters every day except Sunday, and pick up forty Japanese prisoners.

I brought them back to Lolly Beach, and guarded them while they dug latrines, helped with the hangers, and performed other tasks. I had never driven a truck before so it was interesting learning how to double shift the gears. I was given an M-1 rifle to guard them with, but I didn't know how to shoot it. The war was over, and the prisoners soon realized that they were not going to be tortured and were getting good food and clean quarters. They didn't give anyone any trouble knowing they were going to be shipped back to Japan soon so none of them had any desire to escape.

I picked up the same group of Japanese every day, and we started to communicate with each other which resulted in them bringing me gifts such as an airplane made from plastic. Things were going along so well that one day I had to go to the bathroom, so I gave the rifle to one of the prisoners that I had gotten to know well and told him to guard the men until I got back.

If anyone had seen what a stupid move I had made, I think I would still be a prisoner on Okinawa. Even worse, a couple of days later I was guarding the prisoners who were cleaning out the Quonset hut that was going to be used by General McArthur before invading Japan.

For some reason, I had fallen asleep when suddenly the door opened and an officer from headquarters came in and shouted, "Atten-hut!" I immediately woke up dropping the rifle on the floor, and the prisoners started to laugh. Thanks to that officer, he didn't report the incident that could have led to a dishonorable discharge, and a long prison term for me.

When the help from the prisoners was no longer needed, I was assigned to lifeguard the beach. Few of the soldiers in our outfit swam in the morning or late afternoon so I spent most of my time reading the New Testament, another book, or taking a swim in the warm sea. I lifeguarded sometimes on weekends when the doctors from the hospital at headquarters brought some nurses up for the weekend.

One of our officers came down to the beach one day, and told me that some of the doctors and nurses were coming up from the hospital the next day. He wanted the beach to be nice and clean. He showed up the next day with a gigantic bull dozer that had about 12 different gears and a huge blade in front.

I told him I didn't have a clue how to drive such a machine, and he said that I would learn by trial and error. I got up on the machine after he started it, and put it in neutral before he left. I started to change gears until I found the one that made the machine go forward. I planned to take it up to one end of the beach, put it in reverse, drop the blade, then drag the blade down the beach.

I thought I had gone up the beach far enough, but I couldn't find the gear to stop the dozer as it continued to move and get closer and closer to the reef that extended out in the water in front of me. I suddenly panicked and jumped off the dozer just before it hit the reef and started to jump around for a while before it finally stalled. I had never thought to turn the engine off.

When I saw the officer in the mess hall that night, he asked me if I had any trouble with the bull dozer. I told him, "just a little but I figured it out." Nothing was ever said about the bull dozer, but about a day or two later, I was taken off the beach job and sent to a school down at headquarters for a week.

My First Teaching Job is a Failure

The school was an attempt to inform the soldiers of current affairs in the States and about academic opportunities available to them when they returned home. I was never given any such news about what was going on at home, but they did give me a text book to follow. When I returned to Lolly Beach, I was given an hour to talk to the soldiers each week. But having no experience in teaching, I tried to memorize what I wanted to discuss.

I was so nervous that I just stammered through the chapters while the group sat there, and had to listen to me while I made a complete jackass out of myself. I remember that it got so bad that they would groan while I was trying to lecture them, and I can remember only one lecture out of sixteen where I felt they learned a little something from my efforts.

Near the end of the year all the privates in our unit were promoted to corporal except me. I was the only one promoted to private first class because of the miserable job I had done with my presentations.

God Tests Me

I was quite religious, and one morning sitting alone on the beach I prayed to God. I told Him how much I loved Him, and if he wanted to know how much I really cared, to test me. Little did I know that he was going to take me up on my challenge. This was how he tested me in a seven-day period.

One of the soldiers who came over on the boat with us suddenly lost it after a few months at Lolly Beach. He had little to do and was homesick. He was seen running around the base yelling, "Okinawa you, Okinawa you" and acting real crazy.

Captain Michaels told me to fetch the soldier, and bring him back to his office with his duffle bag. I was assigned to drive him down to headquarters to be examined, and to be sent back to the States. He would receive a Section eight and an honorable discharge. I got the soldier and while carrying his duffle bag on my shoulder on the way back to headquarters, we walked behind a hanger that was being torn down. A couple of men on the roof were ripping off corrugated 4'x6' metal sheets and throwing them down to the ground from about twenty-five feet.

72

The men didn't know anyone was below the hanger. They threw one of the heavy metal sheets off the roof that stuck in the coral ground in an upright position about four inches from my foot. The men on the roof looked down in disbelief. They didn't expect anyone to be down there, and I might have been cut in half had I taken another half step. I think it was the first time I ever cussed in my life when I looked up, and called the shocked guy on the roof a stupid son-of-a-bitch.

Captain Michaels assigned me the job of mail carrier to and from headquarters after I finished giving my "brilliant" lectures. I was driving a weapons carrier down to headquarters to deliver and pick up mail the day after the roof incident. As I was going through the mountains on a coral mountain road, I came up behind two M.P.'s who were driving a jeep with a sign on the back that read, "Speed limit 20 miles an hour."

The coral road had a lot of sharp curves so I followed them for about a mile while getting more anxious to get around them at every curve. We came to where the road straightened long enough for me to pass, and after I got by them, I sped up to 40 miles an hour and started to go around some curves.

It had rained that morning, and I wasn't aware of how slippery the coral road was when my vehicle started to skid on a sharp turn. I hit the brakes as I lost control. My vehicle continued to skid until it went off the road, and headed for a cliff that went 200 feet straight down. The carrier went over the edge far enough to be tilting on the under frame. I was so scared that I put both feet on the brake as the engine stopped.

All weapons carriers have a spare tire on the left side next to the driver's seat that requires the driver to crawl over it when getting in and out of the vehicle. Afraid that the carrier would topple over if I tried to crawl over the spare tire, I just sat there trembling. I remembered that the M.P.'s were behind me and when they came around the curve a minute later, they stopped and came over to me.

When they saw my predicament, one said, "Jesus Christ, how in the world did you get out there?" They got their answer looking back at my skid marks. Not wishing to lose the carrier, they suggested that they stand on the back bumper while I started the engine and put it in reverse to gently accelerate and see if the back wheels would get enough traction to pull the frame free.

My vehicle had four-wheel drive, and I put the gear in reverse three or four times to make sure it was in the right place. I started it with difficulty because I was so nervous and gently stepped on the accelerator moving my foot slowly off the clutch. The engine started and the frame moved back off the ledge onto solid ground. From then on I drove down and back from headquarters at a reasonable speed after getting a sound lecture from the M.P.'s.

The next day I was driving a jeep through the mountains on my way down to the post office at headquarters when the windshield suddenly shattered with glass flying everywhere. Though the war was over, many of the Japanese remained in caves in the mountains for years afraid if they came out, they would be tortured and killed. I suddenly realized that I was being shot at so I crouched down in the jeep as much as possible and continued to drive as fast as I safely could to headquarters. From then on, I wasn't too anxious to pick up the mail anymore.

Hilarious Fun and Some Serious Coincidences

One of our soldiers had found a wild monkey, and kept it tied to a tree next to a shack where we took showers. On the fourth day, I was walking past the shack, and the monkey lifted its leg and hit me squarely with a stream of urine from about twenty feet away. Lucky to be close to the shack, I had to take a shower.

The shower worked by heating water in the oil drum on the roof, then pulling a chain in the shack to release warm water for the shower. The oil drum sat with a doughnut stove in it that usually took less combustible kerosene, but because of the war we used high octane gasoline.

I walked over to the stove on the roof, and turned on the gas. Then I lit a match and dropped it down the stack but nothing happened. So, I turned the gas valve a little more, and dropped another match down the stack and again nothing happened. I then turned the valve on all the way, and looking down stack I dropped another match. This time it suddenly exploded, and knocked me out.

I woke up near the edge of the roof, and I could smell foul burnt hair. All the hair on my head and eyebrows had been burnt off, but other than that, I didn't have any other burns or injuries. I must have been out for quite a while because the water was nice and warm after I climbed down the ladder to take my shower.

Everyone wanted to know what happened to my hair when I ate at the mess hall that night. When I told them what had happened, they all had a good laugh. Many believed I was blessed to walk away from such an explosion with no injuries especially to my eyes and face.

Lolly Beach had an outdoor theater down in a cove where the troops could watch movies in the evening while sitting on boards supported with five-gallon gas cans. A day after losing my hair, one of my friends, Brownie, and I were standing on a hill behind the seats where he was showing me some snap shots of his newborn baby that his wife had just sent him. After viewing the pictures and offering my best for his good fortune, I told him that I would see him later as I was going down to the mess hall.

I didn't take more than five steps when I heard a loud roar, and when I turned around, I saw Brownie rolling over and over on the ground about thirty feet away. I ran to where he was lying. He was conscious, but in serious pain holding his side. I asked him what had happened, and he told me that an airplane had hit him. I didn't see any airplane, and thought he might be hallucinating. So, I asked him again, but he insisted that it was an airplane.

The pilots in our squadron often got their air time by flying an L-5 trainer which is a small two seat plane that is easy to fly. They would fly up to Lolly Beach at times, and buzz the area flying under the telephone lines and yell down to someone on the ground, "What's for dinner?"

74

This one day, one of those pilots flew into the theater area, and when starting to fly away, the tail of the plane hit the ground. This caused the plane to yaw just before hitting Brownie, and fly out of the area before I saw it. I stood there in disbelief when the accident occurred because I never saw the airplane.

I ran to headquarters and reported the accident then got a weapons carrier and with the aid of some others, we picked Brownie up and took him down to the hospital near headquarters. We decided to return to Lolly Beach to get some candy and flowers, and visit him in the evening. But just as we were leaving, we received a call from the hospital that told us he had died.

Looking back at the time of the accident, I realized that if I hadn't taken five or six steps at that given moment, I also could have been hit by that plane. The pilot who hit Brownie returned to Lolly Beach as soon as he could, and was really shook up. He was ordered to stand trial a few days later, and was found guilty of manslaughter. He was only given five years in a small compound with a native to tend to his domestic needs. I left Okinawa a few months later and never found out if he served his full sentence. The pilot was really a nice guy and we all felt sorry for him because we all did stupid things.

The whole unit went to Brownie's funeral including the pilot responsible for his death. And not one week later, the officer who was second in command of our unit went up to the barracks that was to be used by General McArthur, and shot himself in the head with a colt 45 pistol. He never left any word why he killed himself, but we ended up going to another funeral within a week. It was unbelievable that we lost two men from our unit in two weeks, and we were no longer at war with Japan.

One of our non-com soldiers was really interested in the ocean, and went scuba diving every day. He had the use of a dinghy, and would shine a big search light on the surface of the water at night. It would attract eels to charge the light looking like a cobra before crashing into the sides of the boat. While we were out one night enjoying this new venture, bullets started hitting the water all around us.

We suddenly realized we had crossed over the line for the leper colony. We immediately jumped out of the boat, and got behind it. We yelled at the Marine guards on the shore not to shoot. But unfortunately, we were too far from shore to be heard as the bullets kept coming. So, we grabbed the top side of the boat and pushed it back toward our base until we were out of the area, and the bullets stopped. We thought we would hear from the Marines about the incident but we never did.

Our Fantastic Pilots

The pilots in our outfit were fantastic. They flew P-40 or P-47 fighter planes up Lolly Beach flying low behind the reefs where the water was calm. They would prop wash the water flying 340 miles an hour. They challenged each other to see who could fly the closest to the mess hall and make the corrugated roof rattle.

One of the pilots was very eccentric. He went down to headquarters and came back with a motorcycle. We never found out how he got it, but we all could guess. One day he asked me if I would like to take a ride with him. I knew he was a wild man, and didn't want to go. But since he was an officer, I thought I should to placate him.

Sure enough, we hardly got started when he started to speed up and go real fast. He hit a bump on the dirt road that sent me flying about 75 feet through the air, and I landed on my back in a field. When he came over to find if I was all right, I told him I was okay except for a few scratches.

I talked to God soon after that incident, and thanked Him for watching over me for the week when I had so many close shaves with death. I then asked Him if he had to test me so hard? After that I never had a life-threatening ordeal again during my stint in the service.

A while later the same pilot was driving his motorcycle too fast and lost control when he hit a tree, and broke his back that put him in the hospital for about a month. The pilot wanted to go home so bad that when he got out of the hospital, he went down to the Navy yard and stole a small boat. He used that small boat to steal a big P.T. boat (the same boat that President John F. Kennedy was on.)

It took him all night to tow the boat up to Lolly Beach to hide them in a cove for nearly a year while trying to get the engine to work, but never succeeded. I think Captain Michaels knew all about his capers, but never brought them up because it would have caused a real mess that would have ended up in court and get him court martialed and thrown in jail. The strangest thing about the whole ordeal was that the Navy never missed the ship or the small motor boat that he stole.

Gifts from Our Government

Everyone was given a case of beer every week whether they drank beer or not. We, who didn't drink, gave our rations to those who did drink. Our cook was an alcoholic, and didn't like me when I first arrived. But he changed his mind when I started to give him my beer rations. He would go on a binge every week end, and be gone for a day or two before sobering up and returning to his job.

He was such a good cook that no one ever complained and, besides, he had two good assistants who covered for him. Sometimes, he would come to work a little drunk and cuss everyone out, including the officers, as they passed through the chow line to get food. He used to call me "professor" because he always saw me reading a book in the mess hall.

Jim Eklem, pictured on the left had come over on the same boat as me and we became friends after arriving at Lolly Beach. He was put in charge of the P.X. and concessions, and would sell me whatever I wanted when the store was closed. We ran around together when we had time, and we often checked out a jeep to visit some of the other military units around the Naha area.

One of our ventures took us to a valley where we saw five-thousand jeeps waiting to be used in the invasion of Japan that was to begin from Okinawa. But with the war over, they were later buried because the government thought it was cheaper than to ship them home.

We also visited the air base and saw around five-hundred P-51 Mustang fighter planes lined up on a very long runway waiting to be scrapped, and buried along with the jeeps. We were told that with the war over, we could buy a P-51 Mustang for a hundred dollars, but the only problem was how to get it back to the states. Jim and I went to another air base another time, where hundreds of B-29 bombers and B-25 mini-bombers were parked in a grave yard never to be flown. I would venture to say that the remains of those planes are still there.

Okinawa – the Worst Military Campaign

Okinawa was known to be the worst campaign in the Far East because of the great number of soldiers that were killed. For example, during the invasion of Okinawa, the commanding officer of the First Marine Division decided to surprise the Japanese by making the first landing on Okinawa by climbing over a coral ridge instead of making the landing on one of the sandy beaches.

This turned out to be a terrible mistake because the Japanese anticipated the attack, and made a half-circle around the ridge. And using all kinds of weapons, they killed every one of the Marines as they climbed up the ridge trying to advance. It was so bad that the last of the Marines had to climb over the dead bodies of their comrades to reach the top of the ridge. Bull dozers were brought in, and buried all the dead bodies after their dog tags were removed and nailed to white crosses displayed on the hillside.

Most of those who lived on Okinawa were of Japanese descent because it was once a part of the Japanese empire. Cement tombs were made above ground, and used for family burials. Many of the tombs were broken into during the war and after throwing the bones out, were used as small bunkers by the soldiers. I remember that we could kick human skulls or other human bones from the tombs down the road near Lolly Beach when we first arrived.

I was on Okinawa for four or five months when a notice was sent out to the military units that a ping-pong match was going to be held to determine the best player on the island. I had played a lot of ping-pong at the Y.M.C.A. in Erie so I decided to enter the contest held in a hanger near headquarters. I made the finals in the singles play, and went on to win the doubles playing with the player that had beaten me in the singles game.

My Ping-Pong Excursion to Manila

As winners, we were flown to Manila in the Philippine Islands in a DC-3 plane to compete in the Southern Pacific Championships. We stayed in a nice thatched hut. I ran into Dick Moss, who was in the service and living in the hut next to mine. Dick was a cousin of John Wolford and a classmate of mine at Strong Vincent High School. We had been good friends in high school, but for some reason, he ran off after we had a short discussion.

Manila was a very interesting place to visit. It had been bombed a lot during the war that left the town torn to pieces, and without any sanitation. When a person had to relieve themselves, they would walk over to the curb and do what they had to do but not draw attention from anyone. The roads in and out of the city were in terrible shape with chuck holes everywhere so no one drove very fast.

I did see one case when a jeep was traveling at great speed, and ran into the back end of a truck that decapitated the jeep driver. I turned the other way when I saw what happened and never looked back. The people obtained many of the American jeeps from the war, and made them into taxies. They fixed them so people could board them from the back end, and gave them identity by putting a colored surrey over the top.

I found them still using the same jeeps when I returned to Manila fifteen years later, and the roads had never been fixed. The people thought that America was going to help them rebuild their war-torn country like we did for Germany and Japan, but that didn't happen. Thus, many of the people learned to hate Americans and that made it seem dangerous for anyone to visit the country.

We didn't do well in the ping-pong tournament and got beat in the second round. But visiting Manila was a real treat. The contest was held in a building that was located next to Rizal Stadium that was the place where my brother had dropped from a plane during the war while shooting the Japanese. He was in the 11th Airborne, and made that jump into Rizal Stadium about six months before I arrived.

People at Lolly Beach suggested that I buy a case of liquor while in Manila because there was no liquor on the island of Okinawa, and I could sell it for a good price. So, I bought a case of Seagram Seven and put it into a large linen bag, and brought it back to the base. I made five times what I paid for it by selling a fifth for twenty dollars.

I took a couple of bottles of whiskey down to the Navy yards, and found a sailor who was ready to pour gasoline on a large pile of new Navy flight jackets with fur collars. I told the sailor that I would trade him a bottle of liquor for one of those beautiful jackets, but he said he couldn't do it because if caught, he could be court martialed.

I thought what a shame it was to destroy such beautiful jackets that couldn't hurt anyone by giving them away. His reaction told me that none of the millions and millions of dollars of military equipment that was brought to Okinawa for the invasion of Japan was ever going to be returned to our country.

My Side Trip to Diving Competition in Tokyo

Our unit received another notice a couple of months later that a swimming and diving meet was going to be staged in Tokyo, Japan. Captain Michaels gave me permission to compete in the meet, so I was flown up to Tokyo and checked in at the Meiji Park Hotel where I shared a room with two Australian athletes.

They turned out to be wonderful guys with a great sense of humor, and we spent most of our free time together laughing at our different accents. The meet was held outdoors in the Meiji Park pool that had a separate diving well with good equipment next to the hotel. I didn't dive tower so I only competed on the three-meter springboard.

I was really surprised when my good friend John Boyd (pictured far left) showed up. I hadn't seen him since I had graduated from Strong Vincent. He was at Shepherd Field, Texas, the same time I was, but with 30,000 soldiers it would have been pure luck if we would have run into each other. He said he was shipped out to Tokyo from Texas, and remained there until I met him.

I spent three days with John and we had a marvelous time together, but I had to train for the meet. I don't remember how well I did in the meet, but I never heard or saw John again until fifty-nine years later.

I was assigned to be a telephone operator when I returned to Lolly Beach from Tokyo, and I really liked the job because I was learning something new. That was in the days when a line was plugged into an insert to receive or obtain the number of another party.

While working at my new job in the orderly room, one of our officers came walking in while a non-com was listening to some country music on the radio that was not yet popular in our country. The officer hated that kind of music so he told the non-com to either change the station or turn the radio off. When the non-com objected, the officer pulled out a 45 pistol, and shot the radio with pieces flying all over the room and calmly walked out.

I received a call from headquarters about ten o'clock in the evening a couple of weeks later that notified us that, due to an eruption in the ocean, a huge tidal wave 100 feet high was heading toward Okinawa and we should evacuate our quarters immediately and head for the hills. I quickly contacted Captain Michaels and he called everyone together on the base, and ordered us to get in a motor vehicle to form a convoy and head for the hills.

No one took any of their belongings and we had no idea where we were going. We found a road that went up a mountain and parked in a vacant area near the top waiting for the wave to hit. We sat there for about four or five hours before we decided that the wave was not going to hit Okinawa, and returned to our base at about three in the morning.

We were informed a couple of days later that a high-ranking officer was coming up to Lolly Beach for an inspection that meant we had to wear our uniforms and be clean shaven with haircuts. One of our slightly built soldiers said that he had worked nearly a year to grow his beard, and refused to shave it off.

He was told that if he didn't shave it off, he would be sent down to headquarters and thrown into the brig. He showed up the next day for a dress rehearsal with his face completely covered with bandages. We asked if he had badly burned his face, and he told us the bandages were to cover his beard so he wouldn't have to shave it off. Captain Michaels showed up and read him the riot act, and he finally shaved it off.

It was in November 1946 that the group I had arrived with on Okinawa was given notice that we were being sent home to be discharged. Everyone was happy to get the news, but I was a little sad because I had become accustomed to living on this beautiful island. It was unbelievable to find ourselves going home on the same ship that had brought us to Okinawa.

This time, it took only thirteen days for the U.S.S. Altman to arrive in San Francisco when we saw the same sign "Welcome Home Job Well Done" still on the hill. We were immediately put on a train and had to sleep on cots in open air cattle cars. It was a terrible trip because the train engines were run on coal, and the smoke from the coal filtered back to the cattle cars that covered all the troops with soot.

We arrived at Fort Dix, New Jersey five days later, and were led into a large gymnasium where we were ordered to empty our duffle bags on the floor for inspection. The inspection turned up hundreds of rifles, hand grenades, bazookas, automatic weapons, knives, Samurai swords, etc. all of which were confiscated. We all showered and received clean clothes before going to the medical ward where we received a complete physical examination for malaria, venereal disease, and other physical problems.

They fed us before giving us our discharge papers and when a soldier handed me my mustering out pay of $150, he said that I would be back and I replied, "Don't bet on it" as I walked out the door on December 8, 1946. Being in the service was a great experience despite its ups and downs, and I felt it was well worth it because it gave me a chance to travel to places where I would have never visited as a civilian.

CHAPTER 8

Returning to Ohio State

After leaving Fort Dix in New Jersey, I immediately boarded a Greyhound bus and headed for New Haven, Connecticut to visit my dear friend, John Wolford. He was going to Yale University under the Navy V-12 program for those who were above average intelligence. They attended the best universities in the country with the intent that they would stay in the Navy as officers.

John had gone out for the wrestling team and had seriously broken his arm, and no longer qualified for active service. But he could complete the four-year program. I went to the Yale admissions office the next day to see if I could get into the divinity school, and they told me to come back in five years and they would consider it.

With nearly several hundred thousand G.I.'s getting out of the service after the war, most of them were taking advantage of the G.I. Bill, and started to attend college at the expense of the government. That resulted in most of the colleges and universities in the country becoming over crowded. I had no choice but to return to Ohio State and make different plans for my future.

I went home to Erie after visiting John in New Haven, CT, and decided to return to Ohio State for the spring quarter in 1947. I hung around the house for about a month before deciding to visit John again who had been transferred to the University of Pennsylvania in Philadelphia. He had decided to be a lawyer and was accepted by the law school while still under the V-12 program.

I learned a lot from John during that visit one of which was how to study. We got up at seven in the morning and studied to around ten o'clock before he left for class and returned at about four o'clock. He then studied until six o'clock and went out for dinner after which he studied until midnight when the local radio played, "The Bluebird of Happiness" by Jan Pierce, before signing off.

He didn't take time out for any kind of entertainment until he had finished his school work so we didn't go out much. John suggested that I try to read some classics and gave me a huge book entitled, "From Beowulf to Thomas Harding." It took me a while to get used to such a reading, but I eventually got used to it. I went back home a couple of weeks later, but I never forgot how much he had taught me to get started in the right direction.

The Influence of John Miller Wolford

John Wolford was an honorable man. He was the kind of person who befriended people who were not going anywhere in their lives, and encouraged them to fight for things

that would make them better and I was one of them. He started to encourage me when I was around thirteen years old on the "Y" swim team together, and he became one of my best friends.

I wasn't going anywhere in my life until he took me under his wing, and convinced me that I could do great things with myself. We used to sit in the car at night for hours in high school and talk about what we would like to do with our lives. He constantly encouraged me to think good about myself.

Looking back, I watched him talk and encourage others like Swede Carlson who was also on the Vincent swimming team with us. Everyone in the school made fun of Swede, and called him "the dumb Swede." This caused him to have a terrible inferiority complex until John convinced him that he was a good person and with hard work, he could make something of himself.

Swede joined the Merchant Marines as a seaman when he graduated from high school, and sailed on many ships called "Liberty Ships" that took munitions and soldiers over to Europe during the war. Hundreds of the ships were sunk by German U-Boat submarines that made it very dangerous for their crews. Swede lived through the whole ordeal, and eventually worked his way up to being the captain of one of those ships due mainly through the influence of John Wolford.

I don't think I would have ever ended up the way I did without John's encouragement and faith in me.

John didn't smoke, swear, or drink alcohol until he went into the service when he became an alcoholic, and he never admitted it right up to the time of his death. He ended up being one of the best lawyers in the state of Pennsylvania, and won around thirty straight cases when he started practice. He was a fierce competitor, and did his homework well when in court.

Nancy was John's youngest sister who also attended Vincent High School. She didn't like me when I started to run around with John. I remember she used to like insulting me when I visited John at his home, but then things changed between us.

I was having a milkshake in a dairy bar that was run by a good friend, John Meehan, when one night Nancy walked in and sat down with me to eat an ice cream sundae. Suddenly, we had an air raid that was common during the war days when we were still in high school. This meant that all the lights in the city were turned off, and the windows covered to prevent any light from getting out so the enemy airplanes couldn't spot us.

I held Nancy's hand to give her a little comfort while sitting in the dark, but as I found later, she didn't take my gesture the same way as I did. Suddenly, I had a girl that had a crush on me, and she hinted how she had felt about me for a couple of years. But I didn't respond because her brother was one of my best friends.

She later met a nice guy and went with him for a couple years before deciding to marry him. She asked me to take her for a ride in my car on her wedding day just before the wedding because she said she had something important to tell me. We drove down to the city dock and parked when she said that she loved me, and would break off the wedding and marry me if I wanted her to.

I had no idea that she felt that strongly about me, and I told her that I had very warm feelings for her but I wasn't ready for marriage. I took her back home and she got married that lasted for about ten years before she died from cancer. I didn't think of it then, but later felt she had a lot to do with my naming my daughter "Nancy" when she was born.

John Meehan

John Meehan was the manager of the dairy bar that Nancy and I had sat in during an air raid. He had bad teeth and everyone called him "horse teeth" and looked upon him as a clown and a social misfit. He was another person that John Wolford took on and changed his life.

John Meehan was a genius when it came to American History. He showed his intelligence when he took a course in the subject at Vincent. When the teacher brought up a specific incident or battle that occurred in our early American history, she would call on John to explain what happed, and he would give all the details concerning the activity to the amazement of the rest of the class. John was later drafted during the war, and went over to Europe in the infantry and had half of his leg blown off while fighting in Germany.

At Ohio State

Mike Peppe got me my lifeguard job back at the Scioto Country Club for the summer. John Wolford and John Meehan had also recently gotten out of the service, and decided to visit me. While guarding at the Scioto Country Club, I told them to put on their suits, and go swimming when John Meehan hesitated.

I asked him what was the matter, and he said that he was embarrassed because he only had one leg and the people around the pool might be offended. I told him that there wasn't one person in the whole club that ever came close to what he had sacrificed for his country, so if they saw him differently, I would tell them they could go to hell. Strangely, losing his leg was one of the best things that ever happened to him because he learned, through John Wolford, to hold his head up and develop confidence in himself. He later went to Washington D.C. after graduating from college and got a high-level government job.

Since I was on the G.I. Bill when I returned to Ohio State in the fall, I didn't have to work as a life guard at the Ohio State pool anymore. But I still wanted to lifeguard at the

Scioto Country Club pool during the summer. I had gone through three algebra texts in the service, so I took the course over again and got an "A plus" and "B" in psychology that helped my GPA move up to 2.5. I took courses that kept my GPA around 2.5 for the next two quarters remembering that I almost flunked out of school before going into the service.

I went home to Erie just before spring quarter started in 1948 to get a tooth fixed and to see my mother. My dentist was Doctor Balthasar. He suggested that I consider dentistry as a career so I changed my major to pre-dent when I returned to Ohio State.

I soon realized that I had made a terrible mistake because I took a qualitative analysis course that required analyzing the contents in ten different bottles, and I didn't get any of them right. I also took another course in comparative anatomy where, with the aid some written instructions, I was to dissect a dog fish. I must have asked the student next to me a hundred questions on how I was supposed to cut my fish up.

It got so bad, he wouldn't talk to me anymore. It didn't take me long to figure that I might as well have taken the fish home and cooked it. The two subjects accounted for five credit hours each, and it was obvious that if I flunked both courses, I would flunk out of school. So, I went to the admissions office and requested that I drop out of school to train for the 1948 Olympic tryouts and they accepted my request...phew!

A Minor Miracle

I went back to working as a life guard at the Scioto County Club in the summer of 1948 and I was living under the pool again. Everything was going well until half way through the summer. I woke up in the middle of a Monday night with both ears swollen completely shut which was probably caused by the dampness in the room.

I was screaming with pain and threw up just as the door to my room opened, and Dr. Rosenow walked in. He was the father of two young children I had taught how to swim and dive, and they were very close to me. With all the country clubs closed on Mondays and nobody around, how the doctor showed up at the exact moment I woke up in great pain has always been a mystery to me.

There was no way he could have heard my screams from the pool deck or known I was in trouble. Evaluating my condition, he went to his car and came back with some pain killers that put me to sleep until early morning, and took me to see Doctor Means, an ear specialist, whom I knew from teaching his daughter how to swim as well. He opened the canal in my ears, and gave me some medicine to stop the pain and neither doctor charged me anything.

Dr. Rosenow knew I couldn't stay under the pool so he took me to his home where I remained in bed for two weeks.

The Silbernagel Family

The Silbernagel family came for a visit one day and suggested I stay with them until the end of the summer because I couldn't return to the damp room under the pool. Their generous offer was made because I had taught their nine-year-old daughter Evelyn, and five-year-old Gretchen, how to swim and dive at the Scioto Country Club that summer.

Wynn Silbernagel was an obstetrician and a wonderful husband and father. They lived in a nice two story home in Upper Arlington, a suburb of Columbus. They owned two cars, a Packard convertible and Cadillac, a small two-seat airplane, and two horses. He got house calls from his patients through the night, and I used to go out with him on occasion. But I always had to sit in the car while he attended to a patient.

Jane, his wife, was a beautiful and dignified woman who was active in several social clubs and their Methodist Church. I was given my own room, and after living there for a couple of months we became so close that they introduced me to their friends as their son and I called them mom and dad.

I tried to earn my way by doing odd jobs like washing dishes, windows, and cleaning while living there until they hired a maid. I never grew up in a real family, and enjoyed every moment living with them. They were so nice to me.

Since most of the people in the neighborhood belonged to the Scioto Country Club, I decided to form a tumbling club for the neighborhood children in the fall. I went to the local high school, and got permission to use their gym on Saturday mornings. Then I put the word out that the club was for children between eight and twelve years old.

I also told them that it would cost ten cents a week to take part in the club provided they obeyed three rules: pay dues, pay dues promptly, and don't forget to pay dues. About ten youngsters showed up the first Saturday morning. The word spread that they all had such a good time, and the number increased to about thirty kids by the next Saturday.

The club ran through most of the winter, and everyone had a great time learning a bunch of tumbling stunts. Years later I was thrilled when a whole bunch of those kids got together, and showed up to visit me at an Indiana versus Ohio State swimming meet.

My Academic Experiences at Ohio State

Ohio State was on a quarter point system and I did much better with my grades when I started back to school at Ohio State in the fall of 1947 thanks to John Wolford who taught me how to study.

How I Decided My Major

I started school again in the fall of 1947, and did well with my studies. I still didn't have a clue what I wished to do with my life. I asked myself if I wanted to make a lot of money or help others, and I decided on the latter. The university required all students to choose a major field before they started their junior year so I decided to change my major to education with a math minor that would qualify me to be a school teacher. I took a course in differential equations and another in calculus and did well with differential equations, but calculus was much more like Latin to me. I really struggled through the course and managed to receive only a passing grade that told me I would make a lousy math teacher.

It was at this moment in time when I decided, quite by accident, what I wanted to do with my life. One afternoon, while lying on my bed at the Silbernagel's house reading a book with the radio on, a female who coached softball was being interviewed after winning the state championships. When asked how she managed to coach her girls to win the championships, she said she did nothing more than throw the ball out and tell her team to play ball.

I suddenly hit the ceiling with the book I was reading as I got off the bed yelling what an idiot the coach was to say such a stupid thing. I caught my emotion, and asked myself why was I so upset over the coach's statement? And it was at that moment, I decided to be a school teacher and coach in physical education.

I immediately changed my major, for the last time, to Health, Physical Education, and Recreation with a minor in Math in that fall quarter of 1948. I took Zoology as one of the requirements for my major, and the course involved two exams for a grade. One was a practical exam requiring the identity of all sorts of bugs and insects, and was graded by the number of wrong answers from the number of right answers.

I studied real hard for the test that was on a Friday. I was called into the office by my instructor the following Monday. When I showed up, he said he wanted to congratulate me for getting the lowest score ever made on the test since he had been in the department. I had scored a "minus" thirteen. He asked if I had studied at all, and I told him how I had. And he said he couldn't wait to see what kind of a score I was going to make on the written exam at the end of the quarter.

I came up with some stupid excuse that I couldn't take the exam with the class, and the instructor knew I was faking an excuse so I could talk to some of the class members after they had taken the test. I took the test, with true or false and multiple choice questions, in his office knowing a few answers. When I went to hand in my exam, I saw the answer sheet for the exam on his desk while he was talking on the phone.

I just turned around and sat down again, and changed some of the answers on my exam. When the instructor got off the phone, he asked me what I was doing. I said I was doing everything I could to get a passing grade, and he gave me a "C" grade in the course.

More Major Field Courses

A lot of the required courses in my chosen field were also taken by future nurses and doctors already familiar with medical terms, and one of those courses was physiology. The course was generally given by Dr. Anger who informed our class of about seventy students that he was the only one who knew anything about physiology, and the two text books that were required for the course were worthless.

He went on to say he guaranteed fifty percent of the students in our class would probably flunk the course. The course offered three tests with the last being the final. His lectures related to anatomy, the circulatory system, and the final was on the nervous system. He taught three classes on the same subjects for that quarter, and ours was his third class of the day.

When we went in to take the final exam, that everyone had knocked themselves out studying for, he said that since we probably asked the other classes what was on the test, he was giving us an exam on the circulatory system again that no one had studied for. By accident, I found an old exam he had given years ago, on the circulatory system in the files at the Sigma Chi Fraternity, and I casually scanned over it.

Fortunately, I found some of the answers on that old test that were on our test that helped me pass the course with a "D." I thanked God for my luck because half the class flunked the exam, and had to take the course again.

One of the Physical Education courses we had to take was teaching football, and we played the game wearing football gear out on a football field. One day when leaving the classroom to go out and play, I was walking behind the instructor when suddenly the cleats on my shoes caused me to slip on the wooden floor.

As my feet went out from underneath me, I kicked the instructor in the seat of the pants that caused him to land flat on his back, and the whole class started to laugh. Thinking that it wasn't funny, the instructor got up and accused me of deliberately kicking him. and I would pay for my actions. I told him that it wasn't on purpose and apologized. I worked my tail off in the class and got an "A" on my test, but he still gave me a "C" in the course.

Campus Men's Honorary Associations

Ohio State had men's honorary associations for sophomore, junior, and senior male students, and I made two of them: Bucket and Dipper for juniors, and Sphinx for seniors. The honors were given to thirteen students who had made outstanding contributions in various activities related to the school in each year. The chosen ones were recognized as the big men on campus and, though not mandatory, they all wore a shirt, tie and sport coat attending classes.

My teammate and dear friend, Bruce Harlan, was a year ahead of me in school, and he made all three honors. I know that he had much to do with me being selected during my junior and senior years, but looking back at that time, I deserved the honors. The new members of Sphinx were chosen when a member would visit a class in a black cap and gown, and tap the new honoree on the shoulder.

We were taking an exam in my health class when the Sphinx member walked into our room, and thinking that he was going to tap the captain of the football team, I paid little attention as I went back to the exam. I nearly fell on the floor when he suddenly tapped me on the shoulder, and the whole class got up and gave me a standing ovation.

All the new Sphinx honorees walked around the Oval in the center of the campus with their selectors while the students were changing classes and greeting us. I must say that it was one of the most thrilling moments in my young life. I was selected because I was a top diver on the swimming team, competed in three events on the gymnastic team, was the head cheerleader, and participated in a couple of plays for the drama club.

Extracurricular Activities and Humor

I remember one play entitled, "Dangerous Dan Magrue." Bruce Harlan, Joe Marino, and I were dressed in women's dresses. We acted as can-can dancers, and wore falsies in the top of our dresses. One night while doing the can-can by kicking our straight legs up and down, the strap on my dress broke and the falsies fell out on the floor and the whole audience roared with laughter. Since everyone enjoyed the accident so much, we made it happen in the three remaining shows. Looking back, I can see how these kinds of experiences helped form the clown diving shows we would perform later.

Student Teaching Assignments

Physical Education majors had to student teach and coach in a secondary school as a requirement to graduate. I was assigned to teach a class during the fall quarter at a high school in south Columbus that was in the poor part of town. I walked into the school and the boys' Physical Education teacher gave me his class schedule and grade book. Then he walked out, and I never saw him again.

I taught the class how to wrestle and perform gymnastics, and for a change they really enjoyed learning something new. We all had a good time, but I never saw their teacher. When I finished my student teaching, he gave me a "B" when he never saw me teach.

A rare occasion occurred during the winter quarter when I was assigned to coach the swimming team at Kenyon College in Gambier, Ohio about thirty-five miles north of Columbus. Kenyon had lost their swimming coach so the school contacted our Physical Education Department to see if they could find someone to coach the team until they found a replacement. I drove my car up to Gambier every afternoon, and on weekends when they had swimming meets.

Kenyon was a private school for males with about six-hundred elite students that had to be extremely intelligent, and wealthy to attend the college. The buildings on campus were beautiful and like those seen at Princeton University. The swimming pool was in a greenhouse surrounded with glass, and had one and three-meter diving boards.

The school had a terrible dormitory fire killing six students about three months before I arrived. Their one diver had just recovered from a broken leg jumping out a third-floor window onto a mattress he had thrown down to the ground of the burning dormitory.

The athletic director was nice to me, and we got along beautifully all the time I coached there. He often invited me to have dinner with him, and his family that included his gorgeous daughter who had just returned from serving in the Army. She took a liking to me, and I didn't know it until she told me that I was just the kind of person she was looking for to marry. I was flattered with her comment, but told her I wasn't quite ready to make that commitment. I never saw her again after I left Kenyon at the end of the swimming season.

I invited Bill Hess, the chairman of the Ohio State P.E. department, to referee the last swimming meet at Kenyon so he could evaluate my coaching efforts. He did a good job refereeing the meet. When we returned to school, and as I was handing him the twenty-five dollars for his service that the athletic department gave me to give him, I pulled my hand back with the money.

I then asked him what kind of grade he was going to give me for the coaching job I did? And when he said an "A," I gave him the money. Laughing, he asked me if I would have given him the money had he given me a lower grade, and I smiled at him as I walked out. I found out later that the movie stars Jonathan Winters and Paul Newman were also attending Kenyon at the same time I was coaching, but I don't remember ever meeting them.

Roganne McGuire and Mary Drake

In the fall of 1948 when I was attending a free swim in the Ohio State natatorium, I saw a beautiful girl diving from the one-meter board. I made up my mind I was going to meet her. So, I went over and started a conversation. I offered to help her with her diving, and she gave me her telephone number. Her name was Roganne McGuire. I called her up the next day to learn she lived in Bexley, a rich suburb on the east side of Columbus.

She invited me out to her house that afternoon. After we talked for a short time, there was a knock at her door and a nice-looking guy came in. I went into the other room to give them some privacy, and he stayed for about five minutes. When I asked her who the guy was, she said he was her fiancé. Surprised, I told her that I was sorry to have intruded and I left.

I was even more surprised the next day when she called to tell me she had broken off her engagement, and wanted to see me. We went together for nearly a year when I found that she was interested in aquatics. So, I got her a job teaching synchronized swimming to the young girls at the Scioto Country Club that summer.

One night chatting with her father who was a Sigma Chi, he told me if I ended up marrying Roganne, that he would take me into his carpet business and make me his partner. I remember thanking him for his generous offer, and told him his kind of business was not the direction I planned to go in my life. I broke up with her during the spring of 1949, and I started to date another girl in the fall.

When I started to attend Ohio State again in the spring of 1947 after I left the service, I was made the head cheerleader again when the fall football season started. The cheerleaders had always been males up until the fall of 1949 when the athletic department decided to include girls on the squad. Since I was the head cheerleader, I was given the honor to select three girls.

A tryout notice was put out in the school paper, and about 250 girls showed up in a gym at the Physical Education Building. I had girls calling me at the Silbernagel home day and night, and this caused a problem with Dr. Silbernagel because he received night calls from his pregnant patients all the time.

It took me three or four days to select the three girls who were Jean Chard, Sarah Miller, and Carol Crumley. Having girls on the squad worked out fine, but we were not allowed to touch them while cheering. This made doing cheers with any kind of lifts impossible.

Persistence Pays Off

I saw one girl at the tryouts that I thought was cute so I walked up and started to talk to her. I must have said something that insulted her when she told me to back off because she had come with a friend, and wasn't there to try out. I saw the same girl again the next day as she was walking across the campus, and I asked a friend of mine if he knew her? He said her name was Mary Drake and was in one of his classes.

She lived in Baker Hall, a girl's dormitory. I called her up and told her who I was before going over to her dorm that evening, and asked her if she would like to have a cup of coffee with me. She said that she knew who I was, and wasn't interested in going out with me and hung up.

I bought a 1935 Chevrolet Coupe the next week, and now I had wheels. After I selected the three girls to be cheerleaders, I called Mary again and asked if she would like to take ride with me. She said, "no thanks," and added that she didn't want me to call her again and hung up.

A few weeks later, while standing in line to pick up my schedule for the next quarter at the Education building, I saw Mary standing in line a couple of lines from mine. I told a friend with me that the girl in her line hated my guts, and as I pointed her out, I saw her waving at me. So, I went over and had a nice chat with her.

Television had just come out, and Dr. Silbernagel purchased one of the TV sets. They were going to televise the Ohio State versus Michigan football game at Michigan, and the cheerleaders weren't invited. So, I called Mary and invited her out to the Silbernagel house to watch the game. This time she accepted my invitation, and we both had a great time and I dated her for the next year and a half until I graduated.

CHAPTER 9

The Ohio State Diving Program After Returning from the Service

I discovered that the diving program had changed a lot when I returned to Ohio State from the service in 1946. I was not in good physical shape. I walked into the pool and saw Miller Anderson, Bruce Harlan, Jack Calhoun, Jim Strong, and Johnny Simpson working out, and I realized I was going to have to work very hard if I was ever going to beat any of them.

I knew Miller Anderson from when I had first met him at the Scioto Country Club, and he had won at the National A.A.U. diving championships held at Cuyahoga Falls, Ohio, before going overseas. I also knew who Bruce Harlan was when he placed second to Miller at that same meet. But I had never met Jack Calhoun, Jim Strong, or Johnny Simpson before.

Bruce Harlan

Bruce Harlan was born and raised in Lansdowne, Pennsylvania by a family of "carnies" that were people who worked in carnivals and traveled around the country. He had two sisters and two brothers who also worked with their parents in the carnivals. Bruce would do almost anything to draw attention to himself like performing handstands on the top of bridges or buildings when growing up.

He joined the Navy when he graduated from high school, and was stationed in Pensacola, Florida. One day while playing around on the one-meter diving board at the Navy base pool, R. Jackson Smith a.k.a. RJ, who was a Commander and a competitive diver while at Dartmouth College, spotted Bruce and was impressed with his potential talent.

Smith oversaw the Physical Education program at the Navy base, and asked Bruce if he would like to learn how to dive competitively. Bruce agreed, and RJ assigned a female officer, Helen Perry, who was a competitive diver on the base, to teach Bruce how to dive. That resulted in Bruce missing 188 days of active duty.

He quickly learned a full list of competitive dives. RJ was a close friend of Mike Peppe, and had a sister on the Ohio State's teaching staff. He decided to take Bruce to the 1945 outdoor National A.A.U. diving championships at Cuyahoga Falls, Ohio.

Bruce was a sensation, but was beaten out of first place by Miller Anderson who had just gotten out of a rehabilitation hospital for the fighter plane injury that occurred to him in the war. RJ Smith (pictured below) also competed, and took fourth. I took fifth which I thought wasn't bad since I had hitchhiked all night from St. Louis, and had not

dived in three months while in the service. After Bruce placed second at the Nationals at Cuyahoga Falls in Ohio, RJ helped Coach Peppe and Miller Anderson convince him to attend Ohio State knowing he was going to be out of the service in a couple of months.

Bruce enrolled at Ohio State in the fall of 1945, and went on to win 20 major diving titles. He was also the captain of the swim team in his senior year, and graduated first in his class in 1950. It must be remembered that scholarships were not given by universities until after the Second World War, so none of the athletes got paid to compete while in college.

Jack Calhoun

Jack Calhoun was the third best diver on the team, and proved it many times. He was from Ft. Lauderdale, Florida, and was never in a hurry to do anything. He liked art, and later painted a collection of pictures that were displayed in the museum at the International Swimming Hall of Fame in Ft. Lauderdale.

He had a great sense of humor, served in the Navy, and was on a boxing team before attending Ohio State. He made the U.S. 1952 Helsinki, Finland, Olympic Games Team, and was the first diver to ever use a back 2 ½ somersault from the ten-meter platform in an Olympic event. He performed the dive well in the Olympic trials that put him on the team, but missed the dive in the Olympic Games and didn't make the finals. He later told me that he over trained at the Olympics, and was the first American to not win a medal in an Olympic event for the United States since 1920.

He flew his own airplane years after graduating from Ohio State, and one day crashed it into the ocean near the beach at Ft. Lauderdale. Jack crawled out of the plane unscathed after it tipped over on its back, and the bathers on the beach cheered him. He studied to be a lawyer after graduating from Ohio State, but never passed the bar exam. He ended up being a lifeguard on the beach for thirty years, and passed away in 2011.

Jim Strong

Jim Strong was the other diver on the team who had returned from the service and decided to go to college. He was tall and handsome, and a lady's man who wore three hundred dollar suits but didn't have a dime in his pocket. Strangely, he only dated girls with the name "Betty" and eventually married one.

He was a good diver and considered himself to be among the top divers in the country which he was. He was also an alcoholic that none of us knew about until he performed with us in Al Sheehan's Aqua Follies. Some of the divers would go out to the refreshment area during intermission, and mingle with the spectators and give autographs on their programs.

A group of executives from General Motors attended the show one night, met Jim Strong during the intermission, and offered him a position as general manager for one of their Buick automobile agencies in Springfield, Ohio. Jim took the job, and worked there for several years while making a good living. However, when the price of gasoline jumped from 29 to 83 cents a gallon, fewer people bought Buicks.

Frustrated, alone, and depressed he started to gamble. He lost a lot of money that only depressed him more, and he ended up shooting and killing himself. Sadly, I heard that nobody picked up his ashes after the funeral.

Johnny Simpson (pictured next page)

Johnny Simpson grew up in the South, was very intelligent and gifted in music. He could play several musical instruments, and his favorite was the violin. He was short but an above average diver, and had two children.

One of the most difficult dives in the rule book in those days was a back 1½ somersault with 1½ twists, and Johnny predicted someday divers would perform the same dive with 2½ twists. We all laughed saying it wasn't possible. But the next day Johnny performed that dive he predicted, a back somersault with 2½ twists, from the one-meter low board.

Not one to be outdone, Bruce walked in and saw what Johnny had done so he did the same dive on the low board. Then he did the same dive on the high board. Coach Peppe showed up in the pool while this was going on, and asked me to go up to his office where he showed me a letter from David Browning. He was the father of Skippy Browning, who later won the gold medal on the springboard at the 1952 Olympics. His father stated that his son had just performed a seemingly impossible dive from the three-meter board that should have a degree of difficulty (DD) rating of 3.8. The highest DD for the most difficult dive in the rule book then was 2.5.

David Browning described the same dive that Johnny and Bruce had just performed in our pool, and Mike and I had a good laugh over it. So, Johnny, Bruce, and Skippy came up with the same new dive at approximately the same time. The dive eventually got put in the rule books with a 2.8 DD rating.

Johnny dived in the Al Sheehan Aqua Follies with us for several years. After retiring from diving, he called me in 1964 to inform me that he was going to make a diving comeback. I told him to forget it because he was forty-four years old. He laughed at my comment, and said he knew he could take on any of the present divers. But that dream never happened because the very next day after his call to me he had a massive heart attack and died.

up JOHNY SIMPSON, MILER ANDERSoN, MIKE pEPPE BRUCE HARLW, JIM STRONG - JI

Coach Mike Peppe and His Reputation

I also found that Mike Peppe no longer showed the same interest in his swimmers and divers as he did when I first came to Ohio State. Mike did a fair job of coaching when I returned. But he never scheduled a workout for the divers or swimmers, and left it to them when they wanted to practice. This also let him show up whenever he wanted to.

The swimmers usually practiced in the early morning and early afternoon while the divers practiced in midmorning and late afternoon. We planned our workouts from day to day around our classes, and we coached each other when Mike was not present which was often. When he didn't attend one of our practices, we thought he had practice with the swimmers. And when not present with swimmers, they thought he

95

was with the divers. Believe it or not, Mike came to me in my junior year and paid me seventy-five cents an hour to coach Miller Anderson and Bruce Harlan on Tuesday and Thursday nights. That meant I was coaching my teammates to beat me.

Mike developed the same reputation for coaching divers at Ohio State that was found with the Notre Dame football team. It became known that if you wanted to be a diving champion, you went to Ohio State just as it was if you were a Catholic and wanted to play on a winning football team, you went to Notre Dame. That reputation made recruiting good athletes much easier.

Coaches from other colleges often suggested to those who wanted to be a good diver to go to Ohio State. Not everyone liked Coach Peppe, but I always liked Mike and got along well with him while at Ohio State. He wrote many letters to me on how the team was doing while I was in the service and that meant a lot to me. He was a good leader, and everyone respected him.

Once when we were on a trip, Mike allotted us $1.50 for a meal in a restaurant. Matt Mann, the Michigan coach walked in with his team, and he told them that they could eat anything they wanted if it wasn't more than eighty-eight cents. I thought "Boy was I lucky I didn't go to Michigan."

The dynasty at Ohio State was also made possible because all the college swimming coaches in the country were responsible for coaching their diving program. However, none of them knew a thing about diving, and didn't wish to waste their time trying to coach two or three divers while coaching forty or more swimmers. Swim coaches even tried to get diving eliminated from the swimming program for years, but failed because diving was an Olympic event and most of the Olympic divers came from our universities.

Carl Worthwein (team picture next page top row far right)

Carl Worthwein was Mike's assistant, and a very friendly person but never coached anyone. He was always present in the pool when Mike was there, and he also attended all our meets. Mike had an "in" with the good swimmers from Hawaii, and recruited such greats as Kao Nakama, Hala Hirosi, Dick Cleveland, and Bill Smith.

They all held world swimming records, and made it possible for Ohio State, with the help of the divers, win the N.C.A.A. and National A.A.U. Championships several times. Mike, and many other swimming coaches in those days, believed that the further a swimmer swam, the faster he could swim. That was soon proven not to be true. Most colleges in those days didn't have any good divers, and when one would pop up occasionally, they received little or no coaching from the swimming coach.

I am pictured bottom row second from left next page.

TOP ROW: *Peppe (coach), Bolenbaugh (manager), Webber, Elliott, Bartels, Schauer, Grant, Waltrip (trainer), Wirthwein (asst. coach). ROW TWO: P. Knight, Nakama, Smith, Hirose (captain), deGroot, Congelliere, Rodenbach, R. Knight, Adell. ROW ONE: Thomas, Billingsley, Harlan, Calhoun, Simpson, Henderson*

Diving Coaching Was About to Change

Swimming coaches didn't know how to coach divers, and preferred to spend their time with the swimmers on their teams. This scenario went on until 1954 when Bruce Harlan became the first ever diving coach hired by a college at the University of Michigan. It wasn't long before his divers started to beat the Ohio State divers because he knew more about diving than anyone else at that time.

More About Bruce and the Diving Team

On the team, Bruce was very smart, but had the personality of being a show-off and a jerk at times. About a year after I had returned from the service and was again competing at Ohio State, Jim Patterson, a former Ohio State diver with The Aqua Follies, asked Bruce, Jim Strong and me to do a summer diving exhibition in Fargo North Dakota with him for a thousand dollars.

Patterson accepted the money to prevent us from becoming professionals, and planned to spend the money on a big party in Chicago driving on the way back to Columbus. None of us liked Bruce because he was a show off, self-centered, and always had to be the center of attention. So, while driving up to Fargo, Patterson and Strong started to tell Bruce what a big pain he was. Then they asked me for my opinion, and I added a few more criticisms and told him that he was a great diver but a bigger jerk. The discussion lasted for about a half hour without a single word from Bruce. I think he heard every word we told him, and started to change from that moment on.

Joe Marino

Joe Marino came to Ohio State in 1949 from San Francisco. He was a very handsome Italian young man loaded with talent not only in diving, but also in the field of music. He played a ukulele, and was tremendously popular all over the campus singing songs, especially at sororities where he entertained the girls after dinner.

He won the National A.A.U. three-meter title in Seattle in 1950, and after graduating in Physical Education went into show business. He wound up singing in some national T.V. shows with another Sigma Chi, and later joined a group in Las Vegas where they performed at various casinos on the strip for about seven years. He got married three times, one of which was to a famous Vegas singer, and remained working in Vegas until he retired and passed away in 2011.

The New Replacements

Though I didn't compete with them, I wish to include Fletcher Gilders (3rd from left) and Bobby Clotworthy (pictured below with me) as the two who followed me after my competitive years at Ohio State.

They both started school in 1950 when I was a senior, and we became great friends before I graduated in 1951.

Bobby Clotworthy was from New Jersey and was sort of short, but a very powerful and great diver. He and Miller had similar techniques performing twisting somersault dives that astonished most divers, coaches, and judges. They would start the twist with one arm off to the side,

then reverse the action of the arm when beginning to twist that made it look like an incredible move.

A little on the stocky side, Bob didn't appear to be as graceful as many other divers, but he was a terrific acrobat and a fierce competitor. He later joined the Beta Fraternity, and went on to win the gold medal at the 1956 Olympics in Melbourne, Australia plus a dozen major titles for Ohio State. He was among the great divers

produced at Ohio State, and I followed his career after he graduated and later became the swimming coach at Princeton University.

About a dozen years later, he resigned from his job at Princeton, and coached at a small college in Wisconsin for another decade that didn't offer all the stress found coaching at larger universities. He married a wonderful girl, and they had three children. He finally retired and moved to New Mexico for a long time, before ending up in Fort Collins, Colorado.

Fletcher Gilders was from Detroit, had a great personality, and was liked by everyone. Bruce and I had just finished our show in Delaware, Ohio, one time when Fletcher was there, and introduced us to his younger sister. He said she was a diver, and we thought she was probably a beginner. Instead, we were surprised when she made the 1952 Olympic team, and took third place from the three-meter springboard.

Fletcher went on to be the greatest all-around athlete in the history of Ohio State. He lettered in five different sports in one year, and won the National A.A.U. Championships in diving two years in row. He became a diving coach after graduating, and his first job was at Kenyon College in Gambier, Ohio, that was my first coaching job when I was a senior at Ohio State. Ohio University in Athens, Ohio, later hired him which was the second college job I had as a diving coach. I was beginning to wonder if he would be hired by Indiana if I left for another position.

Fletcher worked at Matt Mann's Camp Chikopi located in Canada during the summers, and later bruised his leg which required surgery. Thinking that it was fixed, he developed a blood clot soon after that killed him in the early 2000's. I really missed him because he was such a good guy. We used to go fishing, and fabulously cook a fish so it tasted really good ... well, almost.

Continuing the Team

Ohio State's swimming team went to the International Swimming Hall of Fame in Ft. Lauderdale to practice in their pool over the Christmas break every year to get outdoors and enjoy warmer weather than winters in Columbus. Coach Peppe found private housing for all of us.

Beyond that, it was a good deal because we were only two blocks from the pool, and ate breakfast every morning in a restaurant that served us bacon and eggs, hash brown potatoes, toast, coffee, and a big glass of orange juice for thirty-nine cents. We practiced in an eight-lane concrete-walled pool with the diving well at one end. It was filled with cold salt water pumped in from the ocean across the street. The diving boards weren't too bad, but we had to share the pool with the swimmers from fifteen other college teams. That created a problem because the swim teams practiced all day long. We were still able to get in two workouts a day, but had to time our dives just right or risk breaking our necks landing on swimmers who continually swam under the boards.

Jim Strong's father lived down the street from the pool, and loaned Jim his car to drive us around. Jim decided to wash and wax the car for his dad before returning it, so the three of us worked on the car the whole afternoon washing and waxing it because in those days the wax had to be rubbed in. We went inside the house to have a cold drink after we finished the job, and Jim asked me to drive the car out of the drive way and park it on the street.

Bruce said he would go along with me, and while driving the car backwards out of the driveway, I hit the mail box that left a long scratch down the side of the car. I about fainted when I saw what I had done, and thought Bruce would run in the house and tell Jim what I had done.

Instead, he told me to get the wax out of the trunk quick, and see if we could rub the scratch out. We managed to rub it out enough in a half hour that made it hard to see, and Bruce never said a word to Jim. From that time on, Bruce Harlan and I became inseparable friends, and we always roomed together for out-of-town meets.

They held the spring Indoor National A.A.U. Diving Championships outdoors at the Daytona, Florida, pool. The one-meter board was mounted on a small cement structure out in the middle of the pool. That meant divers had to swim out to it when practicing and competing. It started to rain real hard in the middle of the contest, so the judges went inside and judged the diving while looking out the window.... oh my!

I remember Al Coffee, who was a great diver, and my little brother in the Sigma Chi fraternity, and was second after the preliminaries. However, when the finals were held late that afternoon, Coffee didn't show up and was disqualified. Peppe later asked him where he had been, and he said he had gone to a movie and didn't want to miss the finish.

Peppe later dropped him from the team and he enrolled at the University of Miami where he placed high in several meets. He was a fantastic diver, and after graduating from Miami dived in the Al Sheehan Aqua Follies with us for several years. A while later the University of Pittsburgh hired him as their diving coach, and then he went on to coach diving at Iowa State.

CHAPTER 10

The Introduction of Aluminum Diving Boards

The Norman Buck Board

All diving boards in the world were made of wood from 1889 until 1947 when a man by the name of Norman Buck came along. He was from Seattle, Washington and read in the Seattle newspaper that Ray Daughters, also from Seattle, was sending six "Ray Daughters" laminated wooden diving boards over to England for the 1948 Olympic Games.

Norman Buck was a maker of aluminum step ladders, and suddenly got the idea that a diving board made of aluminum might offer more spring and last longer than any wooden board. With thirty tons of aluminum from the Army surplus in his garage, he made his version of an aluminum board. Wondering where he could test it, he decided to take it where there were good divers. So, he put it on his old truck and drove all the way East to Ohio State where he mounted it on the one-meter stand.

Bruce Harlan, Johnny Simpson, and I were in the pool when he installed the board, and I was the first person to ever dive from an aluminum diving board. We agreed that the board had much more spring than a wooden diving board, but it had so much torque or twist that a diver could miss landing in the pool with a bad takeoff.

He told us not to worry about it, and took the board back home for a few weeks to make improvements. When he brought it back and mounted it on the stand again, he had placed a thin metal sheet three feet long on the top of the board for stability, and a rubber striping around the edges to keep it from making noise. That became the best board ever made, and the only board that could be repaired if broken.

The board was called "The Buck Board," and it was quickly accepted by all the diving associations throughout the world. He continued to improve the board by baking a non-skid enamel on its surface that eliminated the need for cocoa matting that was used at the end of the board to prevent the diver from slipping doing a forward approach.

The improved board could be set on a level plane instead of being tilted upward two or more inches required of wooden boards. Divers began to perform difficult dives that had not been possible when the wooden board tilted upwards. It also reduced the danger of divers hitting the board when performing reverse and inward dives.

Norman retained control of the board sales worldwide that soon made him wealthy. He and his family went from living in a rundown little old house with a beat-up garage, to the owner of a forty-four-room mansion on Lake Washington where he moored his eighty-foot yacht and flew his own airplane that he used for his new business.   He continued to have a monopoly on the market until Ray Rude entered the scene nearly ten years later.

The Duraflex Diving Board

Ray Rude was an aeronautical engineer in California visiting a friend who was planning to have a diving exhibition at a party one evening. He had painted a wooden diving board in his pool that didn't dry, and was ready to cancel the show when Ray told him to wait until he checked his hanger to maybe find something that could be used for a diving board.

Ray found a part of an aluminum airplane wing, cut it off, and took it back to his friend's house where he installed it on the diving stand. Surprised, he found that it offered a great amount of spring, and the show went on with great success. Knowing that he had discovered something that had great promise, Ray decided to make diving boards, and called them "Duraflex."

The Duraflex board was a great improvement over the Buck Board, and eventually put Norman out of business. The Duraflex board has since been improved to the point that further improvements are no longer needed, and it has become the world standard used in all diving competitions at every competitive level throughout the world since 1958.

CHAPTER 11

Episodes from 1948 to 1951

The 1948 Olympic Trials

An event happened during the spring of 1948 that could have prevented Bruce Harlan from competing in the Olympic tryouts, and winning the Olympic gold medal at the 1948 Olympics staged in England. It happened in the spring at the N.C.A.A. National Championships at the University of Michigan during the finals of the three-meter event. Miller Anderson, Bruce's teammate, performed a reverse one and a half somersault from the three-meter board poorly.

When he got out of the pool, he told the referee, RJ Smith, that people in the audience made some noise that distracted his concentration. So, RJ told him to take the dive over. Miller performed the dive for the second time, and again performed a poor dive. He went to the referee again, and complained that he was distracted by a flash camera from someone in the audience that temporarily interfered with his vision. So the judge gave him permission to perform the dive over for the third time.

Bruce believed that Miller's requests were unjust, and ran straight toward Miller jumping over the one-meter stand. I ran over and grabbed him, and pushed him into the shower room. I convinced him not to hit Miller, especially when it was the Olympic year. If he had hit Miller, he would surely be disciplined, and probably not allowed to compete in the Olympic Trials. His diving career and chance to compete in the Olympics could be over. Bruce finally calmed down, but lost the event to Miller by two points.

Bruce and Miller went on to win every diving title available in the spring and summer of 1948. The Olympic diving trials were staged in August 1948 at an outdoor pool in Detroit. The top three places from the three-meter springboard and ten-meter platform for men and women made the Olympic teams. At that time, the one-meter event was not in the Olympic program.

I didn't know how to dive from the tower, so I only performed on the three-meter springboard. I thought I had an outside chance to make the team if I had a good meet. But I got so nervous doing my forward approach on my first dive that I started off on the wrong foot. I had to stutter my steps before my hurdle which resulted in a poor dive. I still managed to place fourteenth, but that didn't go well with me.

The 1948 London Olympic Games

Bruce and Miller placed first and second with Sammy Lee taking third on the three-meter board at the Olympics. For some unknown reason, the Olympic schedule had the divers perform the ten-dive contest on the three-meter board by performing only two dives a day over a five-day period.

No national championship had ever been conducted that way. That schedule was unheard of, and tough on all the divers and people everywhere to control their emotions and stress level. Everyone had to sweat out the event results for five days. Bruce would have also won the ten-meter event, but his toes tipped the edge of the platform while performing a reverse 1½ somersault in the layout position in the finals. That little error opened the door for Sammy Lee who won the contest with Bruce second, and Miller placing fourth.

About Sammy Lee (pictured in the middle between me and Dick Smith)

Sammy and his wife Roz lived in California where he learned to dive, and went to college to be a doctor. He learned to dive along with Dick Smith before serving

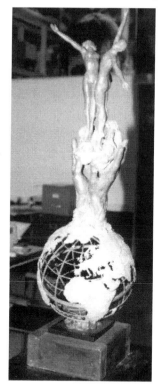

as a U.S. Army Major. He went on to win the 10-meter Olympic gold medal in 1948 and 1952 that were staged in London and Finland. He won the Sullivan and other awards, and served on the President's Commission for sports.

He coached Olympic great Greg Louganis from the time he was very young up until he placed second in the 1976 Olympic Games in Montreal, Canada. He also coached several other prominent divers, and remained connected to diving all his life. He was highly respected by everyone in the sport who knew his accomplishments. He was also a dear friend of mine until he passed away in January 2017 at the age of 95. He will be long remembered as one of the best divers and coaches who ever lived.

The Sammy Lee Award (pictured on right)

Before his death, it was decided that an award be given internationally to a person who has made great contributions to the sport throughout the world. At that time, Sammy was more notable than anyone else coaching diving in the world, and it was decided to be called the Sammy Lee Award.

The award is usually given out every four years, but there have been times when the award wasn't given. Currently, the award has only been given to six persons. In order starting first was Dick Smith, Hobie Billingsley, Klaus Dibiasi of Italy, Greg Louganis, Toivo Ohman of Sweden, and Ron O'Brien. No other diving award has been recognized higher in the world.

Post-Olympic Celebrations

Bruce returned to his home town in Lansdown, Pennsylvania, a suburb of Philadelphia, after returning from the 1948 Olympics. They had a parade, and gave him an eight-millimeter movie camera. Joe Verdeur was from Philadelphia also, and a good friend of ours. Joe won the Olympic gold medal in the 200-meter breaststroke and was given a parade and a new car! I still have Bruce's camera that must have cost about two hundred dollars, but shows the recognized difference between swimming and diving achievements.

My Chance to Win

I never came close to beating Bruce or Miller in a meet except once. We were competing in the 1948 Spring National A.A.U. one-meter championships at Yale University. I was having the best performance in my career, and beating both right up until the last dive. I was performing a forward 1½ somersault with a full twist, and all I needed to win was an average score of seven points from the judges.

Frank Dempsey came up to me just before I was going up to do the dive, and attempted to encourage me by telling me to make sure I had a strong take-off so I wouldn't go short on the dive. Keeping that I mind, I jumped as high as I could in the hurdle. When I landed on the end of the board for the take-off my knees buckled, and I fell off the board and received zeros for a failed dive.

There was absolute silence in the audience as I climbed out of the pool, and the referee, RJ Smith, told me to take the dive over and no one would object. I told him that I didn't have any excuse for my performance, and it would be unfair to repeat the dive. I ran into the dressing room, and after getting dressed, I ran out and found the closest bar and drank a double shot of whiskey. That did nothing to relieve the pain of losing a chance of a lifetime.

Our Gymnastic Team Experience

Bruce and I were also on the gymnastic team in 1949 and 1950. We had a little problem with that because the gymnastic meets often coincided with the swimming dual meets at Ohio State. We competed in two diving events, and three gymnastic meet events. We would start by competing on the flying rings in the gymnasium, and run down to the pool to perform our one-meter dives. Then we would run back upstairs for the tumbling event before running back down again to the pool to compete in the three-meter event. And would finally run back up to the gym to compete on the trampoline, and then finish the day participating in the comedy diving act in the pool.

The stands at the swimming meets were always packed with fans because a comedy diving show was always given at the end of the meet. Jim Patterson used to do the show himself when in school and continued to do so after he graduated. He was famous for his act pretending to be a drunk and fall down the stairs from the top of the stands down to the pool deck.

I had never taken part in a comedy diving act before, but I had watched a few. When one of the divers didn't show up to do the comedy diving after one meet, Bruce came running over, and told me to help and put on a comedy suit. I told him that I didn't know how to do a comedy dive. He told me to follow him, and he would tell me what dives I should try to make funny. I guess I must have done well because I was one of the comedy divers from that time on.

Our Comedy Acts Get Started

Later, Bruce and I created and performed a comedy trampoline act that we did out on the field at Ohio State football game half times, and at basketball games. We also started to perform diving and trampoline acts at local country clubs during the summer. A bunch of swimmers and divers were invited to do an exhibition in Bermuda before the swimming season started in 1948. We all stayed at the Eagles Nest Hotel on top of a hill near the swimming pool.

After we were there for a couple of days, they had a hurricane with winds around 135 miles an hour. Bruce and I shared a very large room with Joe Verduer, from Philadelphia. While Joe was taking a nap one afternoon, a large portion of the plaster ceiling dropped to the floor next to his bed. Showing no concern, he got up and moved his bed on top of the plaster, and went back to sleep. He loved to take baths, and one afternoon Bruce and I walked into the bathroom and found him fast asleep lying in a tub of water. His head was about to go under when Bruce and I woke him up. That may have saved him from drowning.

Bruce suddenly got the crazy idea that we go down to the pool, and dive off the three-meter board in the hurricane. Thinking that he was insane, I agreed. So, we managed to get a door open far enough to get outside of the hotel, and crawled down on our stomachs to the pool about a hundred yards away.

Fortunately, the wind was blowing from behind the board. We climbed up to the three-meter board, and took one step forward before jumping to the end of the board. We took off and flew like a bird about half way down the pool doing a front dive. It was fun so we did it a few more dives before returning to the hotel. Somehow, the New York Times found out about our little stunt, and gave us a nice write up in their paper.

Chummy Hayward, the president of the Lions Club that was sponsoring the show, was a wonderful guy and threw a party one evening for the whole group in the show. Chummy was impressed with our trampoline and diving performances, so he decided to stage a big water show every year for ten years that featured Bruce and me. They built a stage in front of the middle of the pool that we used when we did our trampoline act, and for other acts that were brought in from the United States.

Chummy set us up with a spear fishing trip with Ross Doe. Ross was a large man with a huge chest, and sensational at spear fishing. We saw him go down thirty feet deep in the ocean, and remain there for around three minutes while spearing all kinds of fish that included sharks and other dangerous species. Bruce and I used a hooked steel spear about twelve feet long. At one end was a barb to spear the fish, and the other had a large rubber band so you could stretch the band along the steel spear and release it to spear the fish.

I was so bad at spear fishing that I couldn't have speared a whale. I remember standing on coral reef up to my knees, and when I bent over with my head under water, I saw a barracuda looking at me not three feet away. I suddenly stood up, and yelled to Ross and he said spear it. Knowing I wouldn't spear it, I stood motionless for at least five minutes before getting out of the area.

Ross took part in our show swimming underwater four lengths of the twenty-five-yard-long pool in one breath. One night he was late for his act, and ran up the hill to arrive just as they announced his name. Refusing to get his breath before making the swim, he miraculously swam the four lengths. Sports Illustrated did a feature story on him a couple of years later, and he died when he was only fifty years old.

In the summer of 1948, Coach Mike Peppe was invited to take two divers to perform a diving exhibition for a big party given by Lawrence Hanna. He owned a large estate in Cleveland, Ohio that had a swimming pool with a one and three-meter board, and a large stable of horses. His father was Mark Hanna who helped President McKinley win the presidency back in the 1920's. Lawrence was a bachelor and a wonderful guy in his early seventies. He gave Bruce and me beautiful expensive gold watches after the show, and invited us to come back again and we continued to do our show for him that went on for three or four more years.

The Queen of the Netherlands was so impressed with Bruce's performance at the 1948 Olympics that she invited him to do an exhibition for her at some big affair that was to take place in the summer of 1949.

Bruce was in love with Francis Dillon called "Pinky" who had a conservative and dominating personality, and Bruce was very good looking with blond curly hair and had little trouble making out with girls until he ran into Pinky. He was always trying to seduce her, but she wouldn't give in to his advances and told him she wasn't going to lose her virginity until she was married. He finally asked her to marry him, and the wedding was set for two weeks after the 1949 National A.A.U. Championships in Los Angeles, California.

Bruce showed up from France two days before the meet when it appeared that his trip to Europe really got to him because he lost the three-meter event to Skippy Browning from the University of Texas. It was the first of many national championships for Skippy who went on to win the 1952 Olympic gold medal in Finland. Skippy later became a Navy fighter pilot and when flying to the west coast from Florida, he developed vertigo and was killed when his plane crashed. Skippy has since been recognized as one of the finest divers to have ever competed in the sport.

With Bruce getting married, we decided that Dan Shafer should replace him for the annual show we did in Bermuda, so we got in touch with Chummy Hayward in Bermuda to see if it was okay. Dan wasn't accepted to perform in the show until two days before its opening when Chummy called me in California from Bermuda to tell me he agreed to replace Bruce.

Dan Shafer was a good friend of mine who had graduated from Ohio State, but for some unknown reason, was never on the Ohio State diving team. He had been selling perfume for a big company, and had just purchased a new Ford sedan that he decided to drive out to California from Columbus to dive in the nationals. He asked me if I would like to drive out with him, and share the gasoline expenses. I got permission from the Scioto Country Club to go to the meet and we took off.

We drove to Houston, Texas to see a friend who belonged to the swim club sponsored by the Shamrock Hotel, and had just built a new ten-meter diving tower in their pool. His friend suggested to Mr. Bada, the assistant manager of the hotel, that he invite Dan and me to stop by the hotel for a couple of days, and give a diving exhibition. Dan was also a good tower diver so we were confident we could do a good job of entertaining everyone.

We arrived at the Shamrock Hotel in the evening, and decided to wait until morning before making our entrance. To save our money we stayed in a dumpy motel down the street from the Shamrock that cost about three dollars for the night. We met Mr. Bada in the morning, and he took us up to the thirteenth floor of the hotel. He put us in a beautiful suite fit for a king. We were also informed that we were to eat all our meals at the hotel that included eating with the band members in the main dining room every evening. It was all "on the house."

With very little money, we took off for Los Angeles, using a gas credit card, and headed for the U.C.L.A. Sigma Chi fraternity where we planned to stay because it was open for summer school students. We heard of a restaurant in the city of Los Angeles that would feed anyone for nothing if they didn't like the food. So, we drove downtown, and ate there for the whole time we were in L.A.

Divers often learned to dive from the ten-meter tower by watching others because of the scarcity of diving coaches in those days. The event required all male divers to perform four required dives, and four optional dives that were selected from six different groups of dives. The divers could not repeat any dive from the same group. This allowed divers to avoid performing optional dives from the backward and reverse groups that they found to be the most difficult groups.

I learned to perform a full list of dives by watching everyone else dive from the ten-meter level. I first learned to perform the four required dives from the ten-meter platform in about twenty minutes because they were simple dives. I then learned to perform the more difficult dives by first doing a lead up for each optional dive from the one and five meter levels, and then from the 7½ meter level before attempting it from the ten-meter platform.

It took me about two of the three days to learn four optional dives because I had to gather up enough nerve to try them. Dan was one of about six divers in the world who could perform a forward 3½ somersault from the ten-meter platform. However, three of the four compulsory dives required feet first entry, and Dan had a real phobia about entering the water feet first. He would bend his knees entering the water which would cause a huge splash and resulted in low scores from the diving judges. This, unfortunately, prevented him from winning a national championship throughout his entire diving career.

Before the nationals, Dan and I decided to drive up to San Francisco and compete in the Northwestern Championships staged at the Flyshacker Pool. The pool was known

to be the largest outdoor pool in the world. It was four hundred meters long with lifeguards that used small dingy boats to guard the pool. The water was usually cold because it was filled with salt water pumped in from the Pacific Ocean.

Sammy Lee was the new 1948 Olympic tower champion, and Bruce Harlan placed second. Sammy performed an exhibition at the meet. It was announced that he was the only one in the world who could perform a split forward 2½ somersault. This was performed by first doing a forward 1½ somersault in the tuck position followed by a swan dive, then back into another somersault tuck before entering the water. After he performed the dive, Dan and I jumped up, and said we could do that dive. We didn't hesitate to climb up on the 10-meter platform, and performed the dive in tandem. Sammy Lee didn't forgive me for years because I embarrassed him before a large audience.

One of the funniest things I ever saw was in a comedy act after the meet was over in that huge Flyshacker pool. One of the comedy divers was on the three-meter board getting ready to perform a dive. He looked up and saw a lifeguard four hundred yards away in a life boat. He then started to wave, and yell for the lifeguard to get out of his way so he could perform his dive.

Dan and I returned to L.A. to compete in the Nationals on the springboard and tower, but I don't recall how well we performed. However, I do remember that two Japanese swimmers broke a half dozen world records in the distance swimming events.

After the meet was over, Dan and I left L.A. and took off for Columbus, Ohio. We drove as fast as we could for 40 straight hours to reach Columbus, Ohio in time to board a plane for Bermuda to do the water show. We received only one speeding ticket in Missouri on the way. We made the plane on time, and did a good diving exhibition for the next ten days.

The End of My Collegiate Competition

I completed my competition in sports at the end of my junior year of college in 1950. Although I didn't make the finals in two major championships during my diving career at Ohio State, I still made All-American all four years. I found out later that I was the first collegiate diver to be a four-time All-American.

The reason why I didn't make the finals in one meet occurred when competing on the three-meter board at the N.C.A.A. Championships held at the University of Michigan. The diving rules required the divers to perform in one of three flights, and the divers who scored the highest twelve scores made the finals.

My Time to Move On

I decided to move out of the Silbernagel house in my senior year. I felt it was time for me to move on so after discussing my decision with them, they were reluctant to see me go but they understood. I had spent two years with a family that made me feel like I was their son, and never in my life had I ever known anyone like them that were so kind to me.

I think one of the reasons for moving was that I still felt bad about not being home when they counted on me to watch their daughters when they planned to attend a formal party. I fouled up, and it really hurt them. However, I stayed in touch with the children, and with the parents until they passed away.

I found an apartment on North High Street about two miles north of the campus, and moved in with Howard Curtis who was a fellow senior and a great friend. Howard was very handsome, and had a beautiful voice. He was always walking around the apartment trying to sing like Mario Lanza who had just come out with the top song, "Be My Love." After graduating, Howard moved out to Los Angeles.

Bruce and I later visited him and his family while attending the 1950 Rose Bowl to watch Ohio State play the University of Southern California. He had just bought a new Buick station wagon on the day we arrived, and said he would like to serve us lunch but he was broke. Bruce and I had a good laugh over that so we went out and bought the family some groceries to last them for a few days.

I kept in touch with Howard for years and learned that he had hit it big in television nationally starring in a weekly show entitled, "Rip Cord." He made all his own parachute jumps for the show that lasted for a couple of years. I sent him a Christmas card one year, and his wife replied that he had been killed while making a parachute jump in the show.

CHAPTER 12

The Start of My Life in Show Business

I went home to Erie to visit my mother and friends in late May after finishing my fourth year at Ohio State in 1950. I returned to Columbus about a week later. Bruce showed up after he had finished his first year at Stanford University where he was getting his master's degree. He told me he decided to turn professional and perform diving exhibitions at country clubs around the country, and wanted to know if I would be interested in joining him as his partner.

Since we had performed several exhibitions on the trampoline at the Ohio State football and basketball games, and performed diving and trampoline acts at various social clubs in the area and in Bermuda, I didn't hesitate for a moment to accept his offer.

We decided to start right away, and bought a twenty-eight-foot-high scaffold. We made a special rig to fit on the top with a chair that offered two different heights. We could jump down to a mat with springs like a mini trampoline to dive off into the water. We also purchased a second-hand trailer to transport a full-sized trampoline we could fold up.

We Create Our Show

We created a seven act show that would last an hour. It started with a rendition of "The Fitzsimmons Sisters," a famous synchronized swimming pair. We tried to copy their act, but our form was so bad that we decided to make it a comedy swim act while dressed in women's bathing suits. This act was followed with a series of basic and difficult dives from the one or three-meter diving boards.

The third act was called the "World Traveler" which was a solo comedy routine displaying different kinds of swimming strokes performed in different countries. This was followed with a performance of basic and difficult stunts performed on the trampoline that worked into our comedy routine. After that we went on to perform four dives each from the scaffold that sometimes was

112

difficult because of the different depth of the pools or the placement of the scaffold on the pool deck.

The serious tower diving was followed with our comedy diving routine from the springboard, and we finished the show with me challenging Bruce to a swimming race one length of the pool. I would tell the audience that I could beat him for one length of the pool, and I had so much confidence that I would start in the water. Bruce would stand at the corner of the pool as I jumped in the pool, and picked up a handle on the bottom that was attached to a wire that ran down to the shallow end and continued to an area not seen by the audience.

I would then ask Bruce what number we would start the race, and he said he would count to three. Bruce would start counting, "one for the money, two for the road," etc., and run nearly halfway alongside of the pool and dive in while I was looking the other way and asking the audience what number did we start on?

Then I'd give the wire a jerk that was the signal for three or four big guys at the other end of the wire to pull me through the water so fast that I would always beat Bruce to the shallow end. A lot of those in the audience never did figure out how I could swim so fast, especially with only one arm because they didn't see the wire. With every show, we were rewarded with more laughs, and it was fun to see so many adults and kids happy.

We made up a brochure with pictures of us performing a front dive, and a comedy dive plus a program of our show. We made the mistake of charging too little for our show, just $150, and that was supposed to also cover our traveling expenses.

Bruce Harlan   Hobie Billingsley

WORLD CHAMPION DIVER   AMERICAN DIVING CHAMPION

We mailed the brochures to different country clubs in the bordering states, and sent contracts to those who replied. We also made up a script for the show that was to be used by any local person who would act as the M.C. This included the introduction of each act plus music on our tape recorder that was started and stopped by the M.C for each of our acts.

I remember when we did our show in St. Louis. We had Jack Buck, the radio announcer for the St. Louis Cardinals baseball team for forty years, be the M.C. for our show. We later put our whole show on tape that eliminated a need for an M.C., except for turning the music on and off for certain acts.

Marketing Mistakes

One big problem with receiving a contract to perform our show at a place for the first time was that we never had a clue what kind of facility they had to offer. Finding we weren't making much money for what we were doing risking our lives, we upped the price to $250 a few years later. I don't think I ever performed in a show that I didn't enjoy especially when working with Bruce. Naturally, we had a lot of crazy things happen to us when moving from show to show, and I mention only a few here because of the limited space and time.

One time when pulling into a club in Northern Ohio, we asked where the pool was. The man said, "well, that's a small problem," and whenever we got that kind of answer, we knew we were in trouble. The man pointed to a barge on a narrow river, and wanted to know if we could put our scaffold on the barge and dive from it as it was pulled down the river.

I asked how deep the river was, and the man shrugged his shoulders and said that it all depends. Bruce and I dived to the bottom of the river, and found it to be around eight feet deep in most places with wire cables, oil drums, and other debris lying on the bottom. We decided to give it a shot, put our scaffold up on the barge with no guide wires, and performed a couple of dives from the barge as it was being pulled down the river.

Everything was going fine until small boats started to circle the barge that created waves, and caused the barge to sway from side to side. This caused the scaffold to tip back and forth to the point that Bruce fell off the top, but fortunately landed in the water. It got so bad that we told the man, we couldn't continue any further because of a chance of serious injury or death. He agreed and paid us the full amount for our show anyway.

Another time performing our show in Chicago, we had to set up the scaffold behind a tree. Somehow, we managed to dive over the tree, and clear ten feet of cement to reach the deep end of the pool. We did our show there for around ten years, and never had a problem with that tree.

Bruce was always on the telephone, and while on the road to do our show in New Jersey, he stopped off at a store to make some calls while I waited in the car sitting in the front seat with the door open. It was a real hot day, and when we arrived at the pool, I suddenly got sick and threw up in the filter room before the show was to start before a tremendous crowd.

Bruce suggested that I go up and jump in the pool to cool off which I did. I managed to get through the show as sick as I was. My lips were covered with blisters, and I was light headed the next day. We found a doctor who after examining me, said that I had a heat stroke, and if I hadn't jumped into the cooler water when I did, I might have died.

The sheriffs in Michigan were having a convention in Petoskey, and they wanted some entertainment so they contacted Bruce to do our show for them. We asked where the pool was when we arrived, and a sheriff pointed to a pool that looked more like an oversized baby pool. We checked it out, and found it had a ten-foot-long wooden diving board with a little steel spring under it to give it bounce. The deep end had a drain in front of the board where it was slightly less than six feet deep. The bottom of the pool was in the shape of a funnel so if we didn't land exactly over the drain, the depth instantly became dangerously shallow.

We decided to put the scaffold up only eighteen feet, and we landed on the drain on every dive. Of course, we also had to change the dives we normally performed from the scaffold when it was much lower. We were near the end of our show, and doing some comedy dives off the ten-foot-long wooden board when it pulled loose from its base and fell into the water, and the audience of sheriffs got a big laugh.

We were invited to perform in a big show at the Wykegil Country Club in New Jersey over July 4th before a couple thousand people. This was a famous Jewish club, and they brought in several other shows from places like Florida and New York to perform acts on the deck and in the pool. I remember George Hammond, a famous agent in show business from New York City, brought a seal that leaped over a bar to catch a fish as the bar was raised higher with each jump. We later found that the seal got paid more for its act than the three of us divers who were risking our necks.

Bruce, Dan Shafer, and I were to perform dives from the three-meter board and a tower. After we did our diving on the springboard, we asked the man in charge where the tower was because there wasn't one next to the pool. He said, "well that presented a little problem" so we built a wooden platform on top of the country club building, four stories high, and about twelve feet from the pool, and we could dive from there.

I asked how we could were get to roof, and he pointed to a fire engine with a ladder next to the building. When we got on the roof, we found that they had built a wooden platform about ten feet wide and twelve feet long with a post on each side connected with streamers closest to the pool. The problem was they built the platform above the middle of the pool that meant the only way we could dive into deep water was to take off the platform at an angle and pass over a twelve-foot cement deck.

Bruce and Dan suggested I go first, and I agreed because I decided to perform a reverse somersault, layout, and enter the water feet first in the deep end of the pool. I spread my arms out to perform the dive in a layout position. But as I took off the platform, one of my arms hit the side post that caused me to twist around, and face the building as I descended. I saw each floor of the building pass by as I dropped, and thought that in hitting the post, I wouldn't reach the pool and would probably be killed.

I fortunately entered the water about six inches from the edge of the pool by sheer luck while everyone clapped never knowing how close I had come to death. I refused to go up again and perform another dive, but Bruce and Dan saw what happened to me and managed to perform a couple of forward dives with no further incidents.

A guy climbed up on the roof soon after our act and while making some crazy talk, he dived off the top in a swan dive position, and landed flat on his stomach barely going under when hitting the water. We found later, that he was Henry Lamonth who was famous for landing on his stomach in two thousand successful performances diving off a forty-foot ladder into an oversized baby pool that was only twenty-four inches deep. I always thought that he would have killed himself if he had one unsuccessful dive.

Sports Illustrated Calls

Sports Illustrated called Bruce, and wanted us to take part in the promotion of their new magazine. We had the pleasure to work a week with a whole group of great athletes including Bob Mathias, Crazy Legs Hirsh, Max Bear, and Y.A. Tittle. We were hired to perform in the parking lot at shopping centers in cities across the country.

We performed in the manner that related to our sport then passed out autographed pictures of ourselves to the public. I think Bruce and I did more than any of the other athletes. We performed our straight and comedy routines on the trampoline, dived into

116

a water tank three feet deep from a one-meter board, and into another tank six feet deep from a five-meter board and a scaffold twenty-seven feet high.

The Al Sheehan Aqua Follies

The Al Sheehan Aqua Follies was featured at the Minneapolis Aqua Centennial, and ran annually for two weeks during the summer before five thousand people at the Theodore Worth pool. The show was located on a small lake near the city, and it had a stage over the water with 35-foot-high diving towers on each side. It also had a three-meter diving board under one tower and a five-meter board under the other tower.

The show included 24 dancing girls, 24 synchronized female swimmers, and featured a female swimmer. It also had eight male divers plus a female featured diver, a ten-piece orchestra, and several featured acts on stage that were replaced every year. The show was in the evening with two shows on Saturday night. The show was also performed on Green Lake in Seattle, Washington during the Seattle Sea Fair, four days after the Minneapolis show that was the time needed for the equipment to be moved by train from Minneapolis to Seattle.

The show was presented for twenty summers in Minneapolis, fifteen summers in Seattle, and three summers in Detroit. The show in Detroit was later dropped because their newspaper went on strike every time the show was presented, and few people were aware that it was there. I remember when we did the complete show there one night before only seventy-five people because I counted them.

Jim Patterson, Ohio State's first national diving champion, was the captain of the show's divers. He suggested that Al Sheehan in 1950 hire Bruce Harlan as a featured diver because he was the 1948 Olympic champion. Bruce said he would consider the offer if I was also included, and Al Sheehan agreed after some discussion. Patterson continued as the captain of the divers for four more years when he retired and Bruce was made the captain.

Most of the divers in the show performed dives from the three different levels, and participated in the comedy diving routines near the end of the show. Diving in Minneapolis was difficult because the lake water was so polluted it killed all the fish, and the divers would often yell, "don't flush it" when climbing out of the water after a dive.

The lake was only seven feet deep, and had an all muck bottom. All the shows were at night, and we had to dive into the light from six spot lights that made it almost impossible to spot the water performing a dive. The water bothered me more than any of the other divers. I had to cover my nose with tape to prevent my nose from running all night, and plug my ears with lamb's wool and cover them with modeling clay to prevent an ear ache.

The comedy diving act was known as the "Dillies" that usually had divers perform three rounds of dives in rapid succession each followed by a stall after each round to give the diver's time to get back into position to perform another dive. A stall usually occurred when the music stopped to allow a diver to converse with the M.C. for a couple of minutes.

I remember my first night in the show. Jim Patterson gave me a slot in the order of dives. I was to sneak out to the end of the high platform on my stomach, and watch for a certain diver perform a dive from the five-meter springboard below me before I would perform my dive. We practiced our routines a few times during the day, and I had no problem spotting my diver.

But when I snuck out to the edge of the tower that night, I didn't see the diver that I was supposed to follow so I didn't go. That screwed up the whole routine with divers performing dives in the wrong slots. Al Sheehan was furious after the show, and made us practice the comedy routine several times the next afternoon until things were done right. But unfortunately, I missed my cue again the next night. The problem was finally solved by putting me in a position where I couldn't possibly mess up, and I was delighted because I knew I would be fired if I messed up again.

The Dilly act always used the same "Saber Dance" music, and the whole act usually took about seven to eight minutes. One diver, Charlie Diehl, was featured as the heavy weight diving champion in the world. He was announced as weighing 128 pounds, in each leg, and was a real novelty because of his size. He was from Miami, Florida, and worked as a cabana boy at one of the big hotels. In talking to the people who saw the show, we would ask them if they remembered the diver who went flying off the tower and landed on the stage and killed himself. And they would say, "Oh yeah, where is the big guy?"

The dillies usually included eight divers, with six hired to perform springboard and tower dives in two different sequences of the show. Some of the dives from the tower involved two or three divers diving in tandem fashion. The other two divers were hired to perform only comedy dives.

Orwin Harvey was from Los Angeles, and did stunt work in the movies. He was a likable guy who had some dives rarely performed by other comedy divers. One of his acts was dropping a big wooden yo-yo, about twenty-four inches in diameter, from the high tower that dropped almost to the water before winding back up again

and hitting him in the face knocking him down.

Don Wright, Redwood City, California, was another clown diver who attended Sequoia High School at the same time Bruce was coaching swimming there, and they became good friends. With no diving experience, Don had seen Bruce and I do our show, and after graduating from high school he wanted to be a part of the comedy team. Bruce was captain of the show divers then, and told Don if he could come up with a new comedy dive, he would try to get him into the show.

Don came up with two great comedy dives: One was he stood on the end of the five-meter springboard dressed as a lifeguard and swing a ring buoy on a rope in circles as if getting ready to throw it and save a guy in the water yelling for help. He would toss the buoy letting go of the rope, and the ring buoy would fly off along with his lifeguard clothes towards a swimmer in the water. Still standing on the board embarrassed in under shorts, Don would then fall into the water. He also came up with another dive. As he left the tower, his bunched-up pants would unravel about twenty feet long while diving through the air.

His other brilliant idea for a stunt was to take a piece of galvanized sheet metal and make a large rectangular box in the form of a spotlight that weighed about ten pounds. It was used for a stall when I was supposed to step out on the end of the five-meter board, and request that the music stop. When the M.C. would ask me, what was wrong? I would reply that I would like to dive, but I couldn't see.

The M.C. would then ask for someone to hit me with a spot light, and Don's spotlight would then drop down from the high tower fifteen feet above me, and hit me on the head when I wore a sailor's hat with a towel inside. I avoided injury to my head by a rope attached to the spotlight, and the other end attached to the tower up above. With practice, we could adjust the length of the rope so it would become taut just as it contacted my head.

We practiced the stall several times, and it worked like a charm. Everyone in the show wanted to watch the new stall that night. Unknowingly, the condensation in the night air stretched the rope, and when the spot light was dropped and hit me on the head, it nearly broke my neck. As I fell off the board, the audience loved it. We decided not to try it again after I had trouble moving my neck for about a week.

Don and I formed a close relationship for years after the Aqua Follies closed. He became the top dental student in his class at the University of Michigan. His practice was in Seattle where we got together several more times in my life.

One dive in the act involved riding a bicycle off the high tower with a rope attached to the back end. The rope would become taut, and the diver would go flying over the handle bars leaving the bike dangling in the air from the tower. One night, the rope on the bike broke, and the bicycle went flying through the glass show case where the band was playing beneath the tower. Everyone in the band went running across and behind the stage to escape the crash while Pete, the drummer, kept right on beating the drums.

We kept yelling to the divers to dive out as far as possible to avoid getting cut by the broken glass in the water that may be pointed upward. Fortunately, no one got cut. The next afternoon we went out to gather up the glass on the mucky bottom, but couldn't find the bicycle. After an hour of searching, one of the divers found it underneath the stage. Looking back at that incident, Mr. Sheehan should have had some scuba divers search for the broken glass in the water as it could have badly cut or even killed a diver.

Charlie Diehl was standing on the end of the five-meter board one day in practice waving his arms around. His Elgin wrist watch went flying off into the muddy water. Charlie was almost crying when it hit the water because he claimed that the Elgin Company had given him the watch as a promotion from their watch company. Realizing that he had little or no chance of finding the watch in that mucky bottom, he dived in and found it on the first attempt.

It was during that show in Minneapolis when a slender young lady used to come out, and sit at one end of the stage. She'd watch us practice every afternoon and never said a word. One day I asked one of the stage hands who she was, and he said she was Natalie Wood, the movie star. I can say that she didn't look anything like she did when she starred in "Rebel Without a Cause."

We were often sent to the local radio station in Seattle to promote the Al Sheehan Aqua follies. I was sent to one and walked in to see Clint Eastwood when he was near the beginning of his career. He was doing a commercial for some product, but having difficulty saying it properly. He suddenly said, "Oh shit, I can't get this God-damn commercial straight," and that broke up everyone in the room.

Another time worth mentioning was when I was taking a ferryboat across the sound with my car on board to visit a friend on one of the islands. Standing on the top deck of the ferry, I spotted a woman on the lower deck who kept walking back and forth behind a rope extended across the back end of the ferry.

I mentioned to Mary, my wife then, that there was something wrong with the way the woman was acting, and as we walked away from the railing, a call "man overboard" came over the boat's loud speaker. The boat immediately started to turn around, and it took about twenty minutes for it to return where she jumped off. The captain of the ferry spotted the woman floating about two hundred yards away and ordered for a small boat be lowered.

As some sailors started to board the boat, I ran over and told them that I was a lifeguard and would like to go with them, and they agreed. After searching for a short time, we saw her floating face down. The boat had a deep uneven hull, so when they picked her up and laid her in a very awkward position across one side of the boat, I started to apply artificial respiration.

She had floated face down for nearly a half hour in the water so no one in the boat was surprised when I got no response. I kept up my attempt to revive her until we neared the ferry boat, and thinking she was already dead she suddenly started to cough and respond. A cheer went up as she was lifted onto the ferry boat, and they thanked me for being there.

I knew that it would have been great publicity for the Al Sheehan show if I talked to the press later, but I decided not to. We read in the newspaper the next day that she had fully recovered, and I never brought the subject up to anyone. So, in my career as a lifeguard, I lost one and saved one.

The Aqua-Follies Show Minneapolis-Seattle

The divers drove from Minneapolis to Seattle every year to perform in the Aqua Follies. We always stopped in Miles City, Montana on the way to do a trampoline and diving show for a good friend of ours who was an officer in the National A.A.U. He oversaw a radio station, and used it to inform the people in the city about our show.

He always gave us $250 to do the show that helped pay our expenses, and a little extra for each diver. Although Bruce and I did the trampoline act and performed more dives than any of the other divers, we never asked for any more than what the others received.

After leaving Miles City traveling through Montana one time, Charlie Diehl asked one of two English divers who were featured as comedy divers in the follies for one of their guns they brought along. Charlie spotted a flock of geese about two or three hundred yards from the highway. Going about seventy miles an hour, he opened the window and took a shot at them. Unbelievably one dropped to the ground. A little later one of the English divers was fooling around with his revolver when it accidently went off, and put a hole in his pant leg but didn't hit his leg. His response was, "Hey, I just ruined me trousers."

To save money, three of us divers rented a bedroom with three beds on the third floor of an old house near the University of Washington for one dollar a night. It wasn't the best living conditions, but it was sort of fun in those days. Bruce went out and found a car dealer who loaned him a beat up old car for nothing that helped get us around in our free time when we didn't have a show.

After the Aqua Follies in 1950, Bruce and I finished doing shows at country clubs for the rest of the summer. We did about fifty country club shows in our first year and that greatly increased over the years.

CHAPTER 13

After Graduating from Ohio State

I graduated from Ohio State in late May of 1951. I walked out of the football stadium with my degree, and stuck around Columbus for a week. I wanted to see if someone would offer me a high school teaching job, but no one called. So, I went back to Erie for a week before I returned to Columbus to meet Bruce and start our summer tour. It was then that I decided to go back to school, and work toward a master's degree.

I first applied for a student teacher's position as a graduate assistant at Washington State University in Pullman, Washington because they would pay for my tuition. They accepted my application, but never made much of an effort to hire me. Then I applied to the University of Washington in Seattle and they offered to pay my tuition.

I was glad that it worked out that way because Washington State in Pullman had wicked winters in the eastern part of the state, much like Erie or Buffalo. Seattle had the Japanese trade winds that prevented cold snowy winters, but promised a lot of rain. Besides, I had spent a lot of time in Seattle performing in the Aqua Follies for two years, and I really liked the city.

The University of Washington

I found a room only two blocks from the University, and lived there for a semester before moving in with Joe and Charlie MacIntyre. They were brothers who had taken second place in the pairs World Sculling Championships. We had a real nice apartment right on the edge of Lake Washington, and only a few yards from the campus.

The water in the lake was extremely cold. We could have dived off our deck, but we never tried it. However, we used to take crackers and break them into little pieces to feed ducks that walked up to the entrance of our cottage. After leading them into our living room, we'd close the door, and chase them all around the room with a broom. They were always too fast for us, so we stopped doing such crazy things because the ducks also left feathers and crap all over our furniture and floor.

The University of Washington was the only school in the country that still included boxing in their physical education criteria. They held intermural boxing tournaments every fall. Joe was about six feet two inches tall, and weighed about 220 pounds. He decided to fight in the heavy weight division. Seattle had a great professional boxer named Kid Mathews who was the world's number one contender in his middle weight division, and most of his success was in the way he could move his feet to avoid being hit.

123

So, Joe went to his gym, and got permission to train with him. Joe learned some great foot work that helped him make it all the way to the finals of the tournament without being hit with any good punches. I was doing a trampoline exhibition over on one of the islands the night of the finals, and while coming back on the ferry, I turned on the radio to listen to the fight.

The radio announcer didn't have much to say because about half way through the first round, Joe got hit with a solid punch in the eye that knocked him out. The referee didn't even bother to count because it was obvious that Joe wasn't going to get up. After I returned home that night and Joe walked in, I started to laugh looking at his swollen eye. He said it was a lucky punch and his opponent, Pete Rademacher, would never go any further with his fighting career. We learned later that Pete went on to win the National Heavyweight Golden Glove title before fighting Floyd Patterson for the World Heavyweight Championship in his first professional fight that went thirteen rounds before being knocked out. I believe that his career may have been used to make the Rocky Balboa Hollywood movie series when Rocky fought for the heavyweight championship in his first professional fight.

My Decision to Major in Physical Education

After finishing our summer diving shows with Bruce, I decided to major in physical education for my master's degree. But that proved to be a big mistake because much of the course work at Washington was like the courses I had already taken as an undergraduate at Ohio State. I should have majored in educational administration as that would have qualified me to be a high school principal or superintendent, or a dean or athletic director at some college.

Washington offered me the choice either to do all class work or take some class work and write a thesis. I chose the latter because I wanted to learn more about how to write. My top advisor was Jack Tourney, the swimming coach, who I had met before at the N.C.A.A. Championships. He was a very nice person, and had written a good book on swimming.

He gave me a lot of advice on how to write my thesis along with Chet Palmer, an instructor in the Physical Education department, who was also a member of my advisory committee. Chet and I became good friends in the two years I spent at Washington, and we spent many hours discussing subjects related to physical education.

As a graduate assistant, I was also required to teach some activity classes that would help pay for my tuition. One of the courses I requested to teach was how to sail a boat. The course was offered because the University of Washington was on Lake Washington. Having lived close to Lake Erie while growing up, I had a great desire to learn how to sail a boat, but it had never happened.

Since I didn't have a clue on how to sail, I asked if I could be an assistant to a teacher who knew how to sail. But instead, they gave me three classes on my own. The course allowed a maximum of twelve students in three of the classes because the physical education department had only four dinghy boats that could hold three persons in each boat.

I went to the library and studied how to sail a boat thinking that I could bluff my way through the course, but I soon found that I was wrong. I started with the nomenclature of a boat in my first class, and when I said the sides of the boat were called "gunwales" which is the way it is spelled, one of the students raised his hand and asked if I meant "gunnels."

I then confessed to all three of the classes that I didn't know a thing about sail boats, and how to sail them. Then I asked them to raise their hand if they had sailed before. They all raised their hands. Thinking I would get a different response, I asked how many of them owned their own boat. And everyone in all three classes raised their hands again.

I went on to say that if they would teach me how to sail, I would give all of them A's in the course. The classes met two times a week, and I squeezed into a different boat each time they met so they could teach me. I learned how to sail a boat by the end of the course, and I gave all the students an "A."

When I first arrived in Seattle I went to the swimming pool, and met Bob Buckley who was Jack Tourney's assistant coach. Bob was also in charge of the diving team, but knew next to nothing about diving so he asked me if I would coach his top diver, Merrill Hodges (pictured below).

Merrill was a very talented diver with a great personality, and we became instant friends. I coached him all the time I was at the University of Washington, and he learned enough to place third on the three-meter springboard at the 1952 N.C.A.A. Swimming and Diving Championships. I also taught him our comedy act and diving routines that Bruce and I used in our show. The University had an annual talent show, and we won first prize performing our straight and comedy act on the trampoline.

I went to the dean of physical education one day, and got permission to stage a water show in the varsity pool. With Merrill's help, we came up with one of the best water shows in which I was ever involved. One of the featured acts had Merrill and me performing stunts from a trapeze that swung out from the front of the 3-meter board all the way to the shallow end.

This was possible because the ropes on the trapeze were attached to the ceiling about 42 feet above the water. We did many stunts on the trapeze bar as it swung back and forth. We'd do different dives from the bar to entering the water head first in front of the diving board, and feet first in the shallow end.

Besides making some money for the team, it also brought greater unity between the swimmers and divers. After Merrill graduated from Washington, he went on to perform from the springboard in the Al Sheehan Aqua Follies with me for two summers in Seattle. He later became a commercial airline pilot, got married, and had two children.

My Brilliant Idea to Join the F.B.I.

I got the brilliant idea to join the F.B.I. about six months after arriving in Seattle. The requirements were a person had to be under 25 years old, single, have a college degree, and no police record. Feeling that I qualified, I called up the F.B.I. office in Seattle, and told them that I wanted to apply. They told me to come down to their office the next day at nine o'clock for an exam and an interview.

The largest F.B.I. department in the country was in Washington D.C., and the second largest in Seattle. I went to the address listed in the phone book, but found that they had moved to a new location. When I finally found their new office, the secretary told me I was late for the exam. I don't think she believed me when I told her why I was late.

Disgusted with my reply, she gave me a copy of the exam, and told me to sit down and take it along with three other applicants who had already started. The exam covered some statutes that were used to solve certain cases, and I was to explain how and why they were used. I worked on the test for about twenty minutes when the secretary announced to turn in our papers because the exam was over.

I told her that I had just gotten started, and she said I could take another forty-five minutes. Then I asked her if neatness had any effect on the grade for the exam, and she said about forty-percent. I was in real trouble because I had worked on the first three of the five questions, and crossed them out when I had changed my mind about the explanations.

I handed in my exam, and she told me to report upstairs for an interview with her boss who was the second highest director of the F.B.I. in the country. I walked into a huge office while he was talking on the phone. When he finished, he asked me a couple of standard questions.

When the interview was over, he asked me what I thought about President Truman discharging General Douglas MacArthur who had stepped out of line over some important issues. I said that I thought that the President made the right decision. I turned around to look at a huge picture of MacArthur on his wall. I told him that I guess I didn't have a prayer of becoming an agent, and he said that I got that right and added I wasn't very observant as I walked out the door.

Marriage Talk

Joe and Charlie MacIntyre kiddingly told me not to get married before returning to school in the fall of 1952. I told them not to worry about that because I wasn't that crazy. Bruce had just received his master's degree from Stanford, and got a job

126

teaching and coaching the swimming team at Sequoia High School in Redwood City located south of San Francisco.

I drove down from Seattle to meet him, and we drove our cars back east together where we were contracted to perform some shows. Bruce scheduled us to perform a show in Tucumcari, New Mexico on our way back East. We found the pool to be out in the middle of the desert with no houses in sight. It was getting dark when a large crowd showed up for our show out of nowhere.

We started our show with the Fitzsimons Sister's synchronized act. We did a little dance on the deck to the music of "Flamingo," and bumped into each other making a turnaround pivot to dive into the water. Just as we started to pivot, we looked down and saw a rattle snake about three feet away with its tail rattling. We didn't waste any time diving into the pool.

While driving back East by myself, I got to thinking about getting married, but the problem was, to whom? I thought of five different girls that I liked a lot, and decided to select the one that I believed would make the best wife, mother, and friend, and want children. She would also have to accept my summer job when I would be gone most of the time, and have a good personality and sense of humor.

I had dated a few girls while in Seattle for the year, and two were seniors in the School of Nursing. I liked one of them a lot, and was getting to know her better when I finished the semester, and got ready to go back east. The other nurse was a sweet girl who was more infatuated with me. She suggested marriage to me a couple of times, but I wasn't ready for it at the time. The third girl was the daughter of my landlady. We started to hit it off well, but her mother didn't approve so we didn't date.

Roganne McGuire

On the road for a few days with time to think, I reached Columbus, and decided to speak with Roganne McGuire. I had met her at an open swim one night at Ohio State in 1949, and dated her for over a year. She had a great interest in aquatics and I wanted to see how we would relate after being gone for over a year with no contact.

I arrived in Columbus and called her. I picked her up and we drove over to the front of the Sigma Chi house, and parked. In our conversation, she said that I was a rotten son-of a-bitch because I never took her to any of the fraternity functions or included her in any of the social activities when I got together with my friends while I dated her.

She continued to bring up a couple of other issues that bothered her. I told her what she said was true, and I had grown up a lot in a year. I was sorry that I had treated her so badly, and now saw her in a completely different way. But I realized we were not a good match.

We remained friends, and exchanged Christmas cards every year. She later married a real nice guy, lived in Tampa Florida, and had a bunch of children and grandchildren and passed away in 2010.

127

I Propose to Mary Drake

Mary Drake was smart, good looking, had a nice figure, came from a nice family, and wasn't spoiled. I had also dated her for a little over a year before I graduated. She showed that she really cared for me. But while in Seattle I had little contact with her.

I drove up to Mary's house in Magnetic Springs, Ohio at about two o'clock in the morning. I knew her bedroom was on the second floor, and took a clothes pole to knock on her window until she came to the window. She opened the window surprised to see me, and wanted to know what I wanted at that late hour. I told her I had something important to tell her and she came down to the front door. I told her I wanted to marry her. Obviously surprised, she said she would sleep on it, and give me an answer in the morning. When I showed up again in the morning, she said "yes."

We set the date for August 23rd in her church located in Delaware, Ohio twelve miles from her house. Bruce and I were doing a show in Toledo the night before, and it was the only time we had open that summer. In the Toledo show, I remember Bruce and I had to dive from a thirty-foot tower into about six feet of water. I thought I might not make the wedding because I could get killed. We drove to Akron that night after the show, and stayed with Pinky and her parents before taking off for Delaware in the morning.

Our wedding was something else. Since I was on the road with Bruce all summer, my mother, the Silbernagel family, John Wolford, and Wendy Sheldon were the only ones that represented me. They sat together in the pews on the right-side aisle in the church, and Mary had two hundred and fifty people representing her in the pews on the left side.

John and Wendy arrived without shaving in wrinkled clothes because they had spent the night in jail after they were arrested for speeding and drunk driving coming from Erie. With my luck, I had a good friend of mine take our wedding pictures, but for some reason none of them turned out. When everyone went through the welcoming line after the ceremony, all her friends told me how lucky I was to get such a sweet girl, and I agreed.

After Our Wedding

We left for Seattle the next morning along with Mary's mother. We found a nice apartment in the basement of a house that was a block away from the entrance to the University of Washington. Mary's mother flew back to Columbus after spending a week with us, and we lived there until I graduated a year later. Mary found a job working for Boeing that worked well for us while I was teaching and coaching at the University.

I was still working on my thesis, and one night when it was giving me a lot of grief, I got frustrated, and was ready to chuck the whole thing in. Then Mary asked me a very simple question, "What are you trying to prove?" After stuttering around for a few minutes, I said to myself, "Yeah, what am I trying to prove?".

And with that, I came up with the answer, and finished the thesis without a hitch. The thesis ended up being 186 pages long with a questionnaire that was 26 pages long. My advisors told me a questionnaire shouldn't be more than two pages, and I would be lucky to get a five percent return for anything longer. I stunned them when I received over two thirds return from 133 collegiate swimming coaches around the country. When I took my thesis oral exam, I was told that my thesis should have been for a Doctor's degree, and not a Master's degree.

While teaching at the University, I was called to the phone. When I answered it, I found I was talking to Bud Wilkinson from the University of Oklahoma. He was the UO athletic director, and known to be the best college football coach in the country. He said he was interested in having me be their swimming coach, and asked if I would take a plane back to Oklahoma to be interviewed. I said yes and he picked me up at the airport, and took me to a room in the athletic department.

There were about a dozen coaches sitting around in a circle with me in the center. One of the coaches was an Ohio State graduate, but I still felt uncomfortable because one or two of them would ask me a question while the rest of them sat there staring at me. I learned that they wanted the swimming coach to also be the football team trainer which explains why so many coaches were there.

I told them I had taken a class at Ohio State in training so I could learn from Ernie Biggs, who was known to be the best trainer in the country. When driving me back to the airport, Bud Wilkinson told me that he had another person in mind who was a trainer, and would give me his decision in a couple of days.

He decided to take the other person who knew nothing about coaching a swimming team, and he was fired the next year for illegally recruiting a swimmer. I found later that the reason why Wilkinson called me was because one of his swimmers was from Ohio State and had given him my name.

CHAPTER 14

Teaching and Coaching in High School

San Leandro High School

Bruce Harlan had graduated from Stanford with a Master's degree in 1952, and was teaching physical education classes and coaching swimming and diving at Sequoia High School in Redwood City, California. I earned my Master's degree a year later in 1953.

Bruce wanted me to do our show around his area, and so got me a job teaching physical education classes and coaching the swimming team at San Leandro High School. San Leandro is east of San Francisco Bay, and about fifteen miles south of Oakland. Bruce was a good friend of the principal who had just been transferred to San Leandro. I accepted the job, and soon found out he was a remarkable principal.

Mary got a job teaching fifth grade at a local San Leandro grade school. We packed up our belongings, and left Seattle for Redwood City to pick up Bruce and Pinky, his wife, before heading back East. We were driving Bruce's car and stopped in Las Vegas on the way to see if we could do our show at one of the casino pools.

We went to the Sands Hotel which was one the first hotels on the strip about seven miles south of downtown. After talking to the hotel director about doing our show, he said he would have to be crazy to pull the people away from the slot machines and gambling tables to watch a water show. This was 1953 and the casinos didn't offer any entertainment other than a band at that time.

Upset at this rejection, Bruce and I took off for Denver. About two hours later, Bruce said something was bothering him. He suddenly slammed on the breaks to tell me we had forgotten our wives! We were so used to traveling together before we married that they never crossed our minds. We immediately sped back to the Sands Hotel to meet two irritated women who had been sitting on the pool deck waiting for their husbands for four hours.

We lied, telling them we had visited a couple of other hotels, and got tied up. We never did tell them the truth. As we left driving down along the road, now known as the "Strip," there were signs posted that read, "For Sale, One Acre, $200."

Bruce dropped Mary and me off at Magnetic Springs, and went on to Marion, Ohio to be with Pinky's folks. We got together again a week later to do a show in Akron. Being married for nearly a year, Mary had never seen our show. When it came time for Bruce and me to dive from our scaffold 28 feet high into about six feet deep water, I thought she would be scared to death. Instead, when I looked down at her sitting near the deck, she was reading a book.

After we finished our shows at the end of summer in 1953, Mary and I took off for San Leandro, California to start my teaching and coaching job. San Leandro was a cute little town with nice homes, and an outstanding high school. I didn't want us to live in the same town in which we taught because of school problems that could come up. We decided to live in Hayward a town eight miles south of San Leandro.

I checked in at the main office when school started, and went over to the Physical Education Department that was in a separate building. All physical education classes at that time were not co-ed. Female students were taught on one side by female teachers, and the male students were taught on the other side by male teachers. It took about a week for me to fit in with the six instructors who all turned out to be nice guys.

I had always been told at Ohio State that the size of the gym classes was normally around thirty students. I was really shocked to find about a hundred students running all over in my first class in the gym. Then when I blew my whistle telling the class to line up against the wall for attendance.

They looked at me like I was crazy, and ignored me. But things got better after a couple of days. Since most of the classes were held outside roll was taken while the students stood on an assigned number painted on the ground. This reduced the time it took to start the class.

Things changed after I had been there for a couple of months. Instead of playing basketball, football, and soccer with my classes, I started to teach them gymnastics, wrestling, and volleyball. The kids really liked learning something new. It eventually turned out that I taught the gym teachers a whole new set of activities that were added to the curriculum.

There are far too many stories to tell about my teaching and coaching experiences while at San Leandro High School, so here are some of the highlights. This job gave me the opportunity to develop into the kind of teacher, and coach I was going to be for my entire teaching career.

First, I was a hard-nosed firm but fair teacher and coach. I also had a great sense of humor that I think the students looked for, and enjoyed when everything went well. I was smaller than most of my students. They learned I was very versatile and capable of holding my own in nearly every activity I taught or coached.

I think they knew that I cared about every one of them. I used to show up in the morning a half hour before school started so I could teach ten or twelve kids how to perform giant swings on the monkey bars along with a few other gymnastic stunts not taught in class.

One day, I gave a written test on volleyball rules of the game, and one of my students missed all nineteen questions. I met the youngster, whose parents were Portuguese, after school and asked him what happened because he missed everything. He didn't have an answer, so I asked him to read the first question on the test, and he couldn't do it.

Shocked, I realized he couldn't read, and here he was in the eleventh grade. He had been passed on from grade to grade just to get rid of him. I asked him where he lived, and he pointed his finger in a direction and said, "right down there." When I asked him what street, he didn't know but knew how to get home. Then I read all the test questions to him, and he gave the right answer on all but two of the nineteen questions.

I had another youngster who hated school, and was always a nuisance in class. He made it clear that he hated me, the other kids, and the whole school. Mary and I went to a grocery store to get some empty boxes one day, and saw him working there. I pointed him out to Mary, and told her what a pain he was.

He suddenly spotted us, and came running up to me. With great enthusiasm, he asked if he could help us. I reluctantly told him what I wanted, and he ran off telling me to wait right there while he checked out the back room. When he returned empty handed, he apologized for not having any boxes, and said he would get some for me if we would come back in a day or two. Surprised with his new behavior, I told Mary what a great change he had suddenly made. However, when I saw him in school the next day and greeted him with a smile, he responded in his old sarcastic way. I realized his problem was that he simply didn't like school.

I coached the school's swimming team. We had to walk about a mile after school every day to use the city's swimming pool. Mike was the manager of the team, and suffered from epilepsy. He had a seizure nearly every day at practice.

When I saw his problem, I took the team aside, and explained what was going on. I wanted everyone on the team to see him as not being any different than the rest of us. I went on to say that he had a disease, and they should not to be alarmed when he had to lie down on the ground having a seizure.

Everything worked out fine until the second year when he came to me, and said he wanted to swim on the team. Realizing that this was a serious problem, I went to the superintendent of schools with Mike's request. I explained to the superintendent that it was possible he could have a seizure in the pool while swimming, and maybe drown. Surprisingly, the superintendent said to let him swim. Mike went out for the breaststroke, and never had a seizure again at the pool for the rest of the year.

Our conference championship meet was held at Tech High School in Oakland. When the diving event came up and everyone had performed one dive, I went to the referee and told him to stop the event, and called a conference with all the coaches. Reluctantly, he did as I requested, and all the coaches gathered together. I told them that the diver from Acalanies High School had his father judging his own son. So, I wanted the father of my diver to be a judge, and if they didn't like my proposal they should remove the other father from the judging panel.

I went on to say if they didn't do one or the other, I would take my team out of the contest, and go home. Being the new coach on the block, they told me if I dropped out, I would be fired, and I replied that I would take my chances. They took the opponent's father off the panel, and replaced him with another representative from their school. My diver went on to win the conference diving championship by one point. I think that from that time on, the coaches in the conference were not too anxious to mess with me.

Fight Problem Solved

Because of the overloaded classes, I had to break up a fight nearly every day. I was trying to think of a way to stop them, and finally thought I had figured it out when a fight broke out. I would separate the two and ask one if he was mad at the other. When he said he was, I would ask the other boy the same question and get the same answer.

My solution was to tell one to keep his arms defenseless at his sides, while telling the other boy to punch his opponent in the gut, and hoping the thought of inflicting such pain would be so great they'd never make the punch.

This solution worked out well until two boys got into a fight with one being much bigger than the other. When I told the little guy to hit his larger opponent in the mouth, he smacked the bigger guy so hard that he gave him a bloody nose. And I thought "rats, this isn't working".

I finally figured out how to stop fights after a few days of thought. I found that when a fight was brewing I would tell the class to meet in the auditorium after school for the Wednesday night fights. We met behind the curtains on the stage in the auditorium where they had some gym mats, and everyone in the class showed up.

I had the two boys that wanted to fight put on 16-ounce boxing gloves to fight three one minute rounds knowing that they couldn't hurt each other. They were so tired trying to hit each other with those big gloves, that they were not doing much more than glaring at each other before the first round was over, and all the spectators stood there laughing. From then on, whenever there was a fight, I would say, "Wednesday night fights?" They would stop and apologize to each other, because they didn't want to make fools of themselves in front of their friends.

A Heartfelt Story

The P.E. teachers were assigned an extra after school activity that met once a week, and mine was the varsity club. I put a message in all the teachers' mail boxes, and had it announced over the address system that the varsity club members were to meet in a room at 3:30 after school. I went to the room when school was over, and found three seniors with their varsity sweaters on. We waited a while for more students to show, but none did.

When I asked them where everyone else was, they had no idea why they were the only ones. I then asked if any of them were officers of the club. One said he was the president, and another one said he was the treasurer and had brought along his buddy. Then I asked how much money they had in their treasury. The treasurer said, $1.42, and everyone laughed including me.

My next question was, did they had any idea how they could make some money. And they asked what for. My reply was, had they ever heard of the San Francisco Forty-Niner football team? And if they had, how would they like to go to one of their football games? When they all agreed, we brainstormed ideas to make some money. But none of them wanted to have cake sales, or do car washes. So, I suggested that since it was so hot during the noon hour, they could sell snow cones during lunch hour on every Wednesday. And if they wore their varsity sweaters, I would get them out of class, if necessary, to sell them. They agreed, and I gave them five dollars to get three or four different flavors for the cones, paper cups, and crushed ice from the school cafeteria.

They sold the snow cones for ten cents each and made around twenty dollars the first week, and much more the next week. The word got out, and around 25 more varsity players showed up for our next meeting. The snow cones became so popular after a couple of weeks that people were buying them, and throwing them at each other.

In a matter of weeks, we had over two hundred dollars in our bank account, and around fifty new members. So I suggested we put on a sports show for the school and make a lot more money. Bruce and I had done a sport show at Sequoia High School before I was hired, and it was a huge success.

I told them what was involved in performing such a show. And if we could get their parents to show up, we could possibly make more than a thousand dollars. They all agreed to take part. I told them that Bruce and I would do our trampoline act, and they should go to the school's music department to see if they could make up a band for our show.

I went out and found a few acts that included a juggler, a barbershop quartet, a boxer (who was the number one world middle weight championship contender), a state champion marching group that did a fantastic job marching in a very small area, and finally a hand balancer who, while standing on his hands, would move up and down on a set of blocks to about three feet high. I got that act from Oakland for fifteen dollars. His name was Jack La Lane, who later became famous on television. We also made up a mock gym class skit where all the kids would get into all kinds of trouble in class. This group was necessary so we could to get their parents to come, and see their kids perform in the show.

The two-night show was a tremendous success, and we cleared well over the amount we thought we would get. At our next meeting, I told them I had rented a school bus to take them to the football game. But first, I wanted them to do something else. I said I went down to the court house, and found a family that had no income and would probably have nothing to eat for Thanksgiving that was only a couple of days away.

The family included a mother with two young children who lived in a shack in an alley near the center of town. I suggested the whole gang go down to the grocery store to buy a turkey and enough food to last the family for at least a week. After making sure they bought the right kind of food, we gathered together with everyone wearing their varsity letter sweaters and took the food to the family on an early Friday evening.

The officers and I knocked on the door of the shack which startled the mother. She opened the door with her two children standing behind her. We told her that we knew she had little to eat for Thanksgiving, so we wanted her and her children to accept our gifts.

She started to cry as she invited the three of us in with our arms loaded with bags of food. The kids started to open the bags like they were Christmas presents, and the mother kept saying, "God bless you" over and over. The two club officers and I also started to cry as we told the others outside to bring the rest of the groceries in.

Everyone in the group was sniveling as we walked down the alley after delivering the groceries when one boy in the group said that he never believed people lived like that. We went to the game the following Sunday at Candlestick Park and everyone had a great time. The varsity club was so moved by helping the family that they decided to help a needy family every Thanksgiving if possible. Not bad when starting out with only three varsity students, and $1.42 in the treasury.

We Hire an Agent to Book Our Shows

Bruce and I found a couple agents who contacted hotels and clubs for us to do our trampoline act in the Bay Area during the winter. We did a lot of shows at the Saint Francis Hotel, one of the best hotels in San Francisco. There most of the shows were known as "smokers" meaning when a group of businessmen attend meetings, the smoke in the room got so bad that you could hardly see anything. Bruce and I used to dress up in sailor suits for our act, and mine had hash marks down my arm that continued down my pant leg. Each hash mark represented four years of service, and when added up, I would have been in the Navy for 144 years.

When we arrived to do our act one night, a security guard came up and threatened to throw us out of the hotel thinking we were drunken sailors. It took some real explaining before we finally convinced him that we were there to perform a show. Strippers were brought in to do their thing when we finished our act, and many were mothers from the areas we lived in, and were out to make some extra money for their families.

The agents knew ours was a supporting act before a main feature, and they constantly reminded us that we were going to do a "cheapie" meaning that we were going to get around sixty-five dollars to do our act. An agent called us one night and said he wanted us to go up to Eureka, a town a few miles north of San Francisco. We were to perform in a movie theater that was so old that it must have been built when Lewis and Clark went through California in the 1880's.

The stage in the theater was badly warped from the holes in the roof that dripped rainwater. The show included sixteen acts with eight in the first half of the show, an intermission, then eight more acts in the second half. The show was set for two nights with two shows each night. As usual, we were going to do a "cheapie," and in this case, we got around three hundred dollars. Nobody practiced their acts because they were all pros, and knew exactly what they had to do.

One of the performers came up to us after our first act on the first night, and said our folded trampoline looked awful sitting out in front of the curtain. He suggested that we put the trampoline behind the curtain, and replace it with his marimba that would look better than our ugly trampoline. We agreed, so after doing our act in the second show, we put our trampoline behind the curtain as requested.

In doing so, I hit the curtain with my buttocks that hit the marimba. Being on wheels, it suddenly started to slowly move across the stage due to the warped deck, as the announcer was introducing the next act. Bruce and I were standing behind the curtain when we heard the audience and announcer start to gasp. Wondering what was going on, we peeked out from behind the curtain and saw the marimba slowly moving out to the middle of the stage toward the front edge where it suddenly fell into the orchestra pit with a very loud crash.

I think the audience thought it was part of an act because they started to laugh. They laughed even more when Bruce and I ran out on the stage, and looked down at the marimba in the orchestra pit. Bruce then told me to go back and tell its owner what had happened, and when I refused, he screamed, "God damn it, go back and tell him".

We must have sounded like Abbot and Costello as the audience went wild over what was taking place. I went out behind the theater, and found the owner in his trailer. He was foreign and could hardly speak English. I told him what happened, and he ran out onto the stage yelling up a storm that made the audience laugh more. The marimba wasn't badly damaged as it turned out, and only needed a couple of keys replaced to fix it.

The Master of Ceremonies was Tennessee Ernie Ford, and when he tried to introduce the next number, the audience kept breaking up with laughter that went on for four or five minutes. They had a big party for the entertainers after the second show on the second night, and whenever anyone would look at Bruce and me, they would start to laugh again.

More Shows on the Road

Bruce and his wife Pinky learned they couldn't have children, so they went to Morley Shapiero who was a diver at Ohio State, and his family lived in San Francisco. Morley's father was a Pediatrician. He helped them adopt a cute little blond newborn baby girl. They named her "Laura," after the song by the same name.

It was 1956 after school was over when Bruce and I took off to go east and do our summer shows. We stopped off to do a show in Albuquerque, New Mexico at the same club we had visited the year before. We then performed four more shows on the way to New Orleans, sleeping in the car on the way to save money.

I remember how exhausted we were when we arrived at the New Orleans Country Club when the director of the club decided to take us on a tour of the city. He insisted that we eat with the club members before we were to perform that night. Steaks were served which made it more difficult for us to perform. The weather was so hot and humid that Bruce and I sweated through our whole show, and I don't know how we ever got through it without passing out.

Obviously, we performed in many shows that were outright dangerous, and we both were occasionally injured performing our acts none of which ever stopped either of us from finishing the show. We never worried about being seriously injured or about risking our lives over the years, performing under some deplorable conditions.

One time Bruce slipped off the three-meter board, and landed on his buttocks on the edge of the pool doing the comedy routine. He got up and finished the act in excruciating pain, and went into the shower room and fainted. He had several stitches put in his buttocks that left a huge scar, and kept him out of the pool for a good month.

I was doing the "Lone Ranger" dive on the three-meter board at a country club in Chicago. The dive is done by jumping up and landing on your seat near the end of the board with your legs wrapped around it, and yelling, "High Yo Silver" as the board bounces up and down. However, I had jumped too far forward to land on the end of the board, and caught the corner edge of the board with my back before falling into the water.

I managed to crawl out of the pool onto the deck, and laid on my back with the breath knocked out of me moaning with pain. Bruce came and stood over me with his face two feet from mine, and asked me if I liked to eat. I nodded, "Uh huh". He then told me to get up and finish the act, and somehow, I managed to finish the show. Five years later, I had my back x-rayed. The doctor said I must have broken my back several years before. The transverse processes on two of my vertebrae were broken off, and probably dissolved over the years.

We Do Our Act in Hollywood

We once did our act live in Hollywood on an ABC television series called, "You Asked For It." It was a tough gig because they timed our act right down to the second in a practice, and it had to be done with no mistakes. Our act went over well when Art Baker, our M.C., asked us after we finished if we had ever seen a movie studio. We told him we hadn't, and he took us to the Universal studio.

The first person we met was actor Robert Mitchum who was doing a cowboy scene. I asked him if he rode horses. And he said, "Are you kidding? I'm from Connecticut." We visited another building and watched Charlie Chaplin making the movie "Limelight," which was the last movie he ever made in this country.

We went to a small delicatessen for actors and actresses a short time later, that had five stools to sit on. We were eating a sandwich, and talking about how lucky and thrilled we were to see the greatest comedian of all time making a movie. When I turned around, I almost fell off my stool to find Charlie Chaplin sitting next to me. I managed to say a few words to him that related to his new movie, and he politely replied that he hoped we would find the time to see it. What a great moment in my life, gosh, and a kid from Erie, Pennsylvania.

We later did a personal show for Bing Crosby's twin sons in Spokane, Washington where they lived in a house on a lake near a golf course. Imagine doing a whole one hour show for two kids? We didn't meet Bing because he was out of town. After the show, the twins took Bruce and me out water skiing, and they didn't appear to be spoiled as had been said by the news media.

We did our trampoline act in a big show at the Oakland Auditorium that included many dignitaries. One of them was the former Heavyweight Boxing Champion of the World, Max Bear. His hands were so big that I couldn't see mine when I shook his hand. I kept crossing paths with him when doing other shows, and we became good friends

Allen Park High School in Michigan

Bruce invited me over to his house to have lunch one day in the spring of 1954, and said he had something to tell me. When I arrived, he told me he had received a call from the University of Michigan that told him Matt Mann, the swimming coach, had retired. The athletic department decided to hire Gus Stager, a former swimmer under Matt, as the swimming coach, and wanted Bruce as the diving coach.

No college or university in the United States had ever hired a diving coach. This was the beginning of a new era. I was stunned. I knew Bruce had worked for two years planning to open a swimming and diving school that he hoped would make him a lot of money. I told him if he didn't take the coaching job I would, and he said he was going to sleep on it and tell me what he decided to do the next day. He called me the next morning, and told me he decided to take the coaching job at Michigan.

Bruce's divers were the first to break into Ohio State's dynasty that ended a few years later. With that knowledge, I think Doc realized that his Indiana teams were rarely going to beat Michigan or Ohio State without a strong diving team. Up until then, the swimming coaches were supposed to coach the swimmers and divers. But they rarely tried to help the divers. They didn't have the time, and knew little or nothing about how to coach diving.

After Bruce resigned from Sequoia High School, we took our wives and Bruce's daughter, Laura, and drove to the University of Michigan in Ann Arbor, Michigan to visit our parents. My wife Mary's father died while we were teaching in San Leandro, and she wanted to move back to the Midwest to be close to her family. Moving back also made it possible for Bruce and me to do our trampoline act during the winter, and our whole act throughout the east in the summer.

Bruce found a job for me in the fall of 1954 teaching P.E. classes and coaching the swimming team at Allen Park High School in a Detroit suburb. I remember standing outside of the San Leandro High School, and crying before leaving because I had become so attached to the students.

We moved in with Mary's mother and two sisters during the summer. But I didn't see much of them because Bruce and I were on the road for nearly the whole time performing our shows that included the Al Sheehan Aqua Follies in Minneapolis and Seattle.

In early fall, we moved into an apartment in Dearborn near Allen Park where we lived for six months after Mary got pregnant. Bruce and Pinky invited us out to their house for dinner in Ann Arbor on May eighteenth, the date Nancy was to be born. I told him we couldn't come because Mary was scheduled to have the baby on that date. Bruce and Pinky told me later they got a big kick out of us thinking we could pick the exact date of the birth, but sure enough Nancy was born on that day.

We rented a house near Allen Park High School for another six months. One day, I was walking into the house of one of my swimmers. I looked up and saw a tornado coming just a block from where we lived. I remember running into his house, and calling Mary to find out if the tornado had hit our house. Fortunately, the tornado had jumped over it, but took the roof off the top of a grade school a few hundred yards away. Mary said that all she heard was a loud crash as it went by, but she didn't know what the noise was.

We got along well in Allen Park so we decided to buy a new house for $17,000 in Wyandotte, a small town about eight miles south of Allen Park. We moved into our new white brick home with the help of a few students from school.

A Major Incident

George was the known bully at Allen Park, and everyone was afraid of him, including the teachers. I had him in a class teaching wrestling, and I used him to assist me demonstrating different wrestling holds. He would often get me down on the mat and not let me up to the glee of the students, and I would have to tap him on the back and beg him to let me up.

I had a rough day one time, and was in a bad mood. While sitting in my office in the locker room between classes, I heard a towel snap followed by a yelp from a student in the shower room. I had no idea what was going on, but picked up a yard stick that was the hard wood type with a brass tip on the end. As I walked into the shower room, the kid that got snapped came running out. I found George naked with a towel in his hand, and told him to turn around and bend over.

I backed up against the wall and on the run, I hit him with the yard stick across his butt so hard that it broke the yard stick into several pieces. He must have jumped about six feet from the swat before turning around with great anger on his face. As he started toward me, I remember thinking "was this all worth losing my job over, and being arrested for assault?". I answered myself by saying, "Yes."

As George approached me I knew he would probably half kill me if he wished. I thought that I would at least get a few good shots at him first. Looking straight into each other's eyes, I told him to come and get me, and after hesitating for a few seconds, he walked out of the shower and I gave a great sigh of relief.

George missed my class for two days before knocking on my office door. He came in, and asked me if he could be my gym assistant. I told him I would be delighted. Later, I asked him if he ever told his folks about what had happened. He said he didn't dare because his father would have beaten the crap out of him.

George turned out to be the nicest kid I knew at that school, and we became very close friends. He told everyone not to mess around with Mr. Billingsley because if they did, they would have to deal with him. He used to bring me all kinds of fish when he went out fishing, and would often sit in my office and chat with me after school. I realized later how lucky I was to get away with what I did that day, and he was the first and last student I ever hit in my teaching and coaching career.

Study Hall

I supervised a sixth period study hall for about a hundred students. I stood out in the hall until everyone had entered the room, and then reminded them to be quiet so those who were trying to study were not disturbed. Some would sleep at their desks while others read.

The basketball team was not very good, and had lost most of their games that season. The star of the team was supposed to be in my study hall, but skipped my class several times. One day as classes were changing rooms, he walked by me when he was supposed to be attending my study hall. I grabbed his arm, and asked him why he had missed so many of my classes. He said he was busy doing other things. He was about six feet, four inches tall, and started to pull away from me and start down the hall. I grabbed him by the arm again, and marched him down to the principal's office.

I had never taken a student to the principal's office before because I felt I could take care of my own problems. I took him into the vice-principal's office, and explained what had happened, and asked the vice-principle what he was going to do with the boy. The vice-principle started to make excuses for the kid because he was the star on the basketball team. I told him to forget it, and I would take care of the problem myself.

Study hall was the same as a regular class so the students in the study halls received a passing or failing grade at the end of the semester. I told the ball player that he had just failed study hall which would make him ineligible to play basketball the next year. He told me that I couldn't do that, and I replied that even God could not make me change my mind. I then went to the basketball coach and informed him of what had happened, and added that if any swimmer pulled a similar trick on him, he had my permission to dismiss him from my team. He agreed with me, and the star basketball player did not play the next year.

My Swimming Coach Realization

I didn't realize what a poor swimming coach I was until I left Allen Park. Looking back at that time, I would have never made it as a good swimming coach. My knowledge was limited trying to learn by watching other coaches that resulted in me doing a poor job training the swimmers. I didn't know what I was doing, and disciplined my swimmers in such a way that I should have been fired.

For example, if a swimmer came in late for practice without a legitimate excuse, he had to crawl on his hands and knees between the legs of the whole team who were lined up in a row, and get swatted on his naked bottom. Back in those days, boys swam naked in P.E. classes and on the team.

I began to see that it sure as heck did not make them swim faster or make the team better. Other than those few incidents, I had a very close relationship with my team and the students in my classes, and they all knew how much I cared for them. But in wanting to accomplish something so bad, I overly disciplined some of them to reach my goal.

I found it worked better to make the workouts as entertaining as I could, and we ended up winning half of our meets in the season. We placed about in the middle at the conference meet. I doubt if my record would have ever improved even if I had remained there for the rest of my career. Though I was always a disciplined kind of coach, I changed my ways of coaching, and never touched another diver or student to discipline them. I had a lot of growing up to do, and I feel I did just that as I continued to teach and coach over the years.

CHAPTER 15

Ohio University

Choice I Had to Make

I received a call from Bob Bartels as I was finishing up my second-year teaching and coaching at Allen Park. Bob was a dear friend of mine who was also a member of the Sigma Chi Fraternity, and a swimmer on the Ohio State team. He had taken the swimming coach job at Ohio University in Athens, Ohio. He made a request for an assistant coach, and wanted me to take the job.

Not more than a week later, I received a call from the Air Force Academy in Colorado Springs, Colorado. The Academy was formed in 1952 when I had contacted them about the swimming position, but I never received a word from them in five years. They said they had cut the number of prospects to two, and wanted to fly me out for an interview.

After some thought, I decided not to take the job because those who were recruited by the Air Force were there to make the military their career. Being on the team would be a secondary form of competitive recreation. I also knew I could go further with my career as a diving coach than as a swimming coach, so I accepted the job at Ohio University.

I started in the fall of 1958. Ohio University had about eight thousand students. I went to Bob Bartels, and we agreed that I was going to be the diving coach and not an assistant swimming coach. His decision made me the second person to ever be hired as a diving coach at the college level with Bruce Harlan being the first at the University of Michigan in 1954.

Mary and I found a nice one story house about mile and a half away from the university that made it easy for me to walk to school.

Some Fun at My Expense

I was assigned a half dozen activity classes, and I wasn't very good at teaching two of them. One of those was trap shooting. The class shot clay pigeons with a shot gun along the Hocking River. Most of the students got to be accurate at hitting their targets. At the end of the course, my students wanted to see how good a shot I was. We brought out a box of fifty clay pigeons, and I didn't hit a single clay pigeon as the class broke down in hysterics.

I also asked to teach a golf class with the golf coach who was a pro so I could learn something about the game. I made a few suggestions to the class, but most of my time I spent watching the coach teach. On the last day of the course, the class asked me to hit a few balls. I felt confident after watching the coach, and had made five great shots of 150 yards with a five iron while at Ohio State. I missed hitting the ball twice on my first two attempts, then dubbed the ball and had to dig it out of the dirt. I shanked the next ball that traveled about twenty feet, and finished with a hook shot that hit a house while the students were rolling on the grass laughing.

Coach Bartels

I liked Bob Bartels a lot because he was intelligent, honest, and dedicated to the sport. He was also one of the kindest persons I have ever known, and a nice guy who treated his swimmers like his own children. He also respected and treated me as an equal. One day, something upset him with the team, and he used the word "damn" to express himself. Then he stood there for ten minutes apologizing to the team for using the word.

On team trips he would take us to restaurants. We weren't allowed to eat anything but fruit, vegetables, dried toast, and no meat before a meet. It got so bad that I asked him if my divers and I could eat regular food because we didn't worry about our diet to perform well. He agreed, so we ate what we wanted, that usually included a steak, but we always made sure to eat a little way from the swim team.

Need for Discipline

Though the swimmers loved him, he did little to discipline them when someone got out of line. This irritated me watching the swimmers fool around for hours during a squad meet. I asked Bob if I could talk to the team. I literally chewed the team out for a half hour to the point I was crying. I told them that their lack of intensity in training was so bad that they would never win the conference title, and of course they didn't appreciate my concern.

My First Diving Team

I managed to recruit five boys and one girl diver during my first-year coaching at Ohio University. Chuck Woodley was the best of the recruits, and placed tenth in the N.C.A.A. National Championships after I left to teach and coach at Indiana in the fall of 1960. John Lovestedt from Detroit, was another recruit. He was a tough kid who always wore a black leather jacket. He had long slick hair, and refused to cut it short to make a better competitive appearance for the judges.

One day I went downtown to a barber shop, and told the barber I was going to send him a kid wearing a black leather jacket and long slick hair, and to cut it real short. I asked John to lunch, and on the way back to the pool I pointed out the barbershop. I told him to go there because they did a good job cutting hair and charged less than any other barber in town.

John finally got around to it and afterwards came to the pool with a real short haircut that really upset him. The whole team was in on telling him how much better he looked with short hair, so he kept it that way from then on. He turned out to be a pretty good diver, and I think the sport gave him some direction in growing up to be a respectable adult.

Fred Schlichting was the third diver I recruited who was from Redwood City, California. He was a diver on Bruce Harlan's swimming team at Sequoia High School. Fred and I had become acquainted when he helped Bruce and I set up our equipment for a few diving exhibitions in the area. He decided to attend Ohio University when he graduated from high school because he knew me, and he turned out to be an above average diver. Unfortunately, he had a real problem passing history so was ineligible to compete for the first year at Ohio University.

My fourth diver was John Munn who won the Indiana State High School title, and was a pretty good diver. One day attempting to perform a reverse dive layout he landed on his back on the one-meter board. I asked him if he was okay. After he said he was, I called him a complete idiot, and the rest of the team started to laugh.

The fifth diver was Bob Schneider who I met while walking down the street in town. Bob had just gotten out of four years in the Navy, and during our conversation he showed some interest in diving. I told him to try out for the team. He didn't appear to have much going for him as a diver because he had no experience or talent. However, he did show a lot of enthusiasm, so I kept him on the team. After graduating, Bob coached diving at Princeton University for four years.

The Mid-American Conference Championships were coming up at Kent State. Riding on the team bus up to Kent, I told Bob that if he was nervous and should balk starting to perform a dive, he should have an excuse in mind to tell the judges or he would be penalized. The judges would allow him to start the dive over.

Sure enough, he balked starting a forward approach to his dive. Stunned for a moment while standing on the end of the board, he suddenly bent over and grabbed his leg and said he had a cramp. The referee sitting in front of me asked what he should do. I told him to give him a balk that meant two points would be deducted from each judge when he performed the dive.

I never said a word to him about the balk until we returned to Athens. When we were getting off the bus, I asked him how he was coming along with his cramp. And we laughed about that for years. He graduated from Ohio University and was later hired as the diving coach at Princeton University with Bob Clotworthy who was the swimming coach and the 1956 Melbourne Olympics gold medal winner in diving.

Schneider coached at Princeton University for about a dozen years. In that time, he originated and was editor of the diving magazine called "The Rip" for United States Diving, and did a great job. Bob was intelligent, and after he left the job I don't believe anyone has ever matched the kind of information he gave to competitive diving. He went on to get married and had two nice children who grew up before he retired and eventually returned to Florida where he still lives and has had several editing and publishing jobs.

Female Athlete Programs

There were no diving programs for females in high schools or colleges until Title IX was legislated in 1972. The first college coach who formed a female team aside from his college male team was Dick Pappenguth at Purdue University. He started a girls swimming team in 1935. The second coach was at Mississippi State where a women's black track team was formed in 1944. The only place for females to practice and compete up until Title IX was in clubs.

Women usually joined a club, most of which had a diving coach, and competed in A.A.U. (Amateur Athletic Union) competitions that were available for male and female age groups up to the National Championships, The Pan American Games, and the Olympic Games.

Dick Smith recognized this problem when he was the gymnastics coach at the University of Southern California, and decided to form a swim and diving club in Phoenix, Arizona that included females. The only female competitions at that time were offered by the A.A.U. Therefore, Smith's club drew most of the outstanding divers of all ages in the United States who won several national diving titles.

Bruce Harlan and I were the first to coach female divers at universities beginning in 1958. Of course, they couldn't represent our schools because there were no N.C.A.A. competitions for women. They could compete in only a couple of local A.A.U. meets.

A Funny Pool Incident

I was in the Ohio University pool by myself one morning when the phone rang. The caller said he was university president Baker, and wished to come down and take a swim. The president's home was only about a half block from the pool. He wanted to know if there were any students in the pool, and if there weren't any, would I kindly leave the back door open for him.

Thinking this was a student prank that often happened with questions like, "are there any sharks in the pool or were females required to wear bathing suits when they swam", etc., I said, "Sure sweetheart come on in." After hanging up the phone, I began to think that maybe it really was the president so to make sure, I went to the back door and left it open. Sure enough, President Baker and his wife came walking in with their bathrobes on, and they started to laugh as I approached them to apologize and explain myself. His wife then told me that I was the only person, other than herself, that had ever called the president "sweetheart."

Water Shows at Ohio University

I talked to Coach Bartels about doing a water show during my first year, and he thought it was a great idea. Then I asked the O.U. swimming and diving teams to do the show. I taught thirteen acts for the show to various members on the team that took around ten days because I had to teach them separately after practice. We decided to call the show "Wild Wild World" after a popular T.V. show 'Wide Wide World of Sport." The star in the T.V. show was Dave Garoway. The M.C. for our show was Dan Ogara, who was an announcer at the local radio station.

The Ohio University pool was ideal for the kind of show I had in mind because the bleachers on both sides started about five feet above the pool deck. The ceiling was about forty-two feet high with a board walk that made it possible for rigging the trapeze. We made up show flyers that the team gave out to the campus dormitories, fraternities, and sororities. For about a month the show was constantly announced over the radio that informed everyone the show would start at exactly eight o'clock.

I had a rehearsal with the team the night before the show to put all the acts in their proper order, and to get the music and lighting right. I told the team that we were going to rehearse the show that might take all night, and if anyone didn't want to do it, they could leave and no one left. We finished the final rehearsal about one o'clock in the morning.

Some of the swimmers and divers were so excited about the show that they went down to the dormitories, fraternities, and sororities, and pounded on doors to tell them not to miss this show. I can't go over the whole show because it would be too lengthy. The opening of the show for both years was sort of different than most openings used in any water show.

The place was sold out for the first night, and being a new teacher at Ohio University, few people knew who I was. I poured some liquor on my clothes so those who sat near me in the audience would think I was drunk. When everyone was seated and ready for the show to begin at exactly eight o'clock, nothing happened.

Then a few minutes later, I started to clap quietly, and said loudly, "Let's start the show!" That got me a few dirty looks. I waited for a couple of more minutes when I repeated my requests, but a little louder and some people close to me said the show would start in a minute and to keep quiet. Ignoring them I complained again, but much louder than before.

One of the swimmers, planted on the other side of the pool, yelled to shut up, but I kept yelling. Two ushers came down the aisle and told me to be quiet or they would have to remove me, and when they left I started to yell again. The ushers then returned, picked me up, and threw me out as I kept yelling I had paid my quarter for the show when the cost was a dollar.

I waited a few minutes before returning, and sat in the same seat I had before and started to yell again. When the ushers returned to throw me out again, I ran down the stairs to the railing surrounding the pool where I dared the ushers to come and get me. When the ushers started toward me, I jumped down onto the pool deck.

While I was yelling at the ushers, one of our planted swimmers hit me with a bucket of water from behind. When I started to chase him to the other end of the pool, I picked up another pail on the way, and trapped him in a corner. A similar act was often used in some circuses when wads of paper were thrown from the bucket. But in this case, I threw the whole bucket of water at him.

When he ducked, the water hit a group of people sitting in the stands who pretended to be very angry. Fortunately, the spectators in that area were planted. Then I chased him to the deep end of the pool where he climbed up onto the three-meter board. In the meantime, one of the swimmers started to pull the ropes of a swing that was attached to the ceiling forty-two feet above the pool. The swing swung half way down to the pool, and back near the three-meter board at the deep end.

The swimmer I chased ran out to the end of the board, and jumped to grab the bar on the trapeze as it swung near the three-meter board. Sitting on the swinging trapeze bar, he turned around to face me, and dropped down hanging onto the bar swinging back and forth a couple more times. When he neared the diving board again, I jumped up to the trapeze from the board as he released the bar and passed under me in midair to land feet first on the board. Then he slid to the back of the board, grabbed the railing on the ladder, and swung down to the deck. In the meantime, I grabbed the bar and swung to the shallow end, and did a half gainer into the water when all the lights went out and the show began. The crowd made a lot of "oohs and aahs" between laughs, and applauded loudly.

We did something similar the next year, except I started out by selling drinks on a tray from the pool deck for twenty-five cents a cup. I sold a couple of drinks when a customer, planted in the audience, started yelling at me that I had given him water and I told him it was ice cold so he shouldn't complain. He then threw his drink in my face, and I took the whole tray of drinks and threw them at him that hit others in the stands.

The guy really got mad, and climbed out of the stands and chased me around the pool before I climbed up the ladder to the cat walk with him right behind me. He finally caught up with me, and we got into a big scuffle that was hard to see by the audience. Then he threw a dummy, dressed like me, off the cat walk that landed on the deck when the lights went out to start the show.

Mary and my three-year-old daughter Nancy were attending the show. Nancy didn't realize I wasn't the dummy, and started to scream and cry thinking it was me. Quite a while later in the show she was convinced that it wasn't me when the lights were turned off for a moment during another act, and I traded places with the dummy and I got up and walked away.

Carroll Widows had been head football coach at Ohio State before taking the job as the athletic director at Ohio University. He came to me the next morning, and said he wanted two hundred tickets for the football team for the next show. He wanted them for nothing, and he really got upset with me when I refused to give them to him. The football coach, Bill Hess, came to me that afternoon, handed me a check for the tickets, and chewed me out for not coming to him in the first place. But it was our fundraiser, and I didn't want our team to lose the income.

It rained real hard that night, and people stood in a line that went nearly all around the block to get into the show. The show helped bring the team closer together, and it was by far the greatest show I had ever been in during the fifteen years I was in show business. I had each act come out on the pool deck from the dressing room to be recognized after the show was over, and the fans gave them a standing ovation.

The Birth of my Son Jimmy

My son Jimmy was born on January 28, 1957 during the first year we were at Ohio University. Mary's mother came to stay with us just before her due date. We'd had a big snow that night, and when Mary got up at six o'clock to go to the bathroom she started yelling that the baby was coming. I jumped up and called the doctor. He arrived in a few minutes, and examined her and said she could have the baby any minute.

We both decided to go to the hospital. We picked Mary up and threw a blanket over her body, and ran out into the snow to his car. I told the doctor to jump in the back seat with her while I drove. He said, "The hell with you, I'll drive and you get in the back with her." Jimmy started to come out about half way to the hospital, and I told Mary that since she waited nine months to have the baby, she had to wait another nine minutes for us to get her to the hospital.

At the hospital, we jumped out of the car, picked her up, and ran up a flight of stairs to the delivery room. Just as we put her on the delivery table, Jimmy was born. Unfortunately, I never got to see Jimmy being born because a nurse pulled me out of the room. The doctor came out a few minutes later looking as white as a ghost, and said never in his practice had he ever gone through such a close call.

The doctor and I became good friends soon after, and often had coffee together and talked about that crazy morning. Nancy, my first born, liked Jimmy right away, and they became real close. I remember that as Jimmy began to grow, Nancy would get upset when anyone outside of the family got near him.

Hobie with his children, left to right, Nancy, Hobie, Elizabeth, and Jimmy at 85th birthday celebration.

CHAPTER 16

How I Was Hired by Indiana University

At Ohio University

I was at Ohio University for a short time when I began to write letters to colleges that I thought had better diving programs than Ohio. I wanted to get into the big time at an NCAA Division I school because Ohio University was in Division II. I was a diving judge for the N.C.A.A. and A.A.U. National Championships for a couple of years, so I knew which colleges had decent diving programs and good diving facilities.

I must have written to at least fifty colleges and universities, and always got the same answer from those who responded that politely said, "Thank you for your nice letter, but we don't have such an opening now. However, we will keep your letter on file" ...in the waste basket. It must be remembered that the reason why I received these letters was because at that time, no school had a diving budget for a diving program, and Bruce and I were the only collegiate diving coaches in the country at that time.

Then things began to happen. After I had been teaching and coaching at Ohio University for nearly two years, I received a call from Bill Heusner who had just accepted the head coaching position at the University of Minnesota with the condition that he could have a diving coach, and he suggested my name. That opened the door for me to coach diving at a higher level.

Heusner had resigned from Southern Illinois as their swimming coach. I had known Bill for years when he swam for Northwestern. He asked if I wanted the job. I told him I would think it over. Bill was a wonderful man, and I would have really liked coaching with him. But I wasn't too anxious to move to Minneapolis where the winters are extremely cold, and the pool was always cold and with poor diving facilities.

Meanwhile, Doc Councilman had been hired as the new swimming coach at Indiana University in 1958. Doc and I were good friends on the Ohio State team, so I called and asked him if he was going to hire a diving coach, and if so would he consider me. He told me he would think about it, and he wanted to look around before deciding. He called me back about a week later. He said he decided to take me as the diving coach, but he didn't know if it was possible because Indiana didn't have any job description or money in their budget for a diving coach or for another teacher in the department.

Instrumental in hiring Doc and me was Doc Barton, an Indianapolis dentist who lived next door to the President of Indiana University board of trustees. Doc Barton was a strong proponent of the swimming and diving team at Indiana University for years. He is pictured on the far right with my family on next page.

James "Doc" Counsilman

Doc Counsilman was born in Birmingham, Alabama, and later his family moved to St. Louis. He attended St. Louis High School, and then attended Ohio State. He was captain of the team before entering the Army Air Corps in 1943. After pilot training, he was captain of a B-24. While flying on a mission over Germany towards the end of the war, his plane was  shot down. He instructed his crew to bail out when the bomber was hit and was going to crash, but he told me later that he chickened out and went down with the plane.

Fortunately, Doc wasn't injured when it crashed, and he somehow managed to get back to France and out from behind the enemy lines. He returned to England where he was stationed until 1946 before returning to the United States and discharged from the service. He returned to Ohio State and was made the captain of the swimming team again. He won the Big 10 breaststroke title, and briefly held the 220-yard breaststroke world record. Breaststroke then was swum like the butterfly arm stroke today only with a breaststroke kick.

The Ohio State team had a diving dynasty that helped them win nearly all their Big Ten, N.C.A.A. and National A.A.U Championships as well as most of their International and Olympic titles. Ohio State's divers often scored more points in two diving events in the big meets than the swimmers did in sixteen events.

Doc was a unique person, and wasn't just a great teacher and coach. He was "THE" master coach in swimming. After graduating from Ohio State, Doc went to the

University of Illinois for his master's degree under the direction of Dr. Thomas Kirk Cureton, a renowned professor of exercise physiology. He also helped coach their swimming team.

After Illinois Doc went to the University of Iowa for his Ph.D. doctor's degree in exercise physiology, and helped coach their swimming team. Incidentally, one swimmer that Doc helped at Iowa was my dear friend, John Boyd from Erie. Marge, Doc's wife, whom he married right after the war, helped him all throughout his career. To build team comradery, Marge would cook lasagna Sunday dinners for the whole swimming and diving team at their house. Marge also helped Doc write his books, and never missed a swim meet over the years. She was loyal to him throughout his career, and was helpful to him in many ways. Together they raised four children. As of this writing, Doc passed away January 2004, and Marge is in her 90's living comfortably in an assisted living facility in Bloomington.

Doc's first job as a head coach and assistant professor was at Cortland State Teacher's College in upstate New York in 1954. The college was a Division III school with only 2,000 students. As all good coaches, Doc had an eye for talent, and spotted an unknown swimmer, George Breen, in a physical education swimming class. George had an unorthodox looking stroke because he used a two-beat cross-over kick doing most of the work with his upper body and arms, but had a lot of talent. And with Doc's coaching, George went on to win the 1500-meter national championship, and the Bronze medal in the 1956 Melbourne Olympic Games.

Doc's Transition to Indiana

Due to his curiosity, creativity, and philosophy, Doc began to change training routines and the coaching methods used to correct a swimmer's strokes. When he arrived at Indiana, Doc established a more rigorous training program based on the idea that a young developing person could physiologically accept and adapt to more stress to improve performance. He started weight training and interval training that were foreign to other swimming coaches.

With a meager budget, he converted a small storage room under the pool bleachers into a weight room, and made weights by filling gallon tomato cans with cement on the end of a 3-foot-long pipe. He became a feature coach and speaker at numerous coaching clinics when he wrote the book, <u>The Science of Swimming</u> in 1965. The book has been translated into several languages and used by coaches and swimmers worldwide.

Doc also coached a bunch of young swimmers at the Indianapolis Athletic Club (IAC) for six summers beginning in 1952. One of the IAC swimmers was the daughter of Doc Barton who was a dentist that lived next door to the president of the board of trustees at Indiana University. Bob Royer, the swimming coach at Indiana, had brain cancer, and had little time to live. So, Doc Barton went to his neighbor, and suggested that Indiana hire Doc as Royer's assistant.

Royer was not informed that Doc had been hired, so he went to the athletic director, Bob Allen, and wanted to know why Doc was hired. And Allen, said "because you are going to die soon." That was a terrible thing to say to anyone. Royer was shocked, and said he believed in God and wasn't going to die. But Royer did die a couple of months later, and Doc took over the job as head swimming coach.

Early Indiana Swimming and Diving History

The swim teams at Indiana had never came close to winning a Big Ten Championship even when Royer managed to recruit a couple of good Hawaiian swimmers. Doc was hired in the fall of 1958 after Royer's team placed sixth in the Big 10 Conference meet. Some of the swimmers that Doc had coached at the Indianapolis Athletic Club had graduated from high school, and because of their respect for Doc's coaching abilities that had already made them great swimmers, decided to attend Indiana University after he got the job.

However, they couldn't compete on the varsity team until the fall of 1959 because the N.C.A.A. had rules then that didn't allow athletes to compete until they were college sophomores. But when they became sophomores, his team took second place at the 1959 Big Ten Conference Championships. Michigan won the title by 26 points all of which were scored by their divers. Indiana didn't score any diving points because they didn't have any divers good enough to even qualify in the top sixteen places. But that was about to change.

While waiting to see if I was going to get hired at Indiana, Doc mentioned that he was taking the team out for a picnic in Bloomington. I suggested it might be a good idea for me to get acquainted with the team by doing a trampoline exhibition. He agreed and I drove over to Bloomington with my trailer the next day, and went to the P.E. building to pick up a trampoline and find out where Doc was having the picnic.

I found someone who knew he had taken the team to McCormick's Creek State Park about fifteen miles west of Bloomington. I drove out to the park and found Doc and about twenty swimmers having a picnic, and I set up the trampoline to do my act after they finished eating. I started out with my comedy act that included some jokes and funny stunts as they stood around the trampoline. Not one swimmer even smiled and they seemed bored to death with my act.

Close to the finish of my act, Mike Troy, one of Doc's top swimmers, said, "Hey Doc, when are we going out to the quarries?" I knew right then that the swimming team

153

didn't buy me one bit, and I thought my chances of getting the job at Indiana were zero. Troy's comment that day was brought up many times for a laugh over the years.

Doc Counsilman went to Doctor Barton to see about me getting the job as diving coach at Indiana because he was the one who got Doc his job and thought he might go through the same procedure to get me hired. Doctor Barton then got in touch with Dean Daniels, Chairman of the H.P.E.R Department, and Bob Allen, the athletic director, to see if they could hire me, and they said they would work on it.

Fortunately, Dean Daniels had been one of my teachers when I attended Ohio State. About five years after I graduated from Ohio State, he became the Department Chairman at Indiana. He knew me quite well. Just before graduating, our class chipped in to buy him a gift, and I was selected to give it to him on the last day of the quarter.

Years later after getting a teaching position at Indiana under him, I visited him in his office at Indiana about a week before he died. Dean Daniels asked me if I knew where he got the pipe that he was always smoking. I told him that I didn't have a clue, and he said that it was the pipe our class had given him in 1951. It had been his favorite ever since. Dean Daniels was a real professional with little sense of humor, but for some reason when we got together, I could make him laugh. I felt that I lost a really good friend when he passed away.

Bill Heusner called me in early March of 1959, and told me that Minnesota wanted me to visit them right away for an interview. I flew up to Minneapolis and had the interview. Bill called me about two weeks later to inform me that I had the job, and wanted to know when I would confirm my acceptance. I told him I still wanted to know what Indiana had to offer, and I would tell him by noon on March 22nd the day I was leaving to judge the diving events at the N.C.A.A. Championships at Ohio State.

I received a call from Doctor Barton, and he informed me that he was still working on getting me the job but couldn't guarantee me a thing. I let both schools know that I had been approached by the other school. I was confident I had a good chance to be hired by one or the other schools, and resigned from Ohio University.

I called Doc and told him that Minnesota decided to hire me, and he contacted Doctor Barton who got in touch with Dean Daniels and Bob Allen to see if they were going to hire me. Doc Barton called me about ten minutes before noon on March 22nd, and informed me that he was still working on getting me the job. Everything looked good, but not to count on it. Then I took a real chance and called Bill Heusner, and told him I had decided to accept the job at Indiana... that I didn't have. Looking back at making that decision, with my wife and two children, I would have been in serious financial trouble if Indiana had turned me down. It was a great risk I had to take, and I prayed that things would work out for my family and me.

It took Dean Daniels and Bob Allen about a month to get the details straightened out before they agreed to hire me. Neither department had any money in their budget for my position. However, they managed to pay me around sixty-five hundred dollars a year split equally by the P.E. department and the athletic department. This meant that each department was paying me a little over three thousand dollars a year for me to coach the men's diving team and to teach a full load in the physical education department as an instructor starting in the fall of 1959.

Our Diving Shows Must Go On

The summer of 1959 in Atlanta, Georgia we did our show at a motel that had built a ten-meter tower, and had a beauty contest on television to celebrate the building of the new tower. We performed some dives from the three-meter springboard, and ten-meter platform. Then we finished the show with our comedy diving routine. Atlanta was in the south, and we decided to start the comedy act with a southern joke. Bruce was on the tower, and I was on the three-meter springboard. I would ask him what he was doing up there. And he would say that he would like to dive, but he was scared. I hollered up to him to think of his mother, and he said he didn't have one. Then I asked him to think of his father, and he replied that he was a bachelor.

Again, mind you, we were in the south, and I asked him to think of Robert E. Lee. He replied, "who is he?" The punch line was supposed to be, "Then go ahead and jump you damn Yankee." But for some reason, with the T.V. cameras live, I yelled, "Go ahead and jump, you "damn bastard!" The people around the pool started to howl and whistle as I ran into our guest room, and locked the door. Some people outside came knocking at my door, and said all was forgiven and it was safe for me to come out to finish the show.

Tragedy Strikes

Bruce and I had performed our seven act show about a thousand times which included ten years in Bermuda. During the summer in 1959 we went to Bermuda to perform our ten-day annual show, and took our wives and children with us. However, Bermuda had a bad storm for four days, and we couldn't stay over because we were contracted

to perform a show in Fairfield, Connecticut for the editor of Time Magazine and the people at the Fairfield Yacht Club.

So, we contacted Juaquin Capilla, the 1956 Olympic tower champion from Mexico, and Eddie Cole, the National Trampoline champion to take our places. We had to leave some of our diving

equipment for them to use that included the section we used on top of our 28-foot scaffold. The top had a chair to jump from onto a small trampoline that sprung us into the air to perform our dives.

We called the Fairfield people when we arrived at the New York airport, and had them rent a 28-foot-high scaffold. Then we called the local Y.M.C.A. to borrow a trampolet that we placed on wooden boards on top of the platform to launch our high dives. We dropped our families off at a motel in Fairfield, and went over to the Yacht Club to put up the scaffold. We didn't have our special unit for the top of the scaffold, but improvised with some two by four boards to place across the top of the scaffold to form the platform.

Unfortunately, the only boards we found went about two inches over the edges of the scaffold. We nailed two by fours across the boards, and turned them over to keep them from slipping. We placed the trampolet on top of the boards to jump higher doing our high dives. Other than underwater lights in the pool, the diving area had very little lighting for the evening show so they had to shine spot lights from several of the yachts to help us see what we were doing.

It was a perfect night for the show and everything went well. As usual, Bruce and I decided to take down the equipment, and put it away before joining the people in the club house after the show. So, as the people started for the bar, Bruce and I climbed up the scaffold to dismantle it. Bruce was on top of the boards, and I stayed down with one leg wrapped around a top unit of the scaffold. The upper half of my body was above the boards when Bruce first lowered the trampolet to the ground with a rope.

I suggested we push the boards over into the water, and take them out when we got down. He said he wanted to first pull the one board off that kept all the other boards in place. When he started to pull the board up, with my hands on the tip of the boards, I felt them start to move. Realizing that they were only an inch or two from the edge, I yelled at him to hold it, but I was too late. The edge of the boards in front of me slipped off the scaffold, and Bruce and the boards dropped downward through the middle of the scaffold.

Instinctively, he held on to the board that was still attached to the other boards that turned him upside down, but I was unable to grab him. I screamed as he dropped 28 feet, and landed on his head on the cement. While falling, he grabbed a wire used to set a light on the water, but it broke off like a thread and didn't stop his fall. I screamed again when I couldn't reach him. After watching him fall, I immediately climbed down, and found that he was not breathing.

No one saw him fall because they were all facing the club house when he fell. Someone suddenly pulled me away from him, and applied C.P.R. that started his breathing and kept him alive. I had gone into shock by that time so I don't remember how long it took for the ambulance to arrive, but I do remember getting into it with him and riding to a hospital in Norwalk because there was no hospital in Fairfield.

I went into the emergency room with Bruce where one of the best surgeons in the country was waiting to examine him. Still in shock, I told the doctor to hurry up and get him fixed so we could do a show in Michigan the next week. The doctor asked me what my relation was with Bruce. I said he was my best friend. Then he asked me how tough I was. When I said, I was tough, the doctor put his finger on a big wound on the side of Bruce's head that brought no response to one side of his body, but caused the other half to quiver. The doctor said that one side of Bruce's body was already paralyzed. I asked the doctor what they could do for Bruce, and he said they would inject a dye into his body that would take 24 hours to circulate through his blood system and then follow up with x-rays to determine the nature of his injuries.

I stayed out in the hall until our families showed up, and I don't know how anyone found them because I don't recall us telling anyone in what hotel they were staying. I thought I could be strong about the accident when they arrived, but I completely broke down for most of the evening. I walked by his room once to see how he was, and the side of his head had swollen up like a watermelon. I called Bruce's younger brother, Russell, who lived in King of Prussia just outside of Philadelphia early in the morning, and gave him the sad news about the accident.

His brother wanted to come up to the hospital, and I told him to remain at home until we knew more about the injury. I hung up the phone, and as I started toward Bruce's room, his wife was coming out with her face contorted. It was then that I knew he had died. Strangely, at that moment, I suddenly realized I was still walking around in my bathing suit. It was 1959, and I just lost my partner and best friend.

The people at the hospital held a commercial airplane up for two hours so they could ship Bruce's body back to Detroit and then to Ann Arbor, Michigan. We all went on the same flight, and once off the ground, his son Freddie, four years old, kept running up and down the aisle saying that his daddy had just killed himself. Bruce was just thirty-three years old when they buried him in Marion, Ohio.

Though his accomplishments in life were great, they failed to come close to the kind of person he was. A handsome person with a phenomenal personality, Bruce was a real hustler who liked and helped others far beyond what was expected of him. He was a fierce competitor with a remarkable sense of humor always pulling tricks on people. Bruce was also a natural born leader who was willing to take great risks in life. He had adopted two children during his marriage.

What a pity that such a good young person, who had so much to offer the world, should be taken away from us so early in his life. For years, I asked God why he took him when he had such a great career ahead of him. I wondered "Why not take me, for I hadn't done anything as a coach to brag about?".

The Show Must Go On

As it turned out, I was driven to take over where he left off to honor his career. Little did I know then that I would be challenged with greater odds than any coach has ever known. I wrote this portion of the book on June 22, 2009, the fiftieth anniversary of his death in 1959. It took nearly ten years before I could really talk about his accident. To this day, I have never gotten over his death or those of John Wolford, John Boyd, Jim Pfleuger, and Wendell Sheldon, all of whom were the best friends I ever had.

Bruce and I were scheduled to perform our water show at the Sylvania Country Club in Toledo the week after his death that occurred on June 22, 1959. I asked Dick Kimball, who had just graduated from Michigan and was working on his master's degree, to do the show with me. I remember I cried through the whole show, and tried not to let the audience see my grief.

Kimball and I performed another show at a party in Ann Arbor the next day for a wealthy business man, Mr. Gedes, who was very influential with the University of Michigan. Bruce and I had done our show in a small lake behind his house the year before. We had to walk underwater with a part of the scaffold to the middle of the lake to put it up.

I Make My Decision

After telling me how sorry he was about Bruce, Mr. Gedes asked me if I wanted the diving job at Michigan. He then called the president of the University of Michigan over, and told him that he offered Bruce's job to me and the president said it was fine with him. Then he asked me if I would take the job. I told him I would give him my answer after Kimball and I did the show. After the show, I told him that I appreciated his kind offer, but I decided to accept the position at Indiana. He asked me why I declined his offer, and I said because I had given Indiana my word.

Talk about challenges and doing things the hard way. When I look back on that decision, I must have been out of my mind. But I had three reasons for turning the job down. First, I had taught at Allen Park High School in Michigan for two years, and found the winter weather in Michigan to be horrible, and I didn't want to walk in slush for another thirty years. Indiana was the farthest south of any Big Ten school so it had the best weather. Second, the Michigan pool had a small diving well with the one-meter board on one side, and the three-meter board on the other side. I would I have to stand and coach on a narrow three feet wide walkway while looking one way for the divers on the 1-meter board, then look in the opposite direction for the divers on the 3-meter board. Indiana was also in the process of building a new pool with a separate diving well. And third, I didn't want to continue what Bruce had already accomplished or diminish his legacy because I wanted to build my own reputation for what I could do, win, lose or draw.

CHAPTER 17

I'm Going to Indiana University Fall of 1959

Dick Kimball, My New Water Shows Partner

All the divers in Al Sheehan's Aqua Follies in Minnesota were given a public relation assignment. One year my assignment was to judge a diving contest at the Minnetonka Country Club in 1956. I did this for three summers. When I went there the first year, I was really impressed with one diver who was sort of small, but very explosive and showed great promise. I went to Bruce, who was then the diving coach at Michigan for two years, and told him about the little kid who showed a lot of promise, but Bruce brushed off my comments.

I got the same response from Bruce when I went out to officiate the next year. But in the third year to officiate, Bruce went with me. He was really impressed with the kid when he saw him dive, but I told him that he was too late because Dick Kimball was already on a scholarship from the University of Oklahoma and just finished his freshman year.

Kimball Goes to Michigan (pictured on left)

Ironically, Matt Mann had been the swimming coach at Michigan for nearly forty years, and after retiring at the age of seventy, he was picked up by Oklahoma as their swimming coach. After seeing Dick Kimball dive and hearing what I said about him, Bruce told me to tell Dick to get into his car. When I asked why, Bruce said, "Never mind, just tell him." Now here's where it gets tricky.

Kimball got into Bruce's car, and sat between the two of us. Bruce started to tell me to tell Kimball that he should switch schools, and attend Michigan because no one at Oklahoma knew a thing about diving. And if he would switch schools, he could make him a great diver. I repeated exactly what Bruce said, but had to ask him twice because I forgot some of what he wanted me to say.

Kimball went back to Oklahoma and changed schools that next fall. When Bud Wilkerson, the athletic director and famous football coach at Oklahoma, found out what happened, he called the athletic director at Michigan and told him that if he didn't return Kimball, he would sever all relations with Michigan including playing them in football. Michigan had a big meeting regarding the matter, and Bruce was put before a committee and asked if he had ever talked to Kimball about changing schools. Bruce accurately swore that he never said a word to Kimball... because I was the one who had done the talking. The matter was dropped, and Dick Kimball transferred to Michigan and won the one-meter and three-meter N.C.A.A. diving championships. Dick went on to be one of the greatest acrobatic divers and diving coaches in the world coaching the Michigan diving team.

What If?

Bruce Harlan was the first college diving coach to ever be hired at the University of Michigan in 1954, and had recruited some of the best swimmers and divers in the country for Michigan in 1955. The result was winning the 1956 Big Ten and N.C.A.A. National Championships for three consecutive years.

In retrospect, I wonder what affect it would have had on Michigan's and Indiana's championship teams if I had chosen the established Michigan team. They would have won more Big Ten Conferences and N.C.A.A. Championships when they had just won three in a row.

Plus, they had already hired a proven diving coach in Bruce Harlan. Swimming coaches began to see how teams with divers and knowledgeable coaches would score more championship points. But at the time, there were few university diving coaches who knew much about the sport besides Dick Kimball, Ron O'Brien, and me.

I know if I had taken the job at Michigan, Kimball would have probably ended up coaching at the University of Minnesota with Bill Heusner. However, when I rejected the offer, Kimball, who was a graduate assistant when Bruce died, took his place, and was officially made the diving coach the following year. Kimball only recently retired from Michigan after a forty plus year career.

The 1959 Pan American Games

Before his death in June, Bruce Harlan was selected to be the diving coach for the 1959 Pan American Games in Chicago in early August. The selection committee knew my close friendship with Bruce, and I was chosen to take his place about six weeks before the Games were to begin. The opening ceremony and track events were held at Soldier's Field downtown near Lake Michigan.

The opening ceremony started on a Tuesday morning at ten o'clock during working hours, and most of the people in Chicago had no idea that the Pan American Games were going on in their city. All the athletes, coaches, and officials reported outside of the stadium at eight o'clock to be assigned positions before marching in. We all stood outside the stadium for nearly three hours on a hot summer morning before things got organized.

I stood there with Jack Kelly, (pictured previous page on the left) the famous Olympian rower from the prominent Philadelphia Kelly family. I asked him if he was related to Grace Kelly, the famous movie actress, and later the Queen in Monte Carlo. He said she was his sister, and my mouth dropped. Jack was a wonderful person who never showed that he was from such a famous and wealthy family. He later became the president of the National A.A.U., and was my escort when I was inducted into the International Swimming Hall of Fame in 1983.

The Pan American Games had to be the worst ever staged in its history. The preparation for the opening ceremony was terrible. One can imagine how bad it looked when only eight thousand people showed up for the opening ceremony in a stadium that seated 100,000 people. I couldn't believe it when the torch bearer entered the stadium displaying a light bulb as the burning torch. The rest of the ceremony was not much better.

But I had a great team of divers to work with: Bob Webster, Gary Tobian, Sam Hall, Don Harper, and Dick Conners were among the best divers in the world. There were six slots to fill, but Gary Tobian had qualified to compete on the spring board and the tower so we only had five divers. The first four divers mentioned won gold or silver medals at the Olympics in Rome the following year.

I Use Movies to Coach

I knew all five of these great divers very well, but I had no idea how to coach them in the short time I had with them before the Pan American Games began. I finally came up with an idea. I asked the Pan Am Committee for a Bolex movie camera, and eight-hundred feet of colored film to take movies of each diver's workout. I took one diver at a time into a room, and we watched their dives in slow motion.

In this way, I could look at the movements they used in each dive, and suggest a correction for a movement that they may or may not wish to change. They did a marvelous job in winning both events, and took five of the six medals awarded.

Kimball Turns Professional

Kimball decided to turn professional and do water shows with me after he placed fourth in the Pan American trials. They only took three qualifiers to compete in each of the two diving events in the 1959 Games.

One of the first summer shows we did together was at the Red Roof Country Club in Detroit. Bruce and I had done our show there for nine straight years. We performed the springboard diving from a raft at the end of a long pier for eight years. The raft had a one-meter board at one end, and we always put our scaffold up next to it, and at the other end was a three-meter board.

The raft was kept afloat with oil drums, but one of the drums had a slow leak that caused the raft to tilt to one side a little more each year. Unfortunately, when starting to put the scaffold up this year, the raft tilted enough that the scaffold was in danger of tumbling over. Kimball suggested we put the scaffold up on the pier which would be closer to shore where the people could get a better view of our show. I agreed and wondered why we hadn't done that before.

I soon found out why. Kimball was climbing up the twenty-eight-foot-high scaffold getting ready to perform the first dive from the tower during our show. He asked me to jump in the lake, and test the depth. I jumped in feet first to find myself standing up to my knees in mud with my shoulders still out of the water.

Kimball told me to go down to the bottom, and I yelled I was on the bottom! My legs were in about two feet of muck that meant the depth was only three feet. I knew then why we put the scaffold up on the raft all those years. Kimball asked me what we should do. I told him to go ahead and dive, but do all he could to escape the bottom.

Kimball's first dive was a reverse dive in the pike position. When he tried to touch his feet with his legs in a vertical position, he touched them way too far in front of his body. This meant he would end up hitting the water in a very short position making it nearly impossible for him to avoid the bottom. I was climbing up the back of the scaffold when he was about half way down, and heard him say, "Oh crap!"

He hadn't come up by the time I reached the top. After waiting for minute, he suddenly popped up completely covered with mud with his eyes peeping out that made him look like a mummy. I started to laugh until I realized that I had to dive next. We managed to get through our routine without injury, but diving into the muck caused a large section of the lake to turn grey.

Our World Tour as Ambassadors for the State Department

Bruce and I were supposed to do a world tour giving diving clinics and lectures, and perform our water show as goodwill ambassadors for the State Department in 1959. They called me soon after Bruce died, and asked if I would do the tour alone. I told them if they would postpone the trip for a year, I could get another partner, and they accepted my request.

They were good to their word and called me in 1960. I informed them I had a new partner, and we would like to make the tour after we finished our water shows for the summer. Kimball married Gail a few months before the trip, and about ten days before we were to leave he informed me that he was going to take her along for their honeymoon. I would have also taken my wife, Mary, but she felt she had to stay home and take care of our children.

Our first country was Japan where we were scheduled to visit seven cities that included Osaka, Nagoya, Kanazawa, Komatsu, Takaoka, Kochi, and Tokyo. All our shows were performed outside because there were only four indoor pools in Japan. The mayor in each city had a banquet in our honor after each show. Each time we were introduced like: "We are very honored to have two distinguished diving coaches from the United States. On my right from the University of Michigan, Mister Dick Kimball with a response "áh-so arigato." Then. "On my weft (the "L" was mispronounced) we have from Indiana University, Mister Hobie uh, uh, uh (the "L" again) Biwingsbe." It was always good for a laugh for us because they couldn't pronounce L's.

We carried a lot of luggage from town to town by train that ran on time schedules with computers. We quickly found that if we threw our luggage out the window when the train slowed down for the station, we could quickly get off to gather up all the bags. I remember we did our clinic and show at one town that had long-tailed roosters that were considered sacred. It was unbelievable to see roosters with a tail around six or seven feet long. We really enjoyed our trip to Japan because they were very nice to us, and they did all they could to make our tour as pleasant as possible.

We were supposed to visit Jakarta, Indonesia, next but the State Department canceled our trip because it had just turned communist. A couple of days later the State Department notified us that the trip to Australia was also called off because it was their winter time, and all their outside pools were closed. That left the Philippines as the last country and we soon found it was sadly lacking in gymnastics and diving facilities of any kind mainly because of all the destruction that occurred during the Second World War.

We did our first show in the Rizal stadium that had the only pool in the Philippines with a ten-meter tower. The stadium had the same wooden springboard as when I was there in the service in 1945 and competed in a ping pong match. Rizal stadium had a large grand stand, and when Kimball started our trampoline act performing some basic landing positions, a strange incident occurred.

Their trampoline had been purchased in the Philippines, and the bed on the trampoline was laced with one long shock cord that went completely around the frame. All the trampolines in the states used steel springs to support the mat on the trampoline so this was something different for us. I was sitting in the filled stands dressed up in baggy pants, and waiting for my cue to start our comedy act when the shock cord on their trampoline suddenly came loose while Kimball was jumping up and down.

The single cord unlaced itself much like watching a line of falling dominos. The bed dropped flat to the ground, and Kimball found himself standing there with the trampoline mat under his feet. Thinking it was part of the act, the crowd suddenly went wild. Kimball looked up at me, and asked what we should do next? I remember saying that it beat the hell out of me, so let's go dive from the tower.

We did another show at Santa Tomas University in Manila that had been used as a Japanese torture chamber for American soldiers during the war, and more recently was made into a school for females. The pool was fifty meters long, and the bottom was completely covered with green moss because they had no chemicals, water circulation, or a working filtration system.

We also found that they did not have a diving facility so Dick and I climbed up on top of the filtration shed, and did several dives from a roof that was about eight feet high, ten feet long, and three feet wide. With no room to run for a take-off, we had to perform our dives from a stand while grabbing the metal railings behind us to keep our balance, and could feel the bullet holes that were made from the war. We finished the show with the two of us doing back double somersaults in tandem, and the spectators were very pleased with our show.

163

We then went to Cebu City, south of Manila, where they took us out to a pool that was in the jungle. We saw only monkeys running through the trees when we first arrived at the pool. It had two one-meter cement diving stands that elevated to different heights. Not knowing what a diving board was, they had mounted two twenty-foot long wooden boards ten inches wide on the stands.

When we walked out to the ends of the boards, we ended up standing in water up to our knees. We found a saw, and cut the boards off to a length that we could use for diving. Then we covered the ends with towels so we wouldn't slip diving off in a forward direction. I think we performed more for the monkeys than for people in that show.

When riding in a van that was taking us to do our show and clinic at Santa Maria about a hundred kilometers out of Manila, we found the roads filled with chuck holes from the war that made them very bumpy. The driver suddenly started to accelerate well over fifty miles an hour when Dick yelled at him to slow down because Gail was well into her pregnancy and we didn't want to take the chance of her losing the baby.

The driver said he couldn't slow down because we were passing through "Mao Mao country" where bandits came down from the hills and raped, tortured, and killed people traveling through. So, we had to take our chances with the speed he decided on, and fortunately, Gail didn't lose her baby.

We were free to return home first class after the show, so I decided to complete the trip and go around the world. Unknowingly, Dick and Gail planned to go the same way, but never told me of their plans so we went on our separate ways. I first went to Hong Kong, and bought a whole slew of silk, black velvet paintings, and some wooden statues.

Then I went to Bangkok that still had dirt roads, and found the place dirty. I tried to get out on the first day I arrived, but the travel agency told me they couldn't get me out until the next day. A tour guide suggested that since I had some free time, why not take in a couple of tours? I remarked that tours were for tourists when he reminded me that I was a tourist. So, I reluctantly went on two tours.

I nearly made a horrible mistake wanting to leave as soon as I could because what I saw was hard to believe. I visited several beautiful Siamese temples that seemed like I had gone to a different world.   I also took the floating market tour, and used up all my film taking pictures of the remarkable beauty that I had almost missed. From that time on, I learned that whenever I went to a different country, I would take the tours.

The next city I visited was Calcutta, India.   I spent only one day there because I didn't like looking at the carts that were going around picking up dead bodies on the street in the morning.   I then went to Greece where I saw the Acropolis, and then on to Cairo, Egypt where I visited the pyramids and rode on a camel while the trainer took a picture of me as he yelled, "Hi Yo Silver!" I also went to the Egyptian museum where I was told that if I wanted to really see the precious treasures of Egypt, I would have to go to England.

Rome was my next stop where I saw many historical places, but enjoyed seeing the Coliseum and Saint Peters Cathedral the most. I really enjoyed staying in Barcelona,

Spain for a couple of days because it was a beautiful city with very friendly people. The next city was Monte Carlo that was breath taking before moving on to Paris where I stayed in the same hotel our airline hostess stayed.

She took me to see the Arc de Triomphe one evening. When we arrived, I said how great it was to see where the great armies of the world had marched down Champs Elyse's Street that I read on the street sign. She started to laugh, and corrected me that it was pronounced, "shaump elizae." I later went to visit the Cathedral of Notre Dame, the Eiffel Tower, and the Louvre Museum before leaving for London.

In London, I took two or three tours and really liked the city and the parliament building before flying home. It would take another book to cover what happened and events that occurred while on that trip. But I can say, I don't think I could have made the trip at a better time in my life.

We Continue To Do Our Shows

In the summer of 1961, Kimball, Gail, and I went to Grossinger's, a famous Jewish resort in the Catskill Mountains in upstate New York. Bruce and I had done our water show along with a few other resorts for years over the Fourth of July. This time Grossinger's was sponsoring a world's three-meter diving contest, and the winning prize was a new car.

Around fifteen divers showed up to compete for the car, and I was selected to be the lone diving judge and you may guess who won. I didn't feel guilty about selecting Kimball as the winner because he was, by far, the best diver in the contest.

As always, we went to five or six other resorts before we left to return to Michigan. We stopped to have lunch when we got on the New York State Thruway, and drove for another four hours before we stopped to buy some gas. However, when going to pay for the gas, I couldn't find my wallet. In a state of panic, we pulled everything out of the car and off the trailer, but didn't find my wallet. Luckily there was a state trooper station next to the gas station, so I went over and found a sheriff sitting with his feet up on the desk reading a newspaper.

I told him that I had lost my wallet. Without looking up from the paper, he asked me how much money was in it. When I told him seven hundred dollars in cash, and a thousand dollars in checks, that in those days was a small fortune, the surprised sheriff dropped the paper and asked me where I had lost it. Not knowing the answer, he asked me where was the last place I knew I had my wallet. I told him where we ate lunch near the entrance to the freeway.

He checked a map and found where we got on the freeway. Then he called an officer about an hour from the restaurant, and told him to go over and check it out. It was the Fourth of July weekend with thousands of people on the highway, and the sheriff said that chances of finding the wallet with the money in it were next to none.

About an hour later he got the call from the officer who said, "Is that guy's name Billingsley?" Dick and Gail helped me unhitch the trailer, and I drove back four hours to retrieve the wallet. When the officer handed it to me, he said it was a nearly impossible that all the money was still in it. He found it on the floor under the first table from the buffet line where it had lain for eight hours and nobody had seen it. He said it was unbelievable that someone didn't see the wallet for that long, and he had never heard of such an incident like that before. I tried to give him a hundred dollars for finding it, but he refused the gift because it was against regulations.

We had been up for around 36 hours, an exhausting trip, when we arrived in Ann Arbor. During our return, Kimball said he wanted to go up to Michigan State, and do a 4½ somersault off their outdoor tower. We arrived and unloaded the trailer and car, and I suggested we get some rest. But Kimball said he said he wasn't going to bed because he wanted to go up to Michigan State right way and do the 4 ½ somersault.

Jim Patterson was the only one in the world who had ever performed the dive, and Kimball decided he was going to be the second diver. Thinking he was insane, I agreed to go with him and told him I would call him out of the dive to make sure he knew where he was to prepare for the entry. He successfully performed the dive with the aid of a trampolet that gave him extra spring, and after my call for the first dive, he did the dive two more times without a call.

I well remember when Dick (Kimball) and I did an exhibition for the new pool dedication at the University of Pittsburg in January of 1962. I hadn't dived from a ten-meter tower since the Al Sheehan's Aqua Follies in July, and I was so scared before our show in Pittsburg that I began to get sick. I finally talked myself into performing after pretending it was summer, and Dick told me after the show that it was the best tower diving he had ever seen me do.

We continued to do our own shows at country clubs, and I also took over as captain of the divers in the Al Sheehan Follies for five years after Bruce's death. I decided to retire from doing water shows in 1964 following the end of the Olympic Games. The Al Sheehan show ran for another year after I left, and Dick Kimball took my place as captain of the divers for the last year until Al Sheehan's Aqua Follies folded.

Kimball then teamed up with Ron O'Brien for three years before they also retired from show business. They each started a diving camp in the summer for young divers that made them more money, and used their camps as a means of recruiting divers for their universities. Plus, they could stay home with their families during the summer. I coached four young divers from St. Louis and one from Fort Wayne for nothing while they ran their camps for three years. Then I realized if I was going to compete with them, I would also have to start a diving camp.

CHAPTER 18

The Beginning of My Coaching Career at Indiana

I used to miss a lot of faculty meetings at Ohio University because of attending diving meets away from school. I later found that when taking roll, Carl Nesley would say, "Where's Billingsley?" And he kept right on asking where I was for about a year after I left for Indiana. Years later I heard that he had a heart attack while giving a speech to the graduating class, and dropped dead right on the stage. I always felt sorry that I didn't hear about his loss soon enough to attend his funeral.

Moving to Bloomington

We moved to Bloomington right after the 1959 Pan-American Games. We found the town to be quaint with a court house in the middle of the town square. There were no traffic lights, and had trees over-hanging Kirkwood Street that ran from the court house to the entrance of the university that made it look like a long tunnel.

There were no shopping malls or bypasses around the town, and it had only one high school and post office. There was little growth found in the country during the Depression and World War Two, and that included all the universities throughout the country. Indiana University was no exception. There were only a few dormitories and no outdoor pool. The football stadium held around thirty thousand spectators with a cinder track circling the field, and there were very few parking spaces on the university grounds. The basketball arena was in the indoor fieldhouse, and the eighteen thousand students lived in trailers and small shacks made during World War Two.

Photo Courtesy Indiana University Archives

As mentioned before, the journalism building was named after Ernie Pyle, the famous World War Two newspaper reporter. The addition to the Union offered room accommodations for visitors that were only a couple of years old. The current competition and main pool for students was in the Physical Education building located across the street from the Student Union. It was built in 1919 and looked it. The athletic and physical education departments were bunched in on the second floor along with a gymnasium that was used for classes, and varsity basketball and gymnastic practices.

167

The wrestling team also held their practices in a small room adjacent to the gymnasium. The pavilion was connected to the P.E. building, and had a dirt track that was also used for classes and varsity basketball games when they brought in moveable bleachers that would accomodate eight thousand fans.

To avoid confusion, sports teams varied their seasons with some shorter than others. For example, the football season was in the fall. Sports like swimming, diving, wrestling and gymnastics began in the fall in one year, and ended in the spring of the next year.

Starting a Diving Program in the Old Pool

Right after we moved to Bloomington, I found that the Indiana swimming team didn't have a diving program. The first thing I heard from the athletic department was that they didn't have any money for diving, and as it turned out they never did. Doc's swimmers practiced in the mornings and afternoons with classes using the pool in between.

Photo Courtesy Indiana University Archives

The swimming pool had four lanes with a depth of 8 feet at the deep end and was a hundred feet long with a bulk head that made it 25 yards to meet the standard length for competition. The pool was dimly lit with a ceiling 15 feet above the pool deck. The pool also had a metal diving stand with an aluminum one-meter diving board called a "Townsend board," a brand I had never heard of.

The board projected over the water from one side of the pool. The depth and height made it possible for divers to crack their heads on the ceiling, and hit the bottom performing certain dives. Since the board faced four swimming lanes, it couldn't be used by the divers when swimmers were in the pool. Portable seating for two hundred spectators was brought in for swimming meets.

The ground floor in the P.E. building had dressing rooms for males and females. And like all the other Big 10 schools, the pool was very primitive. Illinois, Indiana and Northwestern were the only colleges that didn't have a three-meter board that meant the three-meter competition was not counted at swimming meets.

Illinois had the worst swimming facility in the country. The pool was eighteen yards long, and located in the men's locker room. The diving stand projected off the corner of the pool with a depth of seven feet. They had to close the men's locker room when they had swimming meets so females could attend.

My First Season 1959-60

There were four eligible divers on the team when I arrived. After coaching them for about three weeks, they came in one day and said they didn't like the way I was coaching them. I was trying to make them champions, and they had come out for diving to receive an easy varsity letter and have a good time. Then they added that if I didn't change my coaching methods, they would all quit.

With that, I said they couldn't quit because they were no longer on the team. I told them to get their things out of their lockers, and get out and don't come back. Why Indiana didn't have any divers was because they didn't have a coach, or decent diving facilities, and very little time to practice.

I still had seven divers to coach, but they were all ineligible. Two were Fred Schlichting, and John Lovestedt (pictured right) who transferred from Ohio University to Indiana. I could coach them, but in changing schools, they were not eligible to compete for a year. The other five were Keith Cradock, Bill Campi, Neal Allen, Dick Schroeder, and John Walker who were all freshmen that I never recruited.

(Pictured below left-right Dick Schroeder, John Walker, Rick Gilbert, Fred Schlicting)

I think the reason why they chose Indiana was because there were only two collegiate diving coaches in the country, and now I was one of them. But being freshmen, none of them were eligible to compete until they were sophomores. That meant I didn't have any divers during my first year at Indiana! Few people knew I was the diving coach for a year because none of my divers were qualified, and we never practiced in the pool when the swimmers were using the pool so they never saw me or my divers. I was also not invited to the swimming party at the end of the season.

Doc had some great young swimmers and the team placed second to Michigan in the Big 10 Conference meet. But Michigan won because they scored 28 more points in diving, and Indiana scored zero. This highlighted the need to develop a good diving program.

The varsity basketball and gymnastic teams practiced in the gym, so I asked Otto Ryser, the gymnastic coach, if I could borrow one of his trampolines. I could put it in the other corner of the gym to prevent any interference with his gymnastic team, and he said no. Not taking no for an answer, I went to George Cousins, the director of the Physical Education Department. I explained my problem, and he got me a trampoline from Otto two days later. This made it possible for me to work the divers out on the trampoline early in the morning, part of the afternoon, and coach diving for a short time in the pool in the evening.

The only time I could coach my divers was early in the evening for one hour. With little pool time to practice, I improvised teaching diving fundamentals using the trampoline in the gymnasium on the second floor of the Fieldhouse above the pool. During the day, I used the trampoline as a training device in the gym to learn basic "take offs" from the board, and aerial movements during dives. I could also teach the basic "lead ups" diving from the one and the three-meter board that we didn't have.

We used the trampoline with the help of a spotting belt that made it possible for the divers to learn the lead-ups for all the three-meter optional dives that included back, reverse, inward double somersaults in the tuck positions, and back and reverse somersaults with 2½ twists with little chance of being injured.

Then, by tilting the trampoline, they also learned a forward 3½ somersault off the front end of the trampoline. By using the spotting belt to stop them, they could land head first with their hands meeting the mat on the floor.

There was a balcony about twelve feet above the trampoline that had a safety rig attached to it. With the divers in the belt, they would try to ring my bell by landing flat on their stomachs on the trampoline. That pulled the ropes up and lifted me up high enough for me to hit my head on the balcony, and they thought it was funny.

Since we practiced in the pool at night and in the gymnasium on the trampoline during the morning and afternoon, the swimmers didn't know I was the diving coach at Indiana for well over a year. I knew things were going to be rough when I took the job at Indiana, but I hadn't anticipated that my divers and I were going to be ignored the way we were.

Only Ineligible Divers to Start

When the swimming season started in the fall of 1959, I went to Doc and told him I had a small problem. I didn't have any eligible divers to compete in any meets. Doc asked me why was I hired. When I said to teach classes and to coach diving, he told me to take care of my own problems and he would take care of his. I then asked if that meant I was my own boss and he replied that it was, but only to a point.

With no eligible divers, the diving event was not announced at any of tho duol mccts. A short break in the meet took its place. Doc then took the swim team into another room for a team meeting, and all the spectators went outside for a smoke or to get some fresh air.

Near the middle of the 1959-60 season Doc told me we had a dual meet coming up in two weeks with Michigan. Doc had a very strong eligible swimming team now with the freshman class recruited the year before, and told me he believed he had a good chance to beat Michigan.

The meet was advertised as the meet of the century because Indiana had never beaten the mighty Michigan teams in swimming. Doc said he had it figured that we could beat Michigan but only by one point and that point would have to come from a diver. For those not acquainted with how points were scored in dual meets then, each team can enter only two athletes in individual events. The top three places score 5, 3, and 1 points respectively so any team competitor in an event is guaranteed at least one point for third.

For those not acquainted with how points are scored in dual meets then, each team can enter three swimmers and divers in a six-lane pool, but only their top two count toward points. The scoring for first, second, and third was 5, 3, and 1 respectively. That meant a team just had to have a competitor complete the event, and they would score one point.

When I reminded Doc that I didn't have any eligible divers to compete in the meet, he said I had better find one and quick. Realizing the importance of the meet, I decided to go over to the journalism building, and advertise for a diver in the school paper. On the way, I ran into Bill Barton, one of Doc's top swimmers. I told him where I was going and why. He said he had a fraternity brother who was a junior who dived in high school, but he was a poor diver and in bad shape. I told him that it didn't matter how bad he was because all we needed was for him to compete against Michigan, and get one point for third place.

Terry Gumz showed up the next day, and performed five compulsory and five optional dives that were needed for him to compete from the one-meter board. His list of dives was so bad that he would have trouble diving against a group of ten-and-under divers, but he was good enough for what we needed.

I told Terry if he would dive in the meet against Michigan, I would give him a varsity letter, and he nearly fell over at my offer. We had an away meet with Iowa the week before meeting Michigan, and he miraculously beat their divers who were worse divers than him! Suddenly, I found that I was working with a person who quickly developed a big head.

The women's pool on campus had a better diving board than ours, so we practiced in their pool. I made a schedule for a two o'clock workout at the pool on Monday after the meet with Iowa. The pool attendant forgot to turn off the hot water in the pool, and the temperature went up to 109 degrees making it too hot to safely work out.

Terry didn't show up for practice on time, so while waiting for him, I had the divers splash water around the deck to make it look like we had been working out. When Terry walked in, I asked him what time it was, and he said it was three o'clock. Then I asked him what time was practice. And he told me it was two o'clock, but he had other things to do. I told him we had already worked out, and to get his suit on and I would coach him for a while.

171

He came out of the dressing room, and started to bounce up and down on the end of the board. He suddenly lost his balance, and fell into the pool. I don't think superman could get out of the pool any faster than he did while cussing and screaming that he felt scalded. We all laughed as I told him that he better not be late again because he may suffer similar consequences.

We took off for Michigan on Friday driving in vans, and by the time we reached Ann Arbor, Terry began to suffer pain from a badly infected tooth that started to make his face swell up on one side. We all stayed at the Michigan Union that night, and it was too late to find a dentist. So, Terry and I sat in their cafeteria all night drinking coffee.

I found a dentist for him early the next morning who said he would see him during his lunch hour. The dentist examined him, and told him he had a badly impacted wisdom tooth. He could either extract the tooth, that may make him sick, or he could inject it with novacain to temporarily kill the pain.

I told Terry that if he decided to have the tooth pulled, I didn't care if he died because I would take his body to the pool and push it off the board six times to get that point. Terry told the dentist to pull it, and with the meet starting at one-thirty, we walked out of the dentist office at one o'clock with blood running down Terry's face and headed for the pool.

The pool was so overcrowded with fans that some were sitting on the edges of the pool cheering for Michigan. We arrived just as the meet was about to start, so Terry didn't get a chance to try out the board before his event. He soon found that he was competing against Bob Webster, two-time Olympic Champion, and Joe Gerlach, a third-place Olympian.

Of course, Terry got slaughtered in the contest, and when the results of the event were announced, Webster took first scoring 387 points, Gerlach was second with 358 points, and Gumz third with 119 points. Terry suddenly jumped up and yelled that he was robbed, and everyone in the pool started to laugh, except me.

I went over to Terry and while pointing my finger at him, I said, "Terry, you are my first diver, and let's see where we go from here!" We won the meet by eleven points, and Terry got his varsity letter then retired. Indiana went on to place second in the 1959-60 Big Ten Championships with Michigan winning by 26 points most of which were made by their divers.

My First Female Divers

The first female diver I coached at I.U. occurred in my first year. Nigel Henry was from Indianapolis competing for a swim club. She placed third on the one-meter board at the National A.A.U. Diving Championships. Doc never knew she was diving with us because of our different schedules. Neal Allen was one of my first male divers and started dating Nigel. When he got her pregnant, they both quit school and got married. Allen enlisted in the Army, and soon afterward stepped on a land mine and was killed in Viet Nam. I believe that he was the first soldier from Indiana to be killed in that war.

Losing both divers, I decided to have a rule that the male divers could not date the female divers. And if they did, the female diver would be off the team because I was being paid to coach male divers, and nothing for coaching female divers. That rule remained through my entire career at I.U. Bill Campi had also joined the team, but quit and that left me with no eligible divers until 1961.

Nancy Lucas (on right in picture) was the second female to dive with us. She was from California and showed up to join my team in my second year. Like Nigel, Doc never knew I was coaching her because he never saw any of our workouts.

We often used the trampoline to practice basic diving skills over in the old Fieldhouse gym. During her second year, Nancy changed her mind doing a back, double somersault on the trampoline, and landed on her head. The injury was severe, but fortunately she didn't break her neck. However, she had to wear a brace for around six months, and her diving career was over. Nancy was very loyal, and we stayed in touch well after I retired. She has always remembered her time with our team, and has never failed to send me a Christmas card.

Hers was the was only serious injury in the thirty years using those trampolines because we gave proper instruction that anticipated what could happen when performing various difficult stunts.

Dibi Everett (pictured previous page on left) showed up when Kimball and I were performing our diving show in Toledo, Ohio. She was a sophomore at the University of Wisconsin, and had taken a bus from Madison. She wanted to know if I would coach her if she changed schools to attend Indiana. Like all the other colleges in the country, Wisconsin didn't have a diving program for females.

I didn't know anything about her, but said I would give her a chance. After she changed colleges, I learned that she had one leg about an inch shorter than the other caused by polio. It didn't slower her down. She learned a full list of dives on the three-meter board, and competed in the National A.A.U. Women's Championships, and the 1960 Olympic tryouts, that I didn't attend.

She married a swimmer from Michigan State soon after graduating from Indiana, and got a job with a T.V. station in Chicago interviewing local people that lasted for around thirty-five years. She had two children and four grandchildren, and at the age of fifty decided to start training to compete in age group triathlon contests.

The contestants were required to swim 1.5K, ride a bicycle 40K, and finish with a 10K run. She won her first USA national age group title, and went on to qualify for the USA team to compete in the ITU World Championships held in Sydney, Australia. She competed in the 65-69 age group, and won her first world title.

She went on to win the world title two more times, and dedicated her second title to me. She told me that she competed at the World Championships against an average of a dozen other women who were younger than her because few women in their seventies could take the physical challenge at her age.

CHAPTER 19

My Teaching Assignments

Teaching Classes at Indiana University

The administration had me teach all kinds of activity classes like gymnastics, swimming, diving, badminton, handball, tennis, and bowling that was in the Student Union. I also taught a course in a classroom entitled, "The Organization and Administration of Physical Education." This course was also taught by two professors. They usually averaged around fifteen students in their classes, and my classes had around seventy students. The reason for the difference in attendance was because I had taught four years in high school, and had a lot of stories that related to the course when neither professor had ever taught in a high school.

A Christmas Story

I remember teaching a swimming class of 45 students in the old pool near Christmas time. I took roll with names of the students in alphabetical order. Not knowing any of the students, I added the name "Claus" to remind the class that it was near Christmas. I then told them since it was Christmastime, I would give an "A" to anyone who could swim a length of the pool underwater. Then I added they had to swim feet first, and if they failed to make the distance they would flunk the course.

Thinking that no one would try it, one student said he would take the challenge, and I warned him again of the consequences if he failed. He pushed off the side of the pool and came to the surface after swimming about ten feet. I told him he flunked, and asked him his name. And he said, "Claus," and we all had a big laugh.

Student Protests

Those were the days in the sixties when students were protesting in colleges all over the country that Included Indiana. Drugs, drinking, sex, and other forms of loose behavior were destroying the education system in our schools until the Kent State incident occurred that resulted in several students getting killed. I got involved in all of this because I really cared for my students and was willing to take my chances in protesting the protestors. Unless you lived through that era, there is no way to describe how bad things were, but I will mention two of the many incidents in which I got involved.

My Protest Over Student Visitation

The first was visitation. This movement involved females who lived in dormitories. They were required to be in their buildings by ten o'clock from Monday through Friday, and could stay out until one o'clock on weekends. Male students had no curfew, and

175

were only permitted to visit females in the reception rooms or lobbies on the ground floor of the dormitories up to a given time. Visitation changed those rules by permitting men to go up into a female's room anytime, and stay if they wished. I was very much against this movement because it eliminated a woman's right to privacy, and placed them in danger of being molested and/or raped. It also interfered with a roommate's privacy when a male could stay overnight with his girlfriend at her roommate's discomfort or resentment.

I was so upset about this that I asked for a few moments to discuss the movement with our faculty at their next meeting. When they were about to adjourn, George Cousins, the chairman of our department, told the faculty to remain, and listen to what I had to say. I told them I wanted to discuss visitation, and some of the teachers started to laugh.

Many in the room didn't know anything about visitation until I explained it to them. I used my sixteen-year-old daughter, Nancy, as an example. I said that I didn't want my daughter to be in a position where a male could be invited up to her room to discuss a subject, like history, only to find that he had something else in mind.

The male student could tell her they weren't going to cover that subject tonight because they were going to discuss biology, specifically sex. It was quickly found that the sexual incidents increased some of which were never reported because the females were afraid, confused, and ashamed when molested or abused.

The faculty no longer thought my presentation was funny when Doc Counsilman suggested that I write a petition protesting visitation to find out how many faculty members would agree or disagree with it. I wrote the petition that night, and passed it out to those working in the physical education and athletic departments the next day, and every person in both departments signed the disagreement except the dean of our physical education department.

Unfortunately, visitation was a national movement, and it turned out to be too late to make any difference as Indiana University accepted the new movement. I went over to see a friend who oversaw all the dormitories on the campus a couple of weeks later, and asked him how things were working out with visitation. He said people were stealing around $50,000 worth of furniture out of the dormitories every month while finding hundreds of people living in the dorms that didn't attend Indiana.

Students Strike Campuses

The second incident occurred in the late 1960's when the students went on strike at universities all around the country. I went over to Bryan Hall to teach a class one morning when I found students locked arm to arm around the whole building. Not knowing that the movement was already happening around the country, I asked the students to let me through so I could teach my class. But they refused because they said they were on strike. I said I wasn't on strike so let me pass, but again they refused. I put my books down and took off my coat, and prepared to fight my way through the line. Just then a couple of students came walking by, and told the striking students to

176

let me through because I was a coach and a good guy and they let me go by. I had forty-four students in the class, and exactly half of them showed up on the second floor.

I rarely took roll because students usually wanted to attend my classes. But I did this time, and told them how proud I was for having the courage to break through the line to attend my class. I also added that they were all going to get an "A" in the course.

I asked one of the students to go down and get someone who was striking to come to our class, so we could discuss the problem. When a student was brought in and I asked why he was striking, he said he had no idea and was only doing it because all his buddies were. The strike went on for a little while longer then suddenly stopped when some students that were striking at Kent State were accidently shot and killed by a few Ohio National Guard troops sent in by the Governor to protect campus buildings.

I Start Teaching Diving Classes

The administration stopped having me teach non-diving courses after a few years at Indiana, so I ended up teaching diving classes along with the Administration and Organization of Physical Education class. I started the diving courses with a short lecture on what was expected of them in class. I described what they were going to learn, and to try not to miss any classes because they were going learn the dives in progression. This meant that they would be introduced to a new dive in every class they attended.

I also told them the course gave them one hour of credit and would meet twice a week for forty-five minutes. I told them that they would find it to be the best course they would ever take at Indiana University. I continued to say that the reason for making such a statement was because they were going to be exposed to fear, and learn how to work with it.

I rarely had any students with competitive diving experience. Most of them were total beginners. I even had a couple of students who wanted to take the course but were non-swimmers, and couldn't take the course until they learned to swim.

The main objective of the course was to have the students learn how to perform thirteen dives from the one-meter springboard, and learning any dives from the three-meter board were optional. I taught the diving class for nearly twenty-five years, and enjoyed every minute. When I got ready for school living up on the hill in Blue Ridge, I used to stand on the front steps of my house overlooking Indiana University, and say, "Good morning, God, I'm ready to mow them down again so step aside because here I come."

It was hard to believe how the people in my class learned to dive so fast when they knew practically nothing about diving. Miss Aldrich, then the Dean of the Physical Education Department, walked into one of my diving classes one day near the end of my teaching career. She watched me teach a class for a few minutes before leaving. She returned about a month later, and asked where was the class I had been teaching earlier? When I said, it was the same group, she didn't believe me, because what she saw now was a bunch of students performing all kinds of dives with good form.

I Challenge My Students

They were challenged from the first class to the last class on how to perform dives they never dreamed were possible for them to learn. I tried to impress those in the diving classes that they were not only learning the fundamental rudiments of diving, but also learning more about themselves. I went on to say they were learning to master and control their fears through sound reasoning, basic explanations, and logic. I also

Come on Bungum, you can make it!!

tried to inject certain basic mechanical principles in their learning process to see if they could understand why certain moves were made to avoid pain and fear that could remain with them for a lifetime.

I used a lot of psychology in teaching, most of which was related to group dynamics. That meant, if a student was afraid to attempt a new dive, he or she should watch another diver in class who could do the dive, but wasn't as good at diving as the one who was afraid. He or she would then think if that person could perform the dive, so could they.

The fear in the activity was related to the possibility of being injured if they landed flat on the water or hit the board. So, I explained how to prevent such an incident, and all that was needed from them was to do what I said and trust me. When they saw how the system worked, they learned very quickly. I also found that a humorous but firm approach to teaching brought good results.

Of course, some students learned how to perform certain dives quicker than others. But with patience and good instruction, the students who learned 13 dives received an "A," a "B" for 12 dives, and a "C" for learning most of the other dives.

We occasionally had a day when we didn't get around to taking the whole time to perform dives because we got into discussing what and where they were going with their lives, and how to meet certain goals by controlling their fears. Looking back at those days, I guess I used diving as a gimmick to help them learn how to handle future challenges in life that involved fear.

On the last day of class, they were given the chance to jump off the five-meter platform. Over the years, they all did it except once when a young student balked. The rest of the students in my class, and another class taking a written test in the bleachers, were all yelling for him to jump. But he wouldn't do it. So, I climbed up on the platform, and held his hand while telling him I was going to jump with him after I counted to three.

I pretended to jump after the count, but I didn't go and neither did he, and everyone had a good laugh. I then told him to sit on the edge of the tower and put his arms above his head, and when he lifted them, I dropped him off the edge and everyone in the pool began to cheer.

All Sorts of People Take My Diving Class

All sorts of people took the course including heavy set and older people with some in their late forties, plus and an occasional faculty member. I once had a female university professor who weighed about eighty pounds and taught Chinese. She took the course four times. Several of our swimmers took the class and that included Mark Spitz, who I had recruited to come to Indiana.

Mark won seven gold medals and broke seven world records at the 1972 Olympic Games in Munich, Germany. One day, while being interviewed, he was asked what was the greatest experience he ever had besides winning all those medals. And he said it was taking my diving class. He was trying to perform a half gainer that scared him to death because he thought he would hit his head on the diving board. After a month of trying to get up the nerve, he finally did the dive then ran all around the pool yelling, "I did it!"

(Side Bar) Story

I think it is worth noting that I used to take the last diving period of each class in the winter semester to talk to my students about the miracle of Christmas. The discussion took the whole period. Some of the highlights were when I told them that the miracle of Christmas was one day of the year when everyone gave to others, and what a shame Christmas didn't occur every day.

I went on to say that the value of the gifts was meaningless unless given unselfishly and to make others happier. That's what Santa Claus and the birth of Jesus Christ was all about. I told the story of when I was five years old, and my mother knitted a sweater for me. The sweater was the only present she could give me for Christmas because she didn't have any money to buy me a toy.

I was never able to tell the full story without breaking up. I suggested near the end of my talk, how they could give their parents the greatest gift of all, and it wouldn't cost them a cent. I told them (particularly the freshmen) that when they went home for Christmas vacation, they probably wouldn't be in the house for more than a few minutes before they would be gone to visit friends and participate in other activities with little concern for their parents.

I finished by suggesting that they select an evening to gather their parents and family together, and turn off the television, radio, phones, and outside lights. Then sit down with their loved ones for one hour and chat with them. I warned them that at times it would be difficult to get their parents to talk because they wouldn't know what to say.

But if that occurred, tell them about things that happened to you at school, and then stop talking. This would let their parents talk about stories and incidents that had happened to them earlier in their lives. And if their parents still didn't talk, to ask them questions about what they were doing when they were young. I told them that they might be amazed to learn things about their folks that they hadn't known before.

I reminded the students that the talk would probably be the only moment they would have in their vacation to fill their parents in on how things were going at college. The whole class just sat there and cried the last time I ever gave that talk and got up and hugged each other saying "Merry Christmas." That last class has always been one of the best Christmas moments I have ever had.

I had one student who took my diving class three times and just before the Christmas holiday one year. As the students returned to Indiana he came into the pool while I was having practice and said he wanted to talk to me. He said he had just returned to school and had ignored my suggestion to spend one hour with his folks until this year.

He went on to say he sat down with his father in the living room. After turning off all the means of communication, they had a couple drinks, and he talked about a few things he was doing at school then stopped talking. He was surprised when his father suddenly opened-up, and told him all kinds of stories that he had never heard before. With tears in his eyes, he told me he had just attended his father's funeral, and wanted to thank me for convincing him to spend that one hour with his loved one when he got to really know his father.

To show how much a teacher can affect a person's life occurred about ten years after my retirement. I received a telephone call from a man in Martinsville who said he wanted to talk to me. I asked him what about, and he said it was nothing really important. I offered to drive up to Martinsville, but he said he would rather drive down to Bloomington and meet me at my house.

After class, he showed up, and said that he had taken my diving class years ago. He recalled one day in class when we had about a twenty-minute discussion about his life, and what he wanted to do with it. He went on to say that he had the largest Chevrolet truck dealership in the country in Indianapolis, and he would have never been successful if I hadn't offered him those suggestions. Of course, I was shocked at what he said, but he said it with great sincerity. And it was times like that, that made me feel teaching and coaching was well worthwhile.

CHAPTER 20

The 1960-1961 Season

My Only Eligible Divers

John Lovestedt and Keith Cradock were the only eligible divers on my team beginning the 1960-1961 swimming season. Indiana had never scored any points in diving at the Big Ten Championships. That ended when Cradock and Lovestedt, went to the Big 10, scored eleven points, and we won our first Big Ten Championship meet by six points.

Next John Walker was a freshman who won the Indiana State High School diving title, but decided to go out for Doc's team as a breaststroker. About half way through the 1960 winter semester he was cut, and decided to try out for the diving team. (Pictured are John Lovestedt and John Walker)

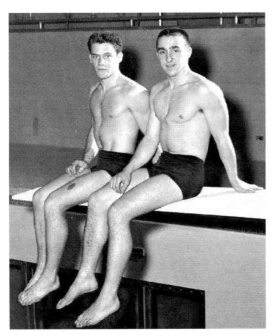

We were working the divers out on the trampoline when John approached me, and I told him to get dressed so I could see if he could qualify for my team. Having never worked on a trampoline, he didn't show me much that would make my team. So, I asked him if he would like to be my manager. He pleaded to let him work out with us for a week, and he suddenly learned to perform some difficult stunts so I decided to keep him.

My next move was to teach the boys how to perform the dives from a three-meter board. The new Royer Pool was not completed and our old pool did not have a three-meter board. I found a pool in an Indianapolis hospital that had a three-meter board, but it was fifty miles away. I taught them how to do all the dives in two days, but they paid a painful price often landing flat on the water. I knew we wouldn't have to travel far if any of them were seriously injured, because they were already in the hospital.

181

I now had three eligible divers. When the diving event was announced at our first dual meet of the season, the spectators in the pool, from habit, started to get up to leave. I was standing by the exit and asked them to please sit down again. Once they were settled, I told them that my divers were doing their best to help the swimming team, and I would appreciate it if they showed a little respect and courtesy for their efforts.

1961 Spring Indoor National A.A.U. Championships

Four new male divers were added to my diving team in 1960, and I took them to the 1961 Spring Indoor National A.A.U. Championships. To show how much our team had improved at the national level, this is how they placed:

One-meter (48 divers entered)			Three meter (38 divers entered)		
8th place	Keith Craddock	357.20	11th place	Keith Cradock	222.15
12th place	John Lovestedt	206.85	17th place	Tom Dinsley	113.50
13th place	Fred Schlichting	204.75	21st place	Fred Schlichting	111.40
20th place	Dean Allen	104.90	25th place	John Lovestedt	103.25
22nd place	John Walker	104.50	26th place	Dean Allen	102.10
24th place	Tom Dinsley	104.35	31st place	John Walker	96.80
37th place	Dick Schroeder	82.90	38th place	Dick Schroeder	75.10

Christmas Break Training

For years, I used to go to Ft. Lauderdale during the Christmas holidays, and give lectures on diving to divers and coaches from different schools. This went on until the director asked me if I could do something different to get away from the same old same old. I decided to give a clinic on how to teach different diving stunts and lead-ups with the use of the trampoline, and used Don Harper as my demonstrator. Don had placed second in the 1960 Olympics diving at Ohio State, and was fantastic on the trampoline.

Half way through the clinic I realized the trampoline method I had been doing to teach diving at Indiana worked. and started a trend used by other coaches. Later I learned that Bobby Clotworthy, the Ohio State Olympic three-meter gold medal winner at the 1956 Melbourne Olympics and the swimming coach at Princeton University, used the trampoline for the same reason. So, we both were given credit for being the first to use the trampoline to coach divers.

CHAPTER 21

The New Royer Swimming Pool

The new Royer Pool was dedicated in the Spring of 1961. The new facility compared to the old pool in the Physical Education building was like night and day. Now we could begin to recruit in earnest because we had a nice facility.

The large new addition to the H.P.E.R building had been started in early 1959. It included a new 25-yard swimming pool that was desperately needed. They decided to name the new complex the Royer Pool after the deceased swimming coach Bob Royer.

New Royer Pool Courtesy Indiana University Archives I had just arrived in Bloomington when Doc took me to see the campus and construction of the new facility. While showing me the hole they had dug to start the new building, he said that we were going to build a dynasty in that hole someday. I was taken by his comment, and never forgot what he said. As I started my job, it was exciting to watch the new addition being built every day.

Doc was just in time to learn that the swimming pool plan called for only five lanes when six lanes was the standard number. The builders corrected the architect's error by widening the pool to six lanes, but that decreased the width of the pool deck. However, they didn't narrow the decks around the diving well. The diving well was to have two one-meter and two-three meter stands with aluminum Duraflex diving boards. These state-of-the-art new boards would make it possible for divers to perform more somersaults and twists than any previously made board.

Unfortunately, the one-meter and three-meter outer boards were installed eight feet from the sides of the pool when they were supposed to be, by standard, ten feet from the edge. So, our divers dived from two boards that were illegal throughout my entire career as a teacher and coach at Indiana.

My 1961-62 Season

Indiana built Assembly Hall in the early 1960's. It was a large arena used for basketball practice and games. The Athletic Department, gymnastic, and wrestling teams moved into the Hall which gave me room to use more trampolines in the old gym in the P.E. building. I used three trampolines with spotters on all four sides, and a fourth with a

183

spotting rig so I could safely teach various stunts before the divers practiced their moves on another trampoline. The only serious injury we had in the thirty years using the trampolines was with Nancy Lucas. This was because I gave proper instruction and anticipated what could happen doing various difficult stunts.

One year later, freshman Rick Earley was warming up bouncing on the three-meter board. He had performed the hurdle but landed on the corner end of board off balance. He had to decide when taking off whether to try to enter the water without hitting the edge of the pool or jump to the deck. He decided on the latter, and landed on the deck hard on his heels.

Unfortunately, he couldn't wear shoes for about two weeks, and that was the only incident that occurred diving from one of the illegal boards. Rick went on to make the 1972 Olympic Team in the platform event at age 28. Other than that, I found the diving well to be ideal for coaching diving because the diving boards were close to the pool sides, and the diving well was small enough for divers to hear my directions without me shouting. We also liked it because the water in the diving well was warm.

I later made some improvements to the pool one of which included installing heating units in the wall behind the boards to keep the divers warm between dives, and I pad for that out of my pocket. During construction, I got approval to install an aluminum five-meter platform above the one-meter boards and ten feet below the twenty-four-foot-high ceiling.

I guessed at the height of the platform with the use of a broom stick and was fortunate to find my guess to be accurate. The builders didn't know anything about diving towers. They extended the platform over the diving well so far that a diver could easily hit the other side of the pool. So they had to shorten its length by about four feet.

The overhead lights in the pool were so dim I could hardly see to coach my divers. If I turned the light switch off and on a couple of times on the wall in the pool, two or three lights in the ceiling would blow out. It was so bad that television groups had to bring their own lighting facilities to cover big meets. The large bay windows on the wall above the pool office offered some lighting from the outside, but not enough to make a difference in the lighting over either pool.

I had enough trouble trying to coach my divers in semi darkness for years, so one day, I went over to the utilities department and talked to the supervisor that I knew quite well. When I complained about using "seconds" bulbs in the ceiling and not able to see, he told me to mind my own business, and get my ass out of his office.

We had a long weekend coming up when the students and faculty were gone from the campus for three days. I went downtown to a hardware store, and had them install nine florescent lights in the ceiling overlooking the diving well. They put them in on the weekend when no one was around, and it cost me three thousand dollars which was nearly half of the salary I was making for the year.

The supervisor found out what I did and was ready to kill me. Then Doc went and told him to put similar lighting over the swimming pool, and it was done for no charge! I had the one-meter and three-meter stands changed from metal to cement years later,

184

and was surprised I wasn't charged for that job too. The seating capacity on both sides of the pools held a little over a thousand fans which made Royer Pool an ideal site for swimming and diving meets.

CHAPTER 22

Four Years on Probation

University President Calls for a Meeting

I was at Indiana for a little over a year when Herman B Wells, the president of Indiana University, requested all the athletic coaches meet with him in the Student Union. He informed us that the N.C.A.A. had just put the entire athletic program at Indiana on probation for four years. Phil Dickens, the IU head football coach, had gotten caught for illegal recruiting in Chicago for the second time in two years.

When caught the first time, he was prohibited from coaching his football players on the field, and had to sit with the fans during games. The team was not permitted to play in a Bowl game for two years. Then Phil turned around and made the same mistake again that resulted in the worst penalty the N.C.A.A. had ever given to a college.

This sort of punishment meant that we probably would not be able to recruit any good athletes for many years because the effect of that period would last longer than the probation period. Thankfully, the penalty allowed athletes to compete in dual meets and the Big Ten Conference, but not in a Bowl game or any N.C.A.A. National Championships.

I remember walking out of the Union with Doc. He asked me if I knew of any other college that needed a swimming coach, and I told him I didn't. I immediately called Gus Stager at the University of Michigan, and asked him if the diving job was still open at Michigan. Dick Kimball had taken the job as a graduate assistant that year, and Gus said they decided to stick with Kimball.

Bob Allen, the Indiana athletic director, and Phil Dickens, along with his entire coaching staff were fired. And Bill Orwig, a Michigan graduate, was hired as the new athletic director. Doc and I moped around for about two weeks when he came to me and said he decided to stick it out with the probation because he had no other place to go. I also didn't have a place to go because there were only two college diving coaches in the whole country, and I was one of them. So I also decided to stick it out with Doc. Doc and I realized the impact of the probation when we drove over to Ohio State in Columbus, Ohio to watch the 1962 N.C.A.A. National Swimming and Diving Championships, and we had to pay to get into the meet.

Scholarships were not given until after the Second World War, and the swimming team received twenty full scholarships every four years. I received one full scholarship every year that couldn't be broken down. That meant if I gave a diver books, it was considered a full scholarship. Keith Craddock was the best diver on the team, so I gave him my first scholarship.

The Mind Set

Realizing that it would probably be many years before I could recruit another decent diver, I decided to change my image to be the kind of coach by which any athlete would like to be coached. I decided not to smoke cigarettes, never go into a bar, tell dirty jokes, or use foul language. And to be respectful to my colleagues, divers and students, I would act as a professional and dress in a coat and tie to work every day before changing into some other duds to coach. I thought if I offered this kind of mind set and gave them the best I had to offer, I could challenge my divers into not only learning to dive and compete well, but also help to make them into better persons.

Knowing there was no way I could recruit a good diver while on probation, I decided to offer a meet for young girls and boys between the ages of ten and seventeen. I had the first meet in the summer of 1960 held in Royer pool that was called "Hobie's Little Nationals," and it was. It drew a tremendous number of divers because age group diving was just beginning to develop in our country, and age group competitive meets were scarce.

I gave trophies to the top three winners, and nice medals to those who finished fourth through six places. Every diver also got a T shirt with the name of the meet on the front. The meets were held through 1971 indoors until the new outdoor pool was built in 1965. But if the weather was bad, we'd go indoors. Kids came from all over the country, and it was soon recognized as the place to go because everyone had a good time and they were well treated.

CHAPTER 23

The L-5 Mumbo Jumbo

My Divers Teach Me

John Lovestedt transferred from Ohio University to Indiana to continue being coached by me. He came into the pool his junior year about two years after I had just started my career at Indiana in 1959. He said he was going to perform a back dive in the pike position while using his "L-5." I didn't have the slightest idea what he was taking about. He told me that after touching his feet at the peak of the dive, he would extend his arms in a lateral direction over his head for the entry.

However, when performing the dive, his arms didn't reach overhead laterally, but instead moved in a semi-lateral direction. Going along with his humor, I told him he didn't do the L-5, but instead, did a G-4 that I made up on the spot. I went on to warn him not to do an S-2, meaning, the arms would extend overhead shoulder width apart, or a B-3, that meant the arms would bend close to the body at shoulder level before extending them overhead for the entry all of which I made up as a joke.

A Charade Turns into Science

I went along with this charade for a few days because it was fun. Then I realized that I could control the movements of the dive while the diver was in the air by shouting a short trigger signal. This opened a new way to communicate with the divers that no one had thought of before.

This new method improved my coaching by reducing the time a diver needed to correct certain movements while in the air I found this greatly improved the learning process for all divers. Prior to this find, all coaches communicated with their divers before and after performing a dive, and never thought to communicate with the diver while in the air for around one and five eights of a second.

My 1961-1962 Team

I suddenly found that I had an army of divers, and the only ones I recruited were Rick Gilbert and Chris Unrue. I gave both a scholarship, but Chris hurt his shoulder and never competed on our team.

Jim Everroad, Jim Blickenstaff, John Walker, Bill Scribner, Bob Keller, Terry Fish, Eddie Doerr, Denny McPherson, Dick Schroeder, and Rick Gilbert all showed up to dive for Indiana in the fall of 1961. Nigel Henry was followed by Nancy Lucas from California, and Dibi Everett from Chicago.

(Left-Right John Walker, Jim Blickenstaff, James Everroad, Dick Schroeder, Rick Gilbert)

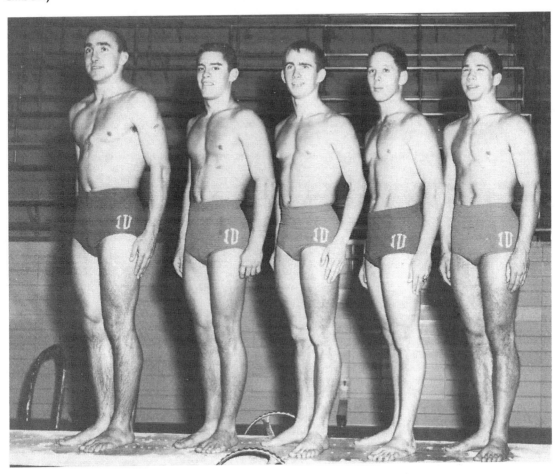

Denny McPherson dived on our team, but didn't make the finals in any of our meets and dropped off the team his second year. However, before quitting, the new football stadium had just been built. Denny had a few hundred parachute jumps in his career, and he and two of my other divers decided to parachute onto the field before I.U.'s first game.

My other two divers were very limited in performing parachute free falls, and they ended up landing in the stadium parking lot. I remember watching Denny pulling his legs up to avoid hitting the side of the stadium. That side was about seventy feet high, and if he hadn't pulled up his legs he probably would have been killed.

Discovering the Use of Science to Coach Diving

The only way diving coaches all over the world taught their divers how to dive from 1889 to the early 1960's was by copying the actions of the better divers, and by trial

189

and error. To this day there has never been a single written word how to perform a perfect dive when a new and better way to coach diving was in the making.

One day in 1961, Doc came down to watch me coach, and asked me if I knew what I was talking about when I was coaching. I told him that I must know something because I had worked with the best divers in the world from the time I started to dive in college. He asked me again if I was sure, and then asked me if I knew who Isaac M. Newton was. Trying to be a smart aleck, I said, "wasn't he the guy who dropped the ball off the leaning tower of Pietsa?" Doc laughed, then said, "No, that was Galileo, and it wasn't Pietsa, it was Pisa." Then I told Doc I knew that and was only joking with him.

Doc planted the seed and I couldn't block out why he had asked me those questions. I was confronted with a similar episode about a week later. I was showing some movies to my divers that I had taken when I coached the Pan American divers after Harlan's death. One of those films was Bob Webster performing an inward dive in the layout position from the three-meter board.

I filmed the dive standing on the deck near the back end of the diving stand that gave me a clear shot of Bob's face. I saw how easily Bob pushed his legs up behind him on the take off. All divers normally contort their face while performing all dives, but Bob had so much strength in his legs his didn't.

Fred Schlichting, my diver from California who had transferred from Ohio, said that Bob wasn't doing the dive with the strength of his legs, but doing it with his arms. I thought Fred was crazy, and had little knowledge of how to perform dives. I asked him how could he have done that. Fred went on to explain.

He said that while standing on the end of the board, the weight of the diver causes the board to bend downward. If the board was made level again without the diver changing position, he would be leaning forward in toward the board. Then, apply Newton's Third Law of Motion that states "For every action, there is an equal and opposite reaction."

When the arms pull down laterally starting the dive from overhead, they would move in a backward direction. This would cause the feet to be pushed forward into the board, and the board would push the feet backward with an equal force. That would cause the legs to be pushed backward and upward in the dive.

I was astounded at what Fred said, and began to realize that I didn't know a darn thing about diving. But neither did anyone else except Fred, and two English bio-mechanic experts. Geoffrey Dyson authored, The Mechanics of Athletics in 1962 on how science is applied to the various motions used in sports such as diving, track, and gymnastics. George Rackham also wrote a book in the late 1950's on how to apply scientific principles to the performance of dives. I started to study their methods and became the first diving coach to apply their scientific principles. For some unknown reason, none of the other diving coaches in the world had picked up on it.

After hearing Fred's simple explanation and studying the information given by the experts in both of those books, I suddenly found that I could coach in the direction of perfection by using scientific principles based on Newton's Laws of Motion that offered a new way of coaching diving throughout the world.

With Indiana still on probation it wasn't long before my divers began to learn to perform dives properly in an amazingly short period. This also reduced the number of repetitions normally used to learn how to perform dives by trial and error. In plain words, the more I applied science to the performance of a dive, the quicker the divers learned how to dive.

I couldn't get to the pool to coach the divers soon enough to learn more how Newton's Laws could be used in the performance of dives. At times, I questioned what Newton meant only to eventually find later that I didn't understand, and had to admit to myself I was wrong. I challenged myself to see how I could use this new technique that was based on irrefutable scientific principles. And I don't think I ever got so excited about anything since I had become a Christian at the age of sixteen.

My new discovery occurred in 1961, and I began to start using some science in early 1962 that permitted me to jump ahead of all the other diving coaches in the world. They were still coaching their divers by copying someone else or using the trial and error method. Learning to master the use of science to coach diving took a couple of years.

I remember listening to Laura Schlesinger on the radio many years later, and I was astounded on how quickly she could answer every question presented to her by troubled people. I believed she could do so because she had a strong psychological base from which she could draw her answers, and that was exactly what I found I was doing when I formed a scientific base for coaching diving. It didn't take long before I could answer any question correctly when asked about the performance of any dive.

CHAPTER 24

Rick Gilbert the Diver Who Made Me a Diving Coach

I Get a Tip

A few days after we were put on probation, one of my divers told me that he heard about a good diver in Lancaster, Pennsylvania. His name was Rick Gilbert (pictured on right). Knowing that there was little to no chance of recruiting a good diver, I got his address and decided to write him a letter. But I got no response. I kept writing Rick several more letters well over a month when he finally wrote back probably because he began to feel sorry for me. I then called him a couple of times, but still had no idea how good of a diver he was. I asked him if he had any diving movies or pictures of himself. He sent a short movie, and I was stunned to see how much talent he had.

Rick Gilbert was a senior in high school when he decided to dive in the 1961 Indoor National A.A.U. Championships at Yale University the first week of April. Fred Schlichting, John Walker and a couple of my other divers went to the meet with me, and competed for experience. The N.C.A.A. rules said I could only wave at Rick, and not have any contact with high school seniors except by phone or mail.

I wasn't surprised when he placed seventh on the one-meter board and that was a remarkable feat for a high school diver. My divers and I went to a restaurant after the meet when Rick walked in with a whole bunch of Ohio State divers, and sat in a booth right behind ours. We could hear them trying to talk Rick into going to Ohio State.

My Communication with Rick

As a senior eligible for a scholarship, he could visit five schools. I phoned him when we got home, and asked if he would include Indiana as one of his recruiting trips. He visited Indiana in late April for his last visit, and I had the chance to spend some time with him. Sorry to say, I didn't think he was impressed with our facilities, the school, or my divers, and after he went home I thought my chances of him attending Indiana were zero.

Scholarships were sent out the first of May, so on the last night of April, I called Rick to learn what college he had decided to attend. I thought it would be either Ohio State or Michigan because they had the best diving programs in the country and were also top schools academically.

After visiting both schools, Rick said that he liked the Ohio State campus more than Indiana's, and I said I could understand that because I had gone to Ohio State for five years. He went on to say that Ohio State was known to have the best diving coach in the world, and who was I. I said that I was new in coaching, and just getting started in my career.

Rick went on to say we had a lousy pool with only a one-meter board when I reminded him that we should have a new pool by next fall about the time he would arrive. Then he reminded me that Ohio State was loaded with top divers who would help him become a better diver, and I didn't have any outstanding divers. I had to agree with everything he said, and my voice got softer and softer with every comment.

He finally came up with the clincher when he said that Indiana was on probation for four years, and he would never get the chance to compete in an N.C.A.A. Championship meet until his junior year, and I agreed with him then went silent.

The Suspense

Waiting for the guillotine to cut off my head, he then said he had made up his mind and was coming to Indiana. I put the phone down, and broke down because I couldn't believe what I had just heard. I asked him, with a broken voice after getting some composure, if he was kidding me, and he said "no" because anyone who had tried as hard as I had to get him to go to Indiana, deserved the chance to make him a champion. Still sobbing, I promised him that he would never be disappointed for making that decision.

The Decision that Changed Destiny

I didn't know it at the time that his decision to come to Indiana changed the destiny of my coaching career plus the careers of a couple of other swimming and several diving coaches. If Gilbert had decided to attend Ohio State, which was his second choice, I would have ended up being his coach later because Bob Bartels, the swimming coach at Ohio University was made the swimming coach at Ohio State after Mike Peppe retired.

I would have gone to Ohio State with him because Indiana was still on probation. That meant all the divers I later coached at Indiana might have gone to Ohio State, and their diving dynasty would have continued for another twenty-five years. It would have also affected the swimming and diving dynasties that were later created at Indiana.

Rick Gilbert showed up on campus in the fall of 1961, and like most college freshmen, had little experience working on a trampoline or diving from a three-meter board because it wasn't an event in high schools. He quickly learned to perform all the lead-up stunts on the trampoline that were needed for him to perform the optional dives on the three-meter springboard except the back somersault with two and a half twists.

He tried to learn the stunt for nearly a month with no success even when all of our divers had learned it. He became so frustrated that he began to cry in practice one day because no matter how hard he tried, nothing worked. I told him that I had tried everything I could think of so he would just have to keep trying.

With that challenge, he got up on the trampoline and unbelievably performed the stunt on his first attempt. What happened was, he had relieved himself of all the frustration, confusion and despair he had built up that had been preventing him from being able to relax and concentrate on the stunt.

Thanksgiving came about two weeks later, and Rick asked me if he could go home to Lancaster for the holidays to be with his folks. I challenged him to learn a full list of dives from the three-meter board, and if he didn't, he would have to stay. Then I asked him if I was being fair. He said I was, and learned them in less than the time we agreed on.

Since the N.C.A.A. at the time didn't permit athletes to compete until they were sophomores, the only meet our freshman divers could compete in was the Men's National A.A.U. Championships that were to be held in Bartlesville, Oklahoma in early April 1962.

The Rest of my 1962 I.U. Men's Diving Team

John Walker, Jim Blickenstaff, Jim Everroad, Dick Schroeder, Rick Gilbert John Vogel, Pete Rhodes, Tom Dinsley.

Vogel was a terrific diver from Columbus, Indiana who attended Purdue University majoring in Engineering, a field that Indiana didn't offer. I coached him during the summers and holidays, so we accepted him as one of us. He was small but explosive with a very limber back, so performing any dives in the layout position was very easy for him. I don't think Doc knew or cared who I was coaching because we all worked out at different times than the swimmers.

We had a small problem preparing to attend the meet in Bartlesville, OK. We didn't have enough money for the trip because it wasn't a collegiate event in our budget, and I couldn't help them because it was against N.C.A.A. rules. However, the Indiana Athletic Department managed to rake up twenty-five dollars for me to go, and I used that to take them to the meet. Then some of the divers managed to get some money from their parents.

We took off in my van that had enough room for all the divers. As I was driving over a bridge in Missouri, I saw a speeding sign of 35 miles posted at the top of the bridge. So, I slowed down as I saw a police officer signaling me to pull over at the other end of the bridge. He said I was driving over the speed limit. I told him I did slow down to the limit when I saw the sign, and he said it didn't matter. He said the fine was twenty-five dollars in cash and to put it in the mail box on the other side of the road. Now having even less funds we rented one room in a motel, and most of my divers slept on the floor through the whole meet.

The first event was the one-meter springboard with Rick taking fourth place, and Vogel eighth in the finals. Walker placed eleventh that was good since he and all our other divers had never competed in a national meet. In three months, all my divers had just learned to perform all the difficult dives from the three-meter board. Realistically, I told the divers that it was going to be extremely difficult for anyone to make the finals. The talented field was loaded with some of the best divers in the world that included one national and four Olympic divers who were also national champions from Ohio State.

I thought it would take a miracle for Rick and Vogel to make the finals in the three-meter event. I think it was one of the hardest contests for me to ever watch in my life. Rick performed brilliantly, and needed to score only one point on his last dive to win the contest. His last dive was a forward 3 ½ somersault in the tuck position. I thought he might be as nervous as I was.

I told him to get a good take-off, and take the dive out a little that would cause him to rotate a little slower than normal. He did exactly what I told him to do, and won the contest by the highest score and widest margin ever scored in a national contest up to that time. Vogel also had a remarkable meet when he placed sixth.

Everyone was shocked with our divers' brilliant performances, but no more than I was especially when it was the first time any of them had ever competed from that height. Rick was also the first diver since 1937 to win a national championship as a freshman. He beat Lou Vitec, five time N.C.A.A. national champion and later an Olympian, Tom Gump, a national champion and an Olympian, Bob Webster, Olympic Champion, Don Harper, Olympic silver medalist, and Ron O'Brien, National Champion all from Ohio State and Ken Spitzbergen, who was a high school sensation at that time.

My feet went off the ground for about a week after the meet. I went home for lunch the following Monday, and was eating a bowl of soup. I suddenly dropped my head face down into the bowl of soup, and came up crying. My wife Mary asked me, what was wrong. I tearfully told her that I was the luckiest man in the world. I had a great wife, wonderful children, was an American, and worked at a university where I loved to teach and coach. I was healthy and had the best diver in the world, and I didn't know why me. Mary answered, "It was because you wanted it so bad for so long."

Mike Peppe became jealous and had the Big 10 check me out for cheating for five straight years when we started to beat his Ohio State divers. But they never found a thing because I never cheated in all the years I coached, and there are few coaches in any sport that can make that statement.

CHAPTER 25

My Home Life

The Birth of Elizabeth

We had been in Indiana for two years when Mary got pregnant with Elizabeth. We lived in a rental house on Matlock Road about a half mile from the University. Mary was getting close to having the baby, and I told her I was going to take her to the hospital the moment she had any pressure or started to dilate.

I didn't want to go through the event again like when she had Jimmy. So, when she told me she felt some pressure one morning, I immediately took her the hospital. When she signed in and was put in a wheelchair, they started to take her to an elevator, and I tried to go with her. But the nurse wouldn't allow me to go with them.

I thought they were taking Mary upstairs to check her out with a doctor who would decide how much she had dilated, and then inform us when she should return that would be closer to delivering the baby. I sat in the waiting room for about a half hour thinking that someone would tell me what was going on, but no one came.

So, I decided to go back to my office, pick up the mail, and then go back and check her out. I was only gone about a half hour, and when I returned, a nurse wanted to know where I had been because Mary already had the baby. We had gone to the hospital several times when Nancy and Jimmy were born, and I couldn't believe that she could have a baby within an hour after her first sign of any pressure. Unfortunately, Mary never did forgive me for not being there when the baby was born. We named her Elizabeth, and she was born on May 27, 1961.

I was home one afternoon about six months after Elizabeth's birth, and Mary was out in front of the house when she let out a scream. I ran out the door and found that Jimmy, then three years old, had crawled into my car and somehow put the gearshift in neutral. The car rolled backwards down our drive and across the street and stopped within inches from our neighbor's house. From that time on, I always applied the emergency brake when parking in our driveway.

We Decide to Buy a House

We decided to buy a house in 1962 after renting the house on Matlock Road for about three years. Kathy Rumple was an incoming freshman at Indiana and lived in Bloomington when she decided to come out for my team. She was a beautiful girl with a perfect body for diving, but had no experience in the sport. So I gave her a chance to make my team. She started out well and one day invited me to her house to meet her mother and father, Shirley and Ken Rumple.

Ken was a contractor who built houses and had just started to develop a large housing project a mile north of the University in a prestigious area called "Blue Ridge." He built a beautiful house for his family on the very top of the hill. After I got to know him and the family, he asked me if I would like to buy the lot next to his, and he would build me a custom-made house from my own plans.

We paid $6,500 for the lot, and for another lot nearby. The house cost $37,500 at that time, and he did a marvelous job. Our new four-bedroom home was finished in the spring of 1963, and it turned out to be everything we hoped it would be. The house included many features we wanted such as a stone fire place we could look through from the dining room into the living room, and a cute little office for me in the basement. We had a view from the top of the ridge where we could look in any direction for miles that included Indiana University lit up at night one mile away.

Kathy was the oldest of their three girls, and they got along really well with my three children after we moved in. That summer, because Kathy had learned to perform a full list of dives on the one and three-meter boards in three months, we took her to the summer National Championships. It was Kathy's first national meet and being new at the sport placed last in both events.

Feeling that she couldn't make the grade in diving, she quit, and didn't try out for our team when she enrolled in the fall. I was really disappointed in her decision. I tried to convince her that she was a beginner and hadn't allowed herself enough time to acquire experience in the sport, but it was to no avail.

My mother from Erie would come over to visit us in our nice house about every other year, and we went to visit her in Erie in the off years. This was wonderful because she could relax and feel good about me because I had three healthy children, a nice wife and house, and a good job.

We loved living in our new house on Blue Ridge Drive and really liked living next to Shirley and Ken Rumple and their three daughters because they were nice people. We got together a lot during the summers exchanging cookouts.

CHAPTER 26

The 1963-64 Season

The 1963 I.U Men's Diving Team

Front Row

Rick Earley, Dan Scullin, Charley Neal, Dickie Morris, Pete Rhodes, Ron Bramble

Back Row

Tom Dinsley, Jim Blickenstaff, Rick Gilbert, Fritz Meyers, John Vogel, Dick Schroeder

*Not shown – Jim Everroad, John Walker, and John Eisel

My Three Strike Rule

By this time, with the increase in the number of divers coming to Indiana to compete, I knew I had to have discipline on my teams. I gave them a set of rules they had to follow and I wanted them to agree that the rules were fair. I made the rules much like three strikes playing baseball. So if a diver broke a rule he got one strike, and if he broke three rules, he would be dropped from the team permanently. (Pictured on following page Jim Blickenstaff and Jim Everroad the Indiana State High School Diving Champion with me)

Over the years, we averaged eighteen divers on my team, and only a few divers ever struck out. Their challenge was to focus on their studies and diving to be on our team. I believed that if they didn't take their work seriously why should I waste my time coaching them.

Our diving program began to change when our swimming and diving teams moved into our new pool, and Gilbert astounded everyone with his incredible performance winning the three-meter event at Bartlesville OK, at the National A.A.U. as a freshman in April 1962.

Female Divers Come to I.U.

The 1962-63 schedule for swimming and diving remained the same every year except when two female divers, Terrie Hauk and Kathy Flicker, showed up and wanted to dive. However, when the girls came into Royer Pool, Doc wanted to know who they were, and I told him that I planned to coach them. Doc was the head coach and said they weren't going to work out in our pool on our time.

So, I was challenged again, and there went my lunch time. They were two short and strong girls. I coached them for nearly two hours before the swim team came to practice, and then they quickly got out of the pool before Doc showed up. This went on for some time plus I had them stay a little later each day. Then when Doc saw what I was doing, he finally said it was okay with him if I coached them as long as it didn't interfere with coaching the boys. So, after that, instead of coaching two or three hours a day, I coached five or six hours.

Dryland Board

I had been coaching diving at I.U. for a little over two years when I still didn't have a facility to teach my divers how to improve their basic board work and take-offs. So, I went to the athletic department and told them I needed a one-meter stand and diving board installed in a corner of the indoor track attached to the physical education building where we did our trampoline work.

This would be convenient to practice on because it was near Royer Pool. I also asked for a pile of dirt to be used for feet first soft landings. I don't believe the athletic department had a clue what I was talking about, as they told the utilities department about my problem and built the diving stand with a non-moveable fulcrum.

The dry land workouts lasted for about an hour or a little more each afternoon. Jim Lavery, the track coach, came to me after we started using the rig and complained that the board was in the way of his runners competing in the sixty-yard dash in meets. He wanted us to remove the stand and install it in some other place. I told him he would have to move it because it had six tons of cement beneath it, and he never moved it.

We used the dry land board a lot during the early season which was great for working on approaches, take-offs, and fundamental moves used to perform somersaults and twisting somersault dives. However, that required them to land on a pile of dirt feet first. One day in 1963, I came in for practice on the dry land board, and found everyone injured with ankle sprains, twisted knees, and whatever that had occurred from the dry land board training.

I thought there must be a better way to use the board without causing injuries. After some thought, I told the team to meet me Saturday morning at the dry land board in old clothes because we were going to dig a big hole in front of the board. The hole looked like a grave with a huge pile of dirt sitting behind it. I never asked for permission to dig the hole because I knew I would never get permission to do so.

I then went downtown to a furniture store that made a lot of their own furniture, and asked if they had any foam rubber I could have. They said they had bins of left overs out back and I could help myself. I got a truck, and we threw the foam rubber in the hole. Like an idiot, I never thought to put a liner in the hole first to keep the divers from getting dirty.

Jumping into a foam rubber pit solved the problems of injury, and made it possible for the divers to land in any one of four body positions - stomach, knees, back, and feet. But didn't include landing in the pit head first.

The Story that Makes Headlines

We nick-named Terry Hauk, "Mighty Mouse" because if she dived with a towel wrapped around her neck, she looked like Mighty Mouse. One day, Terry's roommate, who majored in journalism, came to watch Terry work out on the dry land board. She brought her camera to take some pictures of her jumping into the foam rubber pit.

She wrote a story on Terry and had it published it in the Daily Student, the school paper, with some pictures. The Bloomington newspaper known as the Herald-Telegraph, picked up on the article, and put it in their paper. Then the Indianapolis Star saw the article, and published it in their paper.

The article ultimately found its way to the Stars and Stripes newspaper that was distributed nationally and worldwide, and someone in Los Angeles saw it and realized its potential. From that one article, a manufacturer decided to put foam rubber in large vinyl plastic bags that could be used to improve safety for landings in track and gymnastic events.

At that time, the world's record for the pole vault was below thirteen feet because they could be injured landing flat on their back in sand or sawdust. All high jumpers had to land on their feet for the same reason. The company called their new landing pads the Port-O-Pit.

These foam landing pads enabled pole vault athletes to go as high as twenty-feet while landing on their backs. High jumpers learned the Fosbury Flop which was passing over the bar head first twisting and landing on their backs, and set records over seven feet.

John Nabor, the famous Olympic backstroke swimming champion wrote a book on athletes who had made a great contribution to their sport, and he gave me credit for being the one who first came up with the idea that led to the making of the Port-0-pit using sponge rubber wrapped in plastic bags for all kinds of sports.

Diving Illustrated

I was inspired to start writing a book in 1961 when I found that competitive diving was a sport that didn't offer one word on how to perform a dive, not alone a perfect one. So, judges, divers, and coaches had to teach, learn, and evaluate dives using their own concept of how the dives should be performed. I got the idea when I learned to dive.

When I was a child at the Y.M.C.A., I tried to copy the movements of the dives drawn in sequence that had been taken from the F.I.N.A. rules books and posted on the billboard. However, those dives were drawn in 1908, and they were so badly drawn that it was nearly impossible to copy their movements.

So, I thought I would write a book called Diving Illustrated that would offer everyone a basic concept on how to perform all the dives listed in the diving rule books. My book was originally supposed to be a series of charts to be put on the walls of swimming pools. But when I found that there were going to be so many drawings, I decided to make it a book. I sometimes thought writing it had been a waste of time. But later I learned it was the first book ever written that offered how to perform all the dives.

The drawings showed the dives performed in sequence along with a short explanation of what was happening in each sequence. I had no drawing experience and found it very difficult to draw the movements of dives, especially from different angles.

It took me over five years to draw more than a hundred and thirty different dives. I finished the book and published it at the beginning of the summer of 1965. As years went by, some of the dives I had drawn didn't offer much science because I was still learning how to apply science to teach and coach diving. But the drawings were still good enough to give everyone a better idea of what the dives should look like.

The book is still used by some coaches, divers, and judges throughout the world as a Bible because it offers a basic concept on how dives should be performed. It may continue to be useful until some qualified person improves on it, but that hasn't yet happened.

Doc asked me one day if I had ever gone to the national aquatics convention. I said I hadn't and he suggested I start to attend one if I wanted to know what was going on in the diving world. So I went in the fall and attended several diving committee meetings. I was surprised when I was made the chairman of the national rules committee the next year that went on for six more years. All the suggestions for rules were sent to me and I would put them in order before taking them to the rules committee to be voted on at the convention each year.

A short while later, Doc decided to play music during workouts using the new sound system that had speakers all over the pool and stands. That meant I now had to yell to be heard by my divers. This went on for about ten years until I started to lose my voice. I went to a doctor who told me I had ruined my voice box, and there was nothing that could be done to get it back to normal.

When I went to Doc and told him what happened, he went into the office, picked up a huge bunch of records, and threw them into the pool. Then he told the swimmers music would no longer be played in the pool during practice.

John Walker was about to start his junior year, and learned he was about to flunk out of school. Most universities in the country require students to take general courses for the first two years to be well-rounded students. Then they must choose a major program that relates to their chosen field of interest starting in their junior year.

I persuaded Dean Daniels to take John back in the school on probation, and have him major in Physical Education. I added that I would take full responsibility for his actions. I found a room on the third floor of a home on Thirteenth Street, a block away from the pool, and I told him to study every night. Then go home on weekends, and have his mother help him write his papers because she was an English teacher.

I looked in on him at least once a week until he graduated from Indiana. John went on to earn his Master's and Doctor's degrees, and ended up, of all things, being the diving coach at the University of Minnesota and years later, Harvard University.

The 1963 Pan American Games Trials

The Pan American Games were staged in San Paulo, Brazil in the summer and the trials were held along with the Woman's National A.A.U. Diving Championship at the University of Pittsburgh. I had never attended a women's nationals before because they were held at a different site than the men's in those days. So, my first taste of a

Photo Dick Smith

202

women's national meet was when I decided to take Terry Hauck and Kathy Flicker to Pittsburgh's new pool in April 1963.

I was familiar with the pool because Kimball and I had done a diving exhibition for their dedication a few years before. Dick Smith was the first person I met when I walked into the pool with a large group of good divers from his swim gym in Phoenix, Arizona. Dick Smith's divers were the favorite to win all the top places, and he made a couple of rude remarks about my girls, who were a little overweight.

The Jerrie Adair Incident

This meet was to select the two top divers from the three-meter springboard and ten-meter platform. Since it was a national meet, the one-meter event was also included in the meet, and it was the first event. Jerrie Adair was a great diver from California, and had enrolled at I.U. and won the one-meter event.

The rule for the swimming and diving events required the contestants to place their event entries in a box by twelve o'clock noon the day before their next event. If they failed to do so, they would be disqualified. Something happened during the one-meter event that took up extra time handing out the awards so when Jerrie came to put her entry form in the box it was about three minutes after the deadline.

I was the National Rules Chairman and had just taken the entries out of the box at exactly twelve o'clock. Even though she had enrolled in Indiana, I told her that I couldn't accept her forms because she was too late. What Jerrie didn't know was the meet director was standing right behind me and was watching me when I made the comment.

If I had broken the rule, he would have reported me and I would be in trouble. Jerrie

ran off crying her eyes out because she had worked her entire diving career to compete in a major international meet and was disqualified over a stupid rule. But Jerrie went on to win many more Nationals.

After I had given Jerrie the bad news, the father of two divers who would later come to Indiana, confronted me with all my divers he could gather up behind him. He was Jim Bere president of Borg-Warner, one of the largest corporations in the country. He had two sons, Jim and David (pictured here), and they were two of the finest divers I ever coached. They were normal unspoiled kids that never gave me any trouble, and were very loyal to me and the team.

Jim called me a rotten S.O.B. for disqualifying Jerrie. I told him that all the diving people in the pool area had elected me to be the National Rules Chairman because they believed that I was honest and trustworthy. So if they wanted me to lie and cheat they would never know when I was lying or cheating them.

Something good came out of the incident when the rule for handing in a diving form late was changed the following year from being disqualified to paying a $25 fine. Jerrie never got the recognition she deserved diving for me, and went on to be a successful California lawyer after she finished her diving career.

I Meet Young Ken Sitzberger

When Bruce Harlan and I were doing our shows in the summer time at country clubs in the late 1950's, one was in Chicago where we had to dive over a tree to reach the deep end of the pool. We did our show at that club for ten straight years starting in 1950. Getting ready to do our show the second year or third year, a young boy about eight years old named Ken Sitzberger came up to me, and introduced himself. He did this year after year.

Ken grew up, and developed into one of the best high school divers in the country. Ken was a junior in high school and Illinois State Champion, and won the 1962 one-meter National A.A.U. title in Bartlesville, competing with Rick Gilbert who won the three-meter event. I remember after the event was over, I walked up to Ken and introduced myself as Hobie Billingsley, and asked him if he remembered me.

Obviously, Ohio State and Michigan were aware that Ken was a good diver, and went after him. But I thought I had a better chance of getting him because I had known him and his family since he had been eight years old. However, I soon found I was wrong when he walked into Yale's pool office to compete in the 1963 Indoor National A.A.U. Championships.

I realized then that he didn't plan to attend Indiana, and would probably go to either Ohio State or Michigan. The two divers that placed first and second in the three-meter event qualified to compete in the 1963 Pan American Games that were to be held in San Paulo, Brazil. Gilbert defended his national title and beat Sitzberger, who took second place, by a wide margin.

When the event was over, Ken came up to me and said that he had planned to attend Michigan, but changed his mind and was coming to Indiana. He said the reason for changing his mind was because he was never going to beat Gilbert unless he dived with him every day.

The 1963 Pan American Games

Ken Sitzberger was accepted to Indiana University after graduating from high school, and that summer came to us to practice before going to the 1963 Games. I had no idea who Tom Dinsley was when he showed up at Indiana in the fall of 1961. Then I learned he was one of the better divers from Canada. He didn't show much promise during his freshman year, but qualified for the Pan Am Games back in Canada after school was out for the summer. So we had three divers competing at the Pan American Games that represented Indiana University.

The weather had turned cold in Brazil a couple of days before the meet, and the diving facilities were not good. Dinsley suddenly lost his composure the day before the meet, and got so upset that he decided to quit and return to the States.

Thankfully, Gilbert talked him into staying and competing because he had nothing to lose. The contest ended the next day with Dinsley taking first, Gilbert second, and Sitzberger third. Tom came to my office when he returned to school and threw his gold medal down on my desk, and said, "That was for Canada" as I congratulated him.

Tom won because, like Gilbert who earlier couldn't perform a back 2½ twisting somersault on the trampoline, relieved himself from the frustration and stress caused by the pressure he had built up, and could relax and concentrate that let him perform better than ever before. Unfortunately, Tom never came close to diving as well as he did in Brazil. Diving for Canada in the 1964 Tokyo Olympics the next year, he placed eighteenth. Tom returned to Canada after he graduated from Indiana, and went on to become a successful lawyer.

The 1964 Women's Indoor National A.A.U. Championships

This meet was staged in Pittsburgh again, and was the first women's only national championship I ever attended besides the 1963 Pan American Games trials the year before. During the meet, I saw two girls who got my attention. One was Cynthia Potter (pictured here with her coach Dick Smith) who was thirteen years old. She had a higher hurdle than most boys I had seen, and I decided to chase her down when she got a little older.

The other girl was Lesley Bush (pictured left) whom I had met earlier in Philadelphia. Lesley didn't make the finals in either springboard event, and didn't compete in the tower event. I found later that Lesley had dived for Dick Smith a couple of years earlier, and with Bob Schneider, who was on my team at Ohio University and later was the diving coach at Princeton University.

Terry Hauk didn't make the finals in either springboard event. Kathy Flicker placed eighth on the one-meter board, but failed to qualify on three-meter. Soon after the event was over I started to walk out of the pool to the lobby to wait for the girls. I saw Kathy's mother, and a few of her friends sitting up in the empty stands.

Kathy came from a very wealthy family, and her mother was very sophisticated and dignified. As I walked by, she yelled down, and said she wanted to talk to me. I climbed up the empty seats, and gave her a friendly greeting. Then she started to chew me out for her daughter not making the finals in the three-meter event.

She said that I was doing a lousy job because Kathy made the finals last year, and why she didn't make them this year was my fault. I looked straight at her, and asked her how much money was she paying me to coach her daughter? She was a little taken back with my question, and she said that it was my job.

I then told her that Indiana didn't have a diving program for girls. I was generously coaching them on my own time, and never received a penny from the University or from her. I told her that if she didn't like the way I was coaching her daughter, she should find some other coach.

As I was sitting in the lobby waiting for my divers, Lesley Bush's father walked by, and I grabbed him by the arm. I told him that I liked Lesley's style, and suggested he might like to send her out to Indiana to train with us for the Olympic trials. I went on to say that she had an outside, outside, outside chance of qualifying for the finals, and if not, it would be a good experience for her.

206

He said she was outside of the building, so I should go out and ask her. I gave her the same story I had given her dad. Lesley had the habit of twirling her hair with her fingers, and said she would think about it. I received a call from Don a month later, and didn't know who he was until he said that he had decided to send Lesley out to train with us.

As an afterthought, he asked if she could dive tower, and I replied that I didn't know because she hadn't competed from that height at the nationals. Then I asked him had she ever dived from the tower, and he replied that she had dived off it but didn't know any more about it. I guess her father wasn't aware that we didn't have a ten-meter tower at Indiana until 1965, and we were training indoors on the springboards for the trials that were to be staged outside.

Training for the 1964 Olympic Trials

Sitzberger and Gilbert took first and second in the 1964 Big 10 Conference, the N.C.A.A., and the indoor and outdoor National A.A.U. Championships along with the aid of Rick Earley, Charlie Neel, and Dickie Morris all of whom made the finals in every meet. No other team came close to us, and I thought I would be selected as the Olympic diving coach.

But when the Olympic Diving Committee met after the swimming season was over in the spring, they selected Dick Smith for the women's coach and surprisingly Hank Chapman, from the University of Texas as the men's diving coach. Chapman was a swimming coach, and not a diving coach. But he took credit for coaching his diver, Skippy, who won the 1952 Olympic springboard title in Finland.

He had never coached Skippy Browning, because he didn't know much about the sport. He sent him to the Detroit Athletic Club during the summers and school vacations to be coached by Clarence Pinkston, who won an Olympic Gold medal in diving in 1924. I was doing water shows with Kimball and Ron O'Brien during the summer, and they had to listen to me gripe about how I was cheated out of what I deserved and they agreed.

Then, the unexpected happened. Chapman had a heart attack, and couldn't take the Olympic job. Thinking that I was now a cinch to be selected because of my coaching record, I didn't give it much thought as I continued to coach my team in preparation for the Olympic trials. But I soon found out that I was wrong again.

The 1964 Olympic Games were to be held in Tokyo, Japan so we started to train for the diving trials with the hope that someone might be lucky enough to make the team. We had about six weeks left to train for the trials when Lesley Bush arrived after finishing her junior year in high school. She had little ten-meter tower experience, and Indiana did not yet have an outdoor pool with a tower.

The nearest tower was seventy-seven miles away in Noblesville, a tiny town on the northeast side of Indianapolis. We decided to train there making the trip several times each week. I don't remember any of our divers having any tower diving experience, and Lesley said she had learned a couple of easy dives from the ten-meter platform diving from Dick Smith when she was younger.

The challenge for Lesley and the whole team was to learn to perform a full list of dives for the competition in only a few weeks. We went up to Noblesville three times a week, and used their outside springboard facilities that were not in very good condition. One of the problems learning to dive from ten meters is conditioning the body to take the impact entering the water head first at approximately thirty-three miles an hour.

Our divers learned to perform a full list of dives in six weeks. This included Lesley who essentially who essentially was a novice and unknown as a tower diver. Other exceptions included Ken Sitzberger and Gilbert. Sitzberger pulled some muscles in his triceps, and had to stop tower diving after a few practice sessions. Worse yet, Gilbert had pulled a muscle in his neck while training at home, and didn't get the chance to learn to dive from the tower or practice on the springboard. He came to practice every day and sat on the bench watching the others, and sometimes cried because he couldn't dive. That went on until we arrived in New York City for the trials over a month later.

Terry Hauk, a.k.a. Mighty Mouse, was a gutsy diver, and kept wanting me to teach her how to perform a back 2½ somersault in the tuck position from the ten-meter platform. I kept refusing her request because the bubbler system to soften a diver's entry had not been invented yet. If she missed the dive badly, she could end up in the hospital.

I finally gave in before leaving for the trials, but warned her that she was taking a big chance of being injured if I gave her a bad call. A call is a verbal signal used by the coach to alert the diver when to release the legs from the tuck or pike position, and straighten the body in preparation to see and reach for the entry. Somersaults are more difficult dives because you spin faster, and the timing to break out must be more precise.

Terry surprised all of us when she went up and successfully performed the dive. I remember I was more afraid of her getting hurt than she was. That made her one of a very few women in the world to perform that dive at that time. I also learned from her experience that when a diver wants to learn a difficult dive and has the confidence to try it, then let them.

The day before leaving for the Olympic trials in New York City, we all gathered for a meeting to prepare for our trip. Out of nowhere, Sitzberger said, "Coach, you know us better than anyone, which of us will make the Olympic team?" I said, "Well, the good news, you will and Gilbert has a chance." Sitzberger broke in, and asked me how I knew he would make the team. And I said because I just knew. He refused to back off and said my answer wasn't good enough, and challenged me to prove it.

I got irritated and told him if he wanted proof, I would give it to him. With that, I took three quarters out of my pocket, and gave one to Sitzberger, one to Gilbert, and I kept the third one. I told him that we were going to flip the coins only once with the odd man winning, and that he would be the one to win. The team gathered around to watch us flip the coins, and they were as astonished as I was. After he won the coin flip, he stared at me as I walked away, and said that I really did know.

The 1964 Olympic Trials

The traveling squad included Gilbert, Sitzberger, Vogel, Walker, and Ron Bramble, a freshman, plus our female divers Bush, Flickers, and Hauk. We all piled into my van, and took off for Detroit about five days before the Olympic Trials in New York City were to begin. We planned to stay at Ron Bramble's house overnight in Detroit, and have a practice session in the outdoor pool that was used for the 1948 Olympic trials.

Ron's mother was very nice to put us all up and save us our hotel money. She made us all a nice spaghetti dinner and we were all sitting around the table like the last supper when the telephone rang. Ron's mother answered the phone, and said the call was for me. That was a surprise because no one knew where I was at that time.

I picked up the phone and it was Charlie McCaffrey, the Michigan State swimming coach. I asked him how he found me, and he said he had been trying to find me for over a week. He had finally called my wife, Mary, who suggested where we might be. I asked what he wanted from me. He said he was in New York City with the selection committee to select the men's Olympic diving coach position that was left vacant when Chapman had his heart attack, and he wanted to know Dick Kimball's telephone number.

I couldn't believe my ears knowing how well Gilbert and Sitzberger and my divers had dominated all the national meets the previous year. Quite irritated, I told him that since he lived in Lansing, Michigan, only fifty miles from Ann Arbor, why didn't he call information? And he said, "you'll find out" and hung up.

I was literally stunned as I sat down at the table. I told my divers what was said, and added that I thought Dick Kimball had just been made the Olympic diving coach. Kimball hadn't coached any good divers in his career at that point, but we were good friends. So, I got up and called him, and before he could say a word, I told him he had just been chosen to coach the Olympic Team.

He told me it was crazy because I was the one that deserved it. I went on to tell Dick that he was a darn good coach, and would do a great job. I had all my divers get up and congratulate him, and when they sat back down at the table they started to bad mouth him. I told them to stop because Dick wasn't the one to blame.

We started to eat our dinner again when I suddenly realized what they had just done to me. I suddenly put down my fork and walked out of the house and down the street crying. I came to a park where I sat down, and asked God why they had done such a thing to me. We all had worked so hard, and I never cheated or put anyone down.

I remember it was a beautiful night with a full moon peeking through the clouds, and thinking that it was not worth the pain. I decided to pack up my bag, give my divers my van, and go home and let the divers go to New York City on their own. Then, after sitting there a few more moments feeling sorry for myself, I asked myself why was I coaching?

Was it because I was trying to make myself a famous coach, or was it that I wanted to challenge a bunch of kids to try to be the best they could be? I don't think I went to my heart for the answer, but instead to my very soul. As I got ready to return to the house, I pleaded with God to please let one of my kids make the Olympic team, just one. No one brought up the subject up when I got back to the house nearly an hour later, and we left for New York City the next morning.

(side bar)

The Amateur Athletic Union controlled all amateur competitive sports in America for nearly fifty years and were still in charge. They charged all the athletes in the amateur sports an entry fee to compete in a contest. The fees were then sent to the National A.A.U. office where they were used to help administrate the association.

RJ Smith was the Naval Officer who had discovered Bruce Harlan and sent him to Ohio State, and was now the United States National A.A.U. Diving Chairman. We had a meeting with the officials soon after we arrived for the trials at the Astoria Park Pool in New York City. RJ Smith was going to be the diving referee.

Talking to Ron O'Brien and Dick Kimball before the meeting, we discussed that when RJ Jackson refereed in nine different major contests in the last five years, he allowed divers to do poorly performed dives over again. Coincidently, we knew that Don Harper of Ohio State was allowed to take over and repeat five of his competitive dives when he scored poorly.

As mentioned before, RJ was a close friend of Mike Peppe, the swimming coach at Ohio State, and RJ's sister also taught at Ohio State. So, we thought he showed favoritism for Ohio State. With that knowledge, and as the national diving rules chairman, I asked RJ at the meeting if he was going to tell any diver to take the dive over if he performed a poor dive. Or was he going to obey the rule that states the diver is to make the request to the referee who would decide. When RJ said that it didn't matter, I told him that he had broken the rule nine times in the past five years. As I started to name them, he interrupted me, and said that the diver would have to make the request. That embarrassed him in front of the diving coaches and officials.

The 1964 Olympic Trials Events

We checked into our hotel and put three girls in one room, and the boys and myself in two other rooms. We practiced for three days before the meet. The first event was the men's three-meter springboard. Rick managed to get in some practice before the event after having been injured and not practicing for a month.

He surprised me when he was in second place after the preliminaries with Frank Gorman, (pictured on following page) from Harvard University in first place. Sitzberger was third, and Larry Andreasen, from California, was in fourth place. The top three places made the Olympic team, and Frank had a brilliant meet to take first place in the finals. Sitzberger diving steadily placed second, and Andreasen moved up to third place when Rick went short on a back 2½ somersault and over rotated on a forward 3½ somersault to end up in fourth place.

I was disappointed that Rick didn't make the team, and felt so strongly about him that

I would have given an arm or a leg to have him make the team. Still upset when Rick didn't make the team, I told the other male divers to get their suits on after the event was over so we could practice for the ten-meter event that was scheduled for next day. I waited for them to come out of the locker room for a long time when the only one that showed up was John Walker who told me that they all had gone back to the hotel because they were tired.

The second event that afternoon was the women's three-meter contest and Lesley Bush surprised everyone, including me, when she was in third place up to the last dive in the finals. Unfortunately, Patsy Willard, a diver for Dick Smith, performed a brilliant reverse 1½ somersault with a 1½ twist, and nosed Lesley out of third place by two points. That put Patsy

on the Olympic team along with another one of Dick Smith's divers Jeanne Collier who took first place. (Pictured right with Ken Sitzberger)

Lesley came to me upset after the contest when I told her that she had done a fantastic job, and she still had a chance in the tower event. Then she said, "Oh Hobie, I just learned to do a full list from that height, and I don't have a prayer." I told her that she wouldn't know until she tried. The next day was the ten-meter tower event, and when my male divers came out on the deck ready for a warm up in their practice session they found me sitting in the stands nearby.

They said they were ready, and I said to go ahead while not moving from out of

211

the stands. A little confused, one asked me if I was ready to coach them. And I said that since they didn't think they needed my help yesterday, I didn't think they needed my help today, so they would have to coach themselves and I continued to sit there.

I remembered a lesson about leading that my old coach, Art Weibel had taught me. When I hesitated to take over the team marching in the gym, I thought I would teach my team a similar lesson. They practiced without me saying one word or getting any coaching. Then when the event began, believe it or not, they all performed better than any time they had in practice.

(Pictured diving greats Tom Gompf, Bobby Clotworthy, Hobie Billingsley, Lou Vitucci)

Vogel's last dive was a back 2½ somersault, but he didn't get the scores that everyone there thought he deserved. I think the judges had never seen Vogel dive tower, and felt that Tom Gompf had a better chance of getting a medal at the Olympics. He beat John by only one point which put him in fourth place.

The final event was the ten-meter contest for women. Ron O'Brien was the sixth judge, and I was the seventh judge. Lesley was the last diver to perform, and she executed a beautiful back dive in the layout position for her first dive. The first six judges scored eight's and nines for the dive, and I gave her a seven. Ron looked at me in disbelief, and asked me why in the hell did I give my own diver such a low score? I told him that I didn't know she could dive that well! Lesley went on to perform all her dives with consistency, and placed third to make the Olympic Team. Many of the coaches and divers thought that her making the team was a fluke that prevented another good diver from making the team, and possibly winning a medal. They came to that conclusion because Lesley had never dived in any ten-meter competition prior to the trials, and they didn't know her.

Few people realized after the meet was over that the divers from Indiana nearly took five of the twelve places to make the Olympic team. Rick Gilbert, Lesley Bush, and John Vogel all placed fourth in three events missing third place by narrow margins. I was extremely proud of their performances, and realized we had a great possibility of starting a diving dynasty at Indiana University.

The 1964 Olympic Games

The father of one of my divers had suggested he would buy my plane ticket and lodging to attend the Games since I was overlooked to be selected as the Olympic Team diving coach even though I had the best coaching record for the past two years and had divers make the team. (Pictured Jack Barnett)

Just two weeks before the Games I never got the tickets so I scrapped up enough money to buy a $400 plane ticket on a charter. By this time all affordable lodging had been reserved, and I still had no place to stay. I decided to take a chance I could room with someone I knew as I had done before as a competitor in high school attending the Nationals. I would sleep in the lobby of a hotel if I had to because I was going to go regardless to see my divers compete.

I left with only $100 in my wallet for all my meals and lodging for twelve days, and still didn't have a ticket to see the diving events. As soon as I arrived I went over to the pool, and met Lesley to coach her for a few minutes during practice.

After coaching Lesley I went up to the restaurant for a cup of coffee, and ran into Jack Barnett, my good friend and coach from Australia. He asked me where I was staying, and I told him I had just arrived and had no idea. He told me to follow him, and we took a taxi to his hotel and carried my suitcase to the room so no one would know I was staying there with him as another roommate.

I had to laugh later when we put three different size shoes outside the door every night to be shined for one person. We went back to the pool until about eleven thirty at night when Jack told me he was going out with some of his friends, and would meet me back at the hotel. I was in for a shock when I went out and hailed a taxi to find that I hadn't written down the name of Jack's hotel.

Here I was in a strange country at nearly midnight, and didn't have a clue where I was going to sleep after being up for nearly two days. Waiting for my cab, I suddenly remembered talking to Don Webb, the diving coach from Canada, that Don mentioned he was staying at some hotel that sounded like "eachy." So, I kept saying that to my cab driver, who couldn't understand a word of English.

Then he suddenly said, "ah-so, Dieitchy Hotel." I was surprised to find it was the same hotel that Kimball and I had stayed at when we were on tour in 1960. I went to the hotel desk, and found Don was registered there so I rang his room. I had to ask him if I could stay with him for the night because I didn't know where Jack was staying.

Don was in his pajamas when I entered his room, and after we chatted for a while, he started to take them off and get into his clothes. A little confused, I asked him what he was doing, and he said he was getting ready to go back to the pool. Having also been up for two days without sleep, he was totally exhausted with no knowledge of time.

I told him he must be crazy because it was midnight. When he looked at his watch, he saw that he had put it on upside down and thought it was six thirty in the morning. We both stood there laughing at each other because I didn't know where I was staying, and he didn't know the time of day.

For the next few days I could meet with the coaches at the pool, and all I heard was how bad a diver Lesley was. Dick Smith commented she couldn't hit a dive from tower if her life depended on it, and thought she'd probably finish last. Dick Kimball issued a similar sentiment that Lesley should have never made the team because she was taking away the chance for a serious contender to win a medal. Then, my good friend, Jack Barnett, the Australian coach, echoed the same view after watching Lesley in practice.

But the other divers on the team showed little resentment because they, too, had never seen Lesley compete in tower competitions and felt they could beat her. They had trained hard for years to make the team, and Lesley had only trained for tower for six weeks! The odds were certainly not in Lesley's favor.

But I had a different thought. I knew Lesley was only 16 and a junior in high school. In the eighth grade her parents moved to Phoenix, AZ, and for a few years she found Dick Smith to get some early training in Arizona. But she still had little experience in tower. However, now she was farther from home in another country halfway around the world. And, I wasn't selected to be her coach.

I knew Lesley had just turned 17 and just finished her junior year in high school. I suspect she also accepted me as a surrogate father-figure, Psychologically, it was understandable that she had lost her focus and confidence which caused her to perform so poorly in practice at the Games. That coupled with negative attitudes from her Olympic coaches spelled disaster because they couldn't provide her with the same familiar cues I used to coach her back in Indiana.

But soon after I arrived, Lesley went to Dick Smith, the Olympic coach, and directly asked him permission for me to coach her. I recall that Dick and I looked at each other dumbfounded because such a request had never been made by a diver before. After Dick agreed that gave Lesley a boost in confidence because she immediately started to dive more like her ability making the team.

At this point, I took all the pressure off to perform, and refocused her on doing her list one dive at a time. I also told her that this was a learning experience since the 1960 Olympic Champion. Ingrid Kramer, everyone had as a lock to repeat wins on the three-meter and tower. So she had everything to gain and nothing to lose, and focus on executing each of her dives as she was coached to do and block out all the other distractions. She would have more fun to enjoy the experience.

Someone at the pool gave me an extra ticket to the opening ceremony, and I saw the greatest extravaganza I had ever seen in my life. However, from that time on, I would need a picture ID badge to get into the pool. I tried all day to get in by attempting to sneak in, and bribing the guards but nothing worked.

A while later, Barnett came out from the pool to go home, and saw my predicament. He suggested that after he went to the pool the next morning, he would give his credentials to Sue Knight, his diver, to bring them out to me. Though we both wore horned-rim glasses and were bald headed and looked much the same, I told him I couldn't possibly let him take that chance. If they caught either of us, he would be sent home.

Jack said he was willing to take that chance, and that was how I could get into the pool for the entire time I was in Japan. However, after giving Jack back his credentials, when the security men came around to check I.D.'s at the pool a couple of times a day, I would go into the bathroom and stand on the toilet seat until the coast was clear.

The first event was the women's three-meter springboard. Ingrid Kramer, had won both gold medals at the 1960 Olympics in Rome and broke the women's American diving streak of gold medals that started in the 1920's. Ingrid defended her title on the 3-meter board, and was a cinch to win the ten-meter event unless she broke her leg or got run over by a train. Her event was the first time that an electronic score board was ever used for displaying the scores from the judges. It also gave total scores, and the positions the divers placed after each round of dives. (Pictured Collier the Silver, Kramer the Gold, and Willard the Bronze)

Photo Courtesy https://theolympians.co

Ken Sitzberger Wins Gold

The second event was the men's three-meter springboard. Frank Gorman, Ken Sitzberger's teammate, had beaten Ken on all the first eight dives in the finals. Ken was a mentally tough kid, but realized he was behind by sixty-two points with only two dives to go. He came to me crying on the deck and said he was beaten. I grabbed Ken by the shoulders and while shaking him, I looked over his shoulder and saw his mother and father walking out of the building having given up on their son.

Andreasen Silver, Sitzberger Gold, Gorman Bronze
Photo Courtesy https://theolympians.co

215

I told Ken there was still a chance to win. Gorman had been inconsistent doing his back 2½ somersault. I told Ken if he performed a good reverse 2½ somersault, he could still catch up to Gorman. Unbelievably, it happened just as I had suggested. Gorman landed really short for very low scores, and Ken hit his reverse 2½ somersault to score sixty-eight points for the dive.

Gorman then went on to beat Ken on the last dive with a reverse 1½ somersault in the layout position, but he still didn't score enough points to beat Sitzberger who won by three points. Never in any other time in the history of the sport has a diver ever won a contest losing nine out of ten dives to an opponent in any meet from the age group to the senior contests.

The third event was the men's ten-meter platform held on the next day. Lou Vitucci, Bob Webster, and Tom Gompf, were the three U.S.A. divers favored to take the first three places in that order. However, when performing his fourth basic dive, a front hand stand into a forward somersault, Vitucci didn't push his legs up high enough to perform the hand stand and brought his feet back down on the platform for a balk.

Photo Courtesy https://theolympians.co
Dibiasi Silver, Webster Gold, Gompf Bronze

That meant two points would be subtracted from the scores given by each judge after the completion of the dive. Then he made a fatal mistake. Instead of standing up and gathering his wits before attempting the hand stand again, he immediately attempted the hand stand again...and came down to his feet for the second time making it a failed dive.

His wife was sitting in the stands and let out a scream because she knew he couldn't make up the difference to make the finals and win a medal. Bob Wester went on to win the contest, and Tom Gompf managed to dive well enough to take third place missing second place by only one point.

Lesley Bush Wins Gold

The final event was the women's ten-meter platform. Ingrid Kramer was favored to run away with the title since she had already won the springboard title, and two gold medals in Rome. Lesley Bush was the last diver to perform. I didn't see her perform her first dive, the front dive in the layout position, because I was busy being congratulated for Ken's victory in the three-meter by some of the fans.

Some woman in the stands asked who the diver was that had just performed when another woman said it was Bush from the United States. We had to wait a while for the scores to come up on the new electric scoreboard when everyone, especially me, was surprised to find Lesley in first place by a point ahead of Kramer, and a Russian girl, with a name a mile long in third place. Lesley came over and asked me how she was doing. Without telling her I didn't see the dive, I told her that she was the best diver in the world for one dive and to keep up the good work.

The contest required the divers to perform three required dives and one optional dive in the preliminaries. Then, from those scores, the top eight divers qualified for the finals to be held that evening. In the finals that evening, they were required to perform one compulsory dive and two optional dives to determine the winner.

Lesley performed her second and third compulsory dives, and miraculously remained in first place with the Russian diver second and Kramer third by one point. I then told Lesley that if she performed her optional dive well, that was a forward 1½ somersault with a double twist, she would make the finals. She seemed surprised as she walked away curling her hair with her finger. Lesley performed a beautiful optional dive, and qualified first for the finals while still beating Kramer by one point.

That afternoon I was being interviewed by Keith Jackson, a reporter from Indianapolis who wanted to talk about Sitzberger's sensational win, and half way through the interview, I suddenly broke down. He asked, what was wrong? I told him he just didn't get that I had a sixteen-year-old high school girl, who had learned to dive tower in six weeks. And she was beating the best diver in the world when it was believed by everyone that she would place last in the contest.

And if she should win the contest, it would be the biggest upset in the history of the Olympic Games. I told him I couldn't talk to him anymore and walked away. I was a nervous wreck by the time the finals started. Lesley performed her last compulsory dive and remained in first place. She still had two optional dives to perform.

Her next optional dive was an inward 2½ somersault in the tuck position, and she did it well enough to still lead Kramer who was still within a point. Kramer performed a nice optional dive as her final dive, and the scoreboard showed that Lesley would have to score better than 6½ points from the judges on her last dive to win.

I was beginning to go into shock by this time when Lesley came to me before she was to perform a forward 2½ somersault in the pike position. I blurted out how she should perform the dive when I broke down, and told her that she had already proven to me that she was the best diver in the world. So just go up and do the darn dive.

As she walked away curling her hair and thinking what a crazy guy I was, I suddenly remembered that she tended to over rotate the somersault. So, I ran to her just as she

217

started to climb the steps to the tower. I told her to take the dive out a little and play it a little short to prevent her from over rotating, and if she did as I said, she would win the contest.

I didn't think I could watch the dive, so I went behind the bleachers where I argued with myself to watch the dive and finally decided to watch it. I was still behind the bleachers when I looked up to watch her dive, but I couldn't see the top of the tower because it was blocked from view by a railing. The only part of the dive I saw was when she passed by me at my eye level, and it looked like she had already over rotated with still about six feet to go before entering the water.

Thinking that she had rotated too much, I dropped to my knees and thought what a shame it was that she had just blown a chance of a lifetime. I expected to see scores of three and a half's and fours for the dive at best. It seemed like an hour for the scoreboard to show the scores. When they finally came up, I was stunned to see unbelievable scores of 7½, 7, 8, 7½, 7, and she won by a slight margin of only 1.35 points.

I jumped up and started to run to her when I ran into the wall and hurt my shoulder. When I got to her she was already surrounded with reporters. I finally broke through the crowd when she said that she didn't think she had done anything so great. While hugging her I told her to just wait and see.

The Associated Press (AP) called her father back in Princeton, New Jersey, where it was three o'clock in the morning, and woke him up to inform him that his daughter had just won the Olympic Gold medal. He told them that it was a heck of a trick to pull on someone in the middle of the night, and hung up.

The AP called him back and told him that it was true, she really had won. Lesley didn't realize it at the time, but like Sitzberger, she had also performed a miracle. No one, including her coaches, believed she would ever come close to making the finals or certainly winning the contest. In fact, nearly everyone said Bush would be last!

Lesley enrolled in Indiana in the fall of 1965 and went on to win several International and National diving titles on one-meter, three-meter and tower. At the 1965 World Student University games in 1965 and 1967 she took the silver medal on the three-meter, and the gold medal on tower at the 1967 games. She also won the platform at the 1967 Pan American Games in Winnipeg Canada. This proved she was not a fluke winning the Gold on tower at the 1964 Olympic Games, and learned how to compete.

God's Miracles

It was at that moment that I thought about the night when I learned I wasn't going to be named the Olympic diving coach, and sitting on the park bench in Detroit before the Olympic trials. I had pleaded with God to let one of my divers make the Olympic Team, and He rewarded me with two Gold medals that were both won by performing miracles.

(Lesley Bush on left)

Ingeborg Pertmeyr of Austria (pictured below) placed sixth on the ten-meter platform and decided to attend Indiana University soon after the 1964 Olympics to dive on our team. She dived with us

for two years during which time she was seen in a picture that was in Sports Illustrated when they did an article on me. She stayed with us until after she placed ninth at the 1968 Olympics. Then she retired, and went home to live in Austria with her mother. A few years later, Ingeborg got married and had a son. In 2009, she died from cancer. I mention her in my book now because having dived in two Olympic Games few knew who she was while at Indiana.

My Return Trip Home

Australia invited me to give a series of lectures and clinics in six different cities before returning home from Tokyo after the Olympic Games. I thought it was a great opportunity, and agreed to do it. I hopped on a plane to Sydney where I was to meet the people who oversaw my trip. When I arrived at the airport, a bunch of reporters came running toward me yelling, "There he is!"

I thought they must be looking for some celebrity. I turned around to see who they were looking for, and found it was me. A person representing Rothman Cigarettes handed me a schedule of the places I was to visit, and the first city was Perth, then Adelaide, Melbourne, Hobart Tasmania, Sydney, and Brisbane.

I had no idea where Perth was, and when I asked he said that if Sydney was New York City, Perth would be where San Francisco is in California. The man also handed me a big box as he escorted me downtown to a hotel where I stayed for the night. I took off the next morning for a long tedious flight to Perth where I was well received, and gave a clinic in their pool while using a trampoline to show how it could be used to teach dives.

I opened the box that had been given me, and found it full of cigarettes. I realized that Rothman's was sponsoring my trip, and I was to give them out to the spectators. Not a smoker I opened a pack of cigarettes while giving a lecture or clinic in each city. After lighting up a cigarette and starting to choke, I told the audience to be sure to buy Rothman cigarettes!

After giving lectures and diving clinics in the other cities they treated me very well with a banquet in my honor. Sydney was the last clinic before going home, and the president of F.I.N.A., (the international governing body of aquatics) was Australian, and presided over the banquet.

I really liked the people in Australia, and I've had the privilege of visiting the country several times. In fact, I thought later that I would like to live there, but I changed my mind because it was too late in my life. I would find it difficult to start making friends all over again, and it would also be too far away from my home and family. I was glad to get home after being away from my family and job for over a month.

I Decide to Quit Show Business

When I got back home after the Olympics and travel to Australia doing lectures and clinics, I was tired. A few days later, I decided to quit show business. I was only 38 but getting too old to perform our strenuous seven-act show safely. Kimball teamed up with Ron O'Brien, and they performed our show for another three years. Then they quit, and each decided to start their own diving camp. I eventually figured out that if I was going to compete with them on the collegiate level, I would have to start a diving camp, too. I did coach four divers from St. Louis and Ft. Worth during the summer at no charge. But I didn't get around to starting a camp until 1969, four years after I retired from doing clown shows.

Honors and Awards

The Touchdown Club of Columbus held their tenth annual all sports dinner at the Columbus Athletic Club in January of 1965. They honored some of the greatest athletes in the country and in the world. I was honored because Ken Sitzberger was the Olympic diving champion. Dr. Wynne Silbernagel, whom I had lived with part of the time I was in school at Ohio State, was on the selection committee.

The first person I met coming into the lobby was Joe Namath who had just graduated from the University of Alabama, and received $400,000 to play football for the New York Jets. I started to follow him around when Mickey Mantle walked in, and Joe introduced me to him.

I remember I didn't wash my hands for two or three days when I told people that this was the hand that shook the hand of Mickey Mantle. I met several other great athletes and coaches, such as Dick Butkus, Don Shula, Max Schmeling, Bob Hays, and John Wooden. I was really excited to sit between Joe Namath and Johnny Unites at the banquet. That meeting with so many of the best athletes and coaches in the world was one of the greatest thrills in my life.

The I.U. Outdoor Pool

The IU outdoor pool was built in 1965 when President Wells got five alumni to donate fifty-thousand dollars apiece to help with its construction. The cost ended up being four-hundred-thousand dollars to build the whole complex. When they were ready to install the swimming pool and diving well, I told them to face the diving boards and tower north and south to prevent the sun from getting in the diver's eyes.

However, someone on the staff thought it would look much better from the street if the pools were facing East and West. I was in Australia when they finished installing the pools, and I hit the ceiling when I returned and saw what they had done. But it was too late to make any changes. So, Doc and I spent decades training our swimmers and divers in pools that were facing in the wrong direction. The outdoor pool complex was renovated years later costing well over a million dollars.

I was made the assistant supervisor of the outdoor pool when it opened in 1965. The school hired about six different pool supervisors over the twenty-four years I worked there. Jerry Yeagley, our successful soccer coach, got stuck with the job for two summers when one day a professor came into the pool with his son carrying a big inner tube.

When the boy was about to enter the water with the tube, Jerry informed the father that no floating props were permitted in the pool due to safety measures. The professor suddenly turned on Jerry, and asked him if he knew who he was. And Jerry said he had no idea. The professor started to give Jerry a hard time. I was coaching on the deck and he came to me disgusted. Jerry told me what was going on, and asked me if I could do anything about it.

I went over to the professor, and again politely explained the rules of the pool regarding floating objects that obscure a lifeguard's vision of the pool. The professor came up to me eye to eye, and asked me if I knew who he was. I said, no, then asked the professor if he knew who I was. And I added, if his kid tried to put the tube in the water, I would have security kick his butt off the premises along with his kid.

The professor got upset, and said he was going to go to the president of the university, and have me fired. Then I told him that he could go to God, and his son was still not going to put that tube in the water. The professor walked out with his son, and never returned.

Book Publishing

Doc Counsilman finished his book, The Science of Swimming in 1965. It changed the way of coaching swimming throughout the world. Doc used physics principles to illustrate his points. I had also finished my first book, Diving Illustrated that included drawings of all the dives in the diving rule books. They were all drawn in sequence with a short explanation of each movement using principles of physics also. And these books have continued to influence how we coach swimming and diving using irrefutable applied physics principles.

CHAPTER 27

Teaching and Coaching Diving from 1965 to 1968

Our Depth Began to Show
Diving Team in 1965

Top Row: Hobie, Rick Earley, Rick Gilbert, Ken Sitzberger, Dickie Morris

Front Row: Nick Carlton, Charlie Neel, Chuck Stenbeck

Sitzberger and Gilbert took first and second place on the one and three-meter boards in the Big 10, N.C.A.A., and the Indoor and Outdoor National A.A.U. Championships. The Indoor A.A.U. meet was held at Yale University, and there were 84 divers competing on the low board. Ken and Rick took first and second, and Nick Carlton placed 24th.

I ran over after the meet and gave Nick a hug when Ken and Rick came running over, and asked why I was hugging him when they won. I told them because that was the best Nick has ever done. He beat 60 divers, and of course you placed first and second, that was expected of you but not of Nick.

Our divers continued to show their strength at the 1965 outdoor National A.A.U Championships. Sitzberger and Gilbert were first and second again on the one-meter and three-meter boards, and Earley, Neel, Rhodes, and Zimmerman placed in the top ten.

I was using the trampoline for teaching and coaching divers. I decided to make a film using the trampoline in 1965 that would be helpful for all other diving programs. The film included John Vogel, Charlie Neel, Dickie Morris, Rick Gilbert, and Rick Earley.

(Pictured left to right: John Vogel, Charley Neel, Tom Dinsley, Rick Gilbert, Rick Earley, Dickie Morris, and John Walker)

They demonstrated the proper take offs and movements in the basic dives, and the lead ups for the more difficult dives. And I could show the four different landings on the trampoline bed when it was not possible for divers to land on their head.

A pamphlet was included with the film that offered the advantages, care, safety factors, and all the diving skills performed in progression. It was a lot of fun making the film. I remember they were all standing on the trampoline when I thanked them for doing a job well done. Then as I walked away they all suddenly whistled. When I turned around, they were giving me a "moon shot" and broke out laughing.

The 1965 N.C.A.A. Championship Results

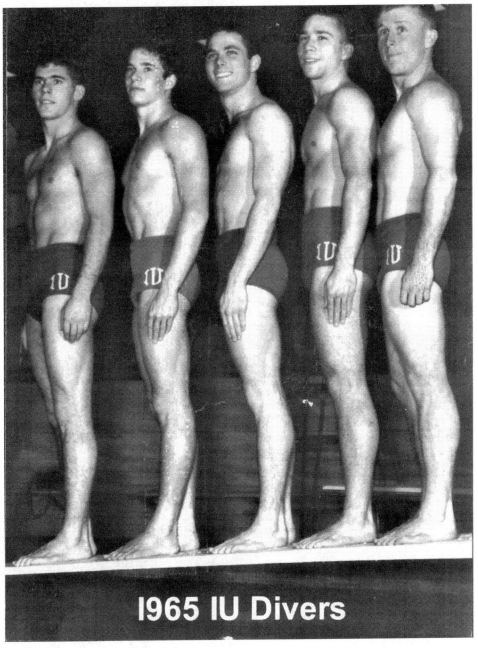

1965 IU Divers

(Pictured left to right: Ken Sitzberger, Dickie Morris, Rick Earley, Rick Gilbert, Charlie Neel) After the 1964 Olympics, we had tremendous depth in our diving program. A high number of diving points was noticeably added to the scores of the Indiana swimming team in major meets. An example of the power and depth of our men's team over a nearly twenty-year period is shown in the following results.

The 1965 N.C.A.A. Championships were held at Iowa State University. We took six divers, and they all performed in the finals. We scored eighty team points in two events compared to 16 swimming events. That would have placed us eighth in the team standings without the aid of the Indiana swimmers.

One-	Meter	Three-	Meter
1st	Sitzberger	1st	Sitzberger
2nd	Gilbert	2nd	Gilbert
5th	Earley	3rd	Earley
11th	Neel	7th	Neel

Our women's team was nearly as good, but couldn't show it because female collegiate athletic teams didn't exist until Title IX was declared in 1972.

The Effect of Title IX

Title IX was enacted by Congress in June 1972 to give equal rights to women's sports and athletes. This meant that the number of sports and scholarships that schools could offer had to be equal with the number applied to the men's programs. To be complying, some schools dropped their men's swimming and diving programs and other non-revenue men's sports so they would have an equal number of women's sports.

Our 1965-1966 Diving Team

Front row: Rick Earley, Charlie Neel, Chuck Stenbeck

Back row: Nick Carlton, Ken Sitzberger, Dick Morris, Luis Niño de Rivera

The Start of 1966 Season

The incredible multi-national champion Jim Henry

This outstanding group from 1965 was followed by Jim Henry who was the only diver that I recruited without leaving the campus. The Athletic Department said there was no money in our budget to recruit divers off campus. I saw Jim dive as a high school senior at a meet in Texas. I was impressed with his amazing leg strength that showed he was well on his way to becoming a great diver.

I began to call Jim in the spring of 1966, and continued until it was time for him to decide where he was going to college. He eventually told me he was coming to Indiana because he had been encouraged by Dave Browning. Dave was the father of Skippy Browning, the 1952 Olympic Springboard Champion, and a good friend of the Henry family. Jim enrolled, and quickly learned a full list of dives from the three-meter springboard, and all the difficult dives from one meter springboard. But he had trouble with his entries, and made a huge splash.

I recognized his problem was that he was muscle bound in the shoulders and arms. This didn't allow him to extend and straighten his arms overhead on the entry. I decided to have him perform two stretching exercises for his shoulders and arms before and after each workout until he finally could straighten them and make entries with little splash.

That simple change eventually made it possible for him to win many major diving contests, and become one of the best divers in the world. He was not only a great diver, but an exceptional person with no bad habits. He was very loyal to me and his family, and never gave me any trouble.

The 1966 Outdoor National A.A.U. Championships in Lincoln, Nebraska

I had my team learn to perform from the ten-meter platform that summer, and Jim was ahead of everyone when he performed the required dives from the three-meter board in Lincoln.

Rick Gilbert and Ken Sitzberger had won a national title as college freshmen, and I wanted Jim to be the third Indiana diver to win a title as a freshman. Jim was leading by 35 points after the five compulsory dives competing from the three-meter board at the 1966 National A.A.U. Championships in Lincoln, Nebraska.

However, when Jim was ready to perform his optional dives after a short break, his triceps had swollen. He was in so much pain he couldn't extend them over his head and had to scratch from the competition. The previous summer, Jim had learned to dive tower. For some reason, he had worked out on tower the day before leaving for the meet, and it took a couple of days for the reaction.

I wanted Ken Sitzberger, in his junior year, to also win a national title for a wedding present. He had recently married Jeanne Collier, who had taken second in the 1964 Olympics. But in the one-meter event he got beat, and took second. That upset me a little, and soon after the event my divers gathered around me except Gilbert.

Gilbert had graduated, and was still in school working on his Master's Degree. He unexpectedly placed fifth on the one-meter, and was whistling while drying off about twenty feet away from us. Still upset, I went over and asked him why he hadn't taken up knitting. Surprised, he asked me why. And still upset, I told him that since he had dived like an old maid, why not be one. I didn't realize at that moment how badly I'd hurt Rick's feelings as he walked away in disgust.

Mary had never gone to an away meet with me before. When she woke up in the middle of the night to find I was awake, she asked me what was wrong. I told her what I had said to Rick, and went on to say he didn't deserve my comment. Rick was the one that made me a coach, and had always shown more loyalty and respect for me and the diving program than anyone else on my team.

The divers, except Gilbert, gathered around me, the next day just before the three-meter event was ready to start. He was standing in the bleachers, and I went over to talk to him. I could see the hate on his face standing only about two feet away.

I told Rick how sorry I was for speaking to him in the manner I had done. I went on to tell him how proud and thankful I was for all that he had done for me and our team, when he also started to cry. We both went behind the stands to be unseen by those around us when the call was made to start the three-meter contest. I loved Rick. He was my first national champion to build my program, and he was the last diver to deserve that treatment.

I sat on the grass with a few other people to watch the contest. It came down to the last dive. Gilbert, Sitzberger, Young, Wrightson (pictured right), and Russell weren't more than a point or two apart from each other.

Rick came over to me just as the round started, and said, "Hobie, today we are going to win our first outdoor national championship!" And I told him I hoped so as he walked away. Rick went on to win the contest, beating his teammate Sitzberger by 35/100 of point. Then he came back the next day and won the ten-meter tower event, and became the first Indiana diver to win a tower title.

Anything Can and Will Happen at a Championship Meet

To show what can happen in major contests, three incidents occurred at the 1966 Outdoor Nationals meet that I think are worth mentioning. The first was when Jim Henry had to scratch. The second incident occurred when Wrightson hit the one-meter board on two different compulsory dives competing in the preliminary rounds.

Wrightson was a good friend, and I thought it was impossible for him to qualify for the finals. I took him behind the stands, and told him not to be discouraged because he was an outstanding diver and things would work out for him. He turned everything around, and not only made the finals but went on to win the contest with Sitzberger placing second. I said to myself, "What a coach."

The third incident occurred when Dick Smith was the referee for the ten-meter platform event. His two divers, Russell and Wrightson, were leading when lightning started to flash in the distance. Everyone wanted to stop the contest because of the danger of being struck by lightning especially diving off a thirty-two-foot high tower.

RJ Smith, the referee, made an announcement that the contest would continue. I think he made that decision because he thought his divers had a better chance of winning. Win Young, also a freshman on our team, was ready to dive when Smith made his comment, and refused to dive so the contest was halted. The contest continued after the lightning and rain passed over, and Rick Gilbert won and Win Young took second place.

N.C.A.A. Would Later Drop Freshman Rule

The N.C.A.A. didn't dropped the freshman ineligible rule until 1972. This meant that all my new recruits could only compete in A.A.U. competitions. Therefore, we had such strong showings in these championship meets in the 1960's.

Rick Earley

Doc Counsilman saw Rick Earley diving in a California meet, and thought he had great promise. Since Doc recruited him, I was surprised when Rick showed up at Indiana because I didn't know a thing about him.

It turned out that he was extremely strong, but not well educated in the sport that was soon to change. He made our team and turned out to be an outstanding diver in his career. But for some reason, Doc didn't let me take him to the Big 10 Championships for two years, even after he placed third in the N.C.A.A. National Championships in both years, and did much better in later years.

Rick enlisted and while serving in the Army he won two national titles on the ten-meter platform, a Gold medal at the 1971 Pan American Games, and placed sixth in the 1972 Olympics on tower. He was a strong diver with great spatial awareness. I believe he was the first diver to perform a back 2½ somersault from the five-meter platform. He also was one of many divers on my team who later became a diving coach. After getting married he had a son who also became a great diver and won several national titles.

Pete Rhodes was a walk-on who came from a very wealthy family that owned the Pittsburgh Plate and Glass Company that none of the divers knew about. He was a quiet kid and easy to coach because he was well disciplined and anxious to learn. He learned fast and scored high in some of our major meets. But unfortunately, I never heard from him again after he graduated.

Another diver who had to work hard to make the team was John Zimmerman from Chicago. John never learned how to be a top diver on my team, but made the finals in a national meet and helped to encourage everyone on the team and stayed in touch with me for years.

A Visit from the Russians

The new I.U. outdoor pool opened in July of 1965. Soon after the pool opened, Doc and I were informed that a group of Russian coaches had arrived on campus to watch Doc and I coach our teams. They heard that we were using scientific principles in our coaching, and came to find out how we used them.

Two swimming and diving coaches showed up with two interpreters, one for swimming and one for diving, and were accompanied by a manager who happened to be a member of the K.G.B. They were staying at the Indiana Union when one day, the K.G.B. manager came running to Doc and me, and said that his group had disappeared and he couldn't find them.

We sat in the lobby of the Union for about an hour waiting for them to show up, but when they didn't show, we decided to go out and look for them. We finally found them in the last place we would have ever guessed. They had gone to a laundromat in town. They had been sitting in there all morning watching people put clothes in the washing machine then take them out put them in a dryer. We were told that no such machines existed in Russia. They thought it was unbelievable that people could clean their clothes in machines, and dry them so quickly while paying only a few coins.

They came to the pool every day for over a month, and observed our coaching and wrote down everything we said and did. Doc had just written his book <u>The Science of Swimming</u>, and I had written my book <u>Diving</u> Illustrated. My divers performed some of the dives from the book for them, and they were amazed to see how quickly the use of

230

the scientific laws helped the divers learn so fast. The books were not yet available anywhere in Russia, so we gave them a couple copies as a gift which they greatly appreciated. Later, we learned that they had our books printed in Russian, and gave them to all their swimming and diving coaches who later passed along copies to the Chinese coaches.

The Housing Situation

Rick Gilbert graduated from Indiana University in 1965 after the 1964 Olympics, and decided to stay at Indiana University another year in 1966 to earn a Master's Degree. Indiana University didn't have dormitories for graduate students yet, so the students lived in house trailers and crappy apartments in older homes that were available near campus.

There was some married student housing in old World War Two Quonset huts and trailers. Rick bought one of the trailers for two years. When he graduated with his Master's Degree he decided to give the trailer to me. This led me to buying four or five more that I rented out to the students.

We Are Recognized

We were recognized in 1966 as the best diving team in the country because we won nearly all the major diving titles, and dominated the finals placing at least four divers in all the finals for a few more years. I was made the National Coach of the Year by the American Swimming Coaches Association seven times in a row until they stopped giving the award. That award was later replaced with the Mike Peppe award, after my coach at Ohio State, and I never won it.

The 1966 World Championships

Bernie Wrightson and Rick Gilbert were selected to compete in the 1966 World Diving Championships in Budapest, Hungary along with a large group of swimmers, and I was selected as the U.S. team diving coach. The meet was held on St. Maria's Island in a river between the old cities of Buda and Pest that are now known as one large city called Budapest.

The meet offered fair swimming and diving facilities. Gilbert won the springboard and tower events making him the best diver in the world at that time, and Wrightson placed second in both events. I think that the reason why Gilbert won both events was because I spent most of my time coaching Wrightson, and Gilbert didn't appreciate it and felt challenged, so he decided to show me he was the better diver.

The team was divided into two groups after the world meet with each visiting different countries where they competed and gave exhibitions on the way home. Rick went with one group, and Bernie and I went with the other group. Our group went to the island of Cyprus in the middle of the Mediterranean Sea where there was a war going on.

We found sand bags piled up on both sides of the main street where the soldiers were fighting each other, but not while we were there. I always thought that they may have stopped the war because of our three-day visit. A large contingent of British soldiers was running the swimming meet. I remember the starter for the swimming events suggested he blow a whistle to start a race instead of shooting a pistol with blanks in fear that the war might start again.

The pool didn't have any diving facilities, so Bernie was invited to dive into the sea. We didn't see any diving facilities when we got to the shore. Instead, we were taken to a long wooden pier where Bernie dived from a sixteen-inch-wide wooden pole about twelve feet above the pier. He had to climb to the top of the post to perform a dive, then swim about fifty yards back to the shore to get back up on the pier.

I did a couple of easy dives to give him time to get back on the pier. It was a crazy show, but the spectators appreciated our efforts to entertain them. Later that night, Bernie managed to dive from an old wooden diving board when the team and I were taken to another pool on the island.

The next stop was Cairo, Egypt for a meet with their swimming team. They had a couple of good divers. Their diving coach wanted us to compete against them, and I refused because they insisted on using only Egyptian judges. I knew they would cheat us to win. They otherwise were very nice to our group, and took us to see the pyramids and the Egyptian museum. We then headed home to the United States.

Charley Neel

Charly Neel, ed in Viet am

Charley was a diver who was sent to me by his coach, Wally Nakamoto in Hawaii in 1965. Wally said he was a nice kid who probably wouldn't score any points for us. But he was wrong, because Charley placed high in many of the major championships.

He was a little guy with a nice build, and liked poetry which he would recite to the team. I taught him several dives from the ten-meter platform at Indiana's new outdoor pool. But he was scared to death to perform a forward 3½ somersault from the top platform. I remember he would stand on the 7½ meter platform until I gave him a sign to dive. Then he would run up to the ten-meter platform, and run off and perform the dive without stopping.

His father was a captain in the Navy. Before graduating from Indiana, Charley decided to join the Marines to fight in Vietnam. I was against his decision and tried to talk him out of it. But he had made up his mind, and was killed when he stepped on a land mine a few months later. As far as I know, he was the second athlete from Indiana University to die in the Vietnam War. Dean Allen, one of my first divers, was the first.

Later, divers from Ohio State had a memorial plaque made in his honor that is displayed in the International Swimming Hall of Fame which recently moved from Ft. Lauderdale, Florida to Santa Clara, California.

Dickie Morris

RICHARD MORSE

DIVING

1964, 1965, 1966 ALL-AMERICAN

Richard Morse was one of several IU divers who shaped the program's legacy. In 1964, Morse joined Richard Earley, Charles Neel and Richard Gilbert to earn a total of eight All-America honors in diving. Prior to that year, Indiana had seen only two divers earn All-American status. That year, Morse finished fourth on three-meter and eighth on one-meter at his first NCAA Championship. In 1965, he claimed a seventh-place finish on the three-meter and 11th on the one-meter. He concluded his career with placing eleventh on three-meter and 10th on one-meter in 1966.

Dickie Morris was from Nashville, Tennessee, and showed up at the pool with his mother after he had graduated from high school. He wanted to know if I would let him dive on our team if he went to Indiana University. I never saw him dive, but agreed to take him. Dickie turned out to be a very steady competitor, and placed well in the more important meets.

Then as a junior, he seriously hit his head on the three-meter board during practice, and he never mentally recovered from the accident and quit diving. He became a Navy seal after graduating from Indiana, and ended up in Hawaii where I believe he still lives.

Our team in 1967

We were recognized as the best diving team in the country winning nearly all the major diving titles, and placing at least four divers in all the finals for a few more years. I was made the National Coach of the Year by the American Swimming Coaches Association seven times in a row until they stopped giving the award.

I was attending the National A.A.U. convention in 1968 when it was decided that all the chairmen of the various sports were to be replaced with new ones. That included the men's and women's national diving chairmen. RJ Smith had been the men's chairman for eighteen years. He wanted to keep the job because he was an architect for a large company in New York that constructed swimming pools, and they paid him a lot of money for his work.

Knowing of the change, the diving coaches got together before the diving committee met, and decided who would bring the matter up at our meeting. We knew RJ was going to try and wiggle around the change. We decided to toss a coin between Jack Roth, a diving coach from California and me, and I lost.

Sure enough, RJ Jackson was aware of the change, and tried to cut our meeting short. He started to adjourn the meeting when I told him we couldn't adjourn until we all voted for a new chairman. He argued that the change didn't include the diving chairman, when we all knew it did. So Dick Smith left the room and returned with one of the top

233

A.A.U. officials who informed us that the changes were meant to include the diving chairmanship. Instead of Jack Roth being our pick, Dick Smith was voted as the new chairman for the men.

Bob Rambo, who was the women's diving chairman and diving coach at the University of Pennsylvania, was also replaced. Bob worked for the Coca Cola Company that paid him well because of his diving chairman position. Unfortunately, Bob committed suicide soon after he was replaced.

(Pictured left-right front row, Win Young, Nick Carlton, Jim Henry, Leslie Bush, Ingeborg Pertmeyr; back row Hobie, Rick Gilbert, Ken Sitzberger, Luis Niño de Rivera, Chuck Stenbeck

The L- 5 Mumbo Jumbo revisited

We had been winning and placing a lot of divers in every National Championship for years when the word got out that I was using John Lovestedt's L-5 mumbo jumbo method in my coaching. I was walking into the pool to compete in the 1967 National Championships in Fort Worth, Texas, and ran into Dick Kimball, Ron O'Brien, and Dick Smith. They started to tease me about what they called the "L-5 mumbo jumbo crap" and I didn't say a word to them.

234

It turned out that all three judged the one-meter event, and my divers placed first, second, third, fourth, seventh, eleventh, and twelfth with Luis Niňo de Rivera winning the contest. As my team and I were walking out after the event, I remember telling the three coaches, "Not bad when using L-5 Mumbo Jumbo." We came back the next day, and placed five divers in the top nine of twelve places. Our divers finished the meet with Win Young and Rick Gilbert taking third and fourth on the ten-meter platform event.

The 1967 Pan American Games

The Pan American Games were in Calgary, Canada and our American divers performed extremely well and took home most of the medals. Dick Smith's divers, Bernie Wrightson and Keith Russell, placed first and second on the three-meter springboard, and Win Young and Luis Niňo de Rivera who was from Mexico but dived for Indiana, took first and second place on the ten-meter platform.

Sue Gossick won the three-meter springboard followed by Micki King who placed second. On the ten-meter platform, Lesley Bush finished first, and Ann Peterson, from Arizona placed third. As it later turned out, these divers also made the 1968 Olympic team.

1967 Indiana's First N.C.A.A. Swimming and Diving National Championship

Indiana swimmers and divers did a great job taking second in 1964 and 1965, and third in the 1966 N.C.A.A. National Championships before finally winning their first N.C.A.A. team title in 1967 at Dartmouth College. Indiana was leading the field going into the last day of the meet, and five Indiana divers scored forty-one points in the finals in the one-meter competition.

Doc couldn't sleep the night before the Saturday events, so he woke me up in the middle of the night, and asked how many points I thought we could count on from the divers in the three-meter event. Still sleepy, I said "five" which startled him, and he really got upset. I told him that diving wasn't like swimming when the coach knew about how fast a person was going to swim by the times he did with a stop watch.

There was no way anyone could predict how well a diver would perform because many mistakes could occur under pressure. I went back to sleep, but I don't think Doc slept a wink that whole night. He was very pleased later that night when we didn't score five points, but instead, scored fifty-five points!

No university had ever had five divers make the finals in the N.C.A.A. Championships, and they scored an unheard of 96 points in two events. That score would have placed our divers in fourth place if the swimmers hadn't been in the meet. Indiana had taken an army of swimmers and divers to the meet. Soon after this meet, the N.C.A.A. ruled to limit sixteen swimmers and four divers to represent a team at the N.C.A.A. National Championships.

Sports Illustrated and a few other magazine and newspaper reporters showed up at Royer Pool to do a story on our amazing win the following Monday. I was down at our diving well with my divers who performed so brilliantly, but none of the reporters came to speak to us nor did Doc say a word about us. Sports Illustrated did a great four-page story on Doc and the swim team's accomplishments that they deserved, but not a word was said about our divers.

I remember the only reporter who gave us any credit was Bob Hammel, the sports editor of the local Bloomington Herald-Telegraph paper. Bob was an excellent reporter who covered all the Indiana University and high school sports events, until he retired and his kind of reporting stopped.

Hammel really loved Doc and Bobby Knight, and wrote fantastic stories about both. He always covered for Bobby Knight when he got into trouble, and he did an outstanding job reporting on Doc, especially when he swam the English Channel. However, he missed a lot of what my divers accomplished that was not his fault.

I made the worst mistake in my career by failing to inform him of the many accomplishments my divers made over the years. I realized, too late, that he couldn't have written about my divers when he was never informed. Sam Bell, the track coach, could have his hat blow off his head, and it would be in the newspaper the next day because Sam would tell Hammel about the incident.

Since our divers rarely got the recognition they deserved I wish to make a comment about them, and the places they took that made it possible for Indiana to win their first N.C.A.A. Championship. The first number next to the diver's name is how they scored in the one-meter event, and the second number is the place they took on the three-meter board.

Jim Henry (1st and 2nd) was from Dallas, Texas and was highly recruited by several colleges because he was a good one-meter diver that showed great promise. He ended up being one of the best divers in the world on the one and three-meter springboard, and the ten-meter tower.

(Pictured left-right Jon Hahnfeldt, Jim Henry, Win Young)

Win Young (2nd and 4th) was a real prize for me while attending Indiana. He had dived for Dick smith as an age grouper. I could write a whole book about him. But here are some of his highlights while coaching him. Win could perform twists in a somersault quicker than any diver in the world. One time in the national championship, he was supposed to do a back 1½ somersault with 2½ twists, and received near perfect scores for the dive.

Observing the dive, Dick Kimball, now the diving coach at Michigan, jumped up and said he had performed 3½ twists instead of 2½ twists. The judges had a meeting, and agreed with Dick after a long discussion. That gave Win a zero for performing the wrong dive even though it was far more difficult!

Win was a fantastic tower diver as well as springboard diver. But one summer, he mysteriously developed a fear of diving from the ten-meter platform. I tried for weeks to challenge him to perform the difficult dives, but he couldn't get up enough nerve to do any of them. I finally called up his old high school coach, Chuck McMahan in Phoenix, and asked if he would take him back and see if he could do anything with him and Chuck agreed.

I called Chuck a week later, and asked him how things were going. He said Win was doing three of the optional dives, and had three to go. I called again two weeks later, and he told me he had finally got Win to perform all but one dive. He also said he wanted to send Win back to me because he was exhausted coaching him. I asked how did he managed to get Win to do the dives, and he said he threw a tantrum and scared him into doing the dives.

The last dive Win had to do was a handstand into a reverse somersault dive. I remembered what Chuck had said, and brought out a wooden chair and placed it on the pool deck close to the cement wall near the tower. When Win continued to balk on every attempt, I suddenly exploded and picked up the chair and smashed it up against the concrete wall behind me.

With one leg of the chair in my hand, I told Win that if he didn't do the dive by the time I got up to the top platform, I would club the daylights out of him. Doc was coaching his swimmers in the pool next to the diving well and calling out the seconds for the swimmers to hear as they were finishing their repeats.

Doc saw me running up the stairs on the tower and started to laugh. My whole team stood there horrified thinking that I had lost my mind. I forgot to tell them that the whole affair was planned. When I got to the top Win was gone, and I asked my divers if he had done the dive. And they said he had.

Win was never taken into the Indiana Hall of Fame because he never graduated from Indiana. Win, later in life, was coaching at the University of Arizona with Michele Mitchell, the head diving coach, when he came down with cancer. Michele called me one day and suggested that I come out and see Win because he was in bad shape.

I put the phone down and took the first flight I could get to Phoenix and spent the day with him talking about old times. He was not able to move his legs without great pain. I was glad I went to see him when I did, because he passed away a couple of days later at age 58.

Jon Hanfeldt (5th and 5th)

Jon made our team when he and his father, Ed, walked into the pool one day as I was getting ready for practice and introduced me to his son. Ed told me he wanted Jon to

237

attend Indiana and dive on my team. I told him that I had never met his son before and I couldn't watch him dive in our pool because it was against the N.C.A.A. rules.

Ed didn't back away and kept telling me I had to take his son and I soon gave in but with one condition. I didn't have a clue how good of a diver Jon was. So, I told him I would coach him for one semester, and if he didn't show any promise he would be dismissed.

Jon was a strong diver who showed promise but kept fooling around in practice. One day he came in and started to give me an attitude problem. I backed him up against the wall, and gave him a chewing out that he had never gotten before.

Fortunately, he heard every word I said, because from then on, he was a member of our team. He turned out to be one of the first divers in the world to ever perform all the difficult non-twisting optional dives from the three-meter board in the pike position when most of them had been performed in the tuck position.

hn Hahnfeldt

Before his last dive, a reverse 2½ somersault, on the three-meter board at the N.C.A.A. Championships at Dartmouth, he confidently walked out to the end of the board and raised thumbs up to the whole crowd. I had never seen a diver do such a thing, and I think the crowd hoped that he would land flat on his back or on his face because of his display. But he wowed them all performing the dive beautifully, and the whole Indiana team stood up and cheered him.

Jon later became a diving coach and was named Coach of the Year when his diver won the state high school title with teammates who made the finals. Jon soon after had a brain aneurism that ruptured and died.

Luis Niňo de Rivera (6th and 6th)

Luis came from a wealthy family in Mexico City. He left Mexico to attend an American high school in Los Angeles for his senior year, and was coached by Jack Roth, a well-known American diving coach and a dear friend of mine.

I first met Luis at a meet when he decided after graduating from high school that he wanted to attend Indiana University, and dive on my team. However, he found that Indiana University denied his admission because one year in high school in America wasn't long enough. His mother was a friend of the President of Mexico, and asked him to help Luis get into Indiana. The Mexican President called a high government official in Washington who knew someone in the Department of Education who called the President of Indiana University, and Luis was accepted.

Luis turned out to be one of the finest divers I ever coached, and has continued to be a close friend of mine after he graduated from Indiana with honors in business. He had five brothers and sisters, and his father was highly respected by some of the most prominent people in Mexico. Luis always scored well in all our dual and championship meets. He made the finals and won the one-meter National A.A.U. championships in 1967. He also placed fourth from the three-meter board, and tenth from the ten-meter platform while competing for Mexico in the 1968 Mexico City Olympic Games.

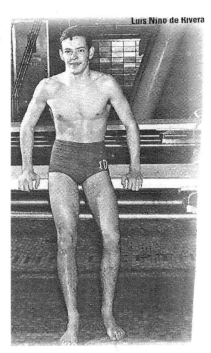
Luis Nino de Rivera

One great memory of Luis was when he was learning to perform a back 2½ somersault from the ten-meter tower at our outdoor pool. We did not have a bubbler system to soften his entry if he made a mistake. I would give him a call to release his legs, and extend his body for the entry. Unfortunately, he didn't hear or respond to my call and over rotated. He landed so flat on the water that he bounced and never went under water. He was in great pain and I didn't know what to tell him. I finally told him to not believe everything he heard, and he started to laugh while still groaning in pain. What a guy!

After graduating from Indiana in 1971, he became one of the best matadors in Mexico for two years, and ended up as their bull fight commissioner after he retired. Luis then went into the banking business, and is now the Vice-Chairman of Banco Azteca, one of the largest banks in Mexico with four-hundred branch banks throughout Mexico and South America. He has three wonderful children by Hortensia, his beautiful wife, and they still live in Mexico City. Luis has always had an infectious personality, and has been the M.C. for all my past birthday parties.

Nick Carlton (8th and 12th) (pictured right)

Nick came from Monroe, Michigan and was another diver I had never met before arriving at IU. He was not recruited by any college, including Indiana, because he was an average diver

239

and came as a walk on. He worked his tail off at every workout, and managed to make the finals in most of our meets in his last two years.

Nick went from twenty-fourth in the National A.A.U. Championship meet in 1966 to making the finals in our first winning N.C.A.A. Championship meet a year later in 1967. He returned to Monroe after graduating from Indiana, and went into business before getting married and having two children.

I Produce Another Diving Film in 1967

I decided to make another film in 1967. This one was called "Diving Champions on Film." I had Ken Sitzberger, Rick Gilbert, Win Young, and Jon Hahnfeldt perform the required and optional dives from the one-meter board at our outdoor pool. They showed different styles, and I offered some written comments for each dive.

Our Indiana divers had just scored an unheard of 96 points helping Indiana win the 1967 N.C.A.A. National Championships. Sitzberger won the 1968 NCAA high and low board titles to end his competitive collegiate diving career on a positive note.

Our Indiana divers then dominated the summer 1967 Outdoor National A.A.U. Championships. Four Indiana divers placed in the top six finals in both events. On the one-meter board, Jim Henry took first, Win Young fourth, Jon Hahnfeldt fifth, and Luis Niño de Riviera sixth. On the three-meter board, Henry was first, Young second, Hahnfeldt fifth, and Niño de Rivera sixth.

They came back again in the 1968 N.C.A.A. Championships held at our home Indiana Royer Pool. On the one-meter, Henry, Young, and Hahnfeldt went one, two, three, and on the three-meter, Young and Henry went one, and two. Hahnfeldt was in a solid third place when he caught his feet on the tip of the board performing an inward 2½ somersault in the pike position, and had to drop out of the event.

Two National A.A.U. Championships Four Months Apart

The 1968 Olympic trials were staged in late August. The A.A.U. had scheduled two National A.A.U. Diving Championships only four months apart. The first one was held indoors in May at East Carolina University in Greenville, North Carolina. But since they didn't have a ten-meter tower, that event was held at the University of Pittsburgh three days later, and all the platform contestants and coaches were furnished complimentary air transportation to Pittsburgh.

Our indoor results proved the dominance of the Indiana divers in the three events:

One-meter - Jim Henry 1st, Rick Gilbert 3rd, Win Young 4th, Luis Niño de Rivera 6th, and Jon Hahnfeldt 8th.

Three-meter – Win Young 1st, Rick Gilbert 2nd, Luis Niño de Rivera 6th, and Nick Carlton 11th.

10-meter platform - Win Young 2nd, Jim Henry 4th, Rick Gilbert 6th, and Luis Niño de Rivera 12th.

The 1968 Summer Outdoor National A.A.U. Championships

The meet was held in Woods Memorial Park in Lincoln, Nebraska a month before the Olympic trials with twelve divers making the finals in each event. The results of the Indiana Divers in the meet are listed for both men and women to show the dominance of the kind of teams we had at that time.

One-meter - Jim Henry 1st, Win Young 3rd, Rick Gilbert 4th, Jon Hanfeldt 6th, and Luis Niño de Rivera 11th.

Three-meter - Rick Gilbert 2nd, Jim Henry 3rd, Win Young 4th, and Luis Niño de Rivera 10th.

10-meter platform - Win Young 1st, Jim Henry 2nd, Rick Gilbert 5th, Jon Hahnfeldt 6th, Rick Early 7th, and Luis Niño de Rivera 9th.

Woman's One meter - Cynthia Potter 1st, Jerrie Adair 3rd, Lesly Bush 6th, Barbara Shaeffer 9th.

Three meter - Jerrie Adair 1st, Lesley Bush 3rd, Cynthia Potter 7th, and Barbara Shaeffer 8th

10 meter – unknown results

Cynthia Potter

The first time I ever saw Cynthia was at the 1964 Women's Indoor Champion-ships in Pittsburgh, Pennsylvania. She was from Houston, Texas and only thirteen years old. I wrote her a letter inviting her to train with my team, and sent it to her coach, Nancy Duty, who didn't give her the letter because she was afraid that she would lose her star diver.

Cynthia was planning to quit diving when she graduated from high school in the spring of 1967 when I gave her a call and invited her to attend Indiana. She came with her mother to look over the school and our diving program. She liked what she saw, and enrolled with us in the fall of 1967. (She is pictured with me and Klaus Dibiasi the great Italian Olympian)

She had never been able to place well in the Nationals or age group meets because she had very poor entries that created a lot of splash. Her arms were muscle bound, and she couldn't extend and close them together over her head for the entry. Like I did with Jim Henry, I had her perform two stretching exercises to loosen the muscles in her shoulders before and after every workout. Eventually she could close her arms, and grab her hands thus eliminating the big splashes on entry. She was exceptionally strong and explosive, and learned all the difficult optional dives needed to compete with the best American divers in a short time.

An example of how competitive she was occurred in the 1970 National A.A.U. Championships. Female divers had to perform five required dives, and six optional dives on the one-meter springboard. The diving rules stated that the divers perform three required and two optional dives in the preliminary round, and the top sixteen divers qualified for the semi-finals. In the semi-finals, they had to perform another required dive and two optional dives, and the top eight divers qualified for the finals. In the finals, they would perform the fifth required dive, and two optional dives to declare the winner.

Cynthia thought she had no chance to qualify. But she managed to perform the two required and two optional dives in the preliminaries well enough to place sixteenth place by a tenth of a point, and qualified for the semi-finals. She then amazed everyone performing her last required dive, and her two optional dives, an inward 1½ somersault in the pike position, and a forward 1½ somersault with one twist that qualified her for the finals in eighth place. Then she performed her final required and two optional dives, and won the contest.

Cynthia Potter is believed to be one of the best divers in the world ever. She was the World Diver of the Year in 1970, 1971, and 1972, and won twenty-eight national championships in her career beating four-time Olympic gold winner Pat McCormick's record who won twenty-seven national titles. Cynthia also won two world championships, a Pan-American title, and made three Olympic teams one of which was as an alternate.

She would have probably won two Gold medals at the 1972 Olympics had she not hit her feet on the practice three-meter platform doing a reverse somersault in the layout position in preparation for performing a reverse 1½ somersault in the layout position from the ten-meter tower.

Using crutches and her feet wrapped in bandages, she decided to try and dive when we got her to the pool. Just before the three-meter board was to start, we went to the board to test if she could dive. Novocain had been injected to numb her feet. She put down her crutches, and removed her bandages, but as I helped her up on the board to see if she could dive, some German officials ran over and said, "Nein, nein, verbotin," and refused to let her try to find if she could dive.

Then just before the event was to start, the officials informed all the diving coaches they could not be on the deck during the diving event because I had made the attempt for her to test her feet. We ended up standing waist deep in a swimming pool next to the diving well behind a glass wall to watch the diving. With no practice and numb feet, she placed sixth on the springboard but did not qualify for the finals on the ten-meter platform and placed 21st.

The 1968 Olympic Trials

The Olympic diving trials were held at the Belmont Plaza Pool in Long Beach California only a month after the outdoor nationals. The pool had windows on both sides that allowed the sun to cast a reflection on the water that hindered the divers' eyesight, and resulted in many diving injuries over the years. I took Mary and the kids to watch the meet, and we stayed with Barbara McAlister-Talmage who dived for Dick Smith.

Barbara had her picture on the cover of Life Magazine that month because she was not only a beautiful woman, but one of the top divers in the country and she and her husband were really nice to us.

We had trained hard for four days before the trials when I decided to take the team to an amusement park for a short break from practice. The park had a great rollercoaster, and we all decided to go on it and Lesley said she wanted to ride with me. Unbelievably, when Lesley went to get out of her seat after the ride, she told me that she couldn't lift her arm above her shoulder.

She had somehow pinched a nerve in her shoulder, and had to wear an arm sling right up to the time of her ten-meter event three days later. She tried to dive in practice, but couldn't dive in head first or do any dive where the arm lifted above her shoulder. That meant she wouldn't be able to compete.

I am the kind of coach who believes that to motivate an athlete one needs to use negative or positive psychology that depends on the situation, and how well you know the athlete. Like in horse racing, when two horses are neck and neck coming to the finish line, one jockey may use a whip on the seat of his horse to signal the best the horse must offer. The whip doesn't really hurt the horse, but it is a way for the jockey to physically communicate with the horse. However, the jockey riding another horse may not be able to use the whip to inspire or motivate his horse because it may confuse or frustrate his steed.

An example of a coach that used a lot of negative psychology was Indiana basketball coach, Bobby Knight, who was very successful in applying a negative approach with his players. But he also knew when to use a positive approach with some of his players that gave him the only college basketball team to have a perfect season.

After using a positive attitude with Lesley for three days, it was obvious that she wasn't going to attempt to compete on the platform. So, I decided to take a chance with her just before they announced her event. I told her how disappointed I was that she was going to let a pinched nerve keep her from competing. I said she should scratch the event, and go back to the hotel because she couldn't take it like a real champion. She got so mad at me that she dived in the meet, and made the Olympic Team.

Top Three Finishers Qualify for the Olympic Team

Jim Henry won the three-meter event and made the Olympic Team along with Bernie Wrightson. But like the last Olympic tryouts in 1964, Rick Gilbert took fourth place in the three-meter event, and missed the cut.

However, for the ten-meter event, Rick qualified third when he beat Jim Henry on the last dive. The judges gave Rick straight nines for a forward 3½ somersault that was only nine tenths of a point better than Henry's final score. Win Young took second, and qualified to make the Olympic team also.

Luis Niño de Rivera, from Mexico City, qualified for the ten-meter event in Mexico.

Keala O'Sullivan from Hawaii, Lt. Micki King from Michigan, and Sue Gossick from California, went 1-2-3 to qualify on the three-meter springboard, and Anne Peterson, Lesley Bush from Indiana, and Barbara Talmage from Arizona placed 1-2-3 to qualify on the ten-meter platform.

Cynthia Potter took fourth on the ten-meter platform, and Jerrie Adair placed fourth on the three-meter springboard. Both were invited to train with us as alternates at the Air Force Academy in Silver Springs, Colorado. The purpose for having alternates was in case one of the female divers should happen to get injured during the training session and couldn't make the trip to Mexico, one of them would replace the injured diver in that event.

Training For the 1968 Olympics at the Air Force Academy

It was believed that the 7,382-foot altitude of Mexico City where the Games were to take place could affect the breathing of the athletes. The Air Force Academy had a 7,000 feet altitude like Mexico City. Dick Smith was the men's Olympic Coach, I was the women's Olympic Coach, and Ron O'Brien was the team manager.

We were put up in a hotel near the Air Force Academy until we left for Mexico City and the Games. The diving facilities at the Academy were not good. Dick Smith coached his divers plus Keala O'Sullivan, and I coached my divers, Lt. Miki King, and Sue Gossick. We trained for nearly two weeks, and we all got along well together before leaving for Mexico City. Since none of the girls got injured during that time, the two alternates, Jerri Adair and Cynthia Potter didn't make the trip to Mexico.

Training for the 1968 Olympics in Mexico City

We were one of the first sport groups to arrive in Mexico City. We were given two cars to use until the top administrators arrived, then the cars had to be returned. Ron and I took one car, and Dick Smith took the other. The car that Ron and I had broke down near the entrance to the Olympic Village after we were there for few days. Mexican people gathered around us as Ron and I checked out the engine. We had no idea what was wrong with it, and we didn't have tools to fix it even if we did know.

An old Mexican showed up, and asked if he could check the engine. After looking it over, he said he thought he could fix it. He worked on that car for at least twelve hours. After dinner Ron and I went back to check on the car. The old man, who had used primitive tools was just cleaning up when we arrived and he said he thought it would run. The car started right up. When we offered to pay him for his hard work, he refused our offer saying that he liked American people, and it was an honor to be helpful.

The Mexicans did a fantastic job in the opening ceremony that was remembered for years by many who attended the event. They were still working on some of their exhibits right up to the time of the first Olympic event, and we found the Mexicans to be very friendly, hard workers, and anxious to impress the visitors from other countries.

The National Amateur Athletic Union (A.A.U.)

To better understand the mood of this Olympic Games, the reader should know that the National A.A.U. controlled all amateur competitive sports in America for around fifty years. Then they lost their control of the amateur sports which led to creating their own federations for their sport. The failure of the A.A.U. started with an incident that occurred during the 1968 Olympics.

Two African-Americans were accepting their medals on the victory stand after placing first and second in their track event. They each raised their arm with a black glove on one of their hands to protest the way blacks were being treated in the United States. They weren't the only ones that felt that way.

Soon after their event, a large group of athletes and coaches, including me, met in a large hall. We were going to boycott the Olympics because of the poor way the A.A.U. officials were running the show. Fortunately, Jesse Owens, the winner of four track gold medals in the 1936 Olympics, took over the meeting, and talked us out of it and the Olympics continued.

The only important person who believed that the Olympics should remain an amateur event was the President of the Olympic Committee, Avery Brundage. Nearly everyone disagreed with him, but he stood his ground up to the day he died a year or two after the 1972 Olympics when professional athletes could compete in the 1975 winter Olympics. That change eventually worked its way into the 1976 Summer Olympics in Montreal, Canada, and became accepted in all the future Olympics.

The 1968 Olympic Games

While coaching Lt. Micki King at the Air Force Academy, I saw her missing the board by only a hair doing a reverse 1½ somersault layout on the three-meter board. She kept reaching back for the water when she was slightly above the level of the board. I suggested that she change the timing of her arm reach by looking back to see the water with her arms remaining close to the front of her body. Then reach for the entry after she passed the board with no fear of hitting the board.

She made the adjustment, and it worked out well. But in the meet, she made the mistake of going back to her old style, and broke her arm hitting the board. One tough diver, she went on to perform her last dive, but missed winning the event that she was leading in up to the second from the last dive and still took fourth place.

Sue Gossick won the contest that I can take partial credit for. Just before the finals, I saw her standing on the three-meter board. I could see that she had panicked. Using a positive approach, I challenged her not to question her ability, and it was natural to lose one's nerve under stress. I continued to challenge her saying now was the time for her to stand up like a champion, and control her fear. And if she would do so, she could win the contest. She thanked me later for showing faith in her, and said she would have not won without me talking her into it.

I felt during my coaching career that if I could get to know my divers well enough, I could positively motivate them to get their best performance. But, I must admit, there were times that I used a negative approach on several of them to get their attention, and to get them to face up to reality.

1968 Olympic Team

I was shocked when the ten-meter tower event for men started because of the crowd's behaviors. Mexico's best diver was Alvero Gaxiola who attended the University of Michigan coached by Dick Kimball. We quickly realized that it was nearly impossible for an American to win the contest due to the reaction of the Mexican people in the stands.

246

They went berserk after Alvero performed a dive. That quickly turned into boos and screaming obscene comments, and throwing articles into the pool before and after Keith Russell, Win Young, and Rick Gilbert did their dives. I remember getting nervous that we might not get out of the pool alive after watching the furious reaction from the crowd.

Klaus Dibiasi, from Italy, won the tower event, and Alvero placed second with 154.19 points that narrowly beat Win Young who was third with 153.93 points and Keith Russell fourth with 152.34 points. We checked the scores of the Mexican judges for the men's springboard and tower events later, and found that their judges had the Mexican divers taking first, second, and third, when the other judges didn't have any of them placing anywhere near the top twelve places. Rick Gilbert didn't make the finals which disappointed all of us because he was good enough to medal. But seeing the behavior of the people in the stands, it would have been highly unlikely.

The next event was the men's three-meter springboard. Ron O'Brien and I were sitting in a hot tub the day before the event when Bernie Wrightson jumped in with us, and broke down crying. He said he was diving so badly that he was going to disgrace himself, family, coach, teammates, and country.

We calmed him down, and did such a good job of it that he won the contest the next day. For the same reason, Dinsley and Gilbert could perform after being frustrated from pressure, and could relax and concentrate before performing. Henry was winning the contest up to the last two dives in the finals when he went short on a back 2½ somersault, and over a forward 3½ and ended up in third place.

The women's 10-meter platform was the final diving event with Lesley Bush defending her title. She had a habit of crimping her legs after the take-off because she didn't jump strong enough from the platform when performing a front dive in the layout position. I kept telling her in practices to get a strong take-off because if she didn't, she would bend her knees some day in an important contest.

Unfortunately, she waited until the Olympic Games to bend her knees on the first dive, and received scores so low that it was nearly impossible for her to make the finals. Lesley placed twentieth with Malina Duchova, from Czechoslovakia, winning the event. Malina's victory was the first gold medal ever won in any sport from her country, and she and her coach, Maria Cermakova, were national heroes when they returned home. Maria also ended up being an Olympic judge for many of the future Olympic diving events.

When Ken Sitzberger won five N.C.A.A. championship titles and after graduating in 1968, he was awarded one of the twenty-two scholarships given out by the N.C.A.A. to the athletes who had contributed the most for outstanding performance and academic achievement.

I told Ken to accept the scholarship and go to law school. However, he refused the scholarship and went into business with his father like his three brothers.

My Election to be Women's National Diving Chairman

At the National Convention in the fall of 1968, Frank Dempsey was elected to be the Men's National Diving Chairman, and I was elected to be the Women's National Diving Chairman. I had been Chairman of the National Diving Rules Committee for six years, and it was great to be in a position that I felt I could help make the sport better. None of the positions paid money, and they took a lot of a person's time. But it was worth it because we had control of many issues that came with the job.

Frank developed some problems and would occasionally change his decisions. I was just the opposite, and would not change my mind once I'd given my opinion or answer. These kinds of conflicts were not good for diving, and I decided to resign both our positions without telling Dempsey. I informed the diving committee at the 1971 National Convention in December that Dempsey and I were resigning. We still had one more year to serve, and he never said a word to me about our resignations.

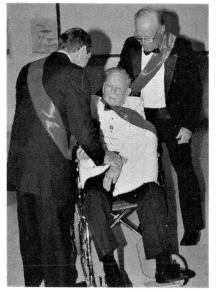

Years later, I met with the selection committee of the International Swimming Hall of Fame, and told them to put Frank Dempsey in the Hall. They asked me, what did Frank contribute to make him eligible. I told them that he had been on their selection committee from the time the Hall was formed. He had won three national diving titles in college, and would have easily made the 1940 and 1944 Olympic Teams if they would not have occurred during the war.

I went on to say he also came out of retirement and competed in the 1948 Olympic trials. He missed making the team taking fourth by less than a point, and used the old style of twisting when performing the forward 1½ somersault. I added that he was deathly sick, and it would be the greatest honor in his life if they would select him. Thankfully, they did before he died two months later.

Frank's wife did not know that I was the person who got him nominated, and called me to ask if I would be his spokesman at his reception party. I brought him into the auditorium in a wheel chair. Frank couldn't move any part of his body. Some of his friends told the audience about what a fine person he was, and everything he had accomplished before I was called to speak.

Finding myself in a spot when everything about Frank had already been said, this is what I said. "One thing everyone wishes to have when growing up or sometime in their lives is a hero, and Frank is one of mine. He was the first diver to help me when I began my diving career in high school, and continued to be a loyal friend when I started coaching. If it hadn't been for him, I would have never been a good diver, coach, or anything connected with diving and probably would have ended up working in a shop for the General Electric Company in my home town."

Duties of the National Diving Chairman

Being the national chairman required us to take some foreign trips that often included some swimmers. On one of those trips we took the team to compete first in Leipzig, Germany, and then Moscow in September of 1971. We traveled to Shannon, Ireland, East Berlin, and Munich on the way, and everyone had a great time except for one incident.

We had a young Russian interpreter in Moscow who had never been to the United States, but knew all the American songs and jokes. He got along with all of us exceptionally well until one night. He had taken us to the Russian square to visit Lenin's Tomb, and was giving us some history about Lenin when one of the swimmers suddenly shouted, "Hey Lenin, come on out and see if you can beat one of our swimmers."

The interpreter suddenly took off on the run. He showed up at breakfast the next morning. He told us that if any Russian official had seen him, he would have been sent to Siberia immediately because no one in Russia was allowed to make any negative remarks about the founder of their country.

CHAPTER 28

The Founding of the World Diving Coaches Association

In the fall of 1967, I was home with Mary and the children when I woke Mary up in the middle of the night, and told her I had a brilliant idea. When coaches went to other countries for competitions, they never treated each other as friends but more like enemies because they had to compete against one another.

I asked Mary, why couldn't they be friends and exchange diving philosophies, concepts, training methods, and ideas on how to coach diving that would help the sport to grow? This would bring the coaches closer together and greatly improve their knowledge of the sport. Mary said it couldn't be done because of the language barrier. But I told her that if one could speak Spanish, German, French, or English, they could converse with anyone in the world. A while later, I told a few other people about my idea, and they all agreed with Mary that it couldn't be done.

It turned out that my idea came at a perfect time when Mexico decided to have a mock Olympic Games in the fall of 1967. The purpose of the mock games was to find and correct errors that could occur in the upcoming 1968 Olympic Games. Several coaches representing different athletic events were selected from around the world, and I was selected to cover the diving events for our country.

Mr. Ostos, was the president of the Mexican Olympic Federation. He oversaw the main meeting for all coaches, officials, and administrators that were to take part in the mock Games. I asked Mr. Ostos if I could have five minutes to make an announcement to the diving coaches before the meeting started, and he gave me permission but only if I didn't exceed my time limit.

I announced to the diving coaches present that I would like to start a world diving coaches' association. This would bring all the coaches in the world together to discuss and solve the problems in our sport, and that would improve and make it better for everyone. I passed a paper tablet around for all the diving coaches to sign and include their address, and affiliation if they were interested in forming the association. There were thirty-seven diving coaches in the room, and they all signed the paper!

The only way of communicating with people living in far off places in those days was to either write a letter or call them by phone. That would be very expensive, so I wrote to every diving coach I knew, and encouraged them to notify other coaches they knew from other countries planning to be at the Olympic Games in Mexico. The letter that I sent to them was:

"Dear Coaches:

You are invited to attend a meeting during the third week of October 1968 at the Olympic Games in Mexico City to help form the "World's Diving Coaches Association." The purpose of this association is to develop closer relationships and create a better understanding of diving among the diving coaches throughout the world. The association will provide the opportunity for diving coaches to exchange ideas, information, and experiences relative to diving methods and other problems concerning the coaching of diving. It will gather and distribute information concerning national and international diving contests, articles, research, new developments, improvements in training equipment, etc. The association will also offer a directory of the diving coaches throughout the world to encourage better communication, and increase the betterment of competitive diving. And finally, it is also hoped that the association will encourage coaches to improve and offer more diving competitions while not directing policy, legislation, or rules concerning competitive diving to diving committees at the national or international level.

It is planned that the association is to meet every four years during the Olympic Games, and if the association is successful, subsequent meetings could be held during various international meets in non-Olympic years. So, it is sincerely hoped that you will be able to attend the meeting in Mexico because the association can be of great value to all of us in competitive diving. However, if you cannot attend the meeting, you can still become a member through a request and application.

Naturally, a great amount of co-operation and interest from many people will be necessary to make such an association possible. Therefore, if you feel that you would like to become a member of the "World Diving Coaches Association" please contact me at your earliest convenience, and feel free to include any constructive ideas or comments that may be helpful in making this a most helpful association.

Sincerely,

Hobie Billingsley"

We met in a room behind the three-meter board on October 14, 1968. 88 coaches showed up. I stood in front of them with my good friend Peter Huber, the coach from

Vienna, Austria, and explained the purpose of the association again and what we planned to do. Then we asked for questions and suggestions related to forming the association.

At first, we received very little response and suddenly realized that many of the coach's present lived behind the Iron Curtain. They feared if they joined the association that was in the free world, their families could be killed. The discussion went on for around two hours when Peter Huber suddenly smashed his fist down on the table and said, "Let's vote!" And it was unanimous. I promised everyone I would send them information where we would all meet again in 1969 to form the association, and we adjourned.

I realized we had to select officers for the Association while everyone was conveniently at the Olympics. So, I went to the building in the Olympic village for German athletes, coaches, and officials about eleven o'clock at night after the meeting, and found Hans Sandhoifer. (Pictured below with me and Cynthia Potter)

Hans had come to Bloomington to watch me coach in the summer of 1966. He was a cute little guy who couldn't speak English. So, he carried an English-German dictionary around with him when he came to the pool every day. I found him a cheap one-room apartment for his six-week visit, and loaded his refrigerator with beer.

He learned a lot from watching me coach my divers, and always thanked me after a workout, saying, "Sank you, Hobie." He had since learned to speak English, and I thought he was the man to be president because he lived in Karlsruhe, Germany located in the center of Europe.

I went to his room in the Olympic Village after the meeting, and asked him to be the president. I told him that the reason why I wanted him to take the job was because no one would accept an American as president. But they would accept him because he knew most of the diving coaches in Europe, and could speak English well enough to be understood by everyone.

I also said that the president had to be one with a friendly attitude, and living in the center of Europe so all the coaches in the surrounding countries could attend a meeting. He kept saying that I should be the president because it was my idea, but I kept telling him it wouldn't work. We talked until about three o'clock in the morning when he finally accepted my offer because he was tired and wanted to get some sleep.

Needing a good public relations man, I made Jack Burnett, from Australia, the vice president because he had a great sense of humor, and was liked by everyone. I took the job as secretary/treasurer because it was going to take years to create a structure that would keep all our members well informed about what was going on in the diving world.

It turned out that Hans was the perfect person for the job. He worked for the city of Karlsruhe that gave him forty-thousand dollars to rent a vacant castle to house and feed all the visiting coaches for a week. The conference met in October 1969, and everyone was surprised when 189 coaches showed up from all over the world. We made Doug Freeman, from New Zealand, the first member of the new association because he put a second mortgage on his house to get enough money to make the trip to Karlsruhe, Germany.

The first meeting was held in a big hall in the castle where Hans thanked everyone for coming. While standing behind a podium, he then said the purpose for the meeting was to have fun while making friends and learning more about diving. Then, he said "Hobie!" I was sitting with the other coaches, and I answered "what?"

Hans said that since it was my idea I should be the one to start telling them about diving. I was not prepared for this, but as I started to walk up to the podium, I quickly realized that I had to say something that would be agreeable with everyone. So, I asked the simplest question I could think of which was, "Where is the best place to place the arms performing a 101-A dive?"

This is a front dive, layout, commonly known as a swan dive. About four different versions were offered by coaches in the group when they started to gather in their defense, and it started to look like it could turn into a riot. Thinking fast, I asked them to please sit down and came up with another approach.

This time, I asked them if they could agree that the easiest way for an object to move from one point to another is in a straight line? And they all agreed except one. Norbert Hatsack, from Romania stood up, and after addressing the coaches, said he disagreed and sat down again. When I asked why he disagreed, he said because it wasn't a law and had never been proven.

To demonstrate my point, I put my hand by my side, and I asked him, "If I wished to touch my nose with my finger, the easiest way would be to move my finger in a straight line, or would I make several gyrations first?" He agreed with my first version, and received applause from the coaches.

I didn't realize until a little later how limited the diving coaches around the world were in knowing how to coach the sport. The reason why they knew so little about diving was because they had little or no information about how dives should be performed. They created their own version, and failed to communicate with coaches in different sections of their countries that had different versions.

I wish I had known how little they knew about diving before this meeting because I had already written my book Diving Illustrated published in 1965 that offers drawings of all the dives performed in sequence found in the diving rule books. The drawings not only gave the divers and coaches a basic concept on how to perform dives, but also helped the diving judges, and officials. During the week, we had several lectures on diving, and made new friends and compared ways of coaching with those from other countries.

We also formed a constitution for our new association during the week. I chose about a dozen coaches from different parts of the world to form a committee. We sat around the table when I suggested that we first find a name for the association. Grunde Vegard

 from Norway suggested that we name it "Wo.D.C.A." that sounded like 'vodka' with a small 'o,' and it was unanimously accepted.

Then I asked suggestions for what should be put in the constitution, and with blank looks on their faces no one had any idea. I had anticipated that this could happen, so I used the American Swimming Coaches Association constitution and converted it into a diving constitution to bring with me.

In the meeting, I started to make suggestions one at a time. The coach sitting across from me was from Russia, and had a German interpreter translate what was being said. He stared at me until he received the correct interpretation, then with some thought, he said "da" with no expression. This went on until near the finish of making the constitution when the Russian suddenly said, "okay" and smiled that changed the whole attitude of everyone in the room.

I was asked in one of our meetings if it was possible to show how a diver could perform a perfect dive when everyone had different concepts. I said "no" but one could get close to perfection if they applied mechanical principles based on Newton's Laws of Motion. I was using the hypothesis that "no move should be made unless it contributes to the performance of the dive." Few understood my suggestions, but it did open their curiosity.

The association went well throughout the world for years. We met at every Olympic Games and at some other important international meets, and discussed various subjects related to diving. What was once a sport that offered an international meet only once or twice a year, became one that offered one nearly every week in the year. The change made it possible for competitive diving to grow by leaps and bounds.

CHAPTER 29

1969 Was a Good Year

10th Big Ten and 3rd NCAA Championship in a Row

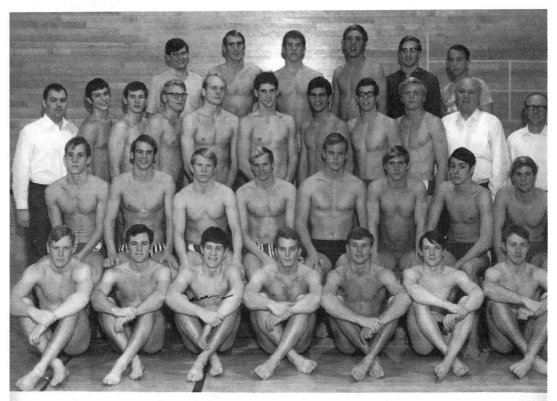

BIG TEN AND N.C.A.A. CHAMPIONS • 1969
INDIANA UNIVERSITY

We had a good year in 1969 when our divers did well in helping Indiana win the Big Ten Championships for the tenth time in a row, and the N.C.A.A. National Championships the third time in a row. The N.C.A.A. Championships were held in Royer Pool, and the Indiana divers took the top three places on the one-meter board. Jim Henry was first, Win Young second, and Jon Hanhfeldt third.

255

This trio was on track to duplicate their performance on the three-meter board when Hahnfeldt, who was in a solid third place, hit his feet on the end of the board performing an inward 2½ somersault in the pike position on his second to last dive. His mother was in the audience and let out a scream, and the crowd gave him a standing ovation as he was carried out from the pool.

He came back on crutches a few minutes later while the event was still going on and whistled, with thumbs up, from the other end of the pool to Win Young who was ready to perform his last dive. Win won the event with Jim Henry placing second. After graduating from Indiana, Jon ended up coaching divers at a high school in Connecticut, and did a terrific job.

He was selected as "Coach of the Year" when his divers took the top three places in the State High School Championships just before he died from a massive stroke in

2010. He was probably one of the best divers in the world because he was the first diver to ever perform all the most difficult somersault dives in the pike position from the first four diving groups on the three-meter springboard.

Indiana Diving Gets Recognized

The I.U. divers were recognized as the best in the country while not only winning nearly all the major diving titles, but also averaging four divers in all the finals that continued for a few years. The only "Coach of the Year" award given for diving up until the middle 1970's was by the American Swimming Coaches Association. Doc and I would have probably been named Big Ten Conference "Coach of the Year" twenty straight times had it been given when we won the Big Ten team championships from 1961 to 1980.

I was the first to be given the award, and continued to receive it for the next six years. The N.C.A.A. started to give a "Coach of the Year" honor in 1983, and I was their first recipient.

CHAPTER 30

Teaching and Coaching from 1969 to 1972

Hobie's Diving Academy

Dick Kimball and Ron O'Brien had stopped performing water shows in 1964, and found that they could make more money running a diving camp than they could doing water shows. They also could recruit divers for their college teams from the camp, and be home with their families during the summer.

They ran their camps for three years before I realized that if I was going to compete with them, I would also have to start a diving camp for teenagers. I coached four young divers from St. Louis, and Mark Virts from Fort Wayne that came to the outdoor pool when it opened in the early summer of 1965. I coached them about four years every day except Sunday for nothing after my divers finished practice.

Mark Virts was not a good springboard diver, and was not good enough for me to give him a scholarship after he graduated from high school. I used to send some of my high school divers up to Purdue. Bob Matus was the Purdue coach at the time, and I suggested he give Mark Virts a scholarship.

But Virts continued to dive with me more from the ten-meter platform, and turned out to be an outstanding diver from that height. He won a couple of national titles, and made the 1980 Olympic team as an alternate.

I Get Promoted to Associate Professor

I was promoted from assistant to associate professor by the physical education department in the spring of 1969, but I was never able to find out why because it didn't change anything including my salary. I started my diving camp that summer and was followed by Doc Counsilman who also started his swimming camp.

We were the first coaches to have summer camps at Indiana. Our campers were assigned to the one dormitory while all the other dorms were closed. The director of dormitories charged the divers fifteen dollars a day for lodging and meals, and I got permission to use Royer Pool for nothing since it was not used during the summer.

I borrowed two trampolines from the I.U. gymnastic coach, and put them outside near the outdoor pool amongst some trees that I used for rigging safety belts over the trampolines. I also put in a one-meter dry land board with a port-o-pit next to the trampolines that made it quite comfortable to train divers outside during the hot summer days.

I named the camp, "Hobie's Diving Academy." I couldn't run the camp by myself, and hired John Eisel as my assistant. John was one of my divers from Canada who had been a national champion in his country. He was a hard worker who could be counted on, and he turned out to be the perfect man for the job. He learned to coach, and did a fine job with the campers who liked him as did I.

The camp was set up for twenty-four male and female divers for five two-week sessions that started when students got out of high school for summer vacation, and lasted until the week before their classes started again. The campers had to attend my camp for two weeks because it took them that long to learn what we had planned to teach them.

The camp required one of us to be with them from morning until night, and since John wasn't married, he had to be their night counselor staying in the dorm. Running the camp made it difficult for me because I had a family that suddenly found they didn't have a husband or father for the whole summer. John and I had to get up at seven o'clock, eat breakfast, and meet the campers by eight o'clock after they had breakfast.

I had no trouble getting campers because they learned more about diving in two weeks than they did in a year or more at home. The cost to attend the camp was $150 that was later changed to $250. I figured out a way that I could handle thirty-two and then forty campers, and hire a counselor and some of my divers to help coach the campers. That allowed John and me to coach for only eight weeks instead of ten. It also reduced our coaching load that was leading John and me towards a breakdown.

Other coaches at Indiana University started camps soon after they saw that Doc and I were making money and recruiting the better athletes from the camp. It wasn't long before the University started to make as much money renting out the dormitories to the campers in the summer as they did during the regular school year.

The opening of the dormitories on the campus caused the price of lodging and meals to go up to a point where I couldn't afford to keep my campers in the dorms any longer because we were a small group. Rick Gilbert was coaching diving at Cornell University and had a diving camp also. He suggested that I put my campers in a fraternity or sorority house, and hire my own cook that would cut our food bills in half. I tried that and Rick was right. I also found we had more control of the campers when not at practice.

259

The divers received schedules at the beginning of each session that covered the time and place they were to report each day, and also given rules they were to observe. No one ever objected to the rules in the twenty-year period I had the camp. Up front, they were asked if the rules were fair, and if anyone objected to a certain rule, we would discuss it until everyone agreed. The campers quickly learned that we were no-nonsense coaches, and our camp really taught them how to dive instead of using it for baby sitters. We consistently had so many campers trying to get into our camp that other coaches around the country were calling me to send those who couldn't get into my camp, to attend their camps.

After reviewing the ground rules, we asked how many of them had ever dived from a three-meter board. All high school divers compete from the one-meter board, but most had not been exposed to the three-meter board because most high schools, if they had a board, had had it removed for insurance liability reasons.

They were told they were all going to learn to perform a complete list of competitive dives from the three-meter board in the first week at camp. They asked why in the first week. I told them learning five required dives was easy. But to learn the five optional dives, they would need a verbal cue to know when to come out of a difficult somersault for their entry.

Our goal was to have them do the optional dives by the end of the second week without a call. We thought their coach at home may not have the experience to make the right call that could result in painful injuries. It also would give them a head start in performing from the three-meter board if they chose to compete in college.

I used to hide in a closet after the first day of practice, and listen to the campers call their parents on the phone. Some would plead with them to let them come home because this guy was trying to kill them. Some parents called me when I told them we were strict coaches for safety reasons, and their child was going to learn to be disciplined. But if they still wanted to leave in a couple of days, they could do so. No one ever quit to go home early in twenty years.

We had a session one year that involved five senior high school male divers. They learned to perform 2½ somersaults as an optional dive from the first four groups of dives, plus a difficult dive from the fifth group that included twists while somersaulting. They were very competitive with each other, and none of them learned the dives without receiving a few welts landing flat.

All five of them ended up being top college diving coaches a few years later, and claimed that it was because they learned how to dive at my camp. Kenny Armstrong was one of the five who made the Canadian Olympic Diving Team before becoming a top diving coach in the United States. His diver, Laura Wilkerson, won the gold medal from the ten-meter platform at the 2,000 Olympic Games in Sidney, Australia. Incidentally, she was the first American woman to win the gold at that height since Lesley Bush won hers in 1964.

The Introduction of the "Bubbler System"

Herb Flewelling was a Canadian from Calgary who came up with the "bubbler system." With the use of a generator, it blew air through a rubber hose connected to a "sparager" that was placed on the bottom of the pool. Air was forced out that formed a large bubble on the surface, and prevented divers from being injured if landing flat on the water.

At first, people thought Herb was insane for such a contraption, but it worked. It made a great contribution to improving the sport because divers could now perform extremely difficult dives from the springboards and ten-meter platforms without being seriously injured. However, the initial cost to have one installed in a pool was around thirty or forty thousand dollars. But coaches found that could make their own bubblers for a very cheap price.

Bill Burgess was a good friend of mine in Seattle, Washington. He coached little kids, and had a self-made bubbler system that cost him under five-hundred dollars to make. So, I made one for my camp and my college divers. Mine was made with a two-horsepower generator that was placed behind a wall to the pool so no electrical unit was on the pool deck.

I projected a one-inch pipe through the wall, and attached it to a rubber hose that was long enough to be attached to an eighteen-foot-long two-inch plastic pipe at the edge of the pool. The pipe was placed on the bottom of the pool slightly in front of the board, and was held down with a ten-pound weight.

The air was turned on and off with a lever attached between the one-inch pipe and the rubber hose near the pool wall. When the air was turned on, a big wave formed on the surface that softened the landing by the diver.

Another person standing at the edge of the deep end could move the plastic pipe to any desired place on the pool bottom. Divers could learn to perform the more difficult dives from as high as the ten-meter tower with little or no fear of being hurt.

I was known to have the best summer diving camp in the country for years because those who attended my camp learned more about diving than at any other camp. They not only learned to dive better, but they also learned how to perform more difficult dives that they could use to compete from the one and three-meter springboards in age-group diving meets.

Ten Big Ten Conference Championships

We had won ten Big 10 Conference Championships in a row in 1969. A reporter asked me how many more team titles I thought we could win in a row since ten was the new record. And I told him twenty-four. He started to laugh, and had to ask why I said twenty-four.

I told him the teams that won the Big 10 or N.C.A.A. title got their picture put on the wall, and there was room for twelve pictures on each side of the Royer pool between the enclosed iron supports for the roof. I don't think he would have laughed very long as we won twenty Big 10 titles in a row, and twenty-three in twenty-four years.

The Founding of the American Diving Coaches Association

At the National A.A.U. Outdoor Championships in August of 1969 in Louisville, Kentucky, I asked that all of those interested in diving to attend a meeting with the purpose of forming an association for American diving coaches. I explained that it would greatly increase the growth and development of the sport by sharing information that would promote and stimulate various areas concerned with competitive diving.

We met in the evening before the competition began on Wednesday, August 12th in 1969. Dr. Bob Rydze, who had two divers in the competition, made the motion that we organize the association. That motion was immediately seconded, and unanimously voted in favor of by the 118 persons attending the meeting.

We also voted for an executive board that would act as the leaders of the association. Dick Kimball, diving coach from the University of Michigan was selected as chairman, Ward O'Connell at Yale University as vice chairman, and Don McGavern from the University of Oregon, the Secretary and treasurer.

They met at the National A.A.U. Convention a couple of months later, and created the constitution for the organization. Then they selected a person to create a newsletter that would send out diving information to every member each month.

Realizing the necessity for the effective functioning of the association, they also created several committees to cover those needs. The association was very successful over the years until people who were not reliable leaders let it fade. But it was later reorganized again, and is now known as the Professional Diving Coaches Association and offers the world's largest video library for competitive diving.

I'll never forget that National Championship meet in Louisville, because I was the National Chairman. There were around 120 divers competing in the one and three-meter events, and all the divers had to perform five compulsory dives in order. That meant, the judges had to judge 120 front, back, reverse, inward, and a front dive with a half twist dives.

This was followed with five optional dives that could be performed in any order, with the top twelve divers making the finals. It took so long to perform all the dives that we didn't finish the one-meter event. It started at ten o'clock in the morning until nine o'clock in the evening.

Most of the scores from the judges of so many compulsory dives from each list fell into a range between four and six. It was so bad, that a judge could go to the bathroom and put a score of five on his seat. The rules for the National Championships were changed at the National Convention that fall when it required divers to compete in a zone located in different parts of the country to qualify for the Nationals. This reduced the number of divers to thirty-six to compete in a national contest.

My 1970 and 1971 Diving Team

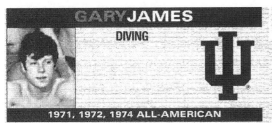

1971, 1972, 1974 ALL-AMERICAN

Gary James was yet another All-America diver at Indiana University as he earned such recognition six times during his career. In 1972, James had his top one-meter performance, finishing fifth. That same year, he placed 11th on the three-meter. As a freshman in 1971, he placed eighth on the three-meter and ninth on the one-meter. He concluded his career with a 10th-place finish on the three-meter at the 1974 NCAA Championships.

1971, 1972 ALL-AMERICAN

Tom Eldredge competed at the 1971 NCAA Championship i[n] [three]-meter diving. He finished ninth. In 1972 he returned t[o] [s]eventh on one-meter.

1972, 1973 ALL-AMERICAN

Don Muir earned All-America distinction in 1972 and again in 1973. In 1972, he finished eighth on the one-meter and followed up that performance with a fourth-place finish on the three-meter and a sixth on the three-meter at the 1973 NCAA Championships.

1971 ALL-AMERICAN

Jack Laughlin finished in 10th-place in the one-meter diving competition at the 1971 NCAA Championships.

Gary James, Tom Eldridge, Don Muir, and Jack Laughlin along with five girls were new freshman divers on our 1970 team. But the girls didn't last long. For a variety of reasons, they did not make my team, and were gone by the semester break.

Gary James came to Indiana in 1971, and he and Tom Eldridge became my two best divers. They made the finals in all the major meets, but never won a title. Don Muir and Jack Laughlin managed to qualify in a couple of the major meets that helped the swimming team win the Big Ten championships in the early 1970's.

Planning the 1971 Pan American Games

I was asked to visit Cali, Columbia in late 1970 to help plan the diving competition program for the Pan American Games that were to be held later in the summer of 1971. I worked with their national coach Sanchez Gomez and I found him to be one of the few people I met in Cali that could speak English. But we still managed to set up a good program. He let me help coach some of his divers by being our interpreter, and I found he was extremely popular with everyone around him.

A Meet with Russia

Russia invited the U.S.A. for an outdoor dual meet in 1970. I was selected as the coach, and Jay Lerew, a young coach from Moultrie, Georgia, was the manager. Being a young and upcoming coach, he wanted to coach so I let him, and that ended with me being the manager.

We had a problem getting into the country at the airport, and were held up for about three hours. So we arrived too late at the hotel to go to the bank to change some of our American money into Russian money.

While having dinner that evening, a waiter whispered to me if I would like to change our money that he could do it for us at black market rates. We agreed. Their food was poor, but we could survive because nearly every member on our team brought a large jar of peanut butter.

They served us some yogurt one night, and having never tasted it before, I thought it tasted more like lard. It was so bad that I didn't eat yogurt for years thinking that all yogurt was that bad. The people were friendly and the young girls were strikingly beautiful.

The thing we all liked most about Russia was their circuses where we saw incredible acts never seen in the United States. We also liked their underground subway travel system after we learned to read the names of some of the areas, and got the chance to see other parts of Moscow.

Pat Jefferies was one of our divers who arrived a couple days late, so some of us took him shopping and told him he could use American money, but to be careful because it wasn't legal. After looking around, he bought a painting and was showing it to us when a man walked up, and said he was the KGB and told Jefferies to go with him.

Being the coach, I said I wanted to go with them and he agreed. He took us down the street and into an alley where we entered a house that was filled with people behind bars. He took us to a vacant room where we sat alone for about an hour wondering what was going to happen to us when a guy opened the door every few minutes to look us over then close the door again.

A couple of KGB members finally came out and told us that using American money was illegal, and if we were caught doing it again, we would be put in prison. So we didn't try it again! But we did continue to use the black market Russian rubles that we had gotten from the waiter at the hotel.

The outdoor meet was supposed to have three divers perform from each country in the one-meter, three-meter, and the ten-meter tower event. However, the Russian coach asked if he could use a couple more of his divers because they needed experience, and I agreed.

We suddenly found that he added about six more divers in each event, and didn't tell us which of his divers were competing against us. I asked who were the three divers we were competing against? He said their names were on the score board, but that didn't help because the names were in Russian and we never did find out who the three divers were.

Not surprising, I'm sure he selected the top three Russians from all his divers who competed the best in every event, and I didn't protest because we were their guests. I don't remember what specific places we took in the meet, but we did manage to win one event and placed in two others. All in all, we had a great time, and it was well worth traveling that far for a dual meet.

The 1970 World Student Games

A World Student Games was held in Turin, Italy during the last week of August in 1970 and the Indiana divers did very well when Cynthia Potter took first and Jerrie Adair placed second in the Women's three-meter event and Cynthia also placed second in the ten-meter event getting nosed out by Galena Kavolanko of Russia. Jim Henry placed second in both the men's springboard events. That wasn't bad when you consider that Indiana divers won five of the twelve medals in the world championship contest.

The women's and men's National A.A.U Championships were held separately and at different locations for years when it was eventually decided to have both events together at the same location beginning in Fort Worth, Texas. A beautiful trophy was given to the best combined team and it all came down to Cynthia performing the last dive on the ten-meter platform to win the trophy.

Cynthia then told me before her last dive that she had injured her shoulder and couldn't perform the dive. Without thinking, I told her to scratch her event when all she had to do was jump off the tower and receive zeroes, and we still would have scored enough points to win the trophy. We weren't very happy when Ohio State won and Ron O'Brien thanked me for giving his team the trophy.

CHAPTER 31

The Water Shows at Indiana 1972-1981

Like at the University of Washington and Ohio University, I decided to have the divers and swimmers perform a water show in Royer Pool that started on the same weekend as the homecoming football game. The purpose of the show was to draw the members of the swimming and diving team closer together, and encourage people to attend our swim meets. The first show was performed in 1972 and they continued until 1981.

Everyone on our teams had a great time taking a part in the show. But we never drew a large audience because it was always given on the Homecoming Weekend, and we had to compete with other campus activities that included the football game. However, it was well received by the whole school and helped our teams to get better acquainted.

Unfortunately, we couldn't do the trapeze act because the diving well was too small and the ceiling too low. As before, I taught them thirteen different acts that lasted for around an hour and twenty minutes because anything longer lost the attention of the spectators. We added a bathing beauty contest in 1977 to try to draw a bigger audience, but it wasn't successful.

Lucinda Fox, a close friend of mine, taught classes for the women's department, and had a synchronized swimming group. She always had a group perform in our show that gave it a little more variety, and continued to teach at Indiana for forty years. I liked her a lot, and we continued to be close friends after I retired years later.

I did my comedy act on the trampoline in the last show after I, unfortunately, sprained both of my ankles the day before the show. I was walking around on crutches, but after I taped my ankles, I managed to perform a back somersault from the trampoline onto the pool deck as the last trick. The show went on for nine years until I told Doc I was getting too old and too busy to perform.

CHAPTER 32

The Rich Lindner Family

(Pictured Carol, Susie, Rich, and me)

Start of a Best Friend

I had a little less than a dozen best friends in my life, and Rich Lindner was one of them. It started when I was painting one of my trailers out in a field to prevent getting paint on any of my neighboring rental trailers when I saw a man crossing the field toward me. I thought he was a bill collector. I asked him if I could help him, and he said he was looking for Hobie Billingsley.

I told him he was talking to him, and he said he was from Cincinnati and had flown over to see me. I asked him if he flew on Ozark Airlines because their planes had problems. He replied that he flew his own plane which was an eight-passenger turbo jet. I started to laugh and told him he must be rich. I asked him what he wanted from me. He said he had a problem, and needed my help.

He asked me if I knew his daughter Carol. I had to think for a moment, and remembered she had competed in Hobie's Little Nationals several times during previous summers. I still had no idea what the problem was. I told him I would be glad to help him, but with one condition. I told him "I think you are rich, but I don't want any of your money. If you don't like my condition, find someone else." He agreed, and told me he needed a diving coach right away for his thirteen-year-old daughter, Carol.

It happened that Carol and Barbara Weinstein, who I knew when she also dived in one of our age group meets were being coached by the same Dr. Weinstein. And for some reason, Lindner and Dr. Weinstein, who was a dentist and later the President of the National Diving Organization, got into an argument. Lindner told the coach he no longer was going to coach both girls, so he had to make a choice, and he chose Barbara.

One of my divers, Win Young, was available, and an excellent teacher. So, I told Lindner to pay him three hundred dollars, plus expenses, for three two-hour lessons a week. A year later, Win left I.U., and I replaced him with Rick Earley who coached her until she graduated from high school in 1974.

Carol Lindner

Carol then decided to attend Indiana University, and she turned out to be an outstanding diver. She placed third and fourth on the one and three-meter boards in the National AIAW Championships when there were eighty divers competing in each event. Then in the 1976 Olympic trials held at the outdoor pool at the University of Tennessee, she needed sevens on her last dive to make the team.

The dive was an inward 2½ somersault from the three-meter board. I remember standing next to Rich, who was shaking and he said, "If she makes the Olympic team, you will never have to worry about money." I didn't look at him, and told him I didn't give a crap about his money, and only wanted her to make the team.

However, she over rotated on the dive, and scored sixes to place fifth in the event. Carol was one of the sweetest girls I ever coached, and she never gave me a problem throughout her diving career. She remained a close friend of mine throughout our lives, and we still get together on occasion.

Rich and I became closer friends when he frequently visited Carol on campus. He was very helpful knowing I didn't have money to spend on the divers going to summer meets. He often flew my divers and me to several meets in his jet plane, and paid the bills for our food and lodging.

Wanna Bet?

He invited me over for a baseball game between Cincinnati and the Los Angeles Dodgers soon after Carol started school at Indiana. I drove over to his house and was surprised to see a beautiful indoor pool with a five-meter platform that, with a push of button, came out of the wall. I was more surprised when he drove us down town to the stadium, and parked his car underneath a large building across from the stadium. I said he must know someone important to use the vacant parking lot. And he said he owned the building that was about forty stories high.

Los Angeles was beating Cincinnati three to one in the last inning with two outs and no one on base. Thinking there was no way Cincinnati could win the game, I asked Lindner if he would like to bet on the game for a dollar. I said I would take L.A. and give him two to one odds, and he took my bet.

Suddenly Cincinnati got a player on base, and the next player hit a home to tie the game. Cincinnati went on to win the game in extra innings, and I paid him two bucks. The bets went on for a couple of months, and I lost every bet until Cincinnati lost a football game. When I asked him for the two dollars I had been betting, he said he didn't carry money, and would pay me later.

I waited for about three weeks before I called him up, and jokingly said I had three kids to feed and I could use the money. And he said he would get the money to me right away. A week later, I received a Fed-Ex package that contained a money bag with two hundred pennies, and a W-2 form.

Rich's wife, Helen, developed a rare disease that the doctors predicted would take her life within eight years. It had been about six years when I first met the Lindner family. Sure enough, Helen suddenly passed away during the eighth year. After attending the funeral, I drove Rich back to their house and he broke down in the drive way.

He was a very strong man and it took time for him to accept her death, but he managed to keep his feelings within his family, and not show his loss to the people he worked with. Helen was an extraordinary woman with a fabulous personality. No one would have ever known that she was the mother of a very wealthy family.

Rich Lindner's Influence

One time when Doc and I were coaching our teams in Ft. Lauderdale during the winter break, Doc told his team to finish practice because they were going to take a ride on a yacht. Rich was standing nearby, and asked me if my team was going with them. I told him that we were never invited by Doc or the swimmers for such occasions. He then told me it was his yacht they were going to use, and to stop coaching and go with him.

We drove down the street to a marina across the street from the Phillips 66 Hotel where Rich was staying. When we walked in, a man named Larry greeted him, and Rich asked if he could get a yacht ready to use in an hour. He took my divers and me for a ride in the marina, but not in the ocean. When he docked the yacht, we all went to shore where a long stretch limousine was sitting nearby. He told us to go sit in limousine, and we were really surprised to see the inside was covered in leopard skin and loaded with sandwiches and drinks for all of us.

Rich's jet plane could travel over four-hundred miles an hour, and was the same plane used by astronauts before taking off in space ships. One time Rich and his pilots flew over to Bloomington to take me somewhere, and as we started to take off, the pilots saw a commercial plane taking off from the other end of the field. The runway had an upward curve, and as both planes approached the middle of the runway the pilots could see each other.

When the two planes were only a few yards away, our pilot made a quick turn off the runway onto a grass field. Thankfully, the other plane started to lift into the air as it passed our plane by a few feet, and no damage was done to either plane. From that time on, when Rich came over to see me, I drove up to the bigger Indianapolis Airport to meet him.

On another occasion, Rich and his crew were flying some of our divers out to California for the National Championships. His daughter and my divers Carol and Jan Gabriel were serving sandwiches and cokes to some of us sitting in our seats. We were about thirty thousand feet up, and I saw Jan suddenly hit the ceiling of the cabin, and Carol go flying by me smashing into the rest room door in the rear of the plane as it started to dive straight down.

No one felt the change in direction at first. The pilots' cockpit door was open, and we could see the two pilots trying to pull the plane out of the dive. They finally succeeded after the plane dropped about eight thousand feet. Fortunately, Carol and Jan were not injured nor any of the passengers because we all had our seat belts fastened as did Rich Linder who was sitting in the pilot's compartment. After we landed in Los Angeles, we found that the automatic pilot unit had broken down, and it was quickly replaced.

Surprise Party

Rich's employees and family decided to have a surprise party on his seventy-fifth birthday, and Nancy, my eldest daughter and I were invited. They had rented a mansion with a huge tent in the back yard that held about four hundred people, and had a wooden floor put in for the band and dancing. All the tables were reserved, so Nancy and I looked around for our table, but couldn't find it. So we went to the far corner of the tent where I saw some people I knew, and they didn't appear to have a reservation.

A few minutes later, a waiter came up to us and told Nancy and me to follow him. I thought he was going to have us thrown out, but instead he took us to Rich's table and told Nancy to sit on one side of him and me on his other side. I told Rich he was losing his mind because he had so many lifelong friends and members of his family honoring him, and they deserved the privilege to sit next to him. Then he told me that he picked his own friends.

Near the end of his life, Rich donated ninety-two million dollars to the University of Cincinnati to build an athletic village in his name that involved a new athletic building eight stories high, a baseball ball and soccer field, a new dormitory, and an indoor parking garage that held a thousand cars. His contribution had much to do with the sudden improvement of the University of Cincinnati football and basketball teams, and other sports, even though he had never gone to college.

Rich developed Parkinson's disease a couple of years after the party, and gradually went from eating out in restaurants to having prepared food brought in for him. I visited him once or twice a month for a few years, and Ellen Lee, the woman I went with for eighteen years, often went with me. She and Rich got along extremely well because she was also a farmer that had raised cows. Bedridden, Rich gradually withered and passed away in 2009.

Pictured are Ellen, Rich, and me.

CHAPTER 33

Events Starting in 1972

Title IX

As I mentioned earlier, Title IX became law on June 23, 1972 with the intention of ending sex discrimination in education. This meant that colleges that received federal funding were to provide women with athletic opportunities equal to men. The law made things complex because few colleges had facilities available for the girl's programs. So that meant that men's program had to figure a way to make room and divide their facilities and time for the women's programs. It has taken around forty years to establish equity in schools.

With colleges looking to save money, men's non-revenue sports such as wrestling, swimming, and gymnastics were first on the chopping block. Much of the concern was not only the number of sports, but more with balancing the number of scholarships that most colleges offered. For example, before Title IX, men's swimming teams received twenty scholarships every four years, and when Title IX became law, the number was reduced to eleven. So, after receiving one full scholarship a year, I only got one every four years for the boys diving program, but received two scholarships for girls.

It also appears that those who passed the law didn't consider how eighty-five men's football scholarships could be equal when the girl's program didn't come near having a sport that gave the same number. So, male non-revenue sports were cut while some female programs were added to establish equality.

The 1972 Olympic Trials

We weren't winning many major championships with our male divers in the early 1970's. But Gary James, Tom Eldridge, Don Muir, and Rick Earley made the finals in nearly every championship meet. Thankfully our girls continued to win with Cynthia Potter leading the way right up to the 1972 Olympic trials. The trials were held in Chicago, and one of my former divers, Jim Blickenstaff was the meet director. Only three divers qualified to make the Olympic team in each event.

Rick Earley (pictured here) was the only Indiana male diver to make the Olympic team on the ten-meter platform. Cynthia made the Olympic team despite badly performing a reverse 2½ somersault from the three-meter springboard. She came up to me after performing the dive, and said, "Oh shit, I just eliminated myself from making the Olympic team!" Then I told her that she could still make the team if she could get eights doing her back 2½ somersault.

Cynthia said that she had never performed the dive well enough to receive eights, and I told her that it was no time like the present. She not only performed one of the best ones I had ever seen her do, but went on to also make the ten-meter platform event.

Other Trials Incidents

Another incident occurred at the Olympic trials that later related to a diver on my team. It started when Jim Blickenstaff (a.k.a. Blick), one of my first Indiana divers, was teaching and coaching in a high school in Elyria, Ohio in 1971. Blick called to tell me there was a good diver that took about seventh place in the Ohio State High School Championships, and would have won had he not missed one dive badly.

Blick said that since the Big 10 Championships were on the same weekend as the state meet, none of the college coaches knew anything about him. Blick told me his name was Phil Boggs, and I thought how could a guy with a name like that be a good diver? I was loaded with top divers, and didn't try to recruit him. But neither did anyone else except Florida State where he won one N.C.A.A. national title in four years.

Boggs then joined the U.S. Air Force in 1971, and became a Lieutenant. For six years, he continued to dive while being coached by Dick Smith until 1972. Smith was weak in teaching divers how to do twisting somersaults. At the trials, Lt. Boggs performed a triple twisting 1½ somersault from the three-meter board, and only scored twos. He failed to make the team when he could have with a simple forward 1½ somersault.

Phil changed coaches in 1973 while attending Michigan's Law School, and was coached by Dick Kimball. Kimball did a terrific job coaching him, and Lt. Boggs went on to win the three-meter 1976 Olympic gold medal in Montreal, Canada along with several world, national, and international titles before retiring. He then became the diving commentator for CBS and ESPN before he passed away from cancer at the age of forty.

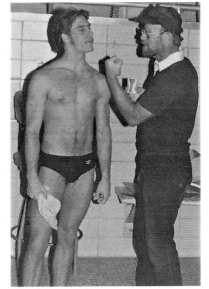

Realizing that I had missed a great diver by not recruiting him because of his name, I decided that the next time I heard of a diver with a crazy name like Phil Boggs, I would recruit him. The time came sooner than I thought when I received a letter from a diver in Bloomington, Minnesota who said he wanted to come to Indiana and be on our team with or without a scholarship. Having never met him and not knowing a thing about him, I gave Brian Bungum my scholarship because of his crazy name. (He's pictured on previous page working on his mental toughness).

273

Brian wasn't a good diver at first, and it looked like he was going to lose his scholarship because he was not showing any signs of progress. But I changed my mind when he competed in the Big Ten Conference meet in 1974. He surprised everyone when he qualified in eleventh place for the finals on the one-meter event.

When our team was leaving for dinner before diving in the finals that night, Brian refused to get dressed to go with us. He sat in a chair next to the diving board for two hours before the finals started, and ended up in seventh place. It was then that I realized Brian had the stuff to make himself a champion before he graduated from college.

It didn't take long for him to prove himself at the 1976 N.C.A.A. Championships at Brown University the next year. There were eighty-four divers competing on the low board. Brian got lost in the air performing a double twisting 1½ somersault and received zeros from the judges for doing the wrong dive. He finished the contest beating only one other diver.

I would have normally gotten upset when a diver made that kind of error. But this time, I put my arm around his shoulder, and said that he had beaten one diver and I was sure that he would do better on the three-meter board the next day. To the amazement of everyone in the pool, he turned around and won the event! I took off my hat and jumped on it because I had never heard of a diver taking eighty-third place in one event, and then turn around to win the three-meter in the next event.

Brian's next three-meter title occurred at the 1977 N.C.A.A. National championships at Cleveland State University, in Ohio the next year. He was diving against Greg Garlich who performed his last dive well enough to win the contest. Brian needed nines from the judges doing a triple twisting 1½ somersault. I wondered what I could say to him that would help him perform the dive well enough to win. I pulled him aside just before he climbed up on the board, and said that everyone in the pool saw him go from 83rd to first place at Brown University last year. Then I asked him if he believed that was a fluke. He received nines from the seven judges, and won the contest.

The 1972 Olympic Games in Munich, Germany

Dick Rydze, Micki King, David Bush from the University of Wisconsin, Craig Lincoln from the University of Minnesota, Mike Finneran from Ohio State, Janet Ely from Los Angeles, California, and Cynthia Potter and Rick Earley from Indiana made up the 1972 Olympic diving team.

Ron O'Brien and I were the diving coaches. We gathered the team together in Philadelphia before going to Washington D.C. to meet the President, and then take off for Munich.

When we arrived in Munich, a bus took us to the Olympic Village. Sitting next to me was a young African-American boy. I asked him what sport he was in. And he said wrestling, then went on to tell me he was from Erie, Pennsylvania, that he lived on the east side of town, and attended East High School. He was really surprised when he asked me the same questions, and got the same answers!

Our swimming and diving teams roomed on the fifth floor of the building for the American athletes, officials, and coaches in the Olympic Village. Our divers shared rooms across the hall from Ron and me. I don't remember how, but I managed to sneak Mike Brown, Jan Gabriel, and Doc Lewis into the Village. Jan and Mike stayed with the divers, and Doc Lewis slept on the floor in our room.

(Pictured left-right Tom Eldridge, Jan Gabriel, Mike Brown, Cynthia Potter)

Doc Lewis was from Cincinnati, and had been a close friend of mine for years. He was the diving coach at the University of Cincinnati before taking a government job in the water department where he oversaw giving millions of dollars to different water companies around the country. He had a very high I.Q. and was an excellent amateur photographer which helped him get into the Olympic diving events.

Doc was loved by all the divers and diving enthusiasts around the country because he was so kind. He used to take pictures of the diving coaches and divers, and after having them developed, gave them away. Photos then were very expensive, but the price never bothered Doc Lewis. Ron and I also managed to sneak Dick Kimball into the pool for the diving competitions. He wasn't the U.S. Olympic coach, but he had three divers in the meet. This was much like when I snuck in at the 1964 Games in Tokyo to be with my three divers.

Cynthia Potter is Injured

Cynthia was favored to win both events in Munich, but that didn't happen. She was practicing a reverse somersault in the layout position from the three-meter platform, as a lead up for her reverse 1½ somersault layout from the ten-meter platform. She hit her feet on the edge of the platform four days before the diving events started. Badly bruised, a trainer at the pool wrapped her feet with gauze and tape, and I put her on my shoulders and carried her about a half mile across a marching field to the American medical station.

I never believed that ninety pounds could be so heavy. We walked in to find a nurse who replaced the old bandages with new ones, and gave Cindy a pair of crutches.

275

After taking Cindy back to her room next to ours, I was taking a shower back in our room in the village when someone told me that there was a doctor in the hall that wanted to talk to me. I said to tell him to wait until I finished my shower. When I came out to meet him, he started to bawl me out for the way I treated his nurse, and I should apologize to her for my behavior. I told him he had it all wrong because she should apologize to me for not attending to an injured athlete, and if he didn't like what I said, he could report me to his superiors. Then I would tell them my side of the story, and request that they all be discharged for doing a lousy job. When leaving, the doctor said he was sorry that I felt that way, and I told him I wasn't sorry.

Cindy was on crutches right up to the moment she was to compete on the three-meter board. She still wanted to compete, and had a doctor shoot her feet with Novocain about five minutes before the three-meter event was to begin. I was helping her up on the board to see if she could try out the board with numb feet, and two German guards came over yelling, "Nein, nein, verboten," and would not allow us on the board.

I remember standing behind her as I cussed out the guards who ignored us. Some German officials then came down on the deck just before the first event was to start, and informed all the diving coaches we were not allowed on the deck during the contest. This was unheard of in any diving contest, and much worse in the Olympics. So, we all had to stand behind a window in another pool next to the diving well in water up to our waists to watch the diving. Cindy managed to dive well enough with numb feet to take seventh place on the three-meter springboard. A couple of days later from the ten-meter platform, she failed to qualify for the finals and place twenty-first.

Cindy Potter's injury opened the door for Lt. Micki King (pictured right) who went on to win the three-meter contest. Janet Ely was also ready to compete on the three-meter springboard when she received word two days before the contest that her mother died. Janet and I became close friends over that matter because I spent a lot of time with her. She dived well enough to finish fourth in the finals, narrowly missing a medal. Looking back at that time, it was unbelievable how often we had such bad incidents occur before our girl divers were to compete in a major championship meet.

John Walker was Craig Lincoln's coach at the University of Minnesota. John came up to me as the three-meter event was about to start, and said they had made the decision that I should coach Craig during his event. Normally, the diver's regular coach has the honor to coach his own diver if he can get on the deck, but they thought I could do a better job of coaching him than John. I told them their decision was one of the nicest honors I ever had in my career as a diving coach. The American divers had won the men's three-meter event in the Olympics since 1920, but that ended when Vladimir

Vasin, from Russia, won the event even though he was short on every dive, but ripped all his entries not making a big splash. Craig took third place, and would have won if he hadn't twisted slightly when performing two of his compulsory dives.

On the three-meter, Mike Finneran placed fifth, and Dave Bush was twentieth. Klaus Dibiasi, from Italy, won the ten-meter platform event with American divers Dick Rydze taking second, Rick Earley placing sixth, and Mike Finneran ninth.

A Young Boy on Tower

I saw a young boy thirteen years old dive from the ten-meter platform who nearly made the finals, and I was amazed with his form. His name was Niki Stajkovic from Salzburg, Austria, and was coached by his father, Valadow. After the event, I introduced myself and suggested that he send Niki to Indiana during the summer so I could coach him, and he accepted my offer. (Pictured on left with Mike Brown at Indiana)

After talking to Niki, I found him to be a very nice young boy, and a marvelous diver. I coached him every summer until he was old enough to attend college. For some unknown reason, I never coached him diving from a springboard. Due to Title IX, I had only one scholarship every four years to give out to a male diver, and I gave it to Niki when he decided to go to Indiana. Niki was very talented on the tower, but unheard of on springboard. Doc got upset, and nearly fired me when I gave Niki my scholarship because tower diving was not yet an event in any N.C.A.A. contests.

When I was on sabbatical leave from Indiana, I visited the Stajkovic family in Salzburg. Valadow took me over to the pool where he had coached Niki, and I found two "Buck" boards locked with chains over the fulcrums so they couldn't be used. Then I knew why Niki had never learned to diving from a springboard. It was unheard of that a diver could learn to dive from the tower without first learning to dive from a springboard. Niki earned the scholarship later when he won the Big 10 three-meter event, and placed second in two N.C.A.A. springboard national championships.

The Wo.D.C.A. Conference at the 1972 Olympics

The Wo.D.C.A. Constitution stated that it would have a conference meeting at every Olympic Games to elect new officers, and discuss other matters related to diving and the association. Dick Smith, from America, was elected the new president, Grundy Vegard, from Norway, the new vice president. and Jack Barnett from Australia, was made the new secretary/treasurer.

When it came to voting for the continental presidents, Dr. Ritz, the National Diving Chairman from the United States, whose son dived for Dick Kimball, nominated Kimball, and it was seconded by another American official. Everyone was surprised because that was the only position that got more than one nomination. I was still the secretary and counted the votes for every position, and found that not one American voted for me. However, there were enough votes for me from other countries to win.

Jack Barnett was voted to be the new secretary/treasurer. Jack lived in Australia too far away from the countries on other continents that would made it very difficult and expensive, in those days, for him to communicate with all its members. As was seen over the next four years, coaches began to lose interest in the association, and my prediction for Wo.D.C.A. turned out to be true.

The Terrorists

Our rooms on the fifth floor in the Olympic Village were tiered down in a forward direction. There was a flag pole on the ground in front of our room that was used every morning by the athletes and coaches from different countries to show their honor and respect. I got up early in the morning on September 5th. Ron O'Brien was coming out of the bath room, and while standing on the balcony looking down to see what country was being honored, I asked, Ron if he knew what country had machine guns as part of their uniforms.

It so happened that eight terrorists had climbed over the fence near the entrance to the Olympic village at about four o'clock in the morning, and quickly moved to Block 31, a three-story building across the street from where we were staying. They stormed into the building, and started to kill the Israelis athletes who were weightlifters and wrestlers in Flat 3.

Their reason for the killings was to stage their revolutionary activities, and retaliate against the denial by the Israeli Cabinet to accede to the terrorist's demands to release 200 Palestinians in Israeli jails. When hearing the shots, some of the Israel track and field athletes in Flat 2, located on the same floor, escaped through the back windows, while others were trapped in the building.

Mark Spitz 7 Golds

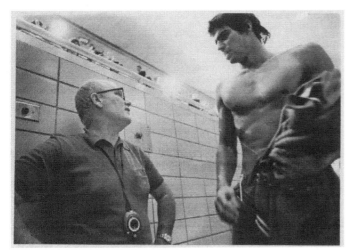

Mark Spitz (pictured here with his coach Doc Counsilman) had just won his seventh gold medal, and broke his seventh world record the day before the attack. Knowing he was a Jew, I went over to see him a few rooms away from ours, and was confronted with two body guards outside of his door. I told them I was his coach, so they knocked on his door, and he told them to send me in.

When I opened the door, I found Mark and his father huddled in the corner saying, "They are going to kill us." I always thought afterward, if Mark had won his seventh gold medal a couple of days sooner, the terrorists might have killed him instead of the Jewish wrestlers and weight lifters because they would have received more attention for their cause.

Our room offered a good view of what was going on in the terrorist's building. Ron and I remained on the balcony all day, and watched the terrorists. They wore face masks, and would run from one room to the other, but we didn't see them kill any more. The Olympic Village was immediately shut down when it became aware of the terrorists, and no one got in or out until the next day.

I was supposed to go out to dinner that evening with some other diving coaches who had rooms near the entrance to the Village. When I went over to see them that night, two or three helicopters landed inside of the Village entrance red lights blinking. A few minutes went by while people were running around in the dark to board the helicopters and take off.

Later, we learned that the terrorists had taken eleven Israeli hostages with them to the Munich Airport. They were all going to board a plane that was waiting for them. However, German military ambushed the helicopters, and the terrorists used hand grenades to kill all the hostages and one German police officer, and destroy the helicopters. German swat teams killed five of the eight terrorists, and captured the other three only to see them released in a prisoner swap three days later.

There was no competitive activity the next day. All the athletes, coaches, and officials met in the Olympic Stadium, and Avery Brundage, the President of the International

Olympic Committee (IOC), informed us that the Games would continue to the cheers from everyone.

Amateur Rules

Professional athletes could not perform at the Olympics at that time because Brundage stuck to his belief that amateurs should be the only athletes eligible for the Olympics. He died a couple of years later and that opened the door for professionals to compete starting with the 1975 Winter Olympics and the 1976 Summer Olympics in Montreal.

After the swimming and diving events were over, Ron and I were watching the United States play Russia for the basketball gold medal on television when the U.S. team won the game in the last second of the contest. Everyone in our building ran out on their balcony yelling and screaming over the victory when everything suddenly became silent. The time keeper of the game said that the game clock was wrong.

The Russian team still had three seconds to inbound the ball from under the U.S. basket after they scored. A Russian player threw the ball the length of the floor to a tall player under the basket who illegally pushed two American players aside, and dunked the ball as the buzzer sounded to win the game. It was an obvious foul by the Russian, but the referees neglected to call it.

The American coaches called for an investigation of the time left to play, so a committee of five officials was formed to decide the outcome. Two of them were from the free world, and three were from countries behind the iron curtain. The vote came out with two officials saying the American team won because the clock had run out, and the other three that included the time keeper who had changed the time to three seconds, voted for the Russian team.

Biased Judges

The men's three-meter diving event was one of the worst bias-judged events in the Olympics. The Italian judge met with the Russian judge. It became obvious that they agreed to give high scores to their divers, and low scores to the American divers. They weren't aware that the judge from England was standing behind them and spoke German, and he told me what they were planning to do.

Sure enough, they cheated, and I made an official protest on prime-time television to explain why and who I had protested. I said that I was protesting the judges not only from Italy and Russia, but also from the United States for cheating. I was asked, why would I protest the judge from America? I replied that when the American judge saw what was going on, he felt the only thing he could do was to cheat and reduce the impact made by the obvious biased scores from the other two judges.

Constantine Domulav, the Russian diving coach and good friend of mine, asked me if I knew what would happen if my protest was accepted. I didn't know. He said the judges would be replaced with other judges from the same countries that would make matters much worse so I withdrew my protest. Sure enough, the judges cheated in the finals, but not as bad as they would have if I had not protested. Having been in seven

Olympic Games, I can say cheating and biased behavior occurs in all sports that are decided with the use of human judgment.

I believe that the German Munich Olympics was one of the worst Games ever held when it seemed that stupid and biased changes were made in many of the events nearly every day. For example, the Americans were winning the pole vault event. In the middle of the contest, the officials informed the Americans they couldn't use their poles because they were only made in the United States, and not available for the athletes in other countries.

It was no surprise when the Americans didn't get a medal in the event. Another incident occurred when two Americans took first and second in the semi-finals of the 200-meter race, and arrived at the stadium track in the middle of the finals because one of their coaches had given them an incorrect old time sheet for the event.

Divine Intervention After the Olympic Games

It was about this time that I was greatly overworked tending to my rental trailers I invested in the late 1960's, my camps, and teaching and coaching more divers. Doc kept telling me if I didn't reduce my work load, I was going to crack. I thought I had my real estate investments under control when I agreed to a business partner to handle all that.

But I learned that he made several deals without my knowledge and was a swindler who took advantage of me knowing my focus was on coaching and camps. I became badly depressed over losing my investments but still incurring liabilities that I believed would hurt my marriage and coaching, and they did.

One day it got so bad I decided to go home after work, pack a bag, throw my wallet down the sewer, and disappear. While driving home to prepare to leave, I passed a sign in front of a lawyer's office that always had a comment on it. This time it read, "Man Is Only Defeated When He Admits It to Himself."

I drove around the block to make sure I read the sign correctly. When I read it again, I asked myself if I was ready to quit or challenge myself? I thought "no," and changed my mind about leaving home. I decided that every problem, no matter how bad, has a solution and I had to find it. But I still had to face the probability that I was going to lose my family, my job, and possibly be put in jail for some illegal things committed by my partner without my knowledge.

I hung around the Olympic Village for a few days after the Games were over with Doc Lewis. I was amazed at the amount of clothing and other souvenirs left behind by all the athletes. I thought how could athletes who worked so hard to achieve this success not care enough to take back home mementos of their experience.

I decided to do a little traveling in Europe for a few days, and Doc Lewis wanted to go along. But I said no because I wanted to be alone to sort out my problems which I was not anxious to return to at home. I was on the verge of financial ruin from poor investments with a real estate partner I had trusted but who swindled me. All that greatly affected my marriage, coaching, and quality of life.

Looking back, I can't say I was running away from reality, but I surely needed time to be alone with my thoughts. What happened next I can only believe was God helping to heal my wounds.

God works in mysterious ways. For true believers, there are messengers to be aware of acting in your lifetime and experience. Some people call "Angelic." What I am about to relate makes sense. But to those of you who have never had a dark period in your life, you will think I had lost touch with reality.

I had purchased a EU rail pass for a week, and decided to take the first train out of Munich that left the train station at six o'clock in the evening. I put most of my belongings in a locker at the station except for a white U.S.A. bag with basic needs.

I walked by eight of the nineteen tracks and found a train leaving at exactly six o'clock, and without looking where it was going, I got on the last car. I found my compartment empty, and after moving a short distance from the station, the train stopped. I began to think I boarded the wrong train headed for the yards, but it started up again.

It was September, and my compartment started to get cold. I couldn't find how to turn the heat on. So, I decided to go to another car, and was really confused when I didn't find anyone in the next six cars that should have been loaded with people leaving after the end of the Olympic Games.

I finally found a car with a man in a dark suit looking out the window from his compartment. I thought he might be a conductor, and opened the door and found it warm inside. I asked the man, would he mind if I shared the compartment with him? He told me to get my luggage, and when I got back and started to enter the compartment, I was stunned to see him staring at me. I couldn't take my eyes off his, he said, "I know you think it is by accident that you come here, but it's not because I have been waiting for you, I am a minister." There is no way I can say how I felt at that moment.

He first wanted to know if I was involved with the Olympics? What sport, etc.? I began to feel that he already knew all the answers. Then he asked me if I was married, and how many children I had? After I told him, he said I had made the mistake of putting my job before my family. I have no memory of how long the conversation lasted when he gave me his card.

He said he was from Albany, New York, and was on his way to Lindow, a small town near the Swiss border, to visit his family. Without looking out the window, he said that we were approaching Lindow, and for me to get off the train with him. It was dark, but I could see well enough to find that no one else got off the train. We walked into a large train station to find no one there.

As we walked toward the front exit, he told me that there were some motels on the other side of a boulevard across from the station, and I should stay in one of them for three nights and get a good rest and visit a restaurant nearby with a German band on a lake. I'll never forget standing next to him on the steps of the train station. One minute he was pointing at the motels lit up between the trees on the boulevard, but when I turned to ask him if those were the ones he suggested and found he wasn't there.

I really freaked out and ran back in the station thinking he might have gone to the men's rest room, but he wasn't there. I must have cried for a half hour before crossing the boulevard and getting a room in one of the motels where I slept soundly in a bed with down feather covers. I got up the next morning, and had breakfast at the restaurant near the lake and listened to the band. I decided to take a ferry to the other side of the lake where I rode a tram to the top of a mountain. I remember how cold it was on top when I told God that this was the closest I had ever been to him standing on this earth.

Three days later and all rested as prescribed by the stranger, I got back on the train going to Zurich, the capital of Switzerland. When I arrived at the train station, I went to the window that offered reserved hotel rooms for visitors. I was the last person in line when I asked for one room, and he said they were all sold out because there were conventions and other activities going on in the city of three million people. After pleading with him for a couple of minutes, he suggested that since I had a first-class ticket, I could sleep on the train.

I got on a train. and sat in an empty compartment. A young woman came in and sat across from me, and put her feet up on the seat next to mine that had a newspaper on it. I knew she thought I was going to talk to her, but I didn't as she kept looking at me until I fell asleep. When I woke up early the next morning, the young woman was gone. Since I didn't have anything to do, I picked up the newspaper on my seat thinking it would probably be written in German. I nearly fell out of my seat when I found the paper was about the New Testament in English.

For a while I didn't know where I was going, so I read the paper and found myself heading back to Munich where I caught a plane for home. On the way home, I called Mary back in Bloomington, and told her about my strange experience. She accused me of making up the story because I was trying to be a martyr.

I kept the minister's calling card for years, and one day when moving to another house, I dropped a box of letters and a single card floated out and landed on the floor a few feet from me. I couldn't believe that it was the card he had given me, so I called the number on the card of the church in Albany, New York. I was told that no such minister ever preached there, and they had no idea who he was. I still have the card.

CHAPTER 34

Some Events and Competitions from 1973 to 1976

Repairing the Damage

Of course, my coaching was badly damaged because of all my personal problems over that period. I don't think I ever fully recovered from those days because I didn't do as good of a job coaching as I did in the 1960's and early 1970's. I had gone through a time when I thought I would have agreed to buy the Brooklyn Bridge if someone tried to sell it to me.

Divers didn't know anything about my personal life, and kept showing up at Indiana. David Bere, Jim Bere's brother, (pictured right) and Scott Cranham (pictured below) were two of them. David never dived well enough to

compete in major meets. Scott had visited Indiana with his family when he was thirteen years old, and decided to attend I.U. when he graduated from high school.

Scott made the finals in several of our important meets, and one day I asked him if he was born in Grand Rapids, Michigan. And he told me he was born in Canada. I immediately called Don Webb, the top Canadian diving coach, and asked if Scott could compete for Canada in national and international contests. And he said he could because he had dual citizenship. Scott kept diving for us at Indiana and did well, but he medaled in the Canadian National Championships and competed for Canada in two Olympic Games. Unfortunately, he didn't make the finals which is extremely difficult to do at the international level. He moved to Canada after he graduated from Indiana, and has over the years worked up to become a top administrator for diving in Canada.

Over Challenged

I remember I put so much pressure on Jan Gabriel and Pat Harrington that they were on the verge of complete breakdowns, and ready to quit the team. I realized this when I went outside and found Jan sitting alone in the upper stands of the old football stadium next to our pool in the Physical Education Building. I called to her, and she came running down from the stadium in tears. She told me she felt she didn't deserve to be on the team, and decided to quit.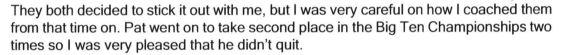

I had a long talk with her, and finally convinced her that she was important to all of us and it wasn't necessary for her be as good as Lesley (Bush) or Cynthia (Potter). I went on to say that I would be just as proud and content with her as I was with the other divers, if she gave me the best she could do.

Pat Harrington had a tough day in practice one day, and started yelling at me and said he was going to quit because he couldn't give what I demanded from him. Recognizing his frustration, I apologized to him for being so tough on him, and told him how much I appreciated how hard he had worked to give me the best he had to offer.

They both decided to stick it out with me, but I was very careful on how I coached them from that time on. Pat went on to take second place in the Big Ten Championships two times so I was very pleased that he didn't quit.

Mike Brown was in our Master's Degree program for physical education, and helping me coach the team while I was going through my challenges. Mike knew Jan (Gabriel) from practice, and they started to date. When Mike got his degree, he was hired as the diving coach at the University of Texas in Austin, Texas, and soon after Mike married Jan. The two of them also formed a diving camp and she also assisted him with the Texas divers. They divorced several years later, and Mike became the diving coach for the University of Hawaii.

Jan who is extremely intelligent, got her master's degree and worked at two jobs in Ft. Lauderdale, Florida. One was at the Pine Crest private school where she has coached several divers to state championships, and the other was working for U.S. Diving in Indianapolis for about fifteen years.

U.S. Diving controls all the competitive diving activities except for those in high schools and universities. She carried a tremendous load for U.S. diving when she single-handedly did most of the administrative work. She would analyze movies of all the important diving competitions world-wide, and share them with the organization's members.

Jan Gabriel's Impact on U.S. Diving

The director of U.S. Diving at that time had no background in diving, and relied on Jan to do most of her work. That included writing a thousand-page book that explained in detail nearly everything you'd want to know about the sport.

The Director of U.S. Diving was replaced with Linda Paul who is a wonderful woman with a fantastic personality. She loved her job, and has made miraculous changes in improving the sport. She was friendly with everyone in diving, and attended all the important competitions and functions. This again has made diving a fun activity.

As of this publication, Linda will have retired, and will surely be missed.

My Sabbatical Leave

I had a large group divers in the 1974 and 1975 school year, and it was the only time I had more females than males. But I decided to take a sabbatical leave in the fall semester of 1974 to do some diving research. I also wanted to get away from the challenges and stress I had gone through in the previous two or three years. I decided to travel through Europe by myself. I had Mike Brown, then a graduate assistant working on his master's degree at Indiana, coach the divers until I returned.

I started my trip by first visiting Johan Knudsen, my friend in Denmark. He visited me to watch me coach a few years ago. I noticed that his father cleaned chimneys for a living, and seeing the way they lived, he was good at his job. I told Johan after staying with him and his family for a couple of days that I planned to rent a car, and drive around Europe. Instead, he loaned me his Volkswagen "Bug" to drive around Europe.

My first stop was Sweden to visit Toivo Ohman, their top diving coach. Toivo had an international meet every year called "The Swedish Cup" that I had taken U.S. divers to compete in on two occasions. I stayed with Toivo for two days, then took off again to see my old friend, Grunder Vegard, in Norway. He was a member and later made president of Wo.D.C.A.

Grunder was a school teacher and coached diving to young kids. I stayed with him and his family for a couple of days when he asked me if I had ever flown in a glider. I said I hadn't, and he had a fifteen-year-old female student take me for a ride. I was a little nervous at first because she was so young. But I could see she was an expert, and it was a marvelous experience. We took off the ground on a tow rope attached to an airplane. When we reached a couple thousand feet, the girl pulled a lever that released the tow rope, and dropped us into flight. I had some fear of it crashing, but that immediately vanished when I found how well we glided. I could feel the lift under the wings. I remember that the seat was tight, and there was no noise. We over her house and around the city before landing on one wheel on an airstrip, and people ran along the wings to keep the glider balanced.

I then took off for Finland where I took a ferry over to East Germany, and was immediately sent to the office of embarkation that was behind the Iron Curtain. Two German guards asked me for my papers that included my passport that I had, but not a visa that they eventually gave me after a long discussion. They told me that I must immediately report to the police station in Berlin in order to obtain permission to stay in East Berlin.

I drove a long distance looking for a sign to Berlin. I didn't find any so I got off at an exit hoping that I was going in the right direction. I drove on the same road for three hours, and was surprised to find myself on the outskirts of Berlin. I located the police station in the middle of East Berlin, and checked in. Across the street was a public swimming pool, and I decided to take a swim. I entered the pool and couldn't believe I saw a group of American divers that I knew, including my diver Cynthia Potter.

They were competing in a meet with the East Germans so I stayed with them for a day before taking off for Western Germany. When I arrived at Check Point Charley, the border of East and West Germany, I exchanged my East German Marks, that I paid twenty American dollars for, into West German Marks. I quickly learned how bad things were in Germany when I found the East German Marks were worth about eighty percent less than the West German Marks.

I drove on to Vienna, Austria to visit Peter Huber who was a diving coach and dear friend who always took me out to drink wine in the evening, then went on to Salzburg (where they filmed the Sound of Music). I visited Niki's mother who was a gracious person, and put me up for three days before I took off to visit a bunch of other countries that included Hungary, Italy, Spain, Switzerland, and France.

I had a marvelous time sightseeing, and slept in the back seat of Johan's VW bug most of the time. I then drove back to Denmark, and gave the car back to Johan. I spent two more days with him and his family before taking a ferry to London, and caught a plane home. The trip helped me to get recharged to create and accept new challenges. I needed that mental and physical rest to refocus on my job preparing young divers for competitions and life.

My Dog Magoo

A friend of mine lived in Texas, and had five fifth-generation golden retriever puppies and sent one to me. I named him "Magoo." He was extremely intelligent. He knew when he did something wrong. When I went to fetch him, I would chase him around in the house in a circle but never could catch him. I found I was too busy to give Magoo enough attention to keep him. After a year, I gave him to Brian Bungum who kept him for a year before he gave Magoo to my daughter Nancy who lived on the edge of Bloomington in a house over a hundred yards away from the highway.

We all loved the dog and when I went to Nancy's house on Christmas eve, we couldn't find Magoo. Leaving Nancy's house to go home, I saw a parked car off the highway next to someone using a flash light, and I didn't know why until I got home. My son Jimmy showed up a couple of minutes later with Magoo dead in the back of his truck. It was a shock because the dog had never gone near the highway before. I loved the dog and I buried him in my back yard.

287

I lived in that house for two years. On a winter day, it started to snow so hard as I was going home that I had to park my car on the road about a half mile from the house because I couldn't get it up a short hill. The wind had drifted the snow waist deep. After walking about a hundred yards up the hill, I suddenly realized that if I didn't get home or find shelter from the wind, I could be trapped and possibly die.

I managed to work my way up to the lawn of a nearby house, and walked in unannounced where I stayed for a while. I eventually got home by walking on everyone's lawn for a couple of blocks, but it was a real scare. Bloomington was closed off from other nearby towns for over a week before the roads were cleared enough for traveling.

And to think I chose to go to Indiana because it was the most southern school in the Big Ten Conference where I thought it would be warmer than Minnesota or Michigan!

The Austrian Federation Asks Me to Coach Niki Stajkovic

Niki Stajkovic was a four-time All-American with the Hoosiers placing on both the one-meter and three-meter boards in 1980 and 1981. In 1980, Stajkovic placed sixth on the one-meter and third on the three-meter. He then placed second on the one-meter and fourth on the three-meter in 1981.

I was asked by the Austrian Federation to coach Niki Stajkovic in Vienna over the Easter holidays for the 1976 Olympics. Niki and I got together with two of Niki's friends to go to a diving contest in Wrenne, France. Two bad accidents occurred during the diving contest. The first was a diver landed flat on his face on the end of the board doing an inward 2½ somersault. They had to put a towel over his face the moment he surfaced knowing that the injury was serious.

The second was the next diver landed flat on his back on the end of the board doing a reverse 2½ somersault that created another bloody mess. Niki was the next diver, and with blood and skin hanging over the end of the board, he dived halfway across the pool doing the same dive to make sure he wouldn't make the same mistake. Those two incidents were the worst I had ever seen in any diving contest.

The 1976 Montreal Olympic Games

I started to coach Niki after I arrived for the Games, and found he began to perform worse in every work out because he didn't appear to have any strength. I found out why when I had lunch with him about five days before his event. I was shocked to find that all he had been eating during that time was strawberries because he liked them.

I ate all my meals with him for the rest of the days before his contest, but it was too late for him to regain his strength and he didn't qualify for the finals. Thankfully, Cynthia didn't make such a foolish mistake, and took the bronze medal in the three-meter event. Niki wasn't the only diver that made an eating mistake at the Olympics. We had heard that one Russian diver, who was supposed to win the three-meter springboard contest, gained over ten pounds before her event from eating too much, and failed to make the finals.

Following the Olympics

Our divers performed very well during the season after the 1976 Olympics despite the loss of some of our divers who had graduated. We outscored all the other teams at the Big Ten, the N.C.A.A., and National indoor and outdoor A.A.U. Championships for men and women. Without going into detail, the divers who competed in those meets were Tom Kenyon, Brian Bungum, Mark Antinoff, Kevin McWhirter, Doug MacAskill, Carol Lindner, Ann Gilmore, Sue Rogers, and Sally Sanguenet.

My Trip to Kiev, Russia

I was selected to coach our United States diving team that competed in Kiev, Russia around 1977. Somehow, I lost my passport after we went through customs in Moscow. I called the American Embassy, and they sent two of their men down from Moscow to give me a new passport. They were two nice guys, and decided to show me around Kiev since I had never been there before.

They took me to an old church that had catacombs where the priests prayed in small cubbyholes below the church until they died. While driving to the church, one of the men driving the car said that the KGB were about five cars behind us in a grey car, and told me not to look back. We parked in front of the church and our driver told me to look at the grey car as it went by, and I saw a man in a white turtle-neck sweater in the back seat.

We went down into the catacombs and walked through a tunnel that was lit up so we could see the priests in the cubbyholes that were perfectly preserved. I turned around to find the man in the white sweater standing behind me. Our men told me that there were four KGB men standing in different places in the lobby. As we were leaving the catacombs, I asked if I should take a picture of them. Then one of our agents grabbed me, and said if I tried to take a picture, we would be taken to their authorities and remain there for a long time. I don't remember how well we did in the meet, but I do remember we held our own.

CHAPTER 35

Events That Occurred Between 1973 and 1982

The 1973 N.C.A.A. National Championships that was a Scam

We had won six N.C.A.A. team championships in a row from 1967 to 1972, and were highly favored to win our seventh title at the University of Southern California. The meet was held at Long Beach State University because they had better facilities. The final team score was U.S.C. 339, and Indiana 338. Remember that score as you read on....

In most of the previous championships we had won, USC was second. They had been frustrated in losing for six years so we believed it was only a matter of time USC was going to beat us even if they had to cheat, and they did in the following ways:

Keep in mind that Title IX was just enacted into law June 23, 1972 that requires gender equity for boys and girls in every educational program that receives federal funding. Previously, Division I swimming and diving teams enjoyed 20 full scholarships over a four-year period. But with the new legislation, schools cut that back to only 11 scholarships. Women's sports now had scholarships, and sometimes not enough quality athletes to recruit and offer a scholarship.

First, they were caught using their allotment of scholarships plus five scholarships allocated for the volleyball team. As the story goes, several of the other PAC 10 Conference schools found out what they did, and were collectively going to report them to the N.C.A.A. U.S.C. told them if they turned them in, they would turn all of them in for violations they had committed in the past. So, the member schools all backed off, and U.S.C. got away with it.

Second, the N.C.A.A. rules stated that swimming competitors had to make out a form for the events they planned to swim in the next day, and put them in the entry box the night before. Only the officials were to open the box until the next day. But some U.S.C. members opened the box ahead of time, and changed their forms after seeing what events the Indiana swimmers were planning to compete in so they could maximize their points.

Third, the N.C.A.A. rule book also stated that a relay team is disqualified if one of the swimmers on the relay team jumps into the water at the finish of the event. A U.S.C. swimmer broke the rule, but the relay was not disqualified by their meet referee. Unfortunately, we made the mistake of not protesting the infraction at that moment.

Fourth, Indiana's Mike Stamm won a silver medal in backstroke at the 1972 Olympic Games and placed second in the backstroke event in this meet. The electronic touch pad was quite narrow, and Mike, on his finish, touched the wall above the pad that failed to activate the electronic circuit. In cases like this, the back-up human watch times are used, and the timers also use an electronic back-up button. The officials did not follow protocol, and had Mike taking fifth place when the fourth-place swimmer was still behind him.

Fifth, to make sure we would lose, in the final event an official disqualified our 800-yard free relay team for jumping on a relay take-off. Relays are scored twice as much as the individual events, and can mean a loss of 14, or 12 points just for placing second or third. There were other violations of the rules that were broken, and one occurred during the three-meter diving event.

What happened requires that I go back a couple of months. Allen Ross was a freshman diver from down south who decided to come to Indiana to dive with me. He was from a prominent family, a little "spoiled," and wasn't eager to accepting discipline. One day he and I got into an argument, and he decided to quit school and attend Louisiana State University.

He wasn't there a week when he realized he had made a very bad mistake because he didn't receive any coaching at L.S.U. So, he called and asked if I would coach him. And I accepted. I coached him when he could find time to come to Indiana on holidays that went on for nearly a year when he became eligible to compete for L.S.U.

Sixth, about two weeks before the 1973 N.C.A.A. National's, I told Allen that I didn't think it was a good idea for me to coach him anymore. I said, because if he dived in the N.C.A.A. meet and beat one of my divers by one point and we lost the meet by one point, I could be fired ... and that is exactly what happened.

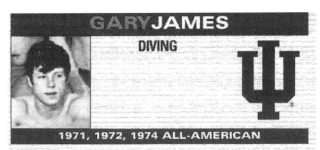

GARY JAMES
DIVING
1971, 1972, 1974 ALL-AMERICAN

Gary James was yet another All-America diver at Indiana University as he earned such recognition six times during his career. In 1972, James had his top one-meter performance, finishing fifth. That same year, he placed 11th on the three-meter. As a freshman in 1971, he placed eighth on the three-meter and ninth on the one-meter. He concluded his career with a 10th-place finish on the three-meter at the 1974 NCAA Championships.

Gary James was my best diver at the time. I didn't know that ninth place would win the meet for us. Every time Gary got up to dive, the lights would go out momentarily which was a signal for about seven hundred U.S.C. fans to scream as loud as possible to distract Gary as he made his approach and performed his dive.

I don't believe that the great Greg Louganis would have been able to dive under such conditions. And as I predicted, Allen Ross beat Gary

James by one point, and we lost the meet by one point.

I was so mad that I went into seclusion, and didn't talk to anyone except members in my family for well over a week. I always felt that if we would have won the meet, Doc and I might have received serious physical consequences. I asked myself for a long time after that meet why I ever got into such a sport where a team would sink so low to beat another team.

The 1974 Season

I recruited nine male divers in the fall of 1974, and all nine showed up along with six girls. I had never met half of them before, and learned several were not very talented. But I decided to coach them. What Jan Gabriel lacked in talent she made up for by being one of the most intense female divers I ever coached.

(Pictured left to right are Tom Eldridge, Cynthia Potter, me, Jan Gabriel, and Mike Brown)

Jan was from St. Louis, Missouri, and came to Indiana after being at one of my diving camps. My program was not easy for the divers because they were challenged to improve themselves every day, not only as a diver but as a person. The ones that had talent caught on quicker and got better than some of the others because they could accept the pressure I put on them. But for others it was almost like a living hell to pay the price to be a great diver.

My Divorce in 1974

I was right in the middle of a workout at the 1968 Olympics in Mexico when I had a premonition that I would be divorced in five years. This occurred before I had any financial or personal problems at home, and I was recognized as the top diving coach in the world. However, things began to change a couple of years later. The first clue occurred when I came home for lunch and was talking to Mary about some problem I had at school.

She interrupted me. I thought she had to go to the bathroom, but she said she didn't want to hear about my problems anymore. I told her she was being ridiculous because we had promised to share our problems when we got married. I asked her, whom should I share my problems with. And she said that I had to figure that out for myself. I didn't realize until much later that our relationship was badly damaged. I didn't know why except that I thought it was because of my job that included spending a lot of time with W.o.D.C.A., my diving camp, and a few other activities keeping up the rental properties.

When Rick Gilbert started graduate school in 1965 he invested in a mobile home next to campus. That saved him a lot of money, and at the same time proved a sure investment because the university was growing and not able to keep up with the housing demand. I learned from that and invested in several mobile homes that I rented out to graduate and married students.

In the course of my real estate investing, I was introduced to Bill Jenkins who was already in the business and suggested we partner. I was busy coaching, and it seemed like a good idea for Jenkins to monitor my properties.

Over a period of several years and with me not minding the store, Jenkins made several terrible investments on our behalf. This left my investments practically worthless. The stress at times was unbearable, and affected my coaching, my marriage, and my finances.

My most profitable adventure was my valuable diving camps where we had to turn students away because of the high demand for my coaching. The lesson I learned from that challenge was to focus on what you are good at, and keep at it. Keep finding ways to improve until you experience success beyond your dreams.

I'm reminded of the Aesop fable of the tortoise and the hare. You may know how the story goes, and it's the plodder tortoise who wins the race. Life has its challenges, but if you keep working to improve what you are gifted to do you will succeed. The flash-in-the-pan schemes seldom work. There is a phrase for that too: If it sounds too good to be true, it probably is.

I often told my students there are three most important decisions you will make in your life. The first is what you want to study in college, the second is which college you will attend, and the third is who you will marry and spend the rest of your life with.

Looking back, I wish I had spent more time with my children while they were growing up. But I think every parent often feels this way. Now I have my grandchildren to enjoy.

I remember leaving the courthouse after my divorce. My lawyer asked me how I felt. I told him I was confused because God had put Mary and me together, but man parted us. I talked to my friend Rich Lindner about my financial affairs because the law stated that our belongings should be evenly divided.

Rich said that since I had three children, I should give it all to Mary and start over again, and that is what I did. I want to say here that Mary was a fine wife and mother, and I don't blame her. I was the one who was at fault throughout this ordeal in my life.

Challenges After My Divorce

After my divorce in 1974, I had gone from a good marriage, living in a nice home, and making a good living to losing it all in two years. I remember sitting on a mattress with only two ripped sheets and no pillow feeling sorry for myself after practice. I was depressed with my life, and had hit rock bottom.

Then one day after waking up, I got up and held myself accountable for my errors. Here I was, challenging my divers to stand up and fight for what they believed in, and have the courage to face any problem that may arise when I was doing just the opposite.

From that time on, I decided that I was going to stand up and face whatever happened to me regardless of the outcome. I believed I had to face whatever challenge came along, and do the best I could to be that positive success for others to model. I took that challenge, and never faltered from that moment on.

Mary kept the house after our divorce for a couple of years, then sold it and bought a small farm near Bloomington North High School where all our children went to school. She found a job working as social worker for a few years before she went home for her fiftieth high school reunion in Delaware, Ohio. She met one of her former boyfriends who had become an anesthesiologist and who had recently lost his wife. She started dating him, and they eventually got married.

Mary lived in a condominium in Bloomington, and he had a house in Lima, Ohio, so they traveled back and forth over the years to visit with their children. Eventually, he got sick and died in the fall of 2012, when he fell down the stairs and broke his neck. She sold the house in Lima, and lives in the Bloomington condo she stayed to be near her children, grandchildren, and great grandchildren.

Mary and the children had continued to live in our home on Blue Ridge until Nancy and Jimmy graduated from high school. I agreed to pay their way through college when they both started at Indiana University.

Nancy, my oldest, is married and living in the Orlando, FL area. She has a career as an interior decorator, with many accounts in the area.

Jimmy met Teresa on the beach at Myrtle Beach, South Carolina. He transferred schools and graduated from the University of South Carolina after getting married. They have three children, and he owns a business storing and repairing boats near Lake Monroe southeast of Bloomington.

Elizabeth has four children from her first marriage, and still works for the city. She has devoted herself to her children as a single parent. Then she remarried and lives in a beautiful home west of Bloomington where she can keep her three horses, a pony, and a miniature donkey. One of Elizabeth's memories of childhood was her sitting on my lap while we watched the Gomer Pyle TV show. We would laugh and laugh and laugh, repeating the remarks of the characters.

Susie Dressler When I Needed a Friend

I was teaching a diving class in Royer Pool when I saw a female graduate student having some trouble teaching a lifesaving class in the pool. I went over to see if I could help. That is when I met Susie Dressler, and we struck up a conversation.

I was 24 years older than her, but we got along fine. She invited me to a couple parties at her apartment that she shared with Rose, another graduate student. I got along fine with all of them despite the difference in our ages, and my position at I.U. Susie had a great personality, and I felt comfortable around her, and her friends when I needed them.

That Christmas holiday break I took my divers, and my children to Ft. Lauderdale to practice. Sally Sangunet was one of my divers, and we all stayed at her house whose parents were fantastic hosts. They fed us and gave us places to sleep for nearly two weeks. Unbeknownst to me, Susie and one of her girlfriends had driven together to Ft. Lauderdale, and we ran into them on the beach. They offered to entertain my children while I was coaching my divers, and they had a lot of fun.

Susie took my diving class the next semester as a student to learn how to coach diving. When she got her Master's degree, I got her a job coaching diving along with another Indiana male graduate who got the swim coach job at the University of Evansville, Indiana. She kept the job for two years then decided to move on to a dive coaching position at the University of Southern California - Santa Barbara.

Starting a New Life

After my divorce, I managed to make enough money to rent a condominium in the Jackson Apartments a mile from the University on the west side of Bloomington. I came home late in the afternoon one day to find a young man sitting asleep on my doorstep. When I woke him up, he told me his name was Johan Knudsen, a diving coach from Denmark. He had come to watch me coach my team. He had been up all night so I invited him in and told him to go to bed, and we would talk after getting some sleep. He turned out to be a very fine person, and stayed with me for nearly two months before he returned home. We met again a few years later.

Caught in the Act - A Little Humor

I happened to be walking by a liquor store in town near the University. I saw Tom Kenyon, another one of my divers, walking out with a six-pack of beer in each hand. Tom was one of the four boys from St. Louis that I coached for four years before starting a diving camp in 1969. He came to I.U. and won a Big Ten Title in his senior year. He went on to be doctor and oversaw the AIDS program in Africa.

Knowing how strict I was about drinking, he nearly dropped both six packs of beer when he looked up and saw me. I asked him what he had in his hands. He said that they weren't really for him. So, I asked him who he was getting the beer for. He said, Brian Bungum, and I had a good laugh after he walked away.

Brian was having a birthday party at his condo after dinner that night, and I was invited. I didn't bring up the incident with Tom, but I casually looked in the closet, under the bed, in the kitchen, and a few other places before we celebrated his birthday. I left early after dinner so they could have privacy without the coach around. At practice the next day, I asked Brian "where was it?". And he acted dumb. He asked me what I meant. And I said, "the beer." He smiled, and said it was in the trunk of his car until I left.

The End of My Financial Woes

I think that one of the reasons for my stupidity making bad business decisions was a result of being overworked. I was trying to do over a dozen different jobs, and was probably having a nervous breakdown but didn't realize it even after Doc kept warning me about it.

I had grown up during the Depression and never had any money to think about investing. Then when I had money to invest, I didn't value that as much as I should have. I always wanted to help others more than myself, and would never think of asking anyone for a dime to help me or our program.

My Mother Gets Sick

My mother had a stroke in 1980. I picked up my brother in Canton, Ohio, on the way to Erie to visit our mother in the hospital. Not knowing better, my brother and I made a terrible mistake. When we met with the doctor in the hospital, he informed us that our mother also had colon cancer, and if he didn't operate on her immediately, she would die within the week.

After a short discussion, we told the doctor to operate. What we didn't know was that she would then live another year in pain, and be put in an old people's home. She eventually died from starvation at the age of 81 because with swallow difficulties, she couldn't eat most of the food they offered her.

My older brother Jimmy passed away in 2011 from a heart attack at age 88. We were very close while we were growing up, and I still have great admiration for what he did for his country and his profession. His wife, Shirley, is in perfect physical condition at the age of 91. Their three children got married, and had children whom I try to visit every year when I return to Erie and talk about the good old days.

Bob Bollinger's Thesis Creating Degree of Difficulty Diving Formula

Bob Bollinger was a gymnast while I attended Ohio State, and was a good friend. Bruce Harlan and I used to do back handsprings down the football field during half-time at the Ohio State football games, and he always beat the two of us. He had a brilliant mind with a fantastic vocabulary that he used to write outstanding poetry. He lived in Rockford, Illinois, and had two sons.

Bob came to visit me at my new house one night. We were sitting in the kitchen when he asked what was in the folder sitting on my kitchen table. I told him that it was a copy

of the new diving formula that gave the correct degrees of difficulty (DD) for all the dives used in competition. The DD's had been decided by experienced divers who assigned what they should be up to the present time.

After looking over the folder, Bob said it was his thesis for his master's degree at the University of Iowa, and was later used for gymnastic events that were officially accepted by the national and international gymnastic associations. Constantine Domulov was a gymnastics coach for Russia, and was also the Russian diving coach at the 1972 Olympics. When he received a copy of the formula, he thought it could be changed into a formula for competitive diving, so he wrote a book about it.

However, it was written in Russian, so very few ever read the book. Fortunately, Herb Flewelling, the inventor of the bubble machine from Canada, found the book, and translated it into English and that version of it ended up on my kitchen table. When he assured me that it was his thesis, I told him that I was going to make him famous.

I took the formula to Berlin, Germany for the World Diving Championships a couple of months later, and Dick Smith and I presented it to the F.I.N.A. Bureau. They turned it down because they said it contained too many errors. So, Bollinger and I got together when I returned home, and worked on it until we thought it was properly written.

We then took it back to the F.I.N.A. group at the next international meet, and they finally accepted it along with all the governing diving bodies in the world. The only dives that could be performed in a meet up to that time, were those in the F.I.N.A. rule books, and it usually took four to eight years to get a new dive accepted. Bollinger's formula changed all of that. Now a diver could perform a very difficult dive not in the rule books, and use the formula that gave the correct degree of difficulty.

Robbie Bollinger

Bob Bollinger's son, Robbie, was also a terrific gymnast, and held the world's title for two or three gymnastic events. However, form was not a big issue at that time, so he could perform difficult stunts and win contests with no form. Robbie won the Illinois State Diving Championship as a senior in high school, and his father needed a scholarship to send him to college. Since Robbie could perform many of the difficult dives, Bob thought Robbie would get several offers from the college coaches after he graduated from high school.

However, Title IX caused cutbacks to men's scholarships, and he was shocked when Robbie was not offered one. So, he took Robbie to the summer National A.A.U. Diving

Championships in Woodlands, Texas, and had him perform some gymnastic stunts from the three-meter board that got a lot of applause but no college offers.

Being a very close friend of mine, he thought I should give Robbie the one scholarship that I got every four years. But I told him I couldn't because Robbie had terrible form with flat feet, and a sway back. I had moved into my new house in Blue Ridge when he came to visit me again, and he tried to talk me into taking his son.

I kept refusing to give him my only scholarship. But Bob decided not to leave my house until I gave my only scholarship to his son. That turned out to be a good decision because Robbie went on to win and score in several national championships.

Leading up to the 1980 N.C.A.A. Championships

I taught Robbie how to point his toes and straighten his back, so when we competed in the 1980 N.C.A.A. Championships in Austin, Texas, we had four of our divers make the finals.

Robbie started school as a freshman in 1979 along with Bill Coleman (pictured right), Pat Harrington, and Tom Mulhern. That gave us a strong team along with Niki Stajkovic, a sophomore, Doug MacAskill (pictured left) a junior, and Kevin McWhirter a senior.

Robbie won the one-meter springboard title followed by Tom Mulhern, Pat Harrington, and Doug MacAskill all of whom made the top six in the finals of eight divers. Bill Coleman failed to keep his legs together on the entry doing a reverse 2½ somersault, and placed ninth. We came close to repeating our one-meter accomplishments when Robbie took second, Harrington third, and MacAskill fourth in the three-meter competition. Sadly, Mulhern hit the board with his feet, and failed to make the finals. This group of divers did a magnificent job of diving that was rarely seen in those days.

Strangely, we had more girl divers on our team than we had boys.

The only year that we didn't score in the N.C.A.A. national championships was 1978 at Long Beach State University in California. Four of my divers had a broken foot. David Aaron, Doug MacAskill, and Kevin McWhirter were the only Indiana divers I had to compete. They ended up failing to score in both events because I had them use a new kind of hurdle that the judges had never seen before, and didn't like. Doc and the whole team wouldn't have anything to do with the divers or me for the whole year after that, so we sort of ignored them and worked real hard all year long.

The next year my I.U. divers scored 44 points in the 1979 N.C.A.A. National Championships at Cleveland State University. Doc's swimmers didn't score any points because most of his good swimmers were focused on training for the 1980 Olympic trials, and didn't compete. Doc asked me how in the hell was I able to take a team that didn't get a point one year, and then score forty-four points the next year? And I told him we worked hard.

I rarely if ever drank any alcohol at a swimming or diving event. But that night after the 1979 meet, I was sitting at the bar at the hotel eating a sandwich with a coke when several of the diving coaches were sitting at a nearby table having a beer. Bob Ritz, the coach from Iowa, came over and insisted that I sit with them and have a beer. As I started to leave after drinking it, I got up to pay my bill when Bob said the diving coaches would never let me pay for it because of what my divers had done that day. He reminded me that no other college qualified more than one diver for the finals when I had three of the four divers they had never seen before.

After the meet, I went up to Doc's room, and told him and Marge that I had something to say. And if he didn't like it, they could kick me out of their room. I suggested that since he was sixty-five years old, he should quit coaching and start giving clinics and lectures all over the world that would help improve swimming for everyone everywhere. I went on to say that he would get first class treatment, and make a lot of money when another championship would do nothing for his reputation.

He hesitated for a moment before saying he couldn't do it because they had other commitments. Doc went on to coach until he was seventy years old when Marge told me a few years later that she thought he should have retired, and given clinics and lectures years ago while not remembering what I had already told them.

Robbie went on to win the second of two N.C.A.A. National Championships in 1980 when the Indiana Varsity magazine mentioned Robbie's feat in the last line of the last paragraph on the last page. Chuck Crab worked for the athletic department, and was the editor of the magazine that year. I ran into Chuck at Assembly Hall where we held all our basketball games and had athletic offices, and voiced my complaint that Robbie should have received more attention for his success representing the university.

The school failed to recognize that Robbie was the only athlete that won a national title that year, and it was because he was in a non-revenue sport. A week later the athletic department had a banquet for the athletes who had been on a winning team, and overlooked Robbie's accomplishment. Robbie Bollinger was the ideal person any coach would love to have coached.

Doc was no longer winning any national team titles after the last one in 1973, but we did place second in 1974 and 1975. He came up to me during the one-meter event at the 1982 N.C.A.A. Championships at the University of Wisconsin, and said if our divers didn't score well, the team wouldn't make the top ten teams in the country. Greg Louganis was winning the one-meter board, and was so far ahead, no one could possibly catch him. Robbie was in eleventh place, and ready to perform his last dive that was an inward 2½ somersault. I was trying to figure out what I could say to him that would help him perform the dive well enough to place higher.

I pointed my finger at Kimball and told Robbie what Kimball had said about him years ago, that he wouldn't be good enough to score a single point for Indiana. Then I asked Robbie if he believed that, and I walked away. Robbie received nines for the dive, and moved from eleventh to fifth place which put our swimming team in the top ten.

Robbie got married soon after graduating, and he and his wife worked in the movie Jurassic Park as stunt persons. Later they were hired to perform and choreograph for the Cirque du Soleil in Las Vegas. Robbie came up with a new idea on how performers could use bungee cords on the trapeze after working for the circus a couple of years.

The idea went over so well that he was promoted to recruiting and training new talent that eventually made him a millionaire living in Montreal, Canada.

Doc's Interviews and My Relationship

We used to laugh watching Doc give an interview on television before an important meet. He always said the same thing every time, and that was, "If the divers come through, we should have a good chance to win." That was some statement when the divers competed in two events, and the swimmers competed in sixteen.

Some people thought Doc and I didn't always get along, but that wasn't true. We both had a sense of humor, and would always have something funny to say or make funny gestures at practices that helped keep workouts fun and positive.

My divers used to tell people that they liked to go to practice because I was always so entertaining. I was close to all my divers because we were communicating with each other four hours at a time at every practice session. I didn't have the pleasure of sitting down or being silent during practice because I had to watch the movements made by every diver and comment on their errors when they performed.

I didn't allow chairs on the deck at my end of the pool because I believed I had to stand while coaching my divers so they knew they had my full attention. I never got into their personal lives unless it related to something that involved our team or when they came to me for advice. I always tried to treat them as I would want them to treat me.

One time I had a disagreement with Doc in all those years was over the number of divers I could take to the Big 10 Championships. I was coaching in Royer Pool, and Doc sent the swimming manager to inform me that he planned to take only one diver to the Big 10 Conference meet. Shocked, I went to the pool office door, and told him the number I was taking to the meet was "zero." I left the office, and went back to the diving well by way of the back door of the pool. I told my divers that I thought I had just gotten fired, and they said if so, they would leave with me and make sure that Indiana never got another diver. Talk about challenges!

I went back to the pool the next day, and walked toward the diving well on the opposite side of the pool from where Doc was sitting. But he saw me and yelled that he wanted to talk to me. I thought he was going to fire me, but he told me he had thought it over and said I could take six divers to the Big 10 meet. I figured that was his way of telling me he was sorry for losing his temper. It was over. We worked together for thirty years, so it was inevitable that we would have our differences.

Significant Sigma Chi

I hadn't been active with the Sigma Chi Fraternity since I had graduated from Ohio State when Jeff Muir, one of my I.U. divers, came to me one day as a member of Sigma Chi Chapter on the Indiana Campus. He suggested that I apply to be selected as a Significant Sig which is the most distinguished national award given by the fraternity for a person who has distinguished themselves in their field of endeavor.

Jeff gave me an application for the award that asked what distinguished contributions had I given to mankind in my career. I didn't feel that I deserved such an honor, so I wrote "none" and sent the application back to the national office in Evanston, Illinois. In August of 1974, I was surprised to get a letter from the national executive committee of Sigma Chi Fraternity. They invited me to attend the Grand Chapter banquet in St. Louis with thirty other distinguished alumni.

I decided not to attend because it included presidents of several universities, and presidents and chairmen of elaborate companies such as Chevrolet. I still felt I didn't deserve the award being a coach of a non-revenue sport that gained little attention, but I later regretted the decision. The Sigma Chi chapter on the Indiana campus asked me to take part in their initiation for new Sigma Chi's over a couple of years when I asked the fraternity president if he had ever received my Significant Sig medal. He said it had been in his drawer for a couple of years, and gave it to me.

The moral of the story is if someone wants to honor you even if you think you don't deserve it, you should accept it and be glad others noticed.

Chapter 36

Diving Dynasties

I found it helpful to see how the growth of competitive diving had progressed by looking at the diving dynasties that were formed in the United States by some of our best divers and coaches over the years. The dictionary states "A dynasty is a group that maintains its position for a long period." About competitive diving, that would mean that divers from a certain competitive group must beat their opposition with some consistency at the level in which they compete. One does not form a dynasty by merely competing in or winning a few contests, but must win with some consistency such as was done by Greg Louganis when he won fifty national titles.

International Dynasties

The first world dynasty in competitive diving started in the United States in 1920, and

continued until 1988. During that time, our divers won forty-four out of sixty Olympic gold medals. It began to fade soon after that when we won three medals in 1992, with one gold from Mark Lenzi (pictured right), two bronze medals in 1996, one gold medal by Laura Wilkerson in 2000, and then did not win any medals from the 2004 and 2008 Olympic Games.

The diving dynasty changed countries when China came on the scene in 1977, and began to win most of the medals at the Olympic Games starting in 1988. Even though we won five medals, two of which were gold by Greg Louganis, a silver by Michelle Mitchell, and two bronze, by Kelley McCormick and Wendy Williams.

The Chinese have continued to be superior in the sport up to the present time that will probably continue if there is world competitive diving because of the intense interest and pressure their country has placed on their divers and coaches. Things looked a little better for the U.S. when we garnered seven medals, six from synchronized diving, and one gold by David Boudia on the ten-meter tower in the 2012 Olympics. But the

Chinese won ten of the twelve events, and the Americans won one. Nothing changed when the Chinese continued to beat the rest of the world at the 2016 Olympics in diving.

The Diving Dynasties of U.S. Coaches Between 1937 and 2013

Ohio State - Mike Peppe

Superior diving started in the United States in the 1920's and 1930's when most of the good divers in the country competed for a club that had a diving coach. Mike Peppe, who was the swimming coach at Ohio State University, started a diving dynasty at Ohio State when Jim Patterson, Mike's first diver, won the one-meter N.C.A.A. Championship in 1937.

Ohio State won a national title in every national meet up until 1956. Peppe drew divers to Ohio State much like Notre Dame drew Catholics who wanted to play football on a winning football team. Peppe realized the importance of diving points to the swimming team so he kept getting divers. Few coaches realized that most of the divers that attended OSU were recruited by the divers themselves.

Peppe had clear sailing in competing for divers because the college and high school coaches were required to coach the swimmers and divers. And with many more swimmers in the pool and only two or three divers diving in the same pool, they had little time to give the divers their attention. And none of the swimming coaches knew anything about how to coach diving up until 1954.

The swimming coaches, for some reason, also didn't appear to recognize that Ohio State won many of their N.C.A.A., Big Ten, and National A.A.U. team titles because of their divers scoring points.

I already mentioned that Mike paid me seventy-five cents an hour to coach Bruce Harlan and Miller Anderson on Tuesday and Thursday nights to beat me. At the 1948 Olympics they placed first and second. We all liked Mike because he had a great personality and did care for all of us. To show how few good divers were from other universities during that period, seven of the eight divers who were in the finals at the 1949 national championships held at Yale University were from Ohio State. And all the judges were former Ohio State divers. I know because I was one of those divers.

Bruce Harlan - Michigan

The next dynasty started when Bruce Harlan, the former 1948 Olympic champion and an Ohio State graduate, was the first to ever be hired as a diving coach by a college. He was well on his way to being a great diving coach when he hustled a bunch of swimmers and divers for the University of Michigan that started in 1954. His divers began to beat the Ohio State divers, and Michigan won the Big Ten Conference, N.C.A.A. and National A.A.U. Championships three years in row that started in 1956.

Bruce (pictured right) was not only a great coach, but he knew a lot about diving. Unfortunately, he was tragically killed in a diving accident in 1959 at age 33.

Dick Kimball - Michigan

Michigan's diving dynasty continued after Bruce was killed. Dick Kimball was a former Michigan diver and as a graduate assistant working on his master's degree he temporarily assumed the coach's position. The Michigan athletic department hired him under contract the next year.

BRUCE HARLAN
Ohio State

Kimball took over and coached his former roommate, Bob Webster, to an Olympic gold medal from the ten-meter platform in Rome, October 1960, and again in Tokyo, 1964. Webster was first coached by Sammy Lee when he was in high school before going to Michigan. Then Harlan coached him up to the time of his death in June 1959. Mike Peppe was a tough competitor, but he knew he was in trouble when Bruce's divers started to beat his divers. His problem continued when my Indiana divers, along with the Michigan divers forced Peppe into retirement.

Dick was a national N.C.A.A. champion at Michigan, and was noted for coaching divers with the use of the trampoline. His personality drew many divers after they had graduated from college, and wanted to continue with their careers in the sport. His divers went on to win many Big Ten, N.C.A.A., and National Champion titles along with winning nine Olympic medals three of which were gold.

Kimball's divers won many major titles that included his son, Bruce, who turned out to be one of the best divers in the world when he placed second behind Greg Louganis on the ten-meter tower at the 1984 Olympics in Los Angeles. Dick dedicated his life to the sport of diving. He was one of the greatest acrobatic divers in the world, and one of the best coaches. After he retired from coaching for 43 years, he has continued to give lectures and clinics and remains one of my best friends in the sport along with Ron O'Brien.

Dick Smith - Dick Smith Swim Gym, Phoenix, AZ

Dick Smith was the gymnastics coach at the University of Southern California (USC) when I first met him in 1950. He decided to move to Phoenix, Arizona, and start what he called the Dick Smith Swim Gym. He managed to draw nearly all the good female divers in the country because there were no colleges that had a diving programs for women. His program was also ideal for females because there were few clubs that coached females, and they could attend Arizona State University in Phoenix.

Dick wasn't challenged by anyone except Bruce Harlan and me when we started to coach women at our schools in 1958. However, none of our girls were good enough to challenge any of Smith's divers. Many of his female divers made the 1964 and 1968 Olympic teams. In the 1968 Olympics Dick's divers Bernie Wrightson won the gold in the three-meter event, and Keith Russell took forth on the ten-meter tower. He was the Olympic coach for both of those Olympics, and continued to coach great divers over the years. He later became a good friend of mine until he passed away January 2, 2006.

Dick Smith Nearly Killed

Dick Smith was returning from a meet in Australia. His plane was landing on the island of Pago Pago, in the South Pacific when it missed the runway because of a bad rain storm. He was sitting in the emergency seat and awoke to find the wings clipping off the tops of the trees. The plane finally stopped, and no one was injured, but then the plane caught fire. Everyone panicked, and ran to the front of the plane to get out, but the door opened inward. With everyone pushing against the door, they couldn't get it open.

Dick was the only one that remained in his seat next to the emergency door. When he opened it, flames hit him in the face. He grabbed a pillow to cover his face and breathe, and crawled over and opened the other emergency door and again was surrounded with flames. He had no other choice so he dived out head first with the pillow covering his face.

He landed on the wing of the plane, jumped off, and ran into the woods waiting for the plane to explode. However, it didn't, and a few people managed to get out but were so badly burned that some later died. Dick survived with nothing but a bump on his head, and a small burn on the side of his face.

Ron O'Brien - Ohio State & Mission Viejo, CA

Ron won a National A.A.U. title as a student at Ohio State in 1960. After he graduated, Ron coached at the University of Minnesota. When Mike Peppe retired, Ron was hired as the diving coach at Ohio State. His divers won several national championships. The irony was that Ron O'Brien, Dick Kimball, and I were very close friends. We all performed a seven-act water show at country clubs, and the Al Sheehan Aqua Follies during the summer, and competed against each other during the winter.

Ron left Ohio State to coach for a city club in Mission Viejo, California in 1977. They had just built a complete diving facility with a ten-meter tower, and several members of the swim team were 1976 Olympians. His new coaching job included Greg Louganis who had just taken second place on the ten-meter platform at the 1976 Games in Montreal, Canada.

Ron was the perfect person for the job because he was intelligent, competitive, well organized, had a lot of experience, and had a good business sense that Kimball and I didn't have. The first thing he did after he was hired was to immediately buy up every available good diver in the country that wasn't in college. It wasn't very difficult because he had a lot of money, and a good reputation of being a great coach and had ideal diving facilities. He even recruited high school divers who left their homes and went to school in Mission Viejo. Other families with talented divers also moved to Mission Viejo to be near their children and to be coached by Ron.

I remember complaining to Ron about what he was doing. He asked me what I would have done, if I had taken the job. With some thought, I told him I would have probably done the same thing he did, and we both began to laugh. He ended up with an army of very good divers that made it extremely difficult for anyone to beat.

Ron went high tech and used diving films, and some scientific coaching knowledge. His divers went to their meets first class, and won all kinds of meets from the age-group level to the Olympics. Louganis won four Olympic gold medals, and forty-nine national titles. He would have probably won two more Olympic gold medals if President Carter hadn't boycotted the 1980 Olympic Games. Greg turned out to be by far the best diver that ever lived, and will probably be looked upon that way for as long as there is competitive diving.

Ron later left Mission Viejo, and started a similar program in Boca Raton, Florida, then moved on down to the Florida Keys. Later he went to work for U.S. diving, and traveled all over the United States helping diving coaches improve their diving programs. He held that job for several years, and has retired to live in central Florida.

307

Hobie Billingsley – Indiana University

As soon as I had arrived in the fall of 1959, the athletic department was put on probation for four years by the N.C.A.A. Phil Dickens, the football coach had been caught violating recruiting rules two years in a row, so all IU athletes paid the price. This made it almost impossible for me to have a good diving program for at least six or more years.

The six of us coaches formed our own diving dynasties in our own way when two coached in clubs and four coached in colleges. We also coached in the period when wooden diving boards were the only diving boards available. These boards were eventually replaced with aluminum boards which made it possible for divers to perform more difficult dives on the one and three-meter springboards and on the ten-meter tower.

Jeff Huber – Indiana University

Jeff Huber took over my job as diving coach at Indiana in 1989, and coached first in Royer Pool (pictured below) for five years then moved into the Counsilman-Billingsley Aquatic Center. The new facility has a separate diving well with a ten-meter tower and one, five, 7½-meter platforms. There are two one-meter and two three-meter springboards.

Tower diving was added as an N.C.A.A. diving event in the program in the early 1990's.

Then synchronized diving was also added to national diving programs that began at the 2000 Olympics in Sydney, Australia. This doubled the number of diving events, and is now used in most major programs throughout the world. For some reason, most of the collegiate diving coaches in our country haven't shown much interest in synchronized diving, so it has not been accepted for N.C.A.A. National Championships.

Jeff capitalized on the events offered by the National and U.S. Diving organization, and his divers won many national titles when the competition was limited. Jeff was a hard-working coach, and his divers won a lot of team titles especially in the Big Ten Conference meets. His divers won five N.C.A.A. titles, and had girls make the Olympic team on four different occasions, but none of them ever medaled. He retired in 2013, and thanks to Jeff Huber the diving dynasty at Indiana University has continued for forty-nine straight years. Pictured below is Counsilman-Billingsley Aquatic Center. Photo courtesy of Indiana University Archives.

John Wingfield – U.S. Diving

I first met John Wingfield when he was the coach at Ball State University. He was doing a good job, but the pool deck was too small for all his training with trampolines and safety belts. In a conversation, John told me his ambition was to be an Olympic Team diving coach. I told him that it would never happen coaching at Ball State, and suggested he start a diving program at the I.U.P.U.I. pool in Indianapolis. This pool, called the "Natatorium," is a world-class facility that has hosted national championships.

(Pictured younger Dave Boudia and Tom Finchem future synchronized diving Olympians with coach John Wingfield)

It has an Olympic sized competition pool and a separate diving well that I had designed. The diving facility includes a five platform ten-meter tower plus numerous diving boards that has been copied by many clubs and colleges around the country. U.S. Diving soon hired John as the national training coach that relates to all the diving contests that are not connected to universities.

John started with nothing and set up a program called Starz, and within a short period he had several hundred divers, mostly in high schools, performing under his program around the city of Indianapolis in two years. He and an assistant started taking six divers that were very young, and taught them how to dive from the springboard and tower that have performed in many national, international, and Olympic Games.

310

(Pictured I.U.P.U.I. Natatorium in Indianapolis, IN – Diving well designed by Hobie)

John was made the Olympic coach in 2008 when Boudia and Tom Fitchum both made the Olympic team, but didn't medal. Fitchum retired briefly, and Boudia chose a new synchronized partner, Nick McCrory. At the London Olympic Games in 2012, this new team went on to win the synchronized ten-meter platform gold medal, and Boudia, McCrory, and Finchem placed gold, silver, and bronze on the ten-meter event. In the 2016 Olympic Games in Rio, on the ten-meter platform, Boudia took the bronze medal, and with synchronized partner Steele Johnson won the silver medal on the platform. Thus, John has coached five divers who medaled in the 2012 and 2016 Olympic Games after all five went to Purdue and Indiana University after leaving his Starz program. He represents the U.S. Diving organization doing clinics and lectures all over the United States. John has not received sufficient credit for having started these divers at a very young age, and teaching them how to perform the dives to compete in the Olympics. Wingfield has since built his own diving program in Indianapolis that includes youngsters and senior divers that may one day develop into one of the best diving programs in the United States.

Drew Johansen - Diving Coach Indiana University

Drew Johansen coached at Duke University when his divers, Nick McCrory and Abby Johnston won medals in synchronized diving events at the 2012 Olympics. Nick teamed up with Dave Boudia to take the bronze on the ten-meter platform, and Abby teamed up with Kelci Bryant to win the silver on the three-meter event.

Drew is the last coach to build a dynasty when he replaced Jeff Huber at Indiana after he retired in 2013. He has since developed the best diving program in the country. Proof was when his divers recently earned seven places in the 2016 Olympic Trials. Together with Wingfield's four divers, the state of Indiana represented nine of the fourteen places to compete in the Olympics in Rio de Janeiro, Brazil. I am confident Drew Johansen will keep the Indiana diving dynasty going at Indiana University. It is possibly the longest running sport dynasty in the world.

Two Significant Changes in Diving

The bubble machine and the degree of difficulty formula were invented near the end of our diving careers that made it possible for us to teach male and female divers how to perform difficult dives that had previously thought to be impossible. All of us were inducted into the International Swimming Hall of Fame in Ft. Lauderdale, Florida, and awarded the Sammy Lee award that is the greatest honor for diving in the world.

I have been trying to get these two pioneers, Bob Bollinger and Herb Fleweling, into the International Swimming and Diving Hall-of-Fame for 20 years because they changed our sport. But they have been ignored.

CHAPTER 37

My Career 1978 to 1990

The Trip to Dunedin, New Zealand

Doc and I were invited to give clinics at the 1978 International Aquatic Congress in New Zealand. The Congress had never been in New Zealand before. We were there for a week in May, and they treated us like royalty. I was the clinician for diving, so I gave a clinic every day, and could do some sightseeing after my presentations. We were told that we were in the best place in the world for trout fishing, but I didn't get the chance to find out during that visit.

I don't know if I was any help to the people at the clinic because, except for two diving coaches, everyone else there were swimming coaches. I was invited back years later to help their top diving coach, and stayed for a month coaching him and his divers. He took me trout fishing a couple of times, and we all had a great time catching a lot of trout. I found New Zealand to be a wonderful country where everyone seemed to be relaxed, and not in any hurry to do anything.

Hobie's Heroes 1980 DVD Movie

The name Hobie's Heroes became popular when an incident occurred at the 1979 outdoor National A.A.U. Women's Championships that were held in Houston, Texas, the home town of Cynthia Potter. Cynthia had won the one-meter title. When the press interviewed me, they asked me how I felt about her performance. I told them that I was delighted, and went on to say that she was my hero.

When the papers came out the next day, the title of their article was, "Hobie's Hero Wins the One-Meter Springboard Championship. Cynthia went on to win the three-meter contest the next day, and the press used Hobie's Hero in their title again. Cynthia then won the ten-meter platform title for a "grand slam," and again, the press used Hobie's Hero in their title for her fantastic performance. Hobie's Heroes continued to be an expression that was associated to my divers, and for years to come.

I received a call from Steve Montgomery who had attended my camp from New York City. Steve was so impressed with the experience that he decided to make a movie about the camp in 1978. He called to tell me what he wanted to do, and I told him I thought it would take about $30,000 dollars to make the film. Then I said to contact Ray Rude, the maker of the Duraflex diving boards to see if they would sponsor the film for at least ten percent of the film's total cost, and they agreed.

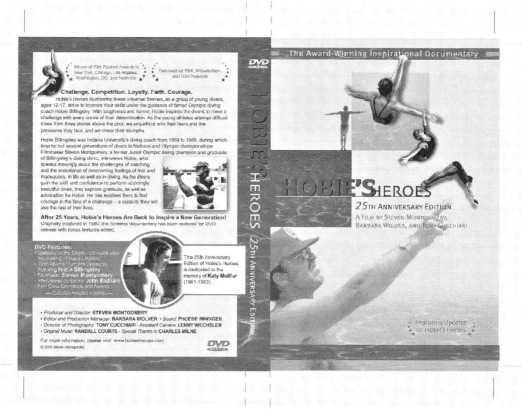

Steve managed to get the rest of the money from some of his friends, and his father. He got his crew together with all their film equipment, and drove to Bloomington in two station wagons. To capture the camp experience from the eyes of the campers, they ate and stayed with the campers.

I asked Steve what he wanted me to do to help make the film, and he said to just be myself and he would take care of what was needed. It took over six weeks for Steve and his crew to film the camp experience. Then he thanked me and went back to New York. A few months later Steve called to tell me he had finished the film.

Steve said he named the movie "Hobie's Heroes," and wanted me to attend the premier in a small theater off Times Square in New York City. I had no idea what to expect. I thought I should attend because Steve had gone through a great deal of time and expense to make the film. I walked into the theater just as the lights were dimed to start the film, and sat alone in one of the side seats.

The documentary film was twenty-nine minutes long, and I could not believe what a great job Steve and his crew had done. I found the film to be accurate and emotional

314

to the point that it brought tears to my eyes, and to many others. They had a gathering after the showing. Seeing the film was one of the most thrilling moments I have ever experienced.

Steve entered the film in several film festivals in America and Europe over the years when it won nearly all the contests. One of the most important and largest festivals in the country was the Datsun Film Festival, and the winner won a new Datsun car. Steve called to tell me that "Hobie's Heroes" was in the top three while the judging was still going on, and I asked him to let me know if his film won.

For about three months, I didn't hear from Steve until he sent me a letter with a picture of him standing next to the new Datsun. When I asked him what he did with the car, he said he gave it to his father who helped pay for making the film. The film was also up for an Academy Award for the less important films that are usually never seen on television, and it took second place. In 2005, the film was released as a 25th anniversary edition. It was honored at sports film festivals in Italy, China, India, Iran, and Poland, and is still shown at various summer diving camps around the country.

The 25th anniversary edition is still being shown and purchased by interested parties. It is now available on Hobie's website: **http://www.HobieBillingsley.com**

Winning the 1980 Big 10 Championship

We had won 19 Big 10 Championships in a row in 1979 and I think we won the last one in 1980 because of what I said during one of Doc's meetings with the team. It wasn't long after Doc swam the English Channel and set the record for being the oldest at age 58. Doc was forthright and told his swimmers at a meeting in the fall that they didn't have a prayer to win the Big 10 meet this year because the team didn't have the horses.

Doc went on to say that they would be third or fourth in the conference meet, even if they performed well. Having never done it before, Doc asked me if I had anything to say to the team. Surprised that he called on me, I didn't have the slightest idea what I was going to say until I started to walk up to the front of the room.

I started to tell my story by pointing at Doc and saying, "Do you see that man over there? He came to me a while back, and told me he was going to swim the English Channel. I thought he was insane because he wouldn't be able to find the time to prepare for the swim, and at the age of fifty-eight, he was a bit old to take on such a challenge."

"Other friends and family also told Doc the same thing, but he had made up his mind and started to train for the event by swimming in Lake Monroe after practice every day. This went on until near winter time when the water got cold, and eventually froze over. Doc then swam in a small unheated pool at his condo near the mall that was around 55 degrees. He never missed a workout during the whole time, and never lost confidence that he could swim the channel."

"Doc sacrificed a lot losing time from activities and home to prepare for the task, but finally accomplished something that no man his age had ever done. So, I say to you, if every one of you in this room would make up your minds like Doc, and dedicate yourself to winning the Big 10 meet next March by giving every practice your best shot, you can pull it off. But, if one of you cheats by staying up late watching T.V., not studying, smoking, or going out to have a couple beers, you will not only cheat yourself but the whole team."

I think they must have heard me because they did the impossible, and won their twentieth Big 10 Conference meet in a row that spring. It was only the second time I ever saw Doc Counsilman cry. The first was when his son Jimmy, who was coaching a swimming team in St. Croix, Virgin Islands, accidently died.

I could only take four divers to the 1980 Big Ten Championships when I had eight good male divers three of which I knew would score well. The five others were questionable, so I held a meet for them each day for a week to decide which one should fill the fourth spot. The five were Bill Coleman, Andy Pollata, Tom Mulhern, Pat Harrington, and Paul Lenihan.

I still couldn't decide after the contests for five days because the winners kept changing. So, I sat them all down on Friday. I looked them over, and selected Paul Lenihan who had become eligible that year but had the least diving experience. The other four had been with me for at least a year, and were upset with my choice.

Andy Pallotta was the one most disappointed. He got married a few years later and at a party at his new bride's family house, Andy's two older brothers introduced themselves to me before they threw me into the backyard swimming pool telling me that was because I didn't select Andy to compete in the 1980 Big 10 Championship meet. Andy and his wife had three children when he started a printing company that included a contract to print the Boston Red Sox baseball team's programs and brochures.

The 1980 Olympic Trials

The Olympic trials were staged at the University of Texas in the early summer. The Olympic boycott hadn't yet occurred. Greg Louganis qualified first on the springboard and tower, and Brian Bungum qualified in third place with Mark Virts fourth as an alternate on the ten-meter platform. The surprise of the meet occurred when Amy McGrath, an Indiana diver, made the Olympic team by placing third on the ten-meter platform.

Eight divers made the finals, and Amy was in eighth place after the preliminaries. The preliminary scores would be added to the finals scores. Amy was twenty-seven points behind the seventh-place diver when she scored nines and tens on her second dive in the finals to pass four divers on that round. Then she passed the third-place diver on

316

her last dive to make the team. That was unheard of for a diver who had been so far behind.

The American Boycott of the 1980 Olympic Games

President Carter made the difficult decision to boycott the 1980 Olympics to be held in Moscow, Russia over a political issue with Russia's aggression in Afghanistan. This shocked the sports world.

I had coached Niki Stajkovic for six years after the 1972 Munich Olympic Games. And I coached Claus Thomsen, from Denmark, when he enrolled at Indiana for a year to improve his diving. Claus had never dived tower so I taught him how in the summer before the Olympic Games, and he was chosen to represent his country.

(Pictured left to right Niki Stajkovic, Hobie, Claus Thomsen, John Shulte)

I attended the Olympics as coach for Claus Thomsen, from Denmark, and Niki Stajkovic from Austria. They were on my team at Indiana University, and neither country had a qualified diving coach.

One day during practice, I saw a man sitting in the empty stands in the pool all by himself. So, I went over to find what country he was from, and nearly fell over when I found he was the athletic director from the Erie Y.M.C.A. and a good friend of mine. He told me that he had ignored the boycott, and decided to attend the Olympic Games despite the President's decision to boycott. He was the only American spectator I saw all the time I was in Russia.

The 1980 Games Highlight in Diving

The highlight of the diving contests occurred during the finals in the three-meter event when a Russian girl performed a dive poorly, and asked the referee if she could take the dive over because she was distracted by someone in the audience that took a flash bulb picture, and the referee gave her permission. A similar problem occurred in the next event again when a Russian male diver performed a reverse 2½ somersault, and landed flat on his back that received very low scores.

Then while taking a warm shower under the three-meter stand, the Russian people in the audience yelled, in Russian, for him to take the dive over when he had no intention of doing so. He went to the referee when he heard their remarks, and told him he had been distracted by the noise coming from the people in a swimming pool in another room that could hardly be heard, and the referee again permitted it. He repeated the dive that was worth nines, but the judges only gave him sevens that was still enough for him to win the contest.

Then while still in the same event, Falk Huffman, the diver from East Germany attempted to perform the same dive. When he did his hurdle before the dive, he was blinded by the sun that had shown through an open curtain at the other end of the pool that resulted in him performing a poor dive. Being an unusual circumstance, he also asked the referee to take the dive over because he was blinded by the sun.

The referee went up on the high board after the request when the sun had already set, and refused his request. I had taken a picture of the dive with my movie camera, but didn't look at the film until I returned home. I found his request was accurate, but it was too late to do anything about it. Niki placed twelfth in the event that was the only time he did not make the finals in five different Olympics.

The 1980 Olympic Diving Team Goes to China

Since the United States boycotted the Olympics, the Olympic diving team was rewarded for their performance by sending them to Japan and China for several diving contests on two different dates. Mike Brown and I were selected to coach the team going to China with Sammy Lee and his wife, Roz, going as chaperones. The divers making the team were Greg Louganis, Amy McGrath, Brian Bungum, Mark Virts, Chris Seufert, and Barbara Weinstein.

We flew to Hong Kong before entering China, and were scheduled to compete in four Chinese cities, and the last was against their national team in Beijing. We were only the third athletic team to ever visit China. President Nixon allowed a team of basketball players in the 1970's, and a ping pong team before us.

1980 UNITED STATES OLYMPIC DIVING TEAM

TOP ROW
l to r
Kevin Machemer, Brian Bungum, Greg Louganis, Dave Burgering, Randy Ableman, Mark Virts

MIDDLE ROW
l to r
Chris Seufert, Kit Salness, Barb Weinstein, Amy McGrath, Megan Neyer, Cynthia Potter, Jennifer Chandler

BOTTOM ROW
l to r
Coaches: Dick Kimball, Bryan Robbins, Ron O'Brien

319

We were supposed to take a plane to Beijing, but somehow ended up taking a train that took thirty-four hours. Thinking about it now, the change may have been planned to tire our team out. We had four people in each sleeper compartment, and I had three of our girl divers in mine that was extremely hot.

All we had was a small fan that moved back and forth to keep us cool, but it didn't help much because we started to sweat when the fan moved away and only got some relief for a moment when it returned to face us. We stopped off in a couple of small towns to get water for the engine. When we got off the train to stretch, the local people would come to us, and check out our clothes. All we saw on that train trip were rice fields.

Beijing was a marvelous city with very wide streets crowded with bicycles ringing their bells constantly. Occasionally a government car drove by. We had plenty of time for site seeing that included the Great Wall of China, the Forbidden City, and some of their factories that made clothes with primitive machines.

We were taken to a school gym where they set up a large screen in the middle of the gym floor, and showed a poor quality American movie. About two-thousand students watched the film from both sides of the screen. They all went wild because it was such a treat. We left before the movie was over because it was so bad. They had gift shops for foreign visitors that were called "Friendship" shops, and the prices were so low that we could buy all sorts of gifts to take home.

All the diving events were judged by the Chinese, and their divers won every event before a huge biased crowd. They showed their hospitality standing on the awards stand when the winners of all the women's events gave their medals to the American divers. We returned to Hong Kong for a day of sightseeing before returning to the States, and it was a trip that none of us would ever forget. A great movie about the Forbidden City was made a few years later that was titled "The Last Emperor," and it showed nearly everything we had seen in our China trip.

CHAPTER 38

Some of the Other Women in My Life

I never remarried after my divorce from Mary in 1975, but I did enjoy pleasant relationships with four amazing women over the course of the next 40 years.

Shirley Smith

Shirley Smith was a teller who worked in the bank I did business with. She had the deepest blue eyes I had ever seen, and I would always get in her line. She eventually got to recognize me when I went to the bank, and we started to talk a bit while she took care of me. I went to Austria to coach a little later, and sent her a post card with a return address.

She eventually married a terrific guy name Mark.

I later made Shirley the secretary for my diving camp that lasted for years, and Mark my photographer who took camp pictures for me. Unfortunately, Mark got very sick with cancer a few years later. When I went to visit him while he was in bed, he told me how much he had enjoyed our friendship, and died a week later.

Bonnie Maurer

I met Bonnie Maurer at the outdoor pool in 1976 when she was a graduate student. I was twenty years older than her, but age didn't seem to matter because we got along very well together. She and her family were Jewish, and Bonnie was sort of a hippie that was obvious from the way she dressed.

Bonnie was also very intelligent, and loved poetry. After dating her for a couple of months, she invited me to meet her mother. She was from Indianapolis, and I soon found out more about her life when we drove north on Meridian street through the wealthy part of town. We pulled into the driveway of one of the big homes. I thought her mother was probably a maid until we walked in the front door and Bonnie called out "Mom."

I went with Bonnie for five years, and enjoyed every minute with her and her family. They accepted me while ignoring my age and religion, and they had a lot of young children that I learned to love like my own. I learned a lot about the Jewish way of life that was very impressive. Bonnie had a stepfather named "Ben" that I learned to adore until he passed away a couple of years after going with Bonnie. I took Bonnie to meet my mother in Erie a couple of times, and the two of them became very attached.

Sheryl McClish

I had met Sheryl McClish seven years before at McDonalds when she was pregnant with her daughter Kirstie. She was so far along with the pregnancy that I thought she was going to have the baby before leaving the restaurant, so I suggested that I sit with her while she ate just in case. I never forgot the chance encounter because she was real nice to me, but I didn't see her again until seven years later.

I saw her in a restaurant, and asked about her pregnancy. She said she was still married, but was getting a divorce and dating others so I started to date her after her husband moved out of their house. She was an excellent dental hygienist, and I took her with me giving lectures and diving clinics around the world.

Sheryl and her daughter lived with me for eight years until she decided to move out and move on. She said she thought the families in our division were snobs, and she didn't enjoy being around them. She wasn't getting along with my children, so they moved out and returned to her house for six years. Later she'd moved to Indianapolis where she married a postman. I never saw her again.

Ellender Lee

I went to the airport to check on the validity of a couple of airline tickets in 1998. The airport corridor was very crowded with people. Then for some unknown reason, I looked up and saw a woman over the crowd on the other side of the corridor waving at me. I looked around to see if she was waving at me, and she kept waving so I thought she must know me. I went over and after exchanging a few words, I asked her if she knew me. And she said she didn't, but added that she lived in Lebanon (Indiana). Fortunately, her plane was about twenty minutes late, so we had a chance to chat a little while longer.

Ellender (Ellen) was four years younger than me. I took her to dinner at the Holiday Inn when she returned from Florida, and found she really liked sports and traveling and we started to date each other. I warned her I was a vagabond, and moved around a lot. I said I could see she had a close relationship with her family, and she would never leave them.

So, she decided she liked the way things were because it gave each other a lot of room to do other things. Our relationship lasted for eighteen years. Sadly, she died in November 2016. I was heartbroken.

CHAPTER 39

Other Noteworthy Events 1980 to 1990

Tbilisi, Georgia Meet 1980

Dick Kimball and I took a team to Tbilisi located in Georgia, a southern Province of Russia, for a dual meet in 1980. We had about eight divers with us, and one was Greg Louganis. RJ Smith and his wife were our chaperones. On the way, we landed in Copenhagen, Denmark for two days. Claus Thomsen, one of my divers, lived in Copenhagen, and arranged for us to work out at his club that had good diving facilities, but not a tower.

Claus came from a wealthy family, and made a wonderful dinner for us at their home and made us feel comfortable until we were ready to leave. I ended up in charge of the money and traveling arrangements. When we got to the airport using taxies, we quickly moved all our baggage near the ticket booth. When I asked someone to give me my satchel that had the tickets and money in it, we couldn't find it. We finally realized that we left it in one of the taxis.

So I went out to the entrance and stood there for a while. I figured it would take at least a week for us to make it back home because the meet would have been cancelled, and we didn't have any airline tickets. Then a miracle occurred. The taxi cab driver found it in his back seat, and circled the airport to bring it back when he saw me standing there to meet him.

When we arrived in Tbilisi, we found we had a nice pool to compete in. Dick and I saw two red diving boards lying on the ground nearby, and we asked the Russians what they were. They started to laugh, and told us they were the Russian version of the Duraflex board. We walked over and got a good look at them, and they looked like they were made of tin and never used by their divers. The springboard events were held first.

While practicing for the ten-meter event, Louganis was performing a reverse dive in the pike position when he hit the back of his head on the edge of the platform. It knocked him out, and he went straight to the pool bottom twenty feet deep. Kimball and I walked over to the edge, and saw he wasn't moving. Someone dove down and hauled him out, and he came to lying on the deck. Fortunately, he recovered.

As we started to walk in, a nurse walked toward us with an apron covered with blood, so we stood outside and called the American embassy for a doctor. The doctor told us if Greg's eyes dilated and/or he started to vomit, to take him to the embassy. But none of this occurred, so we returned to the hotel and didn't return to the pool until the next day.

I had brought two red Indiana caps with me. While wearing one, a Russian saw me and started to follow me around wanting to buy my hat. I refused for a couple of days until I finally gave in, and he grabbed my ears and kissed me on my lips. Red was a rare color in Russia at that time which is why he wanted the hat.

The I.U.P.U.I. Natatorium in Indianapolis

Indiana University – Purdue University – Indianapolis (IUPUI) campus in Indianapolis had around seven million dollars allocated to build a new swimming and diving center in 1981 because Royer Pool had become obsolete. Universities around the country began to build indoor fifty-meter pools with movable bulkheads to operate two 25 yard courses for large meets. These facilities were designed with a separate diving well the same as used in the modern Olympic Games.

The architect department at Indiana asked me if would design their new pool, and I agreed. I was paid $8,000 for the job. The facility was dedicated in 1982 for about 25 million dollars, and has hosted Olympic Trials, NCAA Championships, and Masters National Championships.

My Son-in-Law's Accident Prevents Huge Mistake

While the structure was being built, I had just arrived in Mission Viejo, California for the National Championships when I received a call from a hospital in Indianapolis that Mike Farmer, my son-in-law, had a serious motorcycle accident. I immediately flew home to check on him. After finding that he was going to recover, I decided to go over to see how the construction of the diving well at the I.U.P.U.I. was coming along.

I climbed up a ladder to look over a wall to view the diving well, and what I saw almost made me fall off the ladder. Luckily, all the personal working on the project were having a big meeting in a temporary huge tent. I ran in and got the attention of those working on the diving well. I told them they were building the ten-meter tower so close to the other side of the well, divers would hit the other side.

To prove my point, I knew from having checked out the diving tower in our outdoor pool in Bloomington, that if I ran fast enough on the take-off, I could land in front of the three-meter diving boards on the other side which was where the other side was in Indy. I told them that tower could never be used because it would not meet standards. I asked if there was any way they could move the tower structure back. And they said if they placed the stairway to the tower behind the wall instead of in front of it they could move it back four feet.

Thankfully, the change was enough to make the tower usable. Few will ever know that if my son-in-law had never had his accident, and if I had not arrived just in time for them to correct their mistake, there would never have been any National and Olympic trials held in that aquatic center. Incidentally, a great many of the towers that have been constructed since then have copied my design.

I also designed the bottom of the well to be made in dark blue tile with white seven inch stripes on the bottom to make it easier for the divers to dive in the proper direction. Other diving wells used a bright color that made it difficult to see the surface of the water for better entries. I also had them make a crow's nest on one side of the ten-meter platform so photographers could take pictures from the side rather than directly in front of divers taking off facing the platform. The crow's nest could also be used for directing take offs from the lower platforms.

The pool turned out to be the best indoor pool diving complex in the country, and has been copied by many other institutions since.

The Indiana Hall-of-Fame 1981

All the Indiana coaches had a meeting in 1981 with Ralph Floyd and Leona Hutcheson, the athletic directors. After the meeting, I asked them if I could have a private discussion with them. We met in another room in Assembly Hall, the home of the athletic department built in the 1960's. I told them that I had something on my mind that had been bothering me for a long time.

I told them that Indiana University abused the accomplishments of their athletes, and I had to repeat it twice before they got my point. With their curiosity aroused, they asked for an explanation. I questioned them, if a coach brought a recruit to Indiana University, and wanted to show him or her what our athletes had accomplished, where and what would they to show them.

I then asked them to name the three Indiana athletes that had won the distinguished Sullivan Award, and neither one knew because they didn't know anything about the Sullivan Award. I explained that it was the annual award given to the outstanding amateur athlete in the United States, and two athletes were John Kinsella, 1970, and Mark Spitz, 1971, in Swimming.

I told them whenever we had a meet with Tennessee, I always looked at the pictures of their All-American swimmers and divers that were displayed on the wall in a room with a railing in front that gave their accomplishments. And I read every one of them even when I had no idea who most of them were. I finished the discussion saying I had been on many college campuses in our country, and the only one that I didn't find a Hall-of-Fame was Indiana University.

Ralph Floyd started the Indiana Hall-of-Fame the very next year. Two years later, he took me to one end of Assembly Hall where all the pictures of those in the Hall-of-Fame were displayed on the wall with a railing in front of the pictures that gave the accomplishments for each recipient. Ralph then put his arm around my shoulder, and told me to take a good look because all of that was because of me and my big mouth.

Lesley Bush was the first female to be inducted into the Hall in 1988. She won every gold medal available in her career, and was one of the most outstanding divers of all time. Cynthia Potter was the next female when she won twenty-eight national championships that was the most ever won by a female diver, and had made three Olympic teams.

Amy McGrath was inducted into the Hall in 2013. She won a national championship, and was the first Indiana female athlete-of-the-year and made the Olympic team that was boycotted in 1980. It took eight years for me to get a male diver in the Hall, and that was Rick Gilbert. He was Indiana's first great diver, and had won our first National A.A.U., N.C.A.A., and

Big 10 titles. He was followed by Jim Henry, Ken Sitzberger, and Mark Lenzi.

As many people know, Doc Counsilman and I accomplished the impossible when we developed the best swimming and diving teams in the world that started while Indiana was still on probation for four years. Some of our great swimmers and divers at Indiana have been inducted into the Hall-of-Fame, but many have been ignored over the years to the point where those who have been neglected call it "The Hall of Shame."

I never wished to keep others that made great accomplishments in other sports from being inducted, but Doc I have had many of our athletes who competed in the Olympics, that offers the greatest achievement of an athlete in the world, and have won national titles and have not been inducted. Seven of my divers have been inducted in the last twenty-five years when most of them won at least a Big 10, N.C.A.A., or National title.

Another example of the Hall-of-Fame's negligence is seen when Lona Foss, who had dived for Jim Blickenstaff at Evanston High School in Evanston, Illinois, and won the state championship in 1980. Jim sent her to Indiana to dive with us after she graduated, and in the early 1980's, she helped keep our dynasty alive when she did a brilliant job by winning two Big 10 and two national titles and was an All-American three times.

A Testimonial to My Philosophy of Coaching

The close relationship I've had with my divers may be best described when Jon Hahnfeldt made a comment at an Award Reception on April 13, 1980 at the Westport YMCA in Connecticut. He said, "After being coached by Hobie Billingsley, for the first time in my life, I found what it meant to be a part of a true diving team. The bonds of friendship and fraternity I learned as a member of that team still follow me wherever I go. Hence, my team mates and I became the first generation. Then after coaching for about a year, I came to realize that the team training under me enjoyed the same friendship and loyalty with each other that I had at Indiana that led it to be known as 'The Second Generation,' and is the most terrific age group team I have ever known."

My Last Gripe with the Athletic Department

I went to Ralph Floyd to ask who was the best coach in our department, adding it wasn't Bobby Knight. Getting no answer, I told him it was Doc Counsilman who changed the world of swimming when he wrote his book, The Science of Swimming.

I went on to say he was famous around the world, and had done more for swimming in different ways than any other coach. I then asked him where was Doc's office. I knew it was located across the hall from his, and he didn't know it. Doc and I were told that we would have the first choice of an office when Assembly Hall was built, but we were never given one until eight years later. Doc had been given an office about the size of a small bathroom, and they gave me one on the ground floor that took forever to find. Ralph got the message and eventually moved Doc into a nice office upstairs with Jerry

Yeagley, the best soccer coach in the country. That seemed to satisfy him, and I remained in my little tucked-away office until I retired.

Speeches and Clinics on Diving

When Ron O'Brien, Dick Kimball, Dick Smith, and I became nationally recognized coaches we were called on to give speeches and diving clinics to clubs, high schools, and universities for the National A.A.U., and later U.S. Diving all over the country. I know I gave well over five hundred speeches and diving clinics in my career, and some funny and not so funny things occurred.

One time as I was getting up to speak at a dinner, I knocked over a container of mustard from the table that spread all over the carpet, and the audience had to wait a few minutes for my speech while I and some others cleaned up the mess. A similar incident occurred when the waitresses decided to pick up the table cloth on the table, and shake it out in front of me while I was giving the speech. I had to peek under the table cloth to see the audience that was laughing.

I was going to give a speech for the Masons in Bloomington, and knew one of their members was the treasurer of Indiana University, and a humorless fellow. I decided to see if I could make him laugh so I went to a toy store, and purchased a fake ugly plastic stomach that I strapped on under my shirt that I left unbuttoned half way down.

Fortunately, he was sitting in front of me while I began my speech with a serious look on my face. I was wearing a sport coach that I left unbuttoned, and slowly opened my shirt by pulling it from behind my back as I continued to speak. This got his attention, and his face suddenly started to change from boredom to curiosity. I noticed he started to lean forward in his seat along with everyone else in the room.

Pretending not to notice as the shirt continued to open, he and the others in the room started to smile that turned into laughter when they saw my belly button while I pretended not to know what was going on. He came up to me after the speech, and told me that it was the funniest thing he had ever seen.

I was asked to give a speech about the Olympics at a club on the east side in Erie, PA, my hometown, after returning from the 1972 Games in Munich. I accepted the invitation because I wanted to see my mother, and old friends. It was a thrill to meet some of my old school-mates who I hadn't seen since I left East High School.

About two months later, I was asked to give another speech in Erie at an awards banquet for little children. Before entering the school, I wrote the speech in my car. The speech was entitled, "What are Sports?" that was about me when I was growing up in Erie. It was a very emotional speech, and the kids and their teachers were very pleased with it. Years later, I was invited by the Erie Lions Club to give a speech in a big hotel along with Dick Schaff who was a famous national sports announcer.

Erie decided to form an Athletic Hall-of-Fame, and I was chosen as one of the first recipients to be inducted along with nineteen others representing different sports. My mother and my brother's family went with me, and when I sat down with the others at

329

the head table, I found that they were going to introduce the inductees in the alphabetical order of their sport. Not knowing who I was, they had me down as a swimming coach that meant I would be called to speak late in the program. The inductees were told to not talk longer than seven minutes because of the number of speakers, but most of them talked for more than fifteen minutes that resulted in the program going past midnight.

Eugene Cuneo was a good friend of mine who sat behind me in class at East High School. His son, sport editor of the Erie Daily Times, was the one that was supposed to introduce me. It got so late that he had to leave to make a deadline for the next day's paper, and told the guy next to him to introduce me. Needless to say, it wasn't much of an introduction and my speech at that late hour was not well received.

I wish to suggest that if you ever should give a speech, especially to a large group or for an important occasion, that you have the person inviting you to give you a written time and place for the speech. I received an invitation from the Red Cross in Ann Arbor, Michigan to give a speech on water safety at their national convention before well over a thousand members. The person that called said that the speech was for eight o'clock. I assumed she meant that evening. When I called her at ten o'clock in the morning to inform her I was in town, she told me that the speech was for eight o'clock in the morning, and the meeting had just adjourned.

First Diving Camp for Coaches Only

For the first time in the United States I decided to offer a summer camp in 1988 for diving coaches with the intent of improving their coaching techniques at the age group, high school, and senior levels. They participated in lectures, viewing video tapes, discussion periods, and actual diving activities that covered all the aspects of the sport that were given over five and a half days.

The program included diving rules, how to teach diving safely, conditioning exercises, psychology, teaching aids, motivation and stimulation, organizing a diving program, working with fear, and how to teach divers to compete. I gave the groups Wednesday afternoon off to do anything they wished to do because they were so exhausted from the lectures, and other activities they needed a break to get refreshed.

An average of fourteen coaches attended each of the two summer sessions that I gave for six years, and many who attended were already well-known coaches but wished to improve and learn more. They stayed in the Indiana dormitories, and the fee was $495 which included room and board for the week. We had a party at the end of each session, and all the coaches learned a lot more about the sport and had a good time sharing what they learned. After six years, I stopped the coaching camp because it was a very difficult task, and took a lot of my time to get it organized.

Our Indiana Diving Dynasty Continues

We continued to average four divers in the finals of the N.C.A.A. and National A.A.U. Championships during the 1980's, but didn't win as many titles as we had in the 1960's and seventies. Pat Harrington, Andy Pallotta, Tom Mulhern, John Shulte, Paul Lenihan, and Bill Coleman scored points in those meets, but never won a title. We managed to win a couple of titles in the Big Ten Conference Championships, and won in dual meets. I gave Coleman a scholarship, but he transferred to the University of Wisconsin where he took sixth place in the Big 10 Championships in his senior year. Pat Harrington was tall and lanky and placed second in the Big 10's as a senior. Tom Mulhern placed third in two N.C.A.A. and a fourth in the Big 10 Championships. Paul Lenihan was a good diver starting in his freshman year, and always placed in the top six places in all our major meets.

Cynthia Potter

It was around this time that Cynthia Potter finally retired from diving after winning twenty-eight national championships which was the most any female ever won, and the record still stands. She never left diving, and coached at the University of Arizona in Tucson. She ended up coaching some high school divers at Westminster, a private school in Atlanta, and one of her divers won the state championship. She was hired as an analyst announcing all the major TV diving contests including the Olympic Games.

Hobie's Diving Books

I wrote three books during my career as diving coach. The first one I co-authored the diving portion of the book Swimming and Diving, 1968, written by David Armbruster, the former swimming coach at the University of Iowa, and his assistant, Bob Allen, both of whom have passed away. It didn't sell very well because Iowa never came close to winning a Big Ten Championship until he had retired.

I became the diving coach at Indiana in 1959 and learned that coaches, divers, judges, and diving officials all had different concepts of how to perform the competitive dives. So, I decided to start writing a book in 1960 that gave a basic concept of how to perform every competitive dive listed in the rule books. I made drawings of the dives in sequence with a short explanation of what to do while performing each movement. At the same time, I was learning how to apply mechanical principles to diving based on Isaac M. Newton's Three Laws of Motion. I didn't know enough then about the science of diving to include that analysis in the book, and published the book, Hobie Billingsley's Diving Illustrated in 1965. It became a best-selling book for many years in the diving community. That book is still being sold with a revised third printing in 1994.

My third book, A Comprehensive View of Competitive Diving, 2007, took me 42 years to write that started in 1965. It's available on my website http://www.HobieBillingsley.com and www.USADivingStore.com.

I decided to write about everything I could think about in diving, and cover all the areas that may be helpful to divers, coaches, and judges. Unbelievably, I wrote the chapters with little aid from notes. One of the purposes for writing the book was to simplify knowledge in various areas of competitive diving. I designed the content to help readers and viewers of diving competitions gain a better understanding of what the sport was all about.

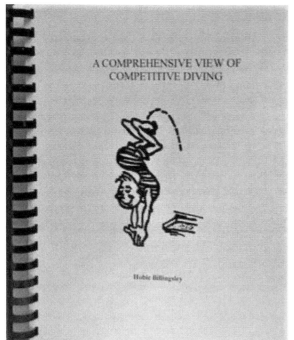

A COMPREHENSIVE VIEW OF COMPETITIVE DIVING

Hobie Billingsley

I also tried to make it simple enough for beginners and still attract the interest of the best divers and coaches. I felt qualified because I had coached champions during the time that there were great changes in competitive diving. After writing the book, I saw that the only thing that didn't change was the method used in judging the dives. That has remained the same for over a hundred years. For years, I have suggested that the range in judging competitions would be greatly increased and made more accurate, if a quarter point system was added. That would make it nearly impossible for ties in the final score.

Peggy Moss and The Moose Moss Family

Peggy Moss showed up to dive with me in 1971 as the Junior National Champion. I had never seen her dive, and she turned out to be very good and made our team as a freshman. But when we started to practice the next year, she didn't show up and had dropped out of school to get married without letting me know. I think her father, Moose Moss from Moultrie, Georgia, sent her to Indiana because he believed I could make her a senior national champion.

Moose Moss owned a large farm, and he coached his children and other youngsters in a diving pool he had built on his farm. I got to know Moose attending several meets, and we became very close friends. He was one of the original Flying Tigers that fought in China against Japan 1941-1942 in the Second World War. He was a real hero after being shot down, and managed to get back to his base.

He met Janie, a beautiful airline hostess, on a blind date when he returned to the United States after the war. They married and had three children while living in Moultrie, Georgia. He was a visionary leader in his hometown, and owned several thousand acres of land that grew mostly tobacco, cotton and peanuts. He loved coaching diving, but knew little about it so he invited me down to his farm and rented a hotel room for me several times. We sat for hours, and discussed diving and how to coach it. (Pictured on right is Peggy with her dad, Moose Moss)

332

Moose loved to fish in one of the five ponds he had on his property, and we would fish for large-mouth bass. He decided to build a diving complex in his home town that included two high and two low boards plus a five platform ten-meter tower with a large grandstand. The project cost well over a million dollars, and he had it made for about a third of that price because he knew every private contractor in town to build it at cost. He also solicited contributions and sold the complex as economic development for the whole town.

(Janie Moss is pictured in the middle with her diving program family)

I was a dealer for Duraflex and sold him all the diving boards at cost. Over one thousand people attended the dedication ceremony. After being praised by several dignitaries for an hour, he was asked to say a few words. I'll never forget when all he said was, "Thank You" and sat down again. He asked me who he should hire to run the program. I told him to get Jay Lerew who was a good coach in Wisconsin, and knew how to get along well with children.

Jay did a great job for around six years until he took a college position. Jay was followed by Wenbo Chen, an Olympic diver and coach from China that helped the program grow into one of the finest competitive club diving programs in the country. Then, he left to coach at Purdue University, and U.S. Diving, and eventually the

University of Minnesota.   Ron Piemonte followed Wenbo and left in 2006 to coach at Virginia Tech.

Today the facility is a non-profit corporation run by volunteer parents, and is financed through diving fees, donations, and an annual Dove Shoot.   The community sees football and diving as their premier sports with the Moose Moss Diving Tigers program drawing divers from all over the world to compete in state, national, and international diving contests.

I was in Ft. Lauderdale, Florida in 1993 when I heard Moose had a heart attack, and passed away while attending a Florida State football game. I immediately took off in my car to attend his funeral, but got there an hour late and missed it. Janie lived eleven more years after his death, and Ellen and I were fortunate to be at her side a couple of days before Christmas when she passed away on December 26th.

The Moss family are outstanding people who have helped the Moose Moss diving program in Moultrie continue to be one of the best in the country. Rick Moss, the son of Moose, allowed me to stay in the Moss home for around a month two different times after Janie's death so I could work on the book I was writing. That showed the kind of people the Moss family were, and it was through the grace of God that I could be a friend of their family for around twenty years.

CHAPTER 40

Closing Out My Career

Mark Lenzi

© AP Photo/Amy Sancetta

I wasn't doing too well with my coaching in 1986. One day after practice, I was talking to Doc at Royer Pool and mentioned that Paul Lenihan had called to tell me about a young diver he had seen diving in a public pool in West Virginia who could spin like a top. Paul went on to say he didn't appear to know much about the sport, but thought I might be able to make him a good diver.

Paul talked to the kid, and found that he had been offered a full scholarship to the University of South Carolina coached by Randy Ableman. So, I told Doc there was no chance I could get him because I only had a half scholarship. Doc had never helped me get a diver before except Rick Early years ago. I was delighted when he said that he had a half scholarship he hadn't given out yet, and he would give it to me.

I didn't know anything about this young diver named Mark Lenzi, but trusted Paul Lenihan's recommendation. I was shocked to learn he was a wrestler who was interested in diving, and I had just offered him a full scholarship that I only received every four years. After he graduated, Mark went down to Ft. Lauderdale to practice with his hero Greg Louganis whose coach was Ron O'Brien.

After coaching Mark for about a week, Ron told him he was too old and too rough to make a good diver and he should take up golf. When Mark told Ron I had offered him a full scholarship, he said take it and started to laugh. After accepting the scholarship,

Mark showed up a week late. Not a good start. Then he got in trouble over a false ID, and was put in jail with 33 others. When I picked him up from jail, Mark thought I was going kick him off the team. While walking back to school I told him about our rules that gave him three strikes after which he would be kicked off the team permanently, and he now had one strike. Though I assume he broke more of my rules in his career while at Indiana, like many of my divers, I never caught him.

I found that Ron O'Brien was probably right about Mark after I coached him for a little more than a week. He was landing all over the pool doing his dives. I told him that if he didn't show any sign of making a diver by the end of the semester, he would lose his scholarship and be sent home.

I sent him to Royer Pool to perform forty line-up dives with ten each in four directions from the five-meter platform to see if he could learn to rip an entry. That meant entering the water with little or no splash. I explained the body alignment needed to accomplish a rip, and had him practice them without me while I coached my other divers on the trampoline and port-o-pit in the gym and pavilion.

About two weeks later, Mark came to me and asked if I would come into the pool and check out what he was doing. Normally, it takes about five months for a diver to learn how to rip one or two dives. But surprisingly he ripped three so I started to change my mind about him.

Mark was no taller than five feet four inches, when I told him I was going to teach him how to perform the most difficult dives listed in the rule books in each of the five groups from the one-meter and three-meter boards. He learned them within a month, but his form and entries were terrible and still needed work.

I took him to Michigan State for his first dual meet. When Mark performed his difficult list from the three-meter board, John Narcy, their diving coach, and I had to stand against the wall to keep from getting wet judging him. Narcy started to laugh when he said I was crazy to think Mark would ever make a diver.

The next week we had a dual meet with Ohio State. Driving over to Columbus, Ohio with Mark and Jim Fisher, one of his teammates, I told Mark he was now going to dive against a two-time national champion who was going to kick his butt from one end of the pool to the other. Instead, Mark performed all his dives so well on the one-meter board that he beat Mike Wantuck, Ohio State's national champion, so bad that Vince Pansano, the Ohio State diving coach, was hitting his head against the wall.

I never saw him come close to performing one good dive in practice before then, but I discovered the reason for his brilliance was because he knew how to compete. I knew then that I had a diver who was going to soon be world class.

I decided to teach Mark how to dive tower soon after that meet. But since we only had a five-meter platform in Royer Pool, I taught him the four simple compulsory dives performed by all the contestants plus the lead-ups for the six optional dives needed to be performed from the ten-meter platform.

We went up to the IUPUI Natatorium in Indianapolis, and in one weekend, he learned to perform the compulsory dives with no difficulty. We went back to Indy the next week to see how many of the difficult dives he could learn after practicing the lead-up dives. I have never known anyone in my career who learned to perform the six most difficult dives from the ten-meter platform in such a short time.

His first dive was a forward 3½ somersault. With the use of the bubble machine, and a call from me to let him know when to come out of the dive, he performed it so well that he said he didn't need any help to perform the dive again. He then went on to perform an inward 3½ somersault, a back 3½ somersault, a reverse 2½ somersault instead of a 3½ because he jumped too far away from the platform. He added a handstand with a reverse double somersault, and a back 1½ somersault with 3½ twists all in forty-five minutes!

A while later, Mark became the first diver to perform a forward 4½ somersault from the three-meter diving board, and to perform the dive in competition from the ten-meter platform! Charlie Casuto and his diver, Pat Evans, came into the I.U.P.U.I. one day while we were practicing. Mark was performing a back 3½ from the ten-meter tower. Mark somersaulted so fast that he came out of the dive well above the five-meter platform, and entered the water with no splash and that left Charlie and Pat in awe.

Mark went on to be a brilliant tower diver, but it didn't last long because he could not hold a hand stand long enough to perform a hand stand dive. I had him practice hand stands before and after every practice, and even took him to a gymnastics coach but he never mastered it.

He went on to be one of the best springboard divers in the world winning eighteen international titles. I remember telling him during a high-powered practice session that if he would listen, and do what I was saying, I could take him to the moon. After he won his first title on the one-meter event by beating the Chinese divers, he didn't realize it was the World Championship. I went over and hugged him after he won, and whispered in his ear, "welcome to the moon."

Bobby Knight Incident

I retired a year before I was sixty-five, but I actually resigned. There were two incidents that occurred in the final year I taught and coached at Indiana. The first incident concerned Bobby Knight who had graduated from Ohio State where he was on one of their national basketball teams. He started his coaching career at the West Military

Academy before accepting the offer to coach at Indiana University in 1971 after Branch McCracken's retirement.

A new portable wooden floor was placed in the pavilion inside the old field house to play their games. The pavilion seated about eight thousand fans, and Bob's teams weren't winning much the first two years he was at Indiana. One day when Doc and I were coming out of the Indiana Union, he approached us and asked how we were winning so much. Doc said he took a scientific approach to his coaching and tried to stay one step in front of everyone else.

When Bobby asked me, I said I was a shouter, and yelled a lot at my divers until they got my way. His team was playing a Big Ten opponent about a week later, and Indiana was winning by twenty points. The other team suddenly caught up, and tied them while our fans remained quiet. Bobby had been a low-keyed coach until at that time. Suddenly Bob walked out to the middle of the basketball floor and started yelling at the audience, if they weren't going to support his team they should leave the pavilion. From that time on the fans screamed for Indiana because they felt they had a coach who was going to fight for his team.

Bobby Knight and Doc became close friends. Doc sold him his house for an unbelievable low price when he first arrived at Indiana, and because Doc was known as the top swimming coach in the country. I really liked Knight and being a fellow Ohio State graduate, I used to stop in his office at least once a week and chat with him for about an hour.

Knight started a basketball camp a few years later. One day when he was talking to all the campers sitting on the basketball floor. He said that some of them would become good players if they were fortunate to have an outstanding coach like two Indiana coaches and one of those coaches was standing right behind him. All the campers stood up, and gave me a standing ovation. I was startled, and very pleased that he saw me that way but my relationship with him changed a few years later.

The day before Thanksgiving he and his assistant coach, Jacoby Wright, were having a closed practice in Assembly Hall. I peeked in to see what was going on as I was leaving to go home. They were taking a break with Knight at one end of the floor, and Jacoby at my end. I walked onto the floor and asked Jacoby if he and his family would like to join me at my house for their Thanksgiving dinner. His family was busy moving into a house about a block from mine.

Jacoby told me his mother-in-law was making their dinner but thanked me for the kind offer. Then he told me I had better leave because Knight was getting upset with me for coming out on the floor, and I left without giving his comment any thought. I later learned that Bobby was not happy that I had interrupted his practice, and we weren't on such friendly terms from then on.

338

Years later when I was asked what I thought of Bobby Knight in an interview I might had said he was a jerk for the way he treated his team. I think that comment got back to him. But I was a cocky coach with a big mouth, too. I learned the hard way that every coach has his own way of handling his team, and if it works for them, who am I to criticize. You have to mind your own affairs before you take time to meddle or advise someone else.

My Female Diver on Scholarship Refuses to Compete in Big Ten Championship

Another incident occurred during my last year of teaching and coaching. I had given a scholarship to a girl diver. For some unknown reason, she missed thirty-two workouts during the season. We were getting ready to compete in the Big 10 Championships, and she refused to dive. So, I told her if she didn't compete, she would lose her scholarship.

A couple of days later while working in my yard, I was called by the school to attend a mandatory meeting with eight faculty members, one of which was Anita Aldrich, the dean of the physical education department, to discuss the problem I had with this diver. Her parents also attended and were all dressed up. I didn't have time to change my clothes, and showed up looking a mess.

Her parents showed them the medals she had won in high school, and what a nice girl she was. After I told my side of the story, the committee, unbelievably, decided in favor of the girl. It was at that moment I decided to resign from Indiana. However, I said I was retiring because I was under the 18-20-year plan that paid my salary for five years after retirement.

My Retirement Parties by the Athletic and Physical Education Departments

Three parties honoring my retirement were given. The first one was a big party at my beautiful house in Blue Ridge. Sheryl, the lady I had been going with for around eight years, did a magnificent job preparing the food and drinks. We had around a hundred guests that included many swimmers and divers that came from seven different countries. Our woman's swimming coach cooked up a hog, and some of my divers set up tables and chairs to eat in the yard and on two decks. It was a fabulous party that went on for two days. I greeted and talked with people I hadn't seen in years. Everyone had a great time, and took pictures of the whole affair some of which I have put in a scrapbook. I was really surprised when my divers gave me a new bass boat that I have used on Lake Monroe outside of Bloomington.

The athletic and physical education departments also decided to have retirement parties for me. When approached earlier, I told them to forget it. I just wanted to leave without any fanfare. But they insisted and the first one was given by the athletic department. The University owns a house near campus that is used for small entertainment groups. Before we met, Doc asked what kind of gift I thought they would they give me. I said it would probably be a gold watch because that's what railroad conductors usually got when they retired. It turned out to be a gold clock.

A group of coaches and their wives showed up, and after having refreshments, Ralph Floyd, the athletic director asked everyone to gather around outside while we stood on a small stair landing with him holding a cardboard box. As I lifted my arm to receive the gift, a bird flew by and dropped some bird drops on the back of my hand and everyone broke out laughing.

Someone in the crowd said that I had better watch what I say because the president of the university was standing right behind me. I said that would be the day, and bent over to look back between my legs to see the president still laughing.

At the physical education department party, Dean Anita Aldrich said that I was the best activity teacher they had ever had at Indiana. I was flattered by her remark, and I also appreciated a portrait painting that they had made of me. Without me knowing it, they had hired an artist who had followed me around the campus for about a month in order to create the painting.

CHAPTER 41

After Retirement

Never Cheated

After I retired, someone came up to me and asked what I liked the most about my career. I told him that I never cheated recruiting, teaching, or coaching because I believed that cheating destroyed the value of success. Like most retirees, I thought I was going to relax and spend time fishing and watching ball games on T.V., but it didn't turn out that way.

World Diving Clinics for F.I.N.A.

F.I.N.A., the governing body of the world for aquatics, sent me all over the world giving lectures and clinics on competitive diving. Three of the rare places I visited were Qatar, Nairobi, and Kuala Lumpur. I really liked traveling and with the exception for a few rare times, I wasn't in Bloomington longer than nine days for eight years. I went to Qatar twice, and found it to be a remarkable country. It had a population of about 250,000 people who live on one side of the country, and all the oil and gas is drilled on the other side. The country was generous with their money because every citizen was given a big house, an automobile, free medical attention, and free educational opportunities.

Someone failed to pick me up at the airport when I arrived in Dao, the capital of Qatar, the second time. It was eleven o'clock at night, and no one was in the arrival area except a man with his little boy, about four years old, who was running all over the place. The man came up to me about a half hour later, and asked me if I was in trouble. I told him what had happened, and he said to come home with him.

He was a Muslim from another country who was doing domestic work in Qatar. When we arrived at his little house after midnight, he kicked his brother out of bed to give me a place to sleep. He spoke English, and we discussed the differences in our religions. We talked until about three in the morning. From what he had said about his God, I told him could be the same as mine, but they had lived at a different time. He took me to my hotel the next morning. The next day when I was giving my lecture, he showed up to see me because we had formed a friendship.

I gave lectures that lasted for around seven or eight hours a day, and I had to stop for ten minutes every hour so they could go to another room and pray. I found that they built new swimming facilities that matched anything we have in our country that included a pool and separate diving well.

One was built in preparation for the Near East Games that were to be staged there the next year. They also built the classiest and biggest mall I had ever seen. The second visit included several women in veils that wanted to learn something about diving, but only understood the basics that seemed to satisfy them. When I asked what they did in Qatar for entertainment, I found that they took their cars out to the sand dunes, and drove them all over the hills. If one tipped over, others would stop and tip it up again.

One of their better divers invited me to his house after diving practice. I thought it was a large school as we drove through the iron gates up to the front door. He said we had to enter a side entrance after he opened the front door, and found his mother entertaining some guests. The side door opened into a huge reception room lit up with outstanding splendor that had sofas all around the room. It also had vases and bowls of fruit on the tables, beautiful paintings on all the walls, and soft thick carpets on the floor all of which must have cost a fortune.

I asked him what his father did for a living. He said he was the ambassador to Iran. All the domestic work done in the homes came from people from neighboring countries who lived in shacks next to the houses. Of course, the citizens all wore beautiful clothes, robes, and turbans. They also treated me as a special guest, and made sure I was well taken care of during my visit. Steve Gerlach was the diving coach in Qatar both times I visited. He was the brother of Joe Gerlach, a great University of Michigan diver.

I found Nairobi a country predominantly of black people. I was put in a nice hotel when I arrived at night. The next morning, I took a walk only two or three blocks up the street before returning to the hotel. When I returned, someone in the hotel asked me where I had been. And he nearly turned white when I told him. He told me I was lucky to be alive because white people were often killed walking alone on the street. They would take their belongings, strip them naked, and throw them into the bushes. This time I was lucky because a mission group from Sweden was nearby, and they probably thought I was one of them.

I went to the pool that afternoon. It had been built by the Chinese along with a separate diving well. They were having a swimming meet, and I asked to see the diving coach. And I was told they didn't have a diving coach. A bit surprised, I asked to meet their divers. And they said they didn't have any. I had to think of something to do, so I asked some of the younger boys who were timers for the swimming meet, if they would like to learn how to dive. Three of the boys agreed. I took them to the diving well that had aluminum diving boards made in China, and were good except they were much heavier than our Duraflex boards.

I taught the three boys how to perform three or four basic dives from the one-meter board in about a half hour. A couple more boys joined in and that started to draw a crowd. The number increased to about a dozen the next day along with a good crowd.

They learned to do a few more basic dives that included a forward 1½ somersault over a couple of days. They seemed to enjoy learning how to dive, so I decided to teach them how to do a back dive from the three-meter board.

I took a diver who had learned the most, and convinced him to perform the back dive by placing his arms over his head, look up at his hands, and lean back slightly while continuing to keep looking his hands. I also warned him several times not to push with his feet because if he did, he would land flat on his stomach. Never having dived from a three-meter board before, he panicked and pushed off to land flat on his stomach. The next day, I only had three divers for another session.

My next stop was the capital of Malaysia. Again, due to poor communication, no one came to pick me up at an open-air airport. I sat around for about an hour and half in the hot sun when someone finally arrived and took me to a hotel. I lied down, and suddenly developed cramps all over my body. I drank a bottle of water sitting on the table before passing out. When I woke up in the morning, my lips were covered with blisters. I was taken to a doctor who told me I had a heat stroke, and if I hadn't drunk that water, I would have died.

I managed to give my lectures for the week without incident, but I had lost a lot of weight and strength. I also worked with a couple of their divers who were appreciative because they learned how to perform a couple of optional dives. But I wasn't there long enough to make much of an impact on their divers or coaches.

The World Acrobatic Society

Bob Bollinger got the idea of forming a World Acrobatic Society in the middle 1990's. It would include all sport activities that involved acrobatics. He asked Dick Smith and me to attend a committee that was gathered in Salt Lake City to create the society. So, we met with them, and I helped form their constitution like I had created for the World Diving Coaches Association. That impressed the group, and they made me their first president. After four years Don Leas, the diving coach from Clarion State University in Pennsylvania replaced me as president.

Mark Lenzi at the 1992 Olympic Trials

The 1992 Olympic trials were a few years away, and Mark decided to come out of retirement and try out for the team. He gave me a call, and asked if I would coach him. I had also retired in 1989, and had just been selected to be a judge at the games. I thought it be a conflict of interest to also coach him, and suggested Ron O'Brien in Florida where he would get excellent coaching.

However, Ron and Mark didn't hit it off, so I had him go up to Ohio State to be coached by Vince Pansano who offered Mark $10,000 to be his assistant, and would also coach him. Mark stayed with Vince for about a year and a half, and decided to leave Ohio State. I then sent him to Dick Kimball, the coach at the University of Michigan, who was a disciplinarian, and Mark needed that. Kimball had several of his own divers trying out for the team, so I coached Mark during the Olympic trials.

The highlight of the trials was the men's three-meter event. The scores from the preliminaries are carried over to the finals. Mark performed well in the finals, but was in fourth place behind Kent Ferguson by a large margin and Mark Bradshaw from Ohio State in second place. Only the two top divers qualified for the Olympics, and it came down to the last dive. Mark had to perform a near perfect reverse 3½ somersault to overtake Ferguson. He did just that scoring 102 points that made him the first diver ever to score over a hundred points on a single dive. Mark beat Ferguson 1,396 to 1,376 points, and Bradshaw ended up in third place.

The 1992 Olympic Games in Barcelona, Spain

The Olympic aquatic pools were located on a high hill overlooking the city, and the view was unbelievably breathtaking. I was a diving judge for the Games, and Dick Kimball was the Olympic coach so I didn't try to coach Mark. The Chinese were favored to win all the diving events as they had done before. The first event was the women's three-meter springboard.

Julie Overhouse, formerly coached by John Narcy of the U.S. was in second place up to the last dive. She did an inward 2½ somersault, and over rotated which knocked her down to fifth place. We did better when Scott Donie, coached by Ron O'Brien, performed brilliantly on the ten-meter tower, and took second place. On the ten-meter platform, Matt Scoggin coached by one of my former divers, Mike Brown from the University of Texas, placed tenth. Doing a back 3½ somersault, Matt's hands slipped off his knees, and he landed flat on his back on the water. He, of course, didn't place, but received more publicity for the crash than if he had won a medal.

I tried to recruit Matt when he graduated from high school. But I didn't know anything about him, and called him Max talking to him on the phone. We have kidded about my error for years when he calls me. He said, "Hobie, if you had known his name was Matt and not Max, he would have come to Indiana."

Mark Lenzi was interviewed a few moments before the three-meter springboard contest was to begin. Based on last year's results, the interviewer asked Mark how he liked diving in the shadow of Kent Ferguson. Kent was believed to have the best chance to beat the Chinese divers. Mark told the interviewer that he had it wrong because Ferguson was diving in his shadow. Unfortunately, Mark's remark about Ferguson was made on international television, and the public was led to believe that Mark thought he was a big shot.

As it turned out, Mark qualified for the finals in second place, and Ferguson who was not diving as well qualified last in twelfth. As we left the pool, Mark asked me where the news media was. And I told him they were behind a nearby building interviewing Ferguson and his coach O'Brien on why he was not diving well.

Mark performed better in the finals than in the preliminaries, and was beating everyone including the Chinese. The only time I tried to coach Mark was when he was ready to perform a forward 3½ somersault. I reminded him to dive out a little so that he could control the dive, and his score ended up being the highest score he had in the meet.

When it came down to his last dive, a reverse 3½ somersault, with the highest degree of difficulty of any dive, he looked over at the diving referee, and smiled. I know if it had been me, I probably would have fainted. Mark performed a beautiful dive, and won the contest to become the greatest diver in the world by beating Tan Liangde of China by forty-nine points.

Kent Ferguson had had a tough meet and ended up in twelfth place. While walking off the deck with his mother and father, Mark asked me how I felt about his terrific performance. I said it was fine, but I was a little disappointed. Shocked, he asked me why. And I told him that he didn't give his best performance. He didn't perform a back and inward 3½ somersault, and could have won the contest by seventy-five instead of fifty points.

But then I told him how proud I was of him for his victory, and that was the frosting on the cake. When I coached, I challenged every diver to give the best they had to offer win, lose, or draw, and he didn't do that. The United States won three medals with Mark taking first on the three-meter springboard, Scott Donie placing second, and Mary Ellen Clark placing third on the ten-meter platform.

CHAPTER 42

The 1996 Atlanta Olympics

Mark Lenzi Comes Out of Retirement

I had been retired for three years, and working at odd jobs. Mark Lenzi still didn't know what he wanted to do. So, he decided to take a shot at making the 1996 Olympic team. He called me up, and asked if I would coach him. I was selected to judge at the Olympics again, so I told him I would, but under the condition that he would do exactly what I wanted him to do and he agreed. Mark had put on about thirty pounds after he retired, and the first thing I told him was that I wasn't interested in his body. I knew he would take off the weight, but I was more interested in how to challenge what was above his shoulders in his head. We only had about eleven months to get ready.

He lost a lot of weight in about three months before competing in international meets in Madrid and Rome. Demitri Sautin, from Russia, was winning nearly all the international contests at that time, and he beat Mark by nearly a hundred points in Madrid and seventy-five points in Rome. Mark told me he had to perform a tougher optional dive if he was going to beat Demitri, and I agreed.

The International Meet in Rome

At the international meet in Rome, (left-right) me, Sammy Lee, and Dick Smith stayed in an apartment in a quaint village outside of Rome. To go to the pool, we had to first take a bus, then change to a street car for about three miles. One day, while standing in the rear of the street car on the way to the pool, three young men, who were obviously from the Near East, got on the street car, and stood close to the three of us.

Suddenly two of them brushed against Dick Smith while putting money in the fare box, and got off again a few blocks later. When Dick Smith got to the pool, he reached into his pants pocket, and found he was missing $600. I gave him money later for the rest of the trip. The very next day when we got on the street car, two similar looking males and a female got on while we were standing in the rear of the street car. They neared us again to put their fares in the box, and when one of them got near Sammy Lee, I told him to hold onto his wallet.

They again got off the street car a few blocks later. When Sammy reached into the pockets of his jacket, he discovered he was missing $400. I later took an American $20 bill, and made about forty copies of the bill before going back to our village apartment. When we made the trip to the pool the next day, I got off and rode the street car back and forth for over a half hour, but none of the pick-pockets showed up again.

After Mark and I returned home, we decided how to beat the Russian diver in the Olympics. He had to learn a dive with a higher degree of difficulty than his reverse 2½ somersault in pike position. I finally came up with a new dive that had just been listed in the diving rule books. It was a reverse 3½ somersault with a half twist that was a perfect choice for him. We first practiced performing a reverse 2½ somersault with a half twist for about two weeks on the one-meter board. When he was ready, I told him to perform the chosen dive from the three-meter board. But he refused to do it. I couldn't believe he wouldn't even try it because that dive was made for him, and there was no way he could be injured.

(Pictured previous page left to right, Ron Kontura, Dick Staufer, Tom Mulhern, Paul Lenihan, Mike Taylor)

Ron Kontura was training with us, and wasn't an elite diver. But in about fifteen minutes, I taught Ron how to perform the dive. Ron didn't do the dive well, but he did it. I argued with Mark for about three days, and finally reminded him that if he didn't keep his promise to do what I wanted him to do, I would stop coaching him. I didn't come back to the pool for a couple of days, but I changed my mind because I couldn't walk out on him when we were so close to the Olympic Games.

The 1996 Olympic Trials

The Olympic trials were held at the I.U.P.U.I. Natatorium pool in Indianapolis. It was an exciting meet because everyone was performing very well, and the points in all the events were very close. The three-meter contest for men ended up being much like the trials in 1992. But this time, Mark was in much more trouble in third place sixty-two points behind Dean Panero. Dean was an excellent diver, and Scott Donie was in second place. Like the last Olympic trials, the scores from the preliminary rounds were added to the finals, so making up enough points for Mark to qualify for the team would be a near miracle.

The three-meter event had the top three divers perform the best dives people had seen in a long time. It came down to the last dive, Panero and Mark were performing a reverse 3½ somersault. Fortunately for Mark, Panero over rotated on his dive, but Mark still had to receive nines for the same dive to make the team. The moment brought a lot of tension from everyone in the pool. When Mark received nine's and nine and a halves for his dive, the crowd went wild and he made the team.

My Greatest Honor - Giving the Oath to Officials at the 1996 Atlanta Olympic Games

I was made a diving judge for the Olympic Games again, but when Mark made the team, it created a big problem. I received credentials for the entrance to the pool as a diving judge. But I needed coaching credentials to coach Mark practicing at an earlier time. They wouldn't give me coaching credentials because their records showed I already had credentials. So, I had to stand in line every day to get a pass into the pool. That resulted in me arriving too late to coach Mark on several occasions.

It happened again on the day of opening ceremonies. Mark came walking out of the pool as I was walking in, and he begrudgingly thanked me for coaching him that didn't occur. I went into the pool totally disgusted with the problem. Randy Ableman, the Olympic coach and the diving coach at the University of Miami, said everything wasn't bad for me because I had just been chosen to give the oath for the officials that night. I told him to stop kidding me because diving coaches were never given that honor, especially when it was given only by officials. He said he wasn't kidding, and when I walked away someone else told me the same thing.

I found out how it happened. Micki King, the 1972 Olympic Champion on the three-meter springboard, was our diving team manager. She happened to walk by a room full of people that morning. She was curious, and stepped in to see what was going on. They said they were trying to decide who should give the oath for the officials. Micki told them a little about me, and they decided to give me the honor.

Micki told me to get a uniform and change in a small building close by. After changing, I found myself sitting with all the Olympic dignitaries. I knew one of them, but everyone kept talking to the guy sitting next to me. I tried to see his name tag, but could only see the word I thought was 'burg.' To start a conversation, I almost told him I used to date a girl in high school by the name of "Sternburg." Luckily, he turned toward me, and I saw his name was "Steinbrener" the owner of the New York Yankees, and a multi-millionaire so I didn't embarrass myself.

We all were taken to a stadium next to the Olympic stadium. As all the athletes arrived, they sat in different sections before being called to march into the Olympic stadium. I was sitting there for a while, and wondering how I was going to give the oath when no one gave me one.

Shortly after, a guy showed up, and put the printed oath in my shirt pocket saying what it was. The athletes from different countries all marched in. When it came to our turn, I found myself walking behind the flag bearer as we went over a ramp to enter the stadium. I decided to drop back behind the dignitaries. Once around them, I stumbled and nearly fell. Then I heard a great roar that came from our athletes marching behind me.

We marched around the track, and took our place on the field. I thought there was no way anyone would find me when a guy came, and led me to a room that had a few T.V. sets showing the ceremony. A tall African-American female, Teresa Edwards a former Olympic team basketball player came in, and said she was giving the oath for the athletes. I asked her how she was going to do it. She said she memorized the oath, and I told her about the guy who gave the oath in Seoul at the 1988 Olympics who suddenly froze about half way through it. The whole thing was put on the main screen, and everyone gave the oath together.

I suggested she read it like I planned to do, and she wouldn't get nervous. I asked a man in the room where we were supposed to go to give the oath. He said out there on the stage in the middle of the stadium. This surprised me as the oath was usually given standing in a booth next to the president of the Olympic Games. I also asked how many people would hear us speak. And he said around three and a half billion people. Then Teresa did as I suggested. She grabbed a corner of the American flag as we were instructed, and read the oath in her hand.

I was next and not scared at all because I knew if I took my time, and read the oath of 37 words slowly it would be okay. I put the written oath, "*In the name of all the judges and officials, I promise that we shall officiate in these Olympic Games with complete impartiality, respecting and abiding by the rules which govern them in the true spirit of sportsmanship*" inside my hat so that I could easily see to read when I took off my hat. I was probably going to be the only diving coach to ever give the oath for the officials because diving coaches are never given an official's position except for this one time.

The next morning, I got a call from Rich Lindner. He flew his jet down from Cincinnati to meet Cynthia Potter and me at the airport to congratulate me for giving the oath. I remember that a couple of coaches and I stood at the exact spot where the next night a bomb exploded near the entrance to the Olympic Games.

Diving was one of the first events at the start of the Olympic Games. The men's three-meter preliminary trials began, and Mark was in 26th place with only three dives to go in an eleven-dive preliminary round. So I had to wait until the event had a break to speak to him. I was so upset over his poor performance that I went into the locker room to talk to him.

After his seventh dive, Mark came in, and I challenged him to start doing what he knows how to do best from all his years of training. He then performed three good optional dives, and moved up to ninth place to make the finals.

In the finals, he performed the five compulsory dives better than I had ever seen him do before. I thought he was on his way to winning the event until he performed a reverse 2½ somersault in the pike position. He had a near perfect dive in the air, but he must have thought he was going to over rotate and pulled his head in. This caused him to reach short with his arms for the entry making a huge splash, and received sixes for the dive. He was still winning when it came down to the last dive. Both Chinese divers received nines doing an inward 3½ somersault, and took first and second place with Mark taking third. Considering that he had come out of retirement to compete again, Mark was very pleased with his bronze medal.

After the Games, Mark took the job as diving coach at Clemson University in South Carolina. Mark got married to Dorothy who was a nurse. They had their wedding in Las Vegas, and I was his best man. He came back to Bloomington, Indiana to coach the children's diving club in the new pool, and Dorothy found a job as a nurse. I had a condo about a block from where they lived so we stayed in touch. He liked coaching children, and was doing a fine job but it didn't last long. He decided to go back to school and become a pathologist so he moved to North Carolina, bought a house, and earned his degree.

I had two ski boats that I used for my diving camp. My son Jimmy had a boat repair and storage business near Lake Monroe. Every early evening, he took five divers out to water ski. I kept the boats for years after I stopped coaching at the camp, and I decided to give one of the boats to Mark in North Carolina so he could use it to go fishing.

The only car I had with a hitch was my old Buick. So, I put the boat on a trailer, and drove the boat down to North Carolina going about seventy miles an hour on the Interstate all the way to Mark's house. Then after dropping it off, I drove a little faster on the way back. I started to cross the Kennedy Bridge in Louisville at about forty miles an hour. I moved into the left lane to Indianapolis. Half way across the bridge, I ran over a bridge expansion divider about a half inch below the road.

I heard a little click but didn't know what it was until I could spin my steering wheel in either direction with complete loss of control of the car. My front wheels turned left into the cement retaining wall, and the car continued to hug the wall until it stopped. It was rush hour, and the bridge was crowded with cars traveling around fifty miles an hour when I managed to climb out of the car.

I walked around to the front end of my car to check the left side. I expected to see the whole side dented, but all the damage was to the left front hub cap. A police car came up behind my car within minutes. We looked under the car, and saw that the engine broke the motor mounts and dropped down to about six inches from the road. The officer called for a wrecker that hauled my car off the bridge, and dropped it in a parking lot. I called Jimmy to bring his truck to pick up the car.

While waiting for him, I began to realize that the only time I had gone slower than seventy miles an hour was crossing the bridge. If my wheels had gone to the right instead of the left, there could have been a multiple-car pileup! We inspected the car after we got home, and could see the engine sat on a cradle bolted down on all four corners. The bolts had rusted and broken which caused the engine to drop.

Considering how many bigger bumps I'd run over at much higher speeds, it was a miracle that the engine hadn't dropped earlier. That experience, along with several other lifesaving experiences I have had in my life, couldn't possibly have been a coincidence. When I got off the bridge, I thanked God for watching over me and giving me another chance to continue with my life.

CHAPTER 43

The New Counsilman - Billingsley Aquatic Center

History to Get the Facility

Doc and I tried to get a new pool for around twenty-five years when Royer Pool built in 1960 had already become obsolete in 1975. The sport had grown so much that most colleges started to build fifty-meter pools with separate diving wells that included a ten-meter tower with five platforms.

In the late 1970's, Doc got a call from the University of Texas offering us a job. Doc asked me if I was interested in changing jobs. I told him that I couldn't do it because my friend, Mike Brown, was their diving coach, and they would have to fire him.

Doc told me to go over to the I.U. Foundation and tell Bill Armstrong that we were considering taking the job. If the administration wanted us to remain at Indiana, they would have to build us a new pool. Bill Armstrong, the President of the Foundation brought in the President of the Board of Trustees the next day and they both agreed to build us a new pool, give us a raise, and a couple of other things we needed. But none of that happened once they learned we weren't really going to Texas.

About fifteen years later, a student came into the pool while I was coaching, and told me that the Board of Trustees was having an open meeting in the Union, and thought Doc and I should attend. We went to the Union, and reluctantly sat in the rear of the room behind two hundred staff members and teachers.

After sitting there for nearly an hour, Doc nudged me to ask what in the hell were we doing there. And I said I had no idea. Just as the meeting was to adjourn, a board member got up, and said there were two coaches present that had been trying to get a new pool for many years and invited Doc to say a few words.

The board was sitting together like a jury in a court room. In a very calm voice, Doc stood in front of them, and said that they had been promised in the past that were plans to build a new facility, but it had not happened. Doc said they were nothing more than a bunch of liars, cheats, and thieves, and then went on to tell them why. No one made a sound except to breathe. I never saw a group of people so stunned like that before. When Doc finished, I was asked to say my piece.

I finished by telling the Board, "I am not talking anymore because you (The Board of Trustees) have never kept your promises to help us out with anything before so why would you help us now?"

I put my arm around Doc's shoulder as we left the Union, and said I thought we just got fired. We both started to laugh when unknowingly, Terry Clapacs, the Vice President at Indiana, and good friend of mine was standing behind us. He said he knew how we felt, and promised us he would somehow get us our new pool. The estimated cost was about twenty-five million dollars.

Terry kept his word, and gathered enough money through donations in two years to build it. Then the problem came up who was going to pay the maintenance to keep the pool going. The athletic department said they didn't have the money to do it. The recreation department said they had enough grants to take care of the pool if the school would build a new recreation building connected to the swimming complex.

The Catch to Building the Facility

But the catch was the recreation department wanted total control of the swimming complex. The estimated maintenance cost was a million dollars a year. To make the complex happen, their demands were accepted and both buildings were finally built in 1995. At first, the swimming complex was only going to be named "The James E. 'Doc' Counsilman Aquatic Center." But that word leaked out, and a campaign got started to name the diving well portion, "The Hobie Billingsley Diving Well." Ultimately the complex was named "The Counsilman-Billingsley Aquatic Center." Unfortunately, neither of us got to enjoy coaching there because we had already retired.

CHAPTER 44

Events and Honors After Retirement

My Birthday Parties

Mark Lenzi and some of the other divers that I had coached at Indiana decided to give me a birthday party every five years. The first one was in the summer of 2006 after I had turned 80 years old. My birthday was December 2, 1926, but because fewer people would attend a party in the winter time, it was set for the summer.

Karl Zacker, of the Alumni department, and Sandy Searcy, the assistant director of the Indiana Athletic High School Association along with my divers Doug MacAskill, Pat Harrington, and Bill Coleman made all the arrangements including notifying everyone. Around 150 people attended the party that lasted four days. We had a picnic buffet at my house that I had bought near Lake Monroe and close to where my son Jimmy and his family lived.

The party also included a free swim at the outdoor pool, an evening in a downtown bar where they roasted me, a comedy/diving show done by all the former divers in Royer Pool, a banquet at a large hall in the football stadium, and finally a Sunday breakfast in the Indiana Union before leaving to go home late Sunday morning. Everyone said they had a wonderful time, and wanted to attend another one. To date we have had five retirement parties.

The second birthday party occurred in the summer of 2011. I was 85 now, and it also went on for four days. All the events were held at the new DeVault Alumni building except for a diving exhibition by some of the old-time divers in Royer Pool, a golf outing, and a gathering at Nick's, a local bar and grill. Karl Zacker again set up all the events, and the banquet was also held in a big room in the Alumni Building.

A third party occurred in 2013. Most of the events were held again in Alumni Hall that included the banquet.

My Bronze Bust in the IU Hall-of-Fame

Curt Simic, the President of the Indiana Foundation and my close friend, attended the banquet, and suggested that a bronze bust be made of me. He said it would cost about $30,000, and he would donate the first $5,000. Then he challenged my divers to come up with $25,000. Surprisingly, all my divers came up with the full amount while still at the banquet.

The bust was made in 2014 so another gathering was made for its presentation. Around a 100 divers and friends attended a banquet at Alumni Hall. The unveiling was in the Counsilman-Billingsley show case, in the Henke Hall of Champions in the Memorial Stadium. Several other coaches that had outstanding careers were also honored. I felt especially honored because my bust was the first and only bust of a head coach at Indiana University.

(Pictured Hobie's bronze bust in display at Indiana University Hall-of-Fame in Assembly Hall on the Bloomington campus)

Mark Lenzi's Death

Three weeks after the celebration of the unveiling of my bronze bust, I received a call from one of my divers. He told me that Mark had died from a heart attack, and the visitation was the next day in South Carolina. I called Chris Unruh, one of my former divers, and we immediately took off for South Carolina. On the way, we stopped in North Carolina to pick up John Walker, another one of my past divers, and stayed overnight before driving on the next morning just in time for the visitation.

Amy McGrath-Watson lived in Charlotte, North Carolina, heard about Mark's death, also showed up. The funeral was held two days later in Fredericksburg, Virginia. Few of us had time to make the trip, and we were glad we could pay our last respects to a great diving competitor who would surely be missed.

Upon reflection, Olympic three-meter gold medalists Bruce Harlan and Mark Lenzi, were both wrestlers and eighteen years old when they started their diving careers. Before Mark came out of retirement to compete in the 1996 Olympics, he had achieved success in all kinds of jobs. I'd like to think that how he was challenged in practices and competitions helped give him the confidence to do whatever he wanted to do in life. I really loved the guy, and feel that it was an honor to coach a kid who learned so much in such a short time to be the best in the world. I'm sure that all who really knew him as did I will continue to miss him for a very long time.

The Rosewell Rotary Air Honor

Kim Smith was one of my finest divers whose father was the head football coach at West Point. After she got married and had children, she became a driver for an ambulance in Atlanta. One of her activities involved a group that took war veterans to Washington D.C. to visit all the war memorials.

She gave me a call and invited me to join a group that had fought in World War Two. About 50 of us met in Atlanta, and took a flight to Washington D.C. and were met by hundreds of people at the airport. One of my best friends and divers, Paul Lenihan, flew down from New York, and pushed me around all day in a wheelchair with the other veterans for a memorable trip.

CHAPTER 45

Some Special Friends I Made While at Indiana University

Curt Simic

Curt Simic was the manager for Otto Riser's gymnastics team when I first started to teach and coach at Indiana. We immediately became good friends. After he graduated I never saw him again for about thirty years. He held top level administrative positions at Oregon, Yale, California at Berkley, and the University of Tennessee. He returned to Indiana and took over as President of the Indiana Foundation after Bill Armstrong retired.

Curt was liked and respected by everyone. He had a great memory, especially for the names of people after meeting them. He became widely recognized as the national leader in fundraising for higher education in the country. During his tenure, he raised more money for Indiana University than all the past foundation presidents combined. He also constantly went out of his way to help others after he retired in 2012.

Curt continued to obtain funds from alumni who consider him to be one of their best friends. He is unselfish and considerate for the feelings of other people while remaining very humble. Over the years, he has not taken credit for the many deeds he has done for Indiana University and many people.

Terry Clapacs

Terry is another person I greatly respected. He is also one of the best persons who ever worked for Indiana University. I met him while he was an undergraduate student at Indiana. Terry worked hard for Indiana University, and became a vice-president and director of facilities and utilities, on the campus and at the

359

Indianapolis medical school. He was also responsible for the construction of over 600 buildings and structures found on both campuses.

Much like Curt Simic, he was a very likable and modest person. Terry did more than anyone else for the university, other than former President Herman B Wells. Without Terry and Curt, Indiana University would have never been in the same class with the other Big Ten Universities.

Terry Clapacs also never left his job after he retired and continued to work in his office in the campus police department building for years. If Terry hadn't got us our new pool at Indiana, I doubt that our swimming and diving programs would have continued to be successful after Doc and I retired.

Karl Zacker

Karl worked for the Alumni department, but was not the head man in his department. He apparently was their work horse. I first got to know him when I received the Bill Orwig award for being a person who had contributed a great deal to Indiana University. Orwig had been the athletic director for years, and when he passed away they started to give a medal annually in his honor.

(Pictured left to right, Hobie, Karl Zacker, and Sandy Searcy)

Karl, time and time again was involved with issues between me and the University. I believed he was one of the best people who ever worked for the Alumni department. He was willing and able to do more than was expected of him on many occasions. He was promoted, and is now the Director of Commencement at Indiana University.

Sandy Searcy

Sandy is a forrmer commissioner for the Indiana High School Athletic Association (I.H.S.A.A.) since 1999, and is currently Director of Sports for the National Federation of High Schools. She is responsible for all girls' softball, boys' and girls' volleyball, and swimming and diving activities in the state of Indiana. She is a marvelous person who played a big part in arranging and organizing my retirement parties.

Sandy started a high school Hall-of-Fame for swimmers and divers in honor of Doc and me that is displayed in the foyer of the I.U.P.U.I. Swimming Pool in Indianapolis. She, like many of my other close friends, was a hard-working modest person with an outstanding personality. Sandy did things for other people with no intent of receiving any appreciation.

Lucinda Fox Cousins

One of my special friends was Lucinda Fox Cousins. She worked in the women's physical education department, and taught swimming and lifesaving for nearly forty years. She had a synchronized group that performed in every one of our water shows, and remained a very close friend of mine throughout my life at Indiana. She was an outstanding athlete in golf when young, and was very humble about it.

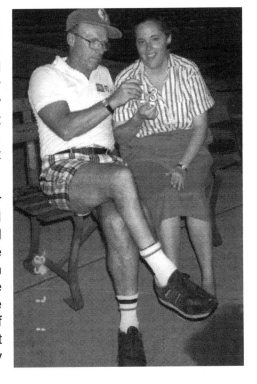

I will never be able to thank her enough for taking me into her home for six weeks after I had an operation on my back, and was well enough to walk again. Lucinda had multiple sclerosis for most of her adult life which affected her walking and balance, but she never complained about her misfortune. She always showed more interest in the welfare of others than she did for herself. I had great respect and loved her like a member of my family.

361

Dr. Alan Sommers

Alan was one of Doc's top distance swimmers who placed highly in the 1960 Olympics. He became a neurologist and treated me a few times for my recurring back injuries from diving. He has always been a good friend, and has tried to find someone to make a movie of the miracles that Ken Sitzberger and Lesley Bush had that will never occur in diving again.

CHAPTER 46

Conflicts and Solutions During My Career

The Athletic Department

When I arrived at Indiana University in 1959 there was no money in the swimming budget for diving, and over the years there never was. Half of my salary was paid by the Athletic Department to coach diving, and the other half came from the Department of Health, Physical Education, and Recreation as an instructor.

The athletic department might have helped me on one occasion. I went to the maintenance department in the spring of 1960, and requested they install a dry land board for me to use in the old field house. It required a one-meter stand, made with two-inch pipe, with a cement foundation for a diving board, and a pile of sand or dirt in front of the board for divers to land on feet first.

Another favor was during the construction of Royer Pool. The plans called for a five-meter-high aluminum diving tower. The plans showed the platform would extend over the pool too far, so that a diver could conceivably run off and land on the deck opposite the platform. I succeeded in having them cut five feet off the end of the platform before it was installed so that people could not run off the platform and land on the other side of the pool.

Stop Winning

A real shock occurred when Bill Orwig, I.U. Athletic Director, called me into his office. He told me to "Stop winning!". When I asked him why, he said because the athletic department couldn't afford to have Doc and I win anymore. He went on to say that when I first came to Indiana, the budget for the swimming team was $8,000. But with all the winning Doc and I started to get, the budget had risen to over a $100,000, and it was obvious that Bill wanted to spend more on revenue sports like football. The message was we cost more than the athletic department could afford, so I should stop winning. I needn't say how I responded to his warning after walking out of his office.

Lack of Regard from Other Coaches

I bought a new port-o-pit for my camp for a thousand dollars, and put it in a storage room until summer when it would be used by my campers. The football players were having spring practice, and went through the storage room on their way to the practice field every day. They tromped over the port-o-pit ripping it to pieces with the cleats on their football shoes, and I never went to the football coach to ask him to replace it because I knew what his answer would be.

No Athletic Salary Increase Despite Success

I coached the female divers for 29 years, and never received a cent for my efforts. Title IX was made a law in 1972, and female athletes were to receive the same equal opportunities as the males in athletics. At some universities coaches were hired to coach the new women's sports teams. But our athletic department told me that coaching females was to be in addition to my existing job duties.

I asked around and learned other colleges hired a separate coach for the female program, or raised the salaries of the present coaches to coach female divers because it doubled their time to coach. I had been teaching a full-time teaching load of physical education classes throughout my entire career when my contract called for only a half-time appointment. That was more classes than anyone else in the department, and I probably received the lowest salary. I can honestly say that it wasn't the money that bothered me as much as the low profile the departments had of me as a teacher and coach because I didn't have a doctor's degree, and they took advantage of it.

In 1977, I felt I had achieved everything I wished to do coaching diving. So, I went to the athletic department and told them that I would like to stop coaching, and just teach diving classes. And they said if I did stop, they would no longer pay me. This meant I would be making around $12,000 a year, so I had to continue to coach until I retired in 1989. A while later I ran out of energy again, and wanted to stop coaching. I thought I would let everyone know that I was going to retire in about in three more years. The word got out, and diving coaches from other schools were happy for my comments because then they could recruit divers that may have attended I.U.

I'll Take Credit for Recruiting Chet and Mark

I humbly take credit for recruiting two great swimmers in my career at Indiana. They were Chet Jastremski and Mark Spitz.

Bruce Harlan and I used to perform our show at the Sylvania Country Club in Toledo, Ohio every summer for about nine years when I got to know Chet Jastremski. Chet was a young boy who lived in Toledo. Bruce and I rarely changed the jokes we used in our show. Chet and his dad must have seen our show many times. We would tell a joke, and just before delivering the punch line Chet's father would shout it out and everyone would laugh. Chet turned out to be a top high school swimmer, and I kept telling him to come to Indiana. So he showed up to I.U. in 1960 and Doc decided to make him a breaststroke swimmer using a new stroke. Two years later, Chet set the world record for the 200-meter event, and was recognized on the front cover of Sports Illustrated as the top swimmer in the world in January 1962.

I used to see Mark Spitz at A.A.U. meets all the time, and would tell him he should come to Indiana because we had a terrific coach, a great school, and very good facilities. At Doc's retirement party, Mark surprisingly gave me credit for convincing him to attend Indiana.

Best Memories of Coaching Colleagues

Some of the better memories I had teaching and coaching at I.U. relate to the people I taught and coached with. The list is so long I can't include everyone except for John Pont and Lee Corso, both head football coaches. I got to know John in the days when the students went on strike, and visitation became an issue for open dorms. I also got to know some of his players that went to the Rose Bowl, and I still run into some of them such as Harry Gonzo who ended up being a lawyer in Indianapolis. I really liked Lee Corso. He used to call me up, and ask if I would sit with him and his family attending social gatherings for the University. He may not have been known as the best football coach, but he had a great personality and was fun to be around. His friendly personality is now seen on television as one of the top college football commentators in the country.

Doc Councilman was the closest to me for thirty years because we worked together many hours a day in and out of the pool. Coaches used to say that we made a perfect team and that what made it possible for us to succeed in our given sport. We were friends, but not close friends for most of our careers. I had to compete for the number of divers I could take to the Big 10 Championships. Doc was always the "head coach," and I usually had no say in the matter. At times that was a shame because if he had let me take divers instead of swimmers, who he knew wouldn't score a point, we would have won a couple more Big Ten Championship titles.

I really loved the man, and was loyal to him because I knew it would have been difficult to coach with someone else. We respected and trusted each other, and worked very well together to accomplish the unbelievable string of twenty Big Ten Championships in a row. Things changed when I retired and Doc became stricken with Parkinson's Disease. This made us closer for the remainder of his life.

The New Athletic Director

I think that the Athletic Department got a real shot in the arm when Fred Glass became the Athletic Director for Indiana University in 2008. I believe he is the only Indiana athletic director to take a genuine interest in all the sports including the non-revenue ones. An example of his interest in swimming and diving was being instrumental in placing banners and large pictures of some of our great swimmers and divers on the walls of the new pool. Included was a huge picture of Doc and me. This kind of recognition and honor for accomplishments was long overdue.

Fred is well known to attend many of the non-revenue sporting events, and invites all the Indiana coaches and athletes to visit with him for any reason in his office. He also has a great assistant athletic director in Eric Neuburger. Eric is the son of Dale Neuburger, the Vice President of F.I.N.A., the world's governing body for all aquatics and a good friend of mine. I truly believe that with the leadership and guidance of these two directors, the improvement in nearly all the sports at Indiana will continue as long as they remain at the university.

My Salary Comparison for the Times

I stayed at Indiana University when it was nearly impossible for me to raise a family of five on the $24,000 salary I was making, so I went to outside sources to make enough to survive. Salaries and incomes have increased with the times and inflation, but even at that time instructors and coaches of non-revenue sports made less than head coaches and assistants of revenue sports and assistant professors.

I made nearly $20,000 doing water shows in the three summer months up until 1964. My combined salaries coaching and teaching was about $24,000 paid out over nine months! I quit the water shows, and later started a diving camp that eventually gave me $25,000 a year. When the Duraflex diving boards came out on the market, they gave me permission to sell them and earn a commission. As busy as I was in those days, I sold two or three boards a year until I stopped doing water shows. I found a way to sell a lot of diving boards by giving $81 as part of my commission to the buyer of the board which most of the time was the diving coach. The number of sales went from three to two hundred in a year along with selling diving stands.

Testimony in Court Cases Involving Diving Injuries

I also got involved in sixteen court cases over insurance claims late in my career that involved diving incidents, and never lost one. I would read their depositions, and if I didn't agree with them, I wouldn't take them. That went on for years when I lost the business with Duraflex around 2005. I was still giving lectures and diving clinics all over the country, and at times in other countries that paid me very little. This travel made it difficult for me to keep the diving boards business going.

I Didn't Coach and Teach for the Money

If I had ever cared about money, I would have never coached girls for nothing for thirty years. Looking back, I probably should have gone into athletic administration because I know I would have been more considerate of the coaches of non-revenue sports. Every time I accomplished something with our divers, I should have gone to the athletic director and asked for a raise like other coaches would do.

In Retrospect

I also would have asked the dean to increase my teaching salary when I was made an assistant and then associate professor. In writing my autobiography, I found it incomprehensible that the university paid me so little for what I had accomplished starting from scratch. However, it no longer bothered me when I was later rewarded in a different way with the number of lives I touched, and made them better people who continued to appreciate my efforts that occurred over sixty years. That feeling is something you cannot put into a paycheck, and I am eternally grateful to all my divers that I challenged to succeed beyond their dreams – as most of them did.

Soon after I retired, I traveled around the world two or three times spreading the scientific way to coach diving. I was recognized by the Russians and Chinese for having given them the system to coach their divers. They claimed that I was the greatest diving coach in the history of the sport and I learned this when I went down to Ft. Lauderdale to see my friend Xu Ximing get inducted into the International Swimming Hall-of-Fame for coaching the divers that won ten Olympic and fifteen World gold medals for China. At the ceremony, I was congratulating him for being the best diving coach in the world. Instead, he pointed his finger at me and said that I was number one because the Chinese coaches had learned the scientific way to coach diving from the Russians, and the Russians had learned when they visited me. I believe that his comment was the greatest compliment I ever received in my coaching career.

My Legacy and Challenge to Diving Coaches

I also found that many of the American coaches felt the same way when I wrote the book <u>Diving Illustrated</u> that offered basic concepts on how to perform all the dives when many coaches and judges didn't have a clear picture of how a dive should be performed. I also wrote the book <u>A Comprehensive View of Competitive Diving</u> that took me forty-two years to write. That book explains how to use scientific principals based on Isaac M. Newton's Laws of Motion to coach diving.

In addition, one of the reasons for such recognition was when I also formed the World Diving Coaches Association in 1968 that brought all the diving coaches in the world together. They became friends and that helped the sport grow. I also created the American Diving Coaches Association in 1971 which aided in the growth of competitive diving in our country.

I never did get away from competitive diving. After I stopped giving lectures and clinics for F.I.N.A. around the world, I gave diving lectures every week to the divers that attended Jeff Huber, John Wingfield, and Drew Johansen diving camps during the summer. I made a little money when I sold my diving books to the campers, and that has held my interest in continuing to give back to the sport I love. I also started to attend the Masters Diving meets around the country, and giving out the awards for the diving events.

My Back Surgery and Aftercare

Ellen and I had been going together for over a decade. We attended the Indiana State Fair a couple of years, and several chiropractors were offering their services. I had arthritis in my back, and one of them said he would take free x-rays of my back to see if he could treat me and I agreed.

I went to his office about a week later. When he looked at the x-rays, he said that my back was in such poor shape, and he couldn't help me. I didn't think much about it again for around three more years until I realized I was beginning to bend forward when walking. So, I decided to get an operation to rid myself of the problem.

There was a doctor in Bloomington who had operated on Lucinda Fox's husband who had a similar problem as mine, and he recovered completely in about eight months. I checked the doctor out, and found he had a great reputation for doing similar operations so I had him operate on me.

Thankfully, my good friend Lucinda Fox insisted that I stay at her house where I remained in bed for six weeks. Lucinda and her husband Gary took really good care of me, and I was very careful on how I moved for about a year. But I ended up with a painful hip that requires I use a cane.

The First Hall-of-Fame for U.S. Diving

It wasn't until June of 2012 that U.S. Diving decided to start a Hall-of-Fame. They called the ceremony "The Rings of Honor" and it was held at the Museum of Flight for Personal Courage in Seattle, Washington. I was invited, but had no idea what the ceremony was for. I didn't think I needed to go, but Linda Paul, the President of U.S. Diving, insisted.

We've been good friends for a long time, so I trusted her request to join her. Don Wright had dived with me in the Al Sheehan Aqua Follies years ago, and lived in Seattle so he went to the event with me. We learned that U.S. Diving was giving an award to six persons, the first six inductees, to honor them for giving the most to competitive diving.

I was surprised to be one of the six people. The other notable inductees were Greg Louganis, Pat McCormick who had won four Olympic gold medals, Sammy Lee, Olympic gold medal diver in 1948 and 1952, Janice Rude, the daughter of Ray Rude the founder of Duraflex Diving Boards and stands that had passed away in 2004, and Lyle Draves who was a hundred years old and husband of Vicky Draves the first female to ever win both the springboard and ten-meter tower at the Olympic Games. It was a great ceremony that had a huge attendance of people that were involved with competitive diving, and I felt honored to be a member of this fine group.

CHAPTER 47

My Greatest Honor

Life is a journey with its own set of challenges. There are fears to overcome. To be a success beyond your dreams requires a strong faith and belief that you are unique, and God has a purpose for you to achieve.

Therefore, do not be a quitter. Face your challenges and become what you dream. Then pass on what you have learned to help others achieve their dreams. That honor is greater than any financial compensation you could ever receive.

I cared for and loved all of you whom I coached and taught. I was tough at times to get you to break through barriers to see the results of your hard work. Each one of you taught me how to coach, and keep improving my skills. Often, it's not what you know, but how you impart your wisdom and knowledge that makes the difference between winning and losing.

I wish you all continued success in the pursuit of your dreams. Take the challenge and hold it up like a torch to light up your path, and you will find your way.

Sincerely,

Hobie

Hobie Billingsley

Summary of Accomplishments, Competitions

Hobie's Accomplishments

Hobert Sherwood Billingsley - accomplishments, honors, and awards teaching and coaching diving at Indiana University 1959 to 1996

Mentor, Coach, Teacher, Author, Leader, Pioneer, Creator, Friend, Pool Designer, and Entertainer

Recognized as the World's Greatest Diving Coach in the history of the sport by Top Coaches from China, Russian, Canada, and the United States

First high school male diver to medal in a senior national diving championship 1944

Big Ten and N.C.A.A. springboard diving champion 1945

First collegiate diver to make All-American in four years at Ohio State University 1945-1950

First diver ever to dive off an aluminum diving board in 1947

First diving coach to use a trampoline as a teaching aid for coaching diving 1956

Second person ever hired as a diving coach at the college level in 1957

First person along with Bruce Harlan to coach girls at the college level starting in 1958

Coached divers to 132 major diving titles in the Big 10, N.C.A.A., National A.A.U. Indoor and Outdoor, Pan American, Olympic, and World Championships

Coached eighteen divers to make Olympic teams that competed in 29 events and won four gold and four bronze medals

First diving coach to use scientific mechanical principles based on Isaac M. Newton's Laws of Motion to coach diving that started in 1961, and offered a new direction in coaching the sport.

First to use foam rubber for a soft landing when performing stunts from a dry land diving board in 1963 that was later adopted for pole vault and high Jumpers in track and gymnastic events

National Chairman for Woman's Competitive diving 1966 to 1970

Founder of World Diving Coaches Association in 1968 and the American Professional Diving Coaches Association in 1971

Olympic Diving Coach five times, Olympic Diving Judge three times

National Diving Coach of the Year Seven Straight years, and first recipient for N.C.A.A. Diving Coach of the year in 1983

Wrote three books on diving that have been used worldwide.

Only diving coach to ever give diving clinics and lectures around the world that included fifteen countries 1985

First and last coach to ever give the Oath for the Officials at the 1996 Olympic Games in Atlanta, Georgia, and it will never occur again

Only coach to have a summer camp for diving coaches that was offered from 1991 to 1996

Founder of the school for national and international diving judges 2004

First president of the World Acrobatic Association

Had five divers make the finals on the one-meter and three-meter boards at the 1973 N.C.A.A. National Championships that scored 96 points, and would have placed fourth in the team standings without the aid of the swimming team

Recognized by Anita Aldrich, the Dean of Physical Education at Indiana University, to be the best teacher of physical education activities in the history of I.U.

First to have a bronze bust unveiled in March 2013 for his Indiana University coaching accomplishments from 1959 to 1990

Was inducted into seven Halls-of-Fame

Designed the I.U.P.U.I. diving well in Indianapolis that has been copied by many colleges, high schools, and clubs throughout the country

Hobie's Indiana-Coached Olympic Divers from 1964-1996

Hobie coached eighteen divers in his career at Indiana University who made Olympic teams. Some dived in more than one event or more than one Olympics. Together, they competed in twenty-nine events, and garnered four gold and four bronze medals. He likes to say that he had divers win four gold medals. Just before her event, Sue Gossick from California, was suffering from stage fright. After she won the 3-meter event in the 1968 Mexico Olympics, she said she wouldn't have won if he hadn't chewed her out to get her refocused on executing each dive just before she competed.

Hobie's Indiana Coached Male and Female Divers That Medaled in Major Contests
AT THE OLYMPIC GAMES

Men	Women
1964 - Tokyo, Japan	
Ken Sitzberger - Gold 3-meter	Leslie Bush - Gold 10-meter
Tom Dinsley (Canada) 24th 3-meter	Ingaborg Pertmeyr (Austria) 14th 3-meter 7th 10-meter
1968 - Mexico City, Mexico	
Jim Henry - Bronze 3-meter	Cynthia Potter - alternate 3-meter
Win Young - Bronze 10-meter	Jerrie Adair - alternate 3 & 10-meter
Luis Niño de Rivera (Mexico) 4th 3-meter, 7th 10-meter	Ingaborg Pertmeyr (Austria) 5th 3-meter, 10th 10-meter
Rick Gilbert - 17th 10-meter	
1972 - Munich, Germany	
Rick Earley 5th 10-meter	Cynthia Potter - 7th 3-meter, 21st 10-meter
Scott Cranham -14th 3-meter, 12th 10-meter	
Niki Stajkovich (Austria) 18th QR 10-meter	
1976 - Montreal, Canada	
Scott Cranham 3 and 10-meter	Cynthia Potter - Bronze 3-meter
Niki Stajkovic (Austria) 12th QR 3-meter	
1980 Moscow, Russia (*U.S. Boycott)	
Claus Thomson (Sweden) 10th 10-meter	
*Brian Bungum - 10-meter	*Amy McGrath -10-meter
*Mark Virts - 10-meter	
Niki Stajkovic (Austria) 12th 3 -meter, 8th 10-meter	
1984 Los Angeles, U.S.A.	
1988 Seoul, Korea	
Niki Stajkovic (Austria) 9th 3-meter	
1992 Barcelona, Spain	

Mark Lenzi - Gold 3-meter	
1996 Atlanta, Georgia U.S. A	
Mark Lenzi - Bronze 3-meter	

AT THE PAN AMERICAN GAMES FROM 1963 TO 1991

1963 Sao Paulo, Brazil	1967 Winnipeg, Canada
Tom Dinsley - Gold 3-meter	Lesley Bush - Gold 10-meter
Rick Gilbert – Silver 3-meter	Win Young - Gold 10-meter
Ken Sitzberger - Bronze 3-meter	
1975 Mexico City, Mexico	**1991 Cuba**
Rick Early - Gold 10-meter	Mark Lenzi - Gold 3-meter

AT WORLD CHAMPIONSHIPS 1965 - 1991

1965 Budapest, Hungary	1981 Berlin, Germany
Rick Gilbert - Gold 3 & 10-meter	Cynthia Potter - Bronze 3-meter
1970 Turin, Italy	**1989 Indianapolis, Indiana**
Cynthia Potter - Gold 3-meter	Mark Lenzi - Gold 1-meter
Jerrie Adair - Silver 3-meter	**1991 Winnipeg, Canada**
Jim Henry - Silver 3 & 10-meter	Mark Lenzi - Gold 1-meter
Ingeborg Pertmeyr (Austria) 10th 10-meter 13th 3-meter	plus, Gold in 18 International Championship Meets
Niki Stajkovic (Austria) 10-meter	

INDIANA N.C.A.A. CHAMPIONS

(Indiana University athletics was on NCAA probation 1959-1963 due to football and not allowed to compete in NCAA Championships until 1964)

Men	*Women
1964 Rick Gilbert 1-meter	1971 Jerrie Adair 1 & 3-meter A.I.A.W.
1965 Ken Sitzberger 1-meter	1980 Amy McGrath 1-meter A.I.A.W.
1966 Ken Sitzberger 1 & 3-meter	1982 Lona Foss 1-meter A.I.A.W.
1967 Ken Sitzberger 1 & 3-meter	
1968 Jim Henry 1-meter	
1969 Jim Henry 1 & 3-meter	*None available until 1973 under Title IX
1970 Jim Henry 1 & 3-meter	A.I.A.W. merged with N.C.A.A. later
1976 Brian Bungum 3-meter	
1977 Brian Bungum 3-meter	
1981 Rob Bollinger 3-meter	
1982 Rob Bollinger 1-meter	

INDIANA BIG 10 CONFERENCE CHAMPIONS

Men	Women
1964 Rick Gilbert 1-meter	1971 Jerrie Adair 1-meter and 3-meter
1965 Rick Gilbert 1-meter and 3-meter	1972 Cynthia Potter 1-meter and 3-meter
1966 Ken Sitzberger 1-meter and 3-meter	1976 Carol Lindner 1-meter
1967 Ken Sitzberger 1-meter and 3-meter	1981 Amy McGrath 1-meter and 3-meter
1968 Jim Henry 1-meter	
1969 Jim Henry 1-meter and 3-meter	
1970 Jim Henry 1-meter	

1976 Tom Kenyon 3-meter	
1980 Niki Stajkovic 3-meter	
1981 Rob Bollinger 3-meter	
1982 Rob Bollinger 1-meter	

Made in the USA
Lexington, KY
26 May 2018